REMEMBERING
THEIR GLORY

REMEMBERING THEIR GLORY

Sports Heroes of the 1940s

James V. Young and Arthur F. McClure

South Brunswick and New York: A. S. Barnes and Company
London: Thomas Yoseloff Ltd

A. S. Barnes and Co., Inc.
Cranbury, New Jersey 08512

Thomas Yoseloff Ltd
Magdalen House
136–148 Tooley Street
London SE1 2TT, England

Library of Congress Cataloging in Publication Data

Young, James V   1936–
Remembering their glory.

Bibliography: p.
Includes index.
1. Sports—United States—History. I. McClure,
Arthur F., joint author. II. Title.
GV583.Y68   796′.09   75-20611
ISBN 0-498-01788-5

PRINTED IN THE UNITED STATES OF AMERICA

To
ROBERT ARTHUR YOUNG and **EDWIN B. STEVENS**
who were so generous with their time and affection,
and instilled in us a love for athletics.

CONTENTS

FOREWORD

Any sports tour of the 1940s is, of course, pleasurable for me personally, but I think any sports fan will find *Remembering Their Glory: Sports Heroes of the 1940s* a delightful escape as well as a serious documentary of that era.

For those of us who were around at the time, there are thousands of memory-joggers. Names we had long forgotten appear on the printed page and suddenly we are transported back through time and can hear the voice of Ted Husing calling the plays, or see the words of a Grantland Rice or a George Trevor in the sports pages.

It's not all nostalgia, though. The authors seek an answer to the absence of genuine present-day sports heroes (as opposed to superstars), and I think they make some logical conclusions.

The year-by-year walk down sport's memory lane makes this book a delight for nostalgia buffs and over-the-hill football players.

Glenn Davis

PREFACE

On several occasions before 1974, Dr. Jim Young, Chairman of the Central Missouri State University Department of Political Science, and Dr. Art McClure, Chairman of that school's Department of History, had discussed what they considered to be a dearth of sports heroes in the 1970s comparable to Glenn Davis, Doak Walker, Charlie Justice, Johnny Lujack, Charley Trippi, and other football greats of the 1940s. In December of 1973, Jim Young gave a talk to an adult Sunday school class in Waterloo, Iowa, entitled "The Importance of Example," in which he reminisced about past experiences in the church and community and discussed the topic of these conversations between Art McClure and himself. A follow-up discussion between Young and McClure about that Sunday talk and their reading of a nostalgic magazine article about Charlie "Choo Choo" Justice led them to resolve to write a book that would be a sort of "scrapbook of memories" about their boyhood heroes.

Both Young and McClure had saved many mementoes from childhood. In addition to these personal memorabilia from the 1940s, they possessed extensive clipping files and personal sports libraries of books, magazines, and programs from or about that period. Those "treasures" both sparked their interest and facilitated their research. Their original conception of the project underwent a change or two, but ultimately evolved into the accumulation of materials for, and writing of, this volume.

ACKNOWLEDGMENTS

The authors wish to thank the following institutions and individuals for their generosity and helpfulness in providing photographs for use in this book:

Colleges and universities (universities unless otherwise indicated).

Ashland College, Baldwin-Wallace College, Bowling Green State, Bradley, Brown, City College of New York, Clemson, Columbia, Cornell, Cornell College, Dartmouth, Denver, De Paul, Detroit, Drake, Duke, Evansville, Georgia, Georgia Tech, Illinois, Indiana, Indiana State at Terre Haute, Iowa, Kansas, Kentucky, Marquette, Marshall (West Virginia), Michigan, Michigan State, Minnesota, Missouri, Navy, New Hampshire, North Carolina State, Northern Iowa, Northwestern, Northwestern State of Louisiana, Northwest Missouri State, Ohio, Ohio State, Oregon, Penn State, Pittsburgh, Princeton, Purdue, Rhode Island, St. Mary's College of California, San Diego State, Seton Hall, South Carolina, Southern California, Southern Methodist, Stanford, Tennessee, Texas, Tufts, Tulane, Tuskegee Institute, UCLA, Villanova, Virginia, Washington, Western Kentucky, West Virginia, Wisconsin, Wyoming, and Yale.

Professional teams

Chicago Bears, Cleveland Browns, Detroit Lions, Green Bay Packers, Los Angeles Rams, New York Giants, St. Louis Football Cardinals, Chicago White Sox, Cincinnati Reds, Cleveland Indians, Detroit Tigers, Los Angeles Dodgers, Minnesota Twins, New York Yankees, Philadelphia Phillies, St. Louis Cardinals, San Francisco Giants, and Kansas City Kings.

Other institutions

Cadaco, Inc., Cracker Jack (Division of Borden Foods, Borden, Inc.), Naismith Memorial Basketball Hall of Fame, National Football Foundation and Hall of Fame, Phillips Petroleum Company, and Pro Football Hall of Fame.

Individuals

Douglas R. Bolton, George Brace, Leland Byrd, Francis X. Cretzmeyer, Lyle Draves, Vicki Draves, George Durham, Dwight "Dike" Eddleman, H. E. "Bud" Foster, Charles Gilbert, Fortune Gordien, Janell Hartley, Sim Iness, John Lujack, Bob Mathias, John W. Nugent, Don Roberts, Don Sayenga, Clyde Scott, Paul K. Scott, Gerald Tucker, and Murray Wier.

Other helpful responses were received from:

Schools and universities

Alabama, Boston College, Colorado, Long Island, Oberlin College, and Southern.

Professional teams

Baltimore Colts, Atlanta Braves, Baltimore Orioles, Boston Red Sox, Chicago Cubs, Pittsburgh Pirates, Detroit Pistons, Los Angeles Lakers, and Philadelphia 76ers.

Individuals

Chet Aubuchon, Bud Browning, Charlie Black, Don Canham, Vaughn Mancha, Don Powers, Russ Smith, and Melford Waits.

Lyle and Vicki Draves and Dr. Tom Hairabedian read portions of the manuscript; Ginger Young listened to it in its entirety; and all four offered constructive advice and information. Dr. Peter Nichols furnished valuable source materials on wrestling; Peary Rader, information about weightlifting; Tom White and Harry B. Robinson, some out-of-print sports volumes; and Francis Cretzmeyer, Ted Wheeler, Francis "Bus" Graham, Roland Smith, and Max Hawkins, materials and information on Iowa and other athletes. The authors are grateful for the permission granted by Lew DeWitt to use his lyrics from the Statler Brothers' *The Boy Inside of Me.* Dr. Gene Aist and Darrell Conway provided invaluable photographic and artistic assistance. Thanks are also owed to Darrell Conway and to Al Mistak for helping to re-create the atmosphere in which the sandlot and parlor games described herein were played by these boys of the 1940s.

Miss Debbie Gorman, Mrs. Joyce MacLean, and Mrs. Marsha Bird faithfully typed portions of the manuscript and innumerable letters, as did Ginger (Mrs. Jim) Young whose initial and continued enthusiasm, encouragement, and faith in the ultimate success of this effort amounted to a *sine qua non* for its completion. Ginger and Ann Young helped in compiling the index. And thanks to Judy (Mrs. Art) McClure, wife and friend.

The following is a list of organizations and terms for which abbreviations are often used:

AAFC	All-America Football Conference
AAU	Amateur Athletic Union of the United States (NAAU Sometimes used for *National* AAU competition)
AL	American League (Baseball)
AP	Associated Press
ASB	All-Star Baseball (TM Parlor game manufactured by Cadaco, Inc., Chicago, Illinois)
BAA	Basketball Association of America
ERA	Earned Run Average
MVP	Most Valuable Player
NAIA	National Association of Intercollegiate Athletics
NAIB	National Association of Intercollegiate Basketball (Name of the NAIA before 1951)
NCAA	National Collegiate Athletic Association
NFL	National Football League
NHL	National Hockey League
NIT	National Invitation Tournament
NL	National League (Baseball)
NBA	National Basketball Association
NBL	National Basketball League
PAT	Point After Touchdown
PGA	Professional Golfers Association
RBI	Runs Batted In
SEC	Southeastern Conference
TD	Touchdown
UP	United Press

Football Positions:

E, LE, RE	End, Left End, Right End
T, LT, RT	Tackle, Left Tackle, Right Tackle
G, LG, RG	Guard, Left Guard, Right Guard
C	Center
B, QB, HB,	Back, Quarterback, Halfback,
LHB, RHB, FB	Left Halfback, Right Halfback, Fullback

Basketball Positions:

F	Forward
C	Center
G	Guard
D	Defense (Used in some Helms Foundation All-American selections)

Conference or League Standings:

W	Wins (or Games Won)
L	Losses (or Games Lost)
	Won-lost records of pitchers are often referred to parenthetically without the "W" and "L" (e.g., 18-5 record).
T	Ties (or Games Tied)
Pct.	Percentage of Total Games Won

"Consensus All-Americans" are athletes who have been chosen more frequently than others on All-America First Teams during a single season in a sport. The National Collegiate Sports Services' *College Football Modern Record Book* is a convenient source for the consensus football selections. Consensus All-American basketball teams can be found in Alexander Weyand's *The Cavalcade of Basketball*. Data for such selections are also included in the *Ronald Encyclopedia of Basketball* by William G. Mokray.

A "unanimous" All-American is a player chosen as a First Team All-American by all of the major selectors of the latter honor teams.

The Helms Foundation and its successor, Citizens Savings Athletic Foundation, are referred to interchangeably in connection with their selection of All-American teams and Hall of Fame members.

I

SPORTS HEROES

Where have you gone, Joe DiMaggio?
A nation turns its lonely eyes to you.
—Paul Simon, *Mrs. Robinson*

In a 1971 column for *Sport* magazine, Paul Hemphill refers to Merle Haggard's song, *Okie from Muskogee,* and country singer Bill Anderson's rendition of *Where Have All the Heroes Gone?* (which Hemphill reports, was written with the help of a Detroit columnist and exsportswriter, Bob Talbert) :

Like *Okie,* [*Where Have All the Heroes Gone?*] is a protest against the cynical new potsmoking American and a call to return to simpler times when it was easier to tell the good guys from the bad guys. The title sums it up.

Whatever Happened to Randolph Scott, The Strand, Cowboy Buckaroo, and *The Boy Inside of Me* are additional titles from the world of country music that convey a similar message and contribute significantly to the popular nostalgia-culture of recent times.

One effect of such songs is a reinforcement of feeling among like-minded individuals who grew up in the 1930s and 1940s—people who might otherwise have believed that their pining for more simple times was an isolated phenomenon.

The enthusiastic response to the above-cited music is exemplified by Hemphill's statements concerning *Where Have All the Heroes Gone?*:

At any rate, everywhere Anderson went to do the song he received foot-stomping standing ovations of almost embarrassing proportions. And even if you don't agree with the politics of *Heroes* you have to admit there is, for better or for worse, a lot of truth in it.

As goes the world of cowboys and the movies, so goes the world of sports. The authors' inspiration for undertaking this project, in part, stemmed from a casual conversation with each other in the halls of academe. The chairmen of the history and political-science departments at Central Missouri State University, with the hope of momentary escape from the problems of the contemporary world in general and administrative dilemmas in particular, began digressing about old-time college football heroes who were publicized so much and so favorably in the 1940s. The names of Tom Harmon, Glenn Davis, Johnny Lujack, Charley Trippi, "Choo Choo" Justice, and other football greats evoked common memories in the minds of two late-thirtyish, balding professors, who had worshipped those and other stars back in their home states of Kansas and Iowa, respectively. The professors concluded their discussion by agreeing that today there are All-Americans, but relatively few *heroes* of the type that they had known in their youth.

Those conclusions of McClure and Young were similar to those of Hemphill:

These are perilous times for heroes. There are too many Jim Boutons snooping around, advising us that Mickey Mantle was something less than a drawling good old boy from Oklahoma. . . . Sportswriters were never widely known as cynical investigators—such a pity that an old pitcher had to show the way.

This remembrance of past heroes is often combined with a recollection by the hero worshipper of imaginary fantasized games in which the solo participant imagined himself to be his various heroes (sometimes simultaneously) while acting out

Covers from ice-cream containers depicting movie heroes and heroines. (From the collections of the authors.)

certain phases of the game involved, such as pitching, or throwing, and catching a ball. In his article, "Growing Up in the Forties," Richard Schickel recounts such a personal experience (when he was "forced to crash a fence, just like Pete Reiser, to make a catch"). He then asserts:

> I was not alone in this pastime. All over town, all over the country, one could observe small boys throwing themselves bodily into their athletic fantasies—looking, I suppose, like escapees from some violent ward for midgets.

And in "Confessions of a Retarded Tiger," Bil Gilbert elaborately describes his bouncing of a tennis ball off a sloping porch roof and a nearby railroad crossing sign (when his father was at home in the evening), while imagining that he was the Detroit Tigers of 1935 playing their American League opponents. Gilbert adds:

> In nostalgic, confessional, usually boozy moments, enough of my contemporaries have admitted to having once behaved as BG [Bil Gilbert] did to suggest that he should be considered as a typical rather than an extreme case of baseball retardation. [A lady with whom he had become acquainted and conversed at a social gathering], though handicapped by her sex, became retarded in a ladylike way by spending her summer afternoons playing a free-form sort of croquet in which the balls, wickets and mallets were Jolly Cholly Grimm and company. [The female conversationalist was as fond of the 1935 Cubs as Gilbert was of the Tigers of that vintage.]

Gilbert then relates comparable "confessions" by others inflicted with this "disease" that he called "nostalgic schizophrenia." He concludes that "based on such a random sampling I suspect that there are still millions of us retards around, including many who would make BG look like Mr. Straight. However, it is difficult to prove. . . ."

Indeed, writers McClure and Young both admit to have been afflicted with this same "illness." And wonderfully so.

That such sports playacting has been a rather common phenomenon is supported by the fact that, shortly after Gilbert's article appeared in *Sports Illustrated*, the letters column of that magazine was crowded with similar confessions by readers.

Quite often this fantasizing was accompanied by a simulated play-by-play account of the game; the announcing being done, of course, by the per-

former. The latter also served as an appreciative audience for the exploits of the sports heroes being imitated. One of the writers of this volume once aspired to be a radio sportscaster, and practice for such a role was part of the athletic simulation. Similarly, Richard Schickel relates:

". . . my brother-in-law is reported to have indulged himself in an unbroken winning streak over imaginary opponents in most of the major sports in far-off California; and I suspect, there is something Richard M. Nixon is not telling when he confesses his secret ambition to be a sportscaster. One imagines him, ahead of his time in this as so many other areas, in the twilight back of the grocery store in Whittier, so solemnly tackling himself while calling the play-by-play in the tones of some legendary broadcaster like Graham McNamee.

It must be emphasized that whether people (or,

Cowboy hero memorabilia of youth from the 1940s. Posters, badges, *Big Little* books, and autographed picture are from the collections of the authors.

perhaps more properly, whether the youth) of today have sports heroes who are comparable to the Doak Walkers and Charley Justices of the 1940s is a matter of opinion and one's perspective. One group of writers who are in disagreement with Messrs. Young, McClure, Gilbert, and the songwriters alluded to *supra,* are the editors of *Sport,* a monthly magazine that has been published since 1946. The latter's philosophy was aptly propounded on *Sport's* editorial page when the editors celebrated the magazine's twenty-fifth anniversary in September of 1971. The editors reaffirmed the commitment of their magazine's founders—to stress "human drama," "truths about sports," and illumination of "the age in which they lived."

The emphasis of the magazine changed in 1952 from the "gee-whiz" (adulatory) school of Grantland Rice to the "new journalism," although the editors claimed in 1971 never to have camped exclusively with either school. They then stated:

Our sense of unity in this magazine over the years has come not from writers as stylists, but from writers as interpreters of the great events in sports, and of the people responsible for those events. The real key to sports, and therefore to our magazine, resides in the word called heroism. A character in Bernard Malamud's novel, *The Natural,* remarked, "Without heroes, we are all plain people and don't know how far we can go." So we spawn heroes. In the end, big-time sports is the *act of heroism constantly repeating itself* [italics mine], and the effects of heroism on the heroes. And that, essentially, is what it will always be about.

. . . .

The athlete must remain true to himself and that truth, as we have said, is encompassed in the word, heroism.

In the same issue, editor Al Silverman asserts:

The fact is, sports in the last 25 years has run head-to-head with rampant technology. Our athletes of today are bigger and stronger and faster and richer *and, on the whole, more heroic than the athletes of any other era* [italics mine]. The golden age of sports they called the 1920's of Dempsey, Ruth, Tilden, Grange and all the others. Possibly it was true then. It is not now. Our athletes have surpassed all the old heroes. *We* are living in the golden age of sports.

Two of the ideas expressed by the *Sport* editors —that sports reflect the changes in the national culture, and that heroes, albeit of a different type, are still with us—were included in an article published in the *Journal of Sport History.* The author, David Voight, thinks that sports can reveal

. . . changing norms and values of American culture. Especially is this reflected in sports heroes and hero

worship, a subject that bears witness to the changing sentiments and lifestyles of Americans. For such a study the sports historian has as his road map some superb studies in American hero worship.

In the changing face of American nationalism the popular choices of sports heroes reflect changing popular tastes for heroes.

Voight cites Dixon Wecter's study, *The Hero in America,* which suggests some expectations that the hero had to conform with in the period prior to 1940. Voight then contrasts the contemporary hero with his counterpart from earlier periods. But the assumption underlying his statements is that heroes are found in every era, even though the changed circumstances dictate that they be of different types.

Even though a reasonable case can be made for editor Silverman's position on contemporary heroes, it is arguable that the stars of today are not and cannot be venerated by youth to the extent that worship of heroes was possible in earlier times. For one thing, the impact of television, reaching the majority of Americans as it did in the 1950s, unalterably changed the perspective in which sports (and other) stars would be viewed by millions of followers.

The first widespread television audience in history, according to Eugene Methvin, followed the 1948 Republican and Democratic conventions and the inauguration of President Truman. It was not until 1951 that the first transcontinental telecast occurred. By 1960, seventy million people had watched the Nixon-Kennedy debates, and in 1966, the World Cup soccer matches were viewed by an estimated five hundred million persons worldwide, via Telstar communications satellite. The percentage of households with at least one television set had jumped dramatically in the early and middle 1950s.

A 1972 *Sports Illustrated* article on "Trivia" quoted singer Mel Torme:

. . . the figures on the movie screen were all 25 to 50 times bigger than life. Now we look at TV, and they're all smaller than life—little guys and girls only seven inches high. At that size they just don't seem very important.

In the same vein, Bil Gilbert, who also lamented the passing of the "good old days," wrote in a 1969 *Sports Illustrated* issue that even though it might seem that television

. . . would create new fantasy fans by the millions . . . it has not. The trouble is that it is very hard to have bigger-than-life imaginary playmates when smaller-than-life but photographically accurate models of the real thing are living-room intimates.

In addition to the difference in perspective, television has brought about an overexposure of sports stars. This point was made by Roger Kahn in his article "Where Have All Our Heroes Gone?":

> Take everything, diffusion, tougher journalism and the rest, and go beyond, to know why the athlete, whom we idolized from great distance, is a callow hero to Stephen, David and April. With his warts and shaky syntax, he is overwhelmingly available, playing too many sports for too many hours on too many television sets.
> Worshiped is the word that goes with hero. Had someone stationed a TV camera on top of Olympus, would anyone have worshiped Zeus?

The same idea was expressed by Edward Hoagland in "Where Have All the Heroes Gone?":

> No bleary succession of games televised daily, no muzzy appearance on "Laugh-In" to confuse us, no chuckling debut on "The Merv Griffin Show" to blur the tall image. Instead, simply "Joltin' Joe," or "Scooter," or "Old Reliable."

And underscoring the same notion were the "Trivia" authors, who thought that in the 1930s and 1940s "movies were 'big'" and "radio fed the imagination [and did not satiate] it, as television is inclined to do." Although the focus of the latter article is on the retention of minor information concerning sports and other aspects of popular culture of the past, many of the same considerations mentioned in it are applicable to a study of heroes.

The "Trivia" authors refer not only to the overexposure of individual heroes, but also to the overexposure of sports in general, and the proliferation of teams and stars:

> Television . . . is not a proper trivia instrument. The programs haven't the staying power, and there are simply too many of them. Trivia players [substitute hero worshippers] saw the world through a smaller focus. There were 16 major league teams, not 24—can anyone recite the starting lineup of the 1971 Milwaukee Brewers? Who, in fact, are they? Professional football was a piddling enterprise in the trivia player's youth. Now the sun rises and sets upon it.

Jim Young recalls watching the current Houston Astros announcer, Gene Elston, broadcast the Waterloo White Hawks away games, all the while secure in the Waterloo, Iowa, studio of KXEL. Elston would read sparse accounts of the action on the teletype. The action might have been occurring as far away as Terre Haute or Evansville, Indiana. He would then embellish the bare-bones teletype account with his imagination of how the play might look were he on the scene in person. Many listeners were aware that the process of broadcasting the away games was done in this fashion, but no objection was made, to the writer's recollection. Radio, thus, provided a vehicle for the imagination of the actual broadcaster to be employed, in addition to that of the listener or the vicarious broadcaster on a sandlot or backyard. Art McClure similarly listened to "Play by Play with Larry Ray" broadcasts of the Kansas City Blues during the 1940s with unrestrained devotion.

Radio broadcasters were apt to stress the positive (or use more restraint in expressing the negative aspects) in their description of athletes. The "new journalist" is apt to emphasize controversy and sensational aspects of the athletes, disregarding the impact of these revelations on the innocent hero worshippers. "Realism" is regarded as a more important objective by the adherents of the newer school. An example is the work of Jim Bouton, referred to by Hemphill above.

In sum, television has brought about changes affecting the concept of the sports hero: (1) It has become a diversion in itself, displacing much of the youngster's creative efforts in the imaginary realm—his efforts to entertain himself by playacting and emulating the distant and aloof heroes; (2) The fact that television has both video *and* audio capabilities reduces the scope of imagination concerning the sporting event and its participants, thus diminishing the chance the athlete might be regarded as "larger-than-life"; (3) The latter result is also effected by the viewer's perspective of the event and participants on the television screen; (4) Radio broadcasters were more apt to be of the "gee-whiz" school than the "new journalist" type; (5) Some of these factors lead to considerable disillusionment. Repeated instances of disillusionment, in turn, discourage placing faith and trust in heroes; (6) Television covers many more sports and teams, and it is difficult for the viewer to follow the sports scene as fully even if he has the time and inclination to do so. (Expansion in number of the major league franchises and the shifting of franchises from one city to another, combined with wholesale player-trades, compound the problem.)

Admittedly, part of the process of maturation is the recognition that things were not always as they seemed to be while one was still young and innocent. The reality of life thus becomes the purveyor of disappointment for youthful dreams. For example, Bill Stern was always the dean of sports broadcasters, so far as Young was concerned in his youth. It was not until the latter began serious research for this study that he learned that Stern's veracity in his broadcasting anecdotes had been seriously questioned, or that he had fought a personal battle with narcotics addiction. The recent conviction of former New York Yankee and St. Louis Brown infielder Gerry Priddy also comes to mind in this connection. However, these and other revelations and developments (some occurring after most of this book was written) do little to dim Young's or McClure's fond memories.

Another admitted weakness in the thesis of McClure, Young, Gilbert, *et alia* is that (at least in the case of the first two) they were leaving their childhood behind them as the events of the 1950s displaced the 1940s in the sweep of history. Therefore, their attitude toward the existence of heroes in different decades arguably was affected by inevitable chronological forces. The fact that others from different age groups have made similar observations concerning the decline of sports heroes offsets this reservation, however. It is also granted that the adult has less time (and possibly less inclination) than the child to focus on sport heroes.

The relative simplicity of life in the 1940s and other past decades, in comparison with the complexity of modern society as a factor affecting attitudes toward heroes, was alluded to previously (page 17). The importance of this factor is underscored by Voight who thinks that as values and lifestyles change, it becomes impossible to arrive at a consensus on the definitions of heroes, villains, and fools.

A parallel emphasis on the contrast between a simpler past and the complex present can be found in country-music themes. The Statler Brothers' lament in *Whatever Happened to Randolph Scott*—that the only movie that they have understood in years is *True Grit,* and that one must take an analyst to the movie to see if the film is suitable—is illustrative.

Like Voight, Hoagland maintains that a decline in traditional beliefs is "bad for heroism, on the whole." Additional factors cited by Hoagland as detracting from hero worship include the above-mentioned point concerning overexposure from television and the audience's lack of patience with, and tolerance of, the mistakes of others.

Although author McClure included among his boyhood sports heroes such stars as Jackie Robinson and Sugar Ray Robinson, some writers have cited the inability of whites to identify with the growing percentage and numbers of black athletes. Although the subsequent breaking of Babe Ruth's career home-run record may have altered his conclusion, Voight states: "That [a black] like Hank Aaron fail[s] to arouse enthusiasm in his mighty efforts suggests that the American social environment is not ready to accommodate a black as Babe Ruth's successor."

Joseph Durso in "What's Happened to Baseball" relates that blacks were able to identify with Jackie Robinson when he broke the color line in baseball, and this helped revive the "folk-hero quality" of the game:

The most important revival of the old-fashioned baseball magic began twenty years ago [1947] when Jackie Robinson arrived in the big leagues. It opened doors to an entire generation of Negroes who had swapped baseball cards, peered at games through knotholes, and dreamed of making it big.

Durso quotes Ed Charles (a black who became one of the stars of the 1969 World Champion New York Mets):

I'll never forget the day the Dodgers brought Jackie Robinson to St. Pete. There were so many people the stadium couldn't hold them. Then after the game we kids trailed him over to the railroad station and stood watching through the train window while he played cards with the white ball players. It was a great, great day because for the first time we realized that it could really happen.

Today, white athletes are in no danger of being excluded because of relative lack of ability from professional and collegiate sports, but the percentage of blacks has obviously been increasing. In a 1971 *Sports Illustrated* article, Martin Kane sets forth some interesting statistics:

Twenty-six years ago there were no blacks on any of the big-league basketball, football or baseball professional team rosters, though on rare occasions in the past, basketball, baseball and football had used black players. Today there are 150 blacks out of 600 players in major league baseball, 330 out of 1,040 in football and 153 out of 280 in basketball.

In a more recent account, Mickey Herskowitz and Steve Perkins note:

The whites have the edge in the NFL, but the color line is closing fast. One of the great ignored stories of pro football is that the black percentage has increased from 28 to 42 per cent in the last five years—by approximation of club officials. Nobody is taking an actual color count for fear of federal agency intervention.

Of more importance for this study's purposes is the fact that blacks are not only contributing more than their "share" of participants to sports in general, but also are contributing *much* more than their share of stars. Kane's 1971 study supplies these figures:

In basketball, three of the five players named to the 1969–70 All-NBA team were black, as were all five of the players named to the All-Rookie team. Blacks have won the league's Most Valuable Player award 12 times in the past 13 seasons.

In pro football all four 1969 Rookie of the Year awards for offense and defense were won by blacks.

In baseball black men have won the National League's MVP award 16 times in the past 22 seasons.

Kane's figures on the Olympic Games are indicative of the fact that one of the most obvious areas of black sport dominance has been the sport of track and field. He also points out that thoroughbred racing is the only sport in which the role of the American black has declined in recent years. That sport was the first in which a large number of blacks became prominent. Their decline has been due in part to their increased physical size.

Grosset and Dunlap's *The Sports Encyclopedia: Baseball* has supplied more recent figures that are supportive of Kane's statistics on sports stars. Rich Koster reported these interesting facts from the *Encyclopedia* to his readers in the *St. Louis Globe-Democrat*:

Jackie Jensen was the last white player to lead either major league in stolen bases, back in 1954. In the past 14 years, Johnny Bench is the National League's only white home run champ. [The article was written in June of 1974.]

In the past five years, white players have hit .251 in the majors; Latins .265 and blacks .270. Since Jackie Robinson broke into baseball in '47, blacks have compiled the best winning percentages by pitchers, the best ERAs, the most strike-outs and the least number of hits allowed.

Although it would seem to the writers that there are sufficient white athletic stars with whom white fans can identify readily, the racial identification matter was the subject of a warning by Wilt Chamberlain years ago, to the effect that "the NBA was getting too many black players for the sport's continued popularity." Moreover, Herskowitz and Perkins quote "an otherwise color-blind" NFL team owner:

It scares me to death, but I don't know what we can do about it. You look at your draft lists every year and you just can't skip down five slots to draft a guy because he's white. If you do, you'll be sitting home on Super Sunday.

Herskowitz and Perkins conclude by alleging that NFL owners "have a fear that maybe Miami knows something they don't know. The Dolphins have only one black on their defense platoon."

Another development making it difficult for some fans to identify with sports stars is the escalating salaries of professional athletes. Dr. Gerald Scully, professor of economics at Southern Methodist University, found that the average NFL player's salary is $27,500; the average major league baseball player's salary is $37,000; and comparable figures for the NHL, NBA, and ABA are $40,000, $90,000 (not a printing error!), and $37,000, respectively.

In responding to a question from a reader (who had been made "a little sick" to read the results of a survey of salaries in New York State that showed Walt Frazier of the Knicks making $225,000 a year while the New York City commissioner of health and medical services made $11,000), sports columnists Mickey Herskowitz and Steve Perkins reported:

It may interest you to learn that Calvin Hill of the Dallas Cowboys, who signed for 1975 with Hawaii of the WFL, was introduced to a Dallas fight crowd the other night—and was booed. Public sentiment is a fragile thing and herein lies the one great concern of thinking people in sports management today. "When the fans stop looking at them as heroes," says a top NFL exec, "and start realizing they are businessmen, that's when they start looking for other forms of entertainment."

In an article entitled "Joe Fan or Mr. Sap," Rich Koster states:

I've been wondering lately just how far professional sports will be allowed to go before the silent partner in the overall equation finally shouts, "Stop!"

In case you haven't noticed, the guy who pays the bills is being had. Joe Fan is being treated like a sap. . . .

How much longer will he continue to pay the increasing box-office freight, while accepting a repeated back-of-the-hand in return?

When will he realize he is a member of a political block, with his own options on turning it all off? *If there are no more heroes—or even the illusion of them—if there is no more rapport, no more loyalty, then why pay for a fraud?* [Italics mine.]

The 1972 major league baseball player strike, which delayed the opening of the regular season several weeks, was the cause of many similar adverse reactions. For many people, including both writers of this volume, the image of most major-league players has been badly tarnished by their participation in that action. (Perhaps it ran counter to their thoughts about sport heroes.) With a 1974 NFL player strike a distinct possibility, Baltimore Colt linebacker Mike Curtis said, "It's a joke for a guy making $150,000 to walk a picket line."

When former St. Louis outfielder Curt Flood attempted to persuade the Supreme Court to set aside the contractual reserve clause binding a player to his club, he argued that the clause relegated him to the status of a chattel slave. Somehow that plea had a hollow ring when one realized Flood had been paid $90,000 by the Cardinals to play for one year. How heroic did it all seem?

Rich Koster also raised another significant and related point concerning forces that allegedly have led to a decline in sport heroes—the process of recruiting athletes today:

> It's a seeding process that begins when a boy is still in grammar school. If he can shoot a jump shot, kick a football or hit a baseball, he is singled out as a resource.
>
> And with the cultivation of the press, of schools with a distorted emphasis and of a public searching for heroes—legitimate or otherwise—the boy becomes an "athlete."
>
> And too often, the athlete becomes a boorish egomaniac. Or, in the words of Bob Cousy, "a monster."

Koster describes why Cousy, one of the all-time greats of college and professional basketball, quit his job as coach of the Kansas City-Omaha Kings during the 1973–74 season. As a product of New York City playgrounds, Cousy had had two college offers when he graduated from high school in 1947.

Today, he says, "a kid who is all-city in New York, like I was, gets 200 offers." That's where it begins.

"It all starts with the recruiting system, spoiling the kids so badly," he stresses. "They're pampered and catered to from the time they're playground players.

"They have an exaggerated opinion of their role in society. They come to expect instant recognition, exposure and financial rewards . . ."

Cousy quit because as a coach he was supposed to mold these highly paid athletes into a "cohesive unit." He concluded that logically it could not be done.

When one-time Yankee great Joe Gordon resigned his position as manager of the 1969 Kansas City Royals, after a creditable year at the helm of that first-year, expansion baseball club, he referred to the changes in the players that had taken place since he had last managed, eight years before:

> Managing was tough on me. I was beat at the end of the season. A lot of change has taken place in players, and it takes a different approach to understand the players today. It's tougher to control them and they are more aware of who is pushing them from the farm system and how things run in the front office. It was very difficult for me to adjust.

The salaries paid professional athletes are seen by the athletes themselves as adversely affecting their performance and pride in their play. Bobby Hull (who is in a position to know) has said:

> Guys today get a dollar in their pocket and they think they've got the world on a string. They say, "Who, me work? Who, me sweat?" Why should a guy with a half-million-dollar contract want to have blood dripping down his face, or sweat, or play with bruises? Hell, they won't even play with bruised feelings now.

As for loss of pride, a statement by twenty-five-year NHL veteran Gump Worsley is illustrative:

> It's not the same anymore. Kids coming up today have no pride. After a loss, they stand around the dressing room laughing. Imagine that. They couldn't care less. All they're concerned with is rushing out and having a few beers.

Sparky Anderson, manager of the Cincinnati Reds, sums up the influence of large salaries on the production of sport heroes today in these words: "The public doesn't want to hear the players talk all the time about money, money, money. It's going to drive fans away. It's pitiful."

It is discouraging that with all of these negative trends seemingly apparent, the need for heroes is as strong now as it ever was. The authors are in agreement with Edward Hoagland who said:

> It's not as if we don't need new heroes, however. They dramatize solutions and help to pave the way through new circumstances; they stumble on a stance that suits nearly everybody.

The need for heroes was also aptly stated by songwriter Lew DeWitt in *The Boy Inside of Me*. DeWitt described a man who had imagined himself to be various heroes as a boy. As a youth, he feared nothing because he could always imagine himself to be a heroic figure capable of combatting any problem. As he grew into adulthood, made his adjustments with the world, and raised a family, he found he had to live in such a way as to be a hero for his own son. In doing so, however, he merely called upon the internal strengths he had acquired as a youngster in his imitation of heroic figures.

In part, the lyrics read:

> When I was just a kid
> I used to wonder all the time
> I had imagination
> And a very active mind.
>
> I had a stack of baseball cards

And I had chicken pox;
I had a red bicycle,
A frog, and smelly socks.

I could be Dick Tracy
In my Daddy's summer hat;
I was Joe Palooka;
I was this 'n' that.

I never feared for anything
For I could always be
Any man I wanted through
This boy inside of me.

Things slowly fell together
I grew into a man;
And I learned to live with politics
And to tie a four-in-hand.

I've taken on a family
And am payin' for a home
And live like so my son can have
A hero of his own.

And sometimes when this hero
Is required to show his stuff,
He just calls on the stuff he learned
While he was growing up.

As recorded by the Statler Brothers. Courtesy of Lew DeWitt.

In songs such as *The Boy Inside of Me, Whatever Happened to Randolph Scott, Cowboy Buckaroo, The Strand,* and *Hoppy, Gene and Me,* popularized by the Statler Brothers, Roy Rogers, and other country music singers, lyricists have emphasized the: (1) simplicity of the past; (2) identification with, and imitation of, heroes, fictional or not; (3) security afforded by certain institutions, traditions, and values; (4) unabashed admiration of, and longing for, these heroes and characteristics; (5) maturation and recognition (albeit regretful) that one "can't go home any more"—recognition of permanent change; (6) related loss of innocence of youth; and (7) use of traits acquired by hero emulation to solve actual problems.

In a speech before an adult coffee-hour class at the First Congregational Church in Waterloo, Iowa, author Young at the age of thirty-seven stated:

Actually, I believe that we have just as many of the same type of heroes today, but for one reason or another, our media pick up the wrong people to publicize or do not want the same type of traits emulated. The *real* heroes are too often played down or ignored.

My first general observation is that *heroes are important,* and that our choice of heroes is likely to reflect the nature of our society.

At the outset, I think that it should be said that human heroes are likely to show feet of clay at some time in their lives. Blind hero worship . . . can thus end in disillusionment. We should not expect our fellow humans to be free of error. *Our main reliance and faith should be in God.* We should not presume that any human can rival Him in stature. The Lord is our Rock, our Strength, and our Redeemer, our Fortress in time of trouble.

Yet it would not be realistic to presume that many of us do not look up to certain humans, as well, for models or examples in our own lives. The world would be better off, in my opinion, if there were more such respect shown and if the right heroes were emulated. Moreover, it wouldn't hurt if we had *more* people setting good examples for others. Each of us could do his or her part. In other words, I think we should stress more the importance of good example.

The unforgettable heroes of the 1940s nearly always stood out as *good examples of quiet dignity.*

In an article entitled "Staubach Throwback to Days of Fiction Heroes," John Steadman quotes Navy coach Rick Forzano concerning Dallas Cowboy star Roger Staubach and his setting of a proper example:

"This is an incredible young man, one of the finest gentlemen you would want to meet," he testified. "He draws respect by the way he lives, by the way he talks and how he acts.

"He is truly a great credit to the Naval Academy, the Naval service and the country.

"In fact he would be embarrassed to know he was being talked of as some kind of model for the youth of America.

"But if more Roger Staubachs were to come along, they have a way of changing the world . . . if only by imitation."

Today, some of the heroes most worthy of emulation are not national figures at all, but are the parents, teachers, bosses, or local leaders, who bring the *real* meaning of love to the upbringing of impressionable youth. Psychiatrists Schwarz and Ruggieri stress the importance of the parents' setting of a good example in their book *You Can Raise Decent Children.*

God, then, has given many of us the ideal. Many of our distant and local heroes, whether famous or not, strive to act in God's image as much as is humanly possible. One anonymous writer thought that day-to-day, unheralded dedication is the most important:

And to most men the call of duty is not uttered in the tones of the trumpet. . . . For most of us the pathway is simple and clear, the work near at hand, and responsibility is constant through the day's toil. For the strength of humanity we look not to our exalted heroes. "Our grand business," as a philosopher says, "is not to grasp at the stars, but to do faithfully life's common work as it comes."

Are there as many heroes today? Are sports stars worshiped as much for their outstanding qualities as they were in the 1940s? Any answer to this would not be free of subjective or normative qualities, and would be difficult to prove by scientific, behavioral analysis. Opinions, however, are not lacking, and several have been examined carefully in this study.

Bob Broeg in his excellent book *Super Stars of Baseball* cites the example of Lou Gehrig (who ended his career just before the 1940s) as a person who was indispensable and, as it turned out, irreplaceable so far as certain positive qualities of the New York Yankees were concerned:

> . . . Lou was the most valuable player the Yankees ever had because he was the prime source of their greatest asset—an implicit confidence in themselves and every man on the club. Lou's pride as a big leaguer brushed off on everyone who played with him. . . .
> The Yankees had that intangible quality called class. It was a tradition perpetuated by guys such as Dickey, DiMaggio, Gordon, Henrich, Rolfe, Gomez and Ruffing, but it stemmed from Lou, and it was the decisive factor in forging their remarkable chain of successes.

The long-term favorable influence that Lou had on the club was underscored by Broeg's statement that:

> It is significant that the Yankees never were involved in night club brawls or drew adverse publicity from clashes between managers and players until DiMaggio and Henrich, *the last men who had been exposed to Lou's influence,* left the club [italics mine].

A modern Diogenes, searching for a counterpart of Gehrig today, however, might seize on the description by John Steadman of Roger Staubach:

> This is an old-fashioned kind of football hero. Roger Staubach reads like one of those make-believe All-American boys we all dreamed about in our long-ago youth and revered from the fictionalized pages of pulp magazines.
> He stands for love of country, love of family, love of God.

According to Steadman, qualities that Staubach deems important in life include dedication and devotion to the above causes, loyalty, humility, honesty, truthfulness, and sincerity.

Reference to such qualities as honesty and humility touches on a distinction that is necessary to comprehend for effective analysis of the relative existence of heroism in two chronologically disparate eras. Whether one thinks that heroes abound today to an equal or greater extent than was the case in the 1940s is apt to be strongly affected by whether he subscribes, on the one hand, to the natural-law theory that there are universally accepted, unchangeable verities or basic truths, or, on the other hand, to the relativist notion that truth is dependent on time and place and changes as circumstances change.

John Steadman, in his description of Staubach, implicitly is adopting a natural-law view that the time-honored virtues of love of country, love of family, love of God, dedication, loyalty, humility, and honesty are values to be cherished in any era or in any place.

On the other hand, David Voight asserts that the hero must "conform to changing value demands." Voight cites Wecter as saying that *formerly* this meant the hero had to be generous, retain the common touch, and be strong without bullying. "In short, he must be human and be patriotic —love his country, be manly and be salty in speech —or earthy." Then Voight concludes: "Of course, some of these expectations which conform to the period up to 1940 have changed."

In other words, some of these values are no longer entertained, and heroes of today must conform to a somewhat different set of expectations. In that view, and in the view of the *Sport* editors, values and times change, and sport figures reflect the times. With these assumptions, it is not difficult to conclude that there are as many or more heroes now as there ever were.

Whether there are as many Staubachs or Steve Garveys (heroes exhibiting traits thought praiseworthy in past generations, as well as by many today) as there were Gehrigs or Doak Walkers is debatable. Few people, after all, die with the grace of Lou Gehrig. It is the writers' view, however, that in recent years the public's focus has not been directed to the older set of values or to those persons that represent them so much as was the case in the 1940s and prior eras.

Thus, one of the purposes of the present study will be to focus on the values represented during the decade of the authors' boyhood by the sports heroes that they venerated. The focus will be on the 1940s and on the personal memories of two young Midwesterners who grew up in that era and were interested in sports nationally, regionally, and locally, and certainly totally. Their reminiscences will thereby reflect their regional and personal biases and will necessarily be fragmentary and not comprehensive so far as the total sports scene of that decade was concerned. Some, but not all, of the gaps can be filled in this volume by others' accounts of the era, and they will be intermingled with the authors' "scrapbook of memories." Honest memories.

The sports, the athletes, the events, the teams; the stadiums, backyards, playgrounds, and other physical settings; and the activities of two boys from Iowa and Kansas, absorbed by all of these and many other things, is what this book is about.

2

BASEBALL

"Here's the windup by Feller . . . and the pitch . . . . Whack! Lombardi lashes the ball deep into left-center field. DiMaggio races for the ball, fields it, and here comes the lo-o-ng throw into Bobby Doerr at second base. Lombardi is held to a single on the play!"

A radio account of the 1942 All-Star Game? No, an eleven-year-old's verbal account that accompanied his playing in 1947 of a popular Cadaco-Ellis (Cadaco today) parlor game, "All-Star Baseball" (ASB). Designed by Ethan Allen, a former Giant and Cardinal star, the game featured a set of forty three-and-one-half-inch flat cardboard "player discs," which fit over a spinner. The periphery of each disc was divided into sections and numbered, with each section and number representing a possible outcome of a time-at-bat—a double, triple, strikeout, etc.—for the "player." Allen had designed the sections mathematically to correspond to the players' actual lifetime batting records in the major leagues. For example, the pitchers' "10" spaces, representing strikeouts, would be large because of the pitchers' relative proclivities to strike out when at bat. Ted Williams and Joe DiMaggio had large "1s," as the "1" stood for home runs.

Cadaco-Ellis appealed to youngsters in their advertising with this message:

Play Ball with Big League Stars! The only game which features real players. All Star American and National League players make up the teams. Each Star plays his regular position on the field . . . bats EXACTLY as he does in the real game. Special Individual Player Discs do the trick. . . . Set-up Bleachers and Score Board authentically duplicate a real Baseball Park.

And play ball (with the game) they did in the

1940s (and, as will be seen, in succeeding decades and generations). Young and McClure both played the game by the hour in their respective Iowa and Kansas homes. With the 1943 version of the player discs (which have since been revised by Ethan Allen annually and sold at a small cost by Cadaco to the avid players of the game), Young played a forty-two-game regular-season schedule between two teams he devised from the National League and American League All-Stars—the Cincinnati Reds and St. Louis Browns, respectively. Unlike most parlor games that he played, however, Young was the "spinner" for both sides, playing each game by himself, accompanied, of course, by a vivid imagination. Several blocks away, a schoolboy friend, Dick Poe (now a psychiatrist in San Francisco) was solo-playing another two-team "regular season" schedule with the same 1943 version of the

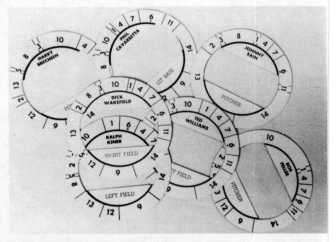

All-Star Baseball player discs from the Cadaco-Ellis All-Star Baseball Game, 1947 and 1949 versions. (Copyright, Cadaco, Inc., Chicago, Illinois.)

game. As might be expected from two youngsters with such imagination, a post-season "world series" was played between the victorious Reds and Panthers. The club "owners" kept elaborate records in addition to giving their imaginary radio play-by-play description of the games.

The writers do not intend to imply by the above description that youngsters do not play this parlor game still, or fantasize athletic encounters as described here and in chapter one. On the contrary, one avid player of the All-Star Baseball game, John Rose, has recently begun quarterly publication of the *All Star Baseball News*. Postal leagues have been organized through advertisements placed in the *News;* Ethan Allen has contributed articles; and the writing of articles by others for this specialized periodical manifests continued enthusiastic interest in the game. Some of the contributors and subscribers have played the game since its inception in the early 1940s.

One contributor, Skip Sesling, in an article entitled "The Cadaco Syndrome or How To Find, Buy or Cheat Your Neighbor Out of Those Discs," lamented the fact that many fans of the parlor game lost their old discs to the trashman through one process or another. Sesling then indicates his continued interest in the game:

Many of us outgrow Tru-Action football . . . our yo-yo's have gone the way of old newspapers . . . baseball cards have been sold to help pay for a date . . . and that treasured Clyde Kluttz autograph has long since returned to its ecological beginnings.

But do we outgrow ASB? Nope. Although I hadn't met another ASB fan for years, two years ago a friend showed me his collection dating back to the 1940's. I hastily convinced him of my undying love for the game. He nearly made me post a bond, but I finally cajoled him into letting me xerox his entire collection of 500 or so discs. I must say it wasn't easy talking him into letting me borrow them for a day in order to copy them. In fact, he only gave me 50 at a time and wouldn't give one batch until I'd returned the previous one.

Sesling then lists six ways an ASB buff can acquire more discs.

The Cadaco Company has always been helpful to the ASB fan, and, upon receiving a request and payment, has sympathetically and promptly mailed new player discs with accompanying lists of those available. From reading a statement on the inside cover of the game box that annual editions of the player discs could be obtained from the company, and by receiving the mimeographed lists and regularized handling of one's requests by Cadaco, the ASB nut realized that he was not alone in his ex-

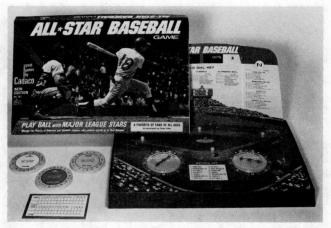

Modern (1975) edition of All-Star Baseball Game. (Courtesy Cadaco, Inc.)

cessive dedication to the game. Publication of the *All Star Baseball News* in 1973, a momentous event in the life of the ASB nut, was, thus, a latter-day confirmation of the validity of that realization.

Accounts in the *News,* such as the following from a twenty-one-year player, have indicated the possible extent of interest in the game:

For 21 years, my friend Ed Lyons and I have been playing ASB. Taped recreations of important games is [sic] among the features of a very elaborate structure we've created over the years.

Since Ed lives in Washington now, the taped games take on a new importance for me. The procedure of how I recreate a game is as follows:

I play the game, keeping complete score of every move. I have 2 records of crowd sounds at a baseball game, one is general background, and the other is cheering, jeering and crack of the bat sounds.

After the game, on one track of my tape machine, I do my elaborated description, adding whatever I can imagine as I improvise using the score sheet as my guide. Sometimes players argue with umpires or get in fights, etc. While I'm doing this, on the same track, I have the general background sounds.

After that's finished, I record, on the other track, whatever cheering or jeering is appropriate to what's happening in the game such as rallys [sic], or homeruns. On this track I also add commercials. (It helps to have access to two tape machines).

The commercials we do are all comedy; Ed excels at this. We even do player interviews before or after the game; these are usually humorous too.

We meet for All-Star games and World Series between our leagues, both major and AAA (we also have B, C and two D leagues). All of the major league games are taped in part, at least, and I enjoy going back and listening to games we played years ago.

The most important part of the ASB is that it provides unlimited opportunity for innovation and creativity . . . all it takes is a love of baseball.

The 1942 World Champion St. Louis Cardinals. Managed by Billy Southworth (front row, fifth from left), the Cardinals possessed one of the strongest pitching staffs ever assembled. Enos Slaughter (front row, second from left) led the NL in hits and batted .318. Stan Musial (to the right of Slaughter) hit .315 in his first full season, and Marty "Slats" Marion (to the left of Slaughter) led the league in doubles. The team's .268 batting average and 2.55 ERA (both first in the NL) indicated its overall strength. But, with 106 wins, the Cards only won the pennant by two games over the Dodgers. Mort Cooper (back row, fourth from right), the loop's MVP, earned that honor by winning the most games (twenty-two), pitching the most shutouts (ten), and posting the best ERA (1.77) in the NL. His brother, Walker Cooper (back row, extreme right), handled most of the catching chores. Rookie Johnny Beazley won twenty-one and lost six (with a 2.14 ERA), and added two Series victories without a defeat. Other fine Cardinal hurlers included Howie Krist, Max Lanier, Harry Gumbert, Howie Pollet, Ernie White, Murry Dickson, and Lon Warneke. (TCMA photo).

Even though the playing of All-Star Baseball is not solely associated with youth of the 1940s, the game was invented during that era when the appeal to the imagination of youngsters was overpowering.

In 1969 Robert Coover published a novel entitled *The Universal Baseball Association*. The protagonist of this fictional work, J. Henry Waugh, spends his evenings playing a parlor baseball game that he has invented. He keeps fantasized newspaper accounts of the games. Unlike most All-Star Baseball nuts, Waugh finds his imaginary players and games both more satisfying and more realistic than baseball itself and the rest of his daily life. As the novel develops, Waugh ultimately loses complete grasp of reality, which becomes equated with his creative fantasy.

Young's first contacts with the sport of baseball included attendance with his family at a minor-league game in 1941 in an old wooden ballpark. The latter was destined to burn during World War II, when professional baseball was already dormant in his hometown of Waterloo. Although his father generously supplied him and his brother with Rip Collins, Frank Demaree, and Pinky Higgins model gloves; Ted Williams and Joe DiMaggio Junior Louisville Slugger bats; official National and American League Spalding and Reach baseballs; and other equipment—the two brothers' actual playing of the game was mainly limited to frequent sessions of playing catch, hitting flies and grounders, and the playing and "broadcasting" of imaginary games by one participant. Games of *softball* at school, Gra-Y, and picnics, and softball games on the grade school playground were common, but organized games of "hardball" were not. Young remembers that playing a few innings for the neighborhood Rosebud (Avenue) Redbirds was his only participation in an actual baseball game.

His interest in the game, however, was considerable, and much of this was manifested in his reading of any available literature on the subject. This began with a perusal of the *1943 Famous Slugger Yearbook*, published by the Hillerich & Bradsby Company, manufacturer of the Louisville Slugger bats. Young's father brought him this valuable collection of data on the 1942 major league season from a local sporting goods store that distributed the yearbooks.

In part because the Cardinals had won the 1942 World Series from the New York Yankees juggernaut, and also because of the geographic proximity of that Middle Western city as compared to other major league sites, Young chose the St. Louis Cardinals as his favorite team. Stan Musial, Whitey Kurowski, Terry Moore, Mort and Walker Cooper, Ernie White, and company were to be his heroes of the baseball world. His admiration for the Cards was not dimmed by the revelation of the *1944 Famous Slugger Yearbook* that the Cardinals had dropped the 1943 Series to the Yankees.

Although Young was never a Yankee fan, he eventually reserved his greatest admiration, of all sports heroes, for the "Pride of the Yankees," Lou "Iron Man" Gehrig. Although Gehrig played professional baseball during the previous two decades, in 1941 he was to succumb to the fatal disease that later was to bear his name. Young's brother, Bob, saw the RKO movie *Pride of the Yankees*, based on Gehrig's life (and starring Gary Cooper), and

The 1942 New York Yankees, American League champions. The Yankees started fast and finished the season nine games in front of the Red Sox. Joe Gordon (second from right, second row) hit .322 and fielded brilliantly to win the MVP award from triple-crown winner, Ted Williams. Joe DiMaggio (top row, third from left) batted .305; and Gordon, DiMag, and Charlie Keller (front row, second from left) all had over 100 RBIs. Bill Dickey (top row, second from right) behind the plate, Phil Rizzuto (front row, fourth from left) at shortstop, Joe Gordon at second, and Joltin' Joe in center gave the Bombers sound defense up the middle. Ernie "Tiny" Bonham (second row, fourth from left) led a solid pitching staff with a league-leading 21-5 mark. In the Series, the Yanks won the opener, 7 to 4; but the Cardinals scored four runs in the ninth inning and went on to shock New York and the nation by sweeping the next four games in this war-year Series. "Marse Joe" McCarthy (front row, sixth from left) lost his first World Series after winning five in the previous six years. Gordon, DiMaggio, and Bonham were picked for the All-Star Major League Team. (TCMA photo.)

Bob related exploits of Gehrig's heroism to Jim before the latter understood the extent of it. At the time, Babe Ruth was more of an idol to Jim, but this was destined to change.

The great Babe, too, was a product of earlier decades (his last playing had been in 1935, a year before Young and McClure were born), but his fatal illness, farewell at Yankee Stadium, and death

The 1943 New York Yankees' World Series starting lineup (l to r): Frankie Crosetti, shortstop; Bud Metheny, rightfield; Billy Johnson, third base; Charlie Keller, leftfield; Bill Dickey, catcher; Nick Etten, first base; Joe "Flash" Gordon, second base; Johnny Lindell, centerfield; and Spurgeon "Spud" Chandler, pitcher. In the regular season, Chandler won twenty while losing only four, with a 1.64 ERA. Leader of the AL in wins, percentage, and ERA (lowest league mark in twenty-four years), he also won the MVP award. Bill Dickey hit .351 at age thirty-six, and Charlie Keller clouted thirty-one homers. Etten led the team in RBIs with 107. The Yankees coasted to the pennant by a thirteen and one-half game margin, and the Cards also repeated, eighteen games in front. In the Series, Chandler was 2-0, and New York obtained revenge by whipping St. Louis in five contests. (TCMA photo.)

The "Iron Horse," Lou Gehrig. The first baseman on the All-Time Team picked by the baseball writers in 1969, Gehrig completed his great career before the 1940s; but his tragic death, caused by amyotrophic lateral sclerosis or "Lou Gehrig's disease," occurred in 1941. Youngsters of the forties admired his exploits as portrayed in the movie *Pride of the Yankees* (1942), starring Gary Cooper. Gehrig's heroic qualities, as manifested in his reaction to the knowledge that he had been stricken with a fatal illness, were prototypic of the character traits admired by youth of the 1940s. He said he was the "luckiest guy in the world." (Courtesy New York Yankees.)

in 1948 were important experiences in the minds of youngsters who had never seen him play. Young followed Ruth's last days closely through the newspaper and learned of his death by that medium while at YMCA Camp Warren in Minnesota. He was later to view the film starring William Bendix, *The Babe Ruth Story*.

Along with Gehrig's death, some of the historic events in baseball in the 1940s prior to this country's entry into World War II were only to be gleaned later by the authors through secondary sources, and were not perceived at the time they occurred.

The triumph of the Cincinnati Reds over the Detroit Tigers in the 1940 World Series occurred before the authors were aware of baseball as a sport, although Red stars Ernie Lombardi and Bucky Walters were to become stalwarts on the Cadaco-style Cincinnati Reds team fashioned by Young from the 1943 version of the game's player discs. Greenberg of the Tigers was to be a star for the parlor-game Browns team in Young's bedroom. Similarly, Mickey Owen's dropped third strike from the bat of Tommy Henrich (the Dodger pitcher was Hugh Casey), which contributed to the Yankee Series championship of 1941, was to escape the authors' notice, basically because of an inability to read at the tender age of five years!

Also in 1941, one of Young's subsequent heroes, the "Splendid Splinter" Ted Williams, was to bat .406—the last time a player has hit .400 or over in

CINCINNATI REDS
WORLD CHAMPIONS
1940

Top Row:—Turner, Ripple, Vander Meer, M. McCormick, Shoffner, Guise, Craft, Frey, Beggs.
Middle Row:—Traveling Secretary Paul, Moore, Joost, Lombardi, Walters, F. McCormick, Derringer, Hutchings, Baker, General Manager Giles.
Bottom Row:—Riggs, Goodman, Thompson, Arnovich, Coach Gowdy, Manager McKechnie, Coach Wilson, Werber, Myers, Riddle, Trainer Rohde.

The 1940 World Champion Cincinnati Reds. Top row (l to r): Jim Turner, Jimmy Ripple, Johnny Vander Meer, *Mike McCormick, Milt Shoffner, Witt Guise, *Harry Craft, *Lonnie Frey, Joe Beggs. Middle row: Traveling Secretary Paul, Whitey Moore, Eddie Joost, *Ernie Lombardi, Bucky Walters, *Frank McCormick, Paul Derringer, Johnny Hutchings, Bill Baker, General Manager Warren Giles. Front row: Lew Riggs, *Ival Goodman, Junior Thompson, Morrie Arnovich, Coach Gowdy, Manager Bill McKechnie, Coach Wilson, *Bill Werber, *Billy Myers, Elmer Riddle, and Trainer Rohde. (*Asterisks denote regulars.*) Lombardi led the team in batting with .319. Frank McCormick and Mike McCormick hit .309 and .300, respectively. Frank McCormick led the NL in doubles and at bats and tied for first in hits. Frey had a league-leading twenty-two stolen bases. Walters posted 22-10 and 2.48 marks to pace the senior circuit in wins and ERA. He also was first in complete games and innings pitched. Derringer was 20-12 on the season. Thompson (16-9), Turner (14-7), and Beggs (12-3) added strength to the staff that led the NL in ERA. Walters (2-0) and Derringer (2-1) were pitching stars in the Series, while Werber, Wilson, Ripple, and Mike McCormick sparkled at the plate. Frank McCormick, Walters, and Derringer made *The Sporting News* All-Star Major League Team. Lombardi, Walters, and Frank McCormick were the National League's MVPs in 1938, 1939, and 1940, respectively. (Courtesy Cincinnati Reds.)

Two-time NL batting champ, catcher Ernie "Schnozz" Lombardi. Playing for the Cincinnati Reds in 1938, Lombardi led the NL in hitting. Representing the Boston Braves in 1942, he duplicated that feat. (TCMA photo.)

33

The 1940 Detroit Tigers, American League champions. Front row: Charlie Gehringer (2b), Dick Bartell (ss), Red Kress (ss-3b), Bing Miller (coach), Del Baker (manager), Merv Shea (coach), Tommy Bridges (p), Barney McCosky (of), Mike Higgins (3b), Pete Fox (of). Middle row: Bobo Newsom (p), Rudy York (1b), Earl Averill (of), Frank Croucher (2b-ss-3b), Dizzy Trout (p), Hal Newhouser (p), Schoolboy Rowe (p), Dutch Meyer (2b), Archie McKain (p), Tuck Stainback (of). Back row: Fred Hutchinson (p), Billy Sullivan (c-3b), Birdie Tebbetts (c), Hank Greenberg (of), Al Benton (p), Johnny Gorsica (p), Tom Seats (p), Clay Smith (p), Bruce Campbell (of). Hank Greenberg cracked out forty-one homers, and Rudy York thirty-three, as the Tigers held off stretch drives by the Indians and Yankees to win the AL pennant by a single game. Greenberg was named the league's MVP, and much-traveled Bobo Newsom (21-5) and Schoolboy Rowe (16-3) paced the mound staff. The Cincinnati Reds edged the Tigers, four games to three, in the Series. (Courtesy Detroit Tigers.)

Mickey Owen of missed third-strike fame. Despite the fact that Owen set NL and club fielding records for catchers, he is best remembered for missing the ball after Tommy Henrich of the Yankees struck out in the ninth inning of the fourth game of the 1941 World Series. If he had held the ball, Brooklyn would have tied the Series at two games apiece. Owen, today the sheriff of Greene County, Missouri, "jumped" to the Mexican League after World War II. (TCMA photo.)

34

The 1941 Brooklyn Dodgers, National League champions. Top row: Casey (p), Camilli (1b), Pfister (c), Wasdell (of), Franks (c), Spencer (c), Coscarart (lf), Fitzsimmons (p), Galan (of), Fred "Dixie" Walker (rf). Middle row: Medwick (lf), Davis (p), Drake (p), French (p), Wyatt (p), Albosta (p), Hamlin (p), Kimball (p), Herman (2b), Allen (p). Bottom row: Wilson, trainer; Lavagetto (3b), Reese (ss), Reiser (cf), Corriden, coach; Durocher, manager; Dressen, coach; Higbe (p), Owen (c), Riggs (3b), Bodner, mascot. The Dodgers broke the two-year Cincinnati dominance of the NL by edging the Cardinals for the flag by two and one-half games, their first pennant since 1920. Brooklyn's Dolph Camilli led the league in homers and RBIs, and was named MVP of the senior circuit. His teammate Pete Reiser led the NL in batting, runs, total bases, doubles, triples, and slugging. Two right-handers, Kirby Higbe and Whit Wyatt, paced the Dodger mound corps with 22-9 and 22-10 records, respectively. *The Sporting News* picked Camilli, Reiser, and Wyatt on the 1941 Major League All-Star Team. The Dodgers dropped the Series to the Yankees in five games. (TCMA photo.)

the majors. And "Joltin'" Joe DiMaggio was to put together his fantastic fifty-six-game consecutive hitting streak in the same year as Owen's famous miscue. DiMaggio's feat was to be deemed "baseball's greatest achievement" in 1969 by leading sport authorities. But all of these prewar baseball gems were to escape the notice of two kindergarten-age boys.

Incidentally, Williams' feat rated fourth place in the same poll. 1941 was also the year Whirlaway won the triple crown of horse racing; Joe Louis

caught up with the challenger, Billy Conn, in the thirteenth round in the boxing ring; and in baseball, Bobby Feller won twenty-five games for the Indians, and Thornton Lee, twenty-two games for the White Sox; Lefty Grove of the Red Sox won his three hundredth, and "Pistol" Pete Reiser of the Dodgers became the youngest player to win the National League batting championship.

As noted, Young's awareness of the 1942 and 1943 seasons was largely a product of after-the-fact accounts in the *Famous Slugger Yearbooks*. It was not until 1944 that he became a devoted follower of the newspaper sports-page box scores and of baseball on a day-by-day basis.

A martial air. The impact of war is apparent in these boyhood photos of co-authors Young (left) and McClure (right). World War II not only had its effect on sports, but also on the impressionable minds of youngsters.

Toy soldiers and equipment from the World War II
era. (From the collections of the authors.)

Ration books and savings bonds from World War
II. (From the collections of the authors.)

As Clem McCarthy was to say in his narrative for the Columbia record album, *The Greatest Moments in Sports*, "the world was now at war." Although Young and McClure were well aware of that fact—as witnessed by their doodling on notepaper at school, "war games" in the backyard and (with toy soldiers) in the house, helping with the victory gardens, taking cans of fat to the store, buying stamps at school toward Victory Bonds, and other war-related pursuits—they were not totally aware of the impact war had had on the sports scene. To be sure, they knew that many baseball and other sports stars were in the armed forces, but they did not appreciate the fact that the quality of play by the oldsters, 4-Fs, and part-time players was far below normal major-league standards.

Clark Griffith, owner of the Washington Senators, and Ford Frick, president of the National League, stayed in contact with seats of governmental power despite Commissioner Kenesaw Mountain Landis' detestation of President Franklin Roosevelt. Griffith and Frick were influential in obtaining a letter from President Roosevelt to Landis in January of 1942 that gave baseball the "green light"—an unofficial authorization to exist during the war. Roosevelt cited, as justification, the healthful effect it would have on civilian morale.

More than 4,000 of the 5,700 players in the major and minor leagues went into the service. Of the forty-one minor leagues existing before Pearl Harbor, only nine were in existence during the war. Night baseball was banned in certain parts of the country until 1944 because of the presence of Nazi submarines off the East Coast. The ban made it difficult for minor-league teams that had employed part-time players, but the major leagues merely resorted to twilight games. Travel restrictions were imposed, and Judge Landis in 1943 ruled out spring training south of the Potomac and Ohio rivers and west of the Mississippi (except for the St. Louis teams that could train anywhere in Missouri).

"For the duration," army camps and naval-training stations fielded their own teams, and Washington encouraged the major-league teams to play the service squads for entertainment of the recruits. Loaded with all-stars, the service teams were formidable opponents. Most clubs dropped all but a few of their scouts, figuring it was not sensible to sign young players who would soon be drafted. But Brooklyn, under Branch Rickey's astute leadership, scouted aggressively and signed every good young player they could "get their hands on," picking up Rex Barney, Carl Erskine, Carl Furillo, Gil Hodges, Clem Labine, and many other outstanding performers for the future.

The war even affected the baseball itself. Because the Office of Price Administration deemed rubber to be a "war-priority product," the A.G. Spalding & Brothers firm came up with what they hoped would be a workable substitute. Under the supervision of a Landis-appointed committee, Spalding devised a baseball core of cork and balata (derived from the sap of a South American tree). Two layers of balata were also used between the core and yarn winding. The result was a ball that had the same size, weight, and shape of a regular baseball. Warren Giles, then general manager of the Cincinnati Reds, demonstrated in an experiment (dropping the regular 1942 balls and the 1943 balata balls from the Reds' grandstand roof to the street fifty feet below) that the newer balls bounced twenty-seven percent less than the old ones. His conclusion was borne out by an unusually low number of runs scored in the first few days of the 1943 season. An investigation by Spalding indicated that the cement used between the layers of wool was faulty, and by 8 May, a new and resilient balata ball was being used. In the meantime, the American League used the dead balata balls, as President Will Harridge had received no formal complaints. The balata ball would have to do; there was a war on. The National Leaguers, however, with President Ford Frick's authorization, found enough 1942-style balls to carry them through. Even with the improved balata ball, Nick Etten was to lead the American League in home runs in 1944 with twenty-two, although this low figure is perhaps explainable by the loss of so many sluggers to the armed forces.

As late as 1943, the major-league teams were able to field some "name players," but by 1944 *The Sporting News* reported that sixty percent of the 1941 starting players on Opening Day had departed. The Yankees had lost all nine starters, eight to the service and one to an Ivy League school coaching staff. By the end of 1944, the major leagues had sent 470 players to war. The fact that the Cardinals were able to retain such notables as Stan Musial, Max Lanier, and Walker Cooper during the 1944 season was an important factor in their winning of the pennant and Series that year. But those stars were lost to the war effort before 1945 (when the Cards did not win the pennant).

During the 1942 season, stars who were not in the service, including the great Joe DiMaggio, were booed by fans on the grounds that if they were sufficiently healthy to play, they were able to serve. With most stars in the service by 1944 and 1945, however, the fans were happier.

Richard Lingeman has noted that, at one point, the teams were loaded with castoffs, rejects, over-

37

The 1944 St. Louis Cardinals, World Champions. Top row: Yatkeman, property man; Donnelly, Wilks, Litwhiler, Sanders, Mort Cooper, Lanier, Musial, Brecheen. Middle row: Byerly, Schmidt, Keely, Fallon, Hopp, Bergamo, Kurowski, Ward, traveling secretary; Harrison Weaver, trainer. Bottom row: Marion, Verban, Jurisch, Gonzalez, coach; Southworth, manager; Wares, coach; Martin, Garms, O'Dea. C. Cooper and Scanlon, batboys. Walker Cooper was not present when picture was taken. (G. S. Gallery photo.)

age fathers, other oldtimers (some of whom were recalled by teams), defense workers playing on a part-time basis, 4-Fs, and foreigners. *Time* rated the calibre of baseball as between the minor league AA and A categories, "but still baseball." And, yet, Lingeman asserts that, despite the quality of play, "major league baseball enjoyed a popularity greater than at any other time in its venerable history."

1944 is remembered in the sports world as the year the Browns won the pennant. The St. Louis Browns (who were to move to Baltimore after the 1953 season) won their only pennant that year with eighteen 4-Fs on their squad. They won the first nine games of the season and led by seven games in June. But they slumped in late season and fell behind the Tigers. The latter were a game ahead as the Browns went into their final four games of the season, all with the Yankees. Amazingly, the Browns swept the Yankees to win the pennant by a game over Detroit.

The famous "Trolley Series" between two St. Louis teams (who shared Sportsman's Park) was

Stan Musial, three-time MVP of the 1940s. *The Sporting News* selected him as player of the Decade in 1956 and named him to their All-Star Major League Team twelve times, including five times in the 1940s. Musial was the NL's MVP in 1943, 1946, and 1948. He played twenty-two consecutive seasons with the St. Louis Cardinals, tying a record, and he led the NL in batting seven times. (Courtesy St. Louis Cardinals.)

The 1944 St. Louis Browns, American League champions. Top row: West, Shirley, Muncrief, Hafey, Hayworth, Kramer, Hollingsworth, Galehouse, Kreevich, Jakucki. Middle row: C. DeWitt, traveling secretary; Caster, Baker, Potter, Zarilla, McQuinn, Laabs, Christman, Byrnes, Gutteridge, Bauman, trainer; Hanley, property man. Bottom row: Paul, Zoldak, Clary, Taylor, coach; Sewell, manager; Hofmann, coach; Moore, Chartak, Stephens, Mancuso, Scanlon, batboy. (G. S. Gallery photo.)

won by the Cardinals, four games to two. The Series has also been dubbed the "Strikeout Series" because of the record number of strikeouts in a six-game Series achieved by both teams' pitchers—forty-nine by Card pitchers and forty-three by Brownie hurlers. In the final two games, all eight Brownie pinch hitters struck out. The Browns also committed ten errors to the Cardinals' one.

Because of the wartime housing shortage, the two St. Louis managers, Billy Southworth of the Cardinals and Luke Sewell of the Browns, had shared the same apartment during the season (Southworth moved into a hotel during the Series when Sewell's family arrived in town).

The Cardinals had become the first National League team to win three consecutive pennants since John McGraw's Giants won four in a row from 1921 through 1924. The Redbirds also became the first Senior Circuit squad to win over one hundred games in three consecutive seasons.

The Cardinals' pitching staff, despite the war, was truly outstanding. During the 1942–1944 period, Redbird hurlers included: their ace, Mort Cooper; Harry "the Cat" Brecheen; Howie Pollet; Max Lanier; Murry Dickson; Ernie White, a hero of the 1942 Series; Johnny Beazley, another hero

of that series while a rookie; Al Brazle; and Ted Wilks. Most of them also did well after the war.

The Cardinals fortunately were also well stocked in the remainder of their lineup with such stalwarts as Terry Moore, Enos "Country" Slaughter, Stan "the Man" Musial, Walker Cooper, Johnny Hopp, Whitey Kurowski, Ray Sanders, Marty "Slats" Marion, Harry "the Hat" Walker, and Danny Litwhiler. *The Sporting News* All-Star Team included outfielder Slaughter and Mort Cooper in 1942; outfielder Musial, and the famous Cooper brothers battery in 1943 (the Coopers learned of their father's death the morning of the second game of the 1943 Series, but carried on anyway with Mort gaining the only Card victory that day); and first baseman Sanders, shortstop Marion, and the Cooper brothers in 1944. Mort Cooper, Musial, and Marion won the National League Most Valuable Player (MVP) award in 1942, 1943, and 1944, respectively.

As for the 1944 Browns, sportswriter Robert L. Burnes of the *St. Louis Globe-Democrat* was to write glowingly thirty years later:

And then there were the 1944 Browns, the only pennant winner. It's a shame that they had to win in a war year when so many friends were away. They were the same kind of hard-nosed guys the more glamorous Gas House Gang had been. . . .

There were some great friends on that team, too, George McQuinn [who led the 1944 Series batters in 1944 with .438] and Don Gutteridge and Gene Moore and Vern Stephens and Mark Christman and Milt Byrnes and Chester Laabs, and Mike Kreevich and Mike Chartak and Denny Galehouse and the toughest pitcher in the clutch I've ever known, Nels Potter.

The Yankee Clipper, Joe DiMaggio. DiMag's 1941 string of at least one hit in fifty-six consecutive games is generally viewed as baseball's most outstanding achievement. In the centennial year for pro baseball (1969), DiMaggio was voted the Greatest Living Player and the Greatest Player Ever—Center Field. He was MVP of the AL in 1939, 1941, and 1947. (TCMA photo.)

"Marse" Joe McCarthy's Yankees, Series winners in 1941 and 1943 and pennant champs in 1942, were led by the great centerfielder, Joe DiMaggio, and catcher Bill Dickey. Other Yanks who played at least part of the 1941–43 period were the famous shortstops Phil "Scooter" Rizzuto and Frankie Crosetti; outfielders Charlie "King Kong" Keller, Tommy Henrich, and Johnny Lindell; second basemen Joe "Flash" Gordon (who batted .500 in the 1941 Series) and George "Snuffy" Stirnweiss (1945 American League bat champ and All-Star); and third baseman Red Rolfe. The pitching staff was solid with Red Ruffing (who broke a record held by Chief Bender, Waite Hoyt, and Lefty Gomez in winning his seventh Series game in 1943), Marius Russo, Ernie Bonham, Spud Chandler, Johnny Murphy, and Hank Borowy. *The Sporting News* All-Star awards went to second baseman Gordon in 1940–1942, third baseman Billy Johnson in 1943, DiMaggio in 1940–42, catcher Dickey in 1941, and pitchers Bonham (in

1942) and Chandler (in 1943). The American League MVP award was won by DiMaggio in 1941, Gordon in 1942, and Chandler in 1943.

An oddity occurring in 1944 that was not well publicized at the time involved Joe Nuxhall of the Cincinnati Reds. Hard-pressed for talent, Manager Bill McKechnie of the Reds called on Nuxhall as a relief pitcher in a game against the Cardinals. Appearing in the ninth inning when the Reds had all but lost, Nuxhall, as a fifteen-year-old junior-high-school student, became the youngest person ever to play in the major leagues.

And it was a disaster. As he struck out the first batter, 3,500 Crosley Field fans cheered. But then the roof fell in as his control deserted him. Before heading to the showers, he walked five, hit one batter, gave up two singles, and was charged with five runs. The Cards won, 18–0, in the worst major-league rout since 1906.

Nuxhall returned to Cincinnati in 1952, and two years later at age twenty-five was named the National League's Comeback Player of the Year. In 1974 he was the regular batting practice pitcher for the Reds.

Although at the beginning of the 1945 season the major-league manpower problem was more serious than it had been since the war began, the subsequent occurrence of V-E and V-J days ameliorated the situation. However, before the return of veterans to baseball ranks was to become a flood, the All-Star Game of 1945 was cancelled. But perhaps a more unique feature of the season was the presence of the Browns' one-armed outfielder, Pete Gray.

As a boy, Pete Gray lost his right arm after he caught it in the spokes of a wagon wheel. A natural athlete (he still shoots golf in the eighties in his old home town of Nanticoke, Pennsylvania), he learned to bat, catch, and throw with one arm. Ultimately the war gave him a chance to play professional baseball, and in 1944 he batted .333 for Memphis in the Southern Association, hit five home runs, and stole 68 bases (which tied a league record). He was named the Association's Most Valuable Player.

In 1945 he became the most discussed rookie in the majors and a boxoffice drawing card for the St. Louis Browns. His expertness as a drag bunter compensated for his otherwise weak hitting, and he proved to be an excellent outfielder. Gray lasted only one season in the big leagues, playing 77 games and batting .218, with fifty-one hits (forty-three of them singles), but he provided an example for the disabled returning veterans by courageously overcoming a handicap.

A veteran who did follow Gray's example was Bert Shepard. As a lieutenant in the United States Army, Bert managed and starred as a pitcher for his base team in England before flying his thirty-fourth mission in a P-38 fighter plane in Germany. Shepard did not return to play in the season opener that day for his base team, as he was shot down by ground fire. Upon regaining consciousness in a German prison hospital several days later, he discovered that his right leg was missing. Mangled by antiaircraft fire, the limb had been hurriedly but properly removed by German doctors.

When the war ended, Shepard's prewar ambition to be a professional player persisted. His dream was realized in 1945 when Clark Griffith of the Washington Senators signed Shepard to a contract. Manager Ossie Bluege called on him to start against the Brooklyn Dodgers in a July exhibition game, and Bert responded with a victory. Later that month Bluege again called on him, this time in relief in a regular-season game against the Red Sox. Watched intently by the crowd, Shepard went five innings, giving up only three hits and one run, striking out two. After this creditable performance, his artificial limb gave him trouble, and he did not play a regular-season game for the Washington Senators again. He was recalled by them, however, after registering a 2–2 won-lost record for Chattanooga, a Senator farm club.

Another true story of heroism involved Corporal Lou Brissie whose legs were shattered by a German shell in the Apennines of Italy, while leading a rifle squad on patrol. Almost left for dead by a search party because of his immobility and inability to speak, Brissie was finally noticed and taken to a Naples evacuation hospital. Having persuaded Dr. William Brubaker, a Cleveland Indians fan, not to remove a leg, Lou subsequently underwent twenty-three operations. (Brubaker had to fit together the pieces of bone, none of which was more than four inches long, like a jigsaw puzzle, using wire.)

Manager Connie Mack of the Philadelphia Athletics had promised Brissie a contract before the war if he would graduate from college first. Mack corresponded with, and encouraged, Brissie while he was in service, telling the courageous soldier, "There will always be a place for you with the Athletics." In 1947 Brissie, with braces for one leg and a sort of artificial leg for the other, won twenty-three games and lost eight for Savannah in the South Atlantic League. He struck out 278 batters and achieved an earned-run-average of 1.91 as the most outstanding pitcher of the league. In 1948 Lou was to win fourteen games for the Philadelphia A's, and he ultimately pitched six full seasons in the majors! His best mark was 16-11 in 1949, and his lifetime major league record was forty-four wins and forty-eight losses. He was selected for the 1948 All-Star Team, but did not play in the game.

Other returning veterans also influenced the outcome of the 1945 pennant race, with returnees Hank Greenberg and Virgil "Fire" Trucks making especially significant contributions to the Tigers who were to become World Champions. Greenberg powered a grand-slam homer on the last day of the season against the Browns to help Detroit win the American League flag. He was the Tigers' batting hero of the Series with a .304 average, three doubles, two home runs (his first one winning the second game, and the second, temporarily tying the sixth contest), and seven runs batted in (RBIs). Trucks joined the Tigers in the last few days of the season and contributed a Series victory over the Cubs after being allowed to play under a special rule for servicemen.

The Chicago Cubs had nosed out the Cardinals for the 1945 National League pennant, but they proceeded to lose their seventh straight World Series. They did improve on their 1938 Series performance when they were swept by the Tigers. (The Cubs' only World Championships came in 1907 and 1908 at the Tigers' expense when Chicago possessed the famed Tinker-to-Evers-to-Chance infield combination. Detroit had Ty Cobb.)

With Charlie Grimm at the helm, the Cubs in 1945 featured good power with the 1943 and 1944 home run and RBI leader, Bill "Swish" Nichol-

The St. Louis Browns' one-armed outfielder, Pete Gray. In 1945, Gray's only year in the majors, the Browns finished third in the league, only six games behind the winning Tigers. (TCMA photo.)

41

The 1945 Detroit Tigers, World Champions. Front row: Doc Cramer (of), Bobby Maier (3b-of), Dizzy Trout (p), Art Mills (coach), Steve O'Neill (manager), Hal Newhouser (p), Paul Richards (c), Eddie Mayo (2b). Second row: Walter Wilson (p), Les Mueller (p), Jimmy Outlaw (3b-of), Al Benton (p), Johnny McHale (1b), Stub Overmire (p), Joe Orrell (p). Third row: Skeeter Webb (2b-ss), Red Borom (2b-ss-3b), Billy Pierce (p), Hub Walker (of), Art Houtteman (p), Bob Swift (c), Rudy York (1b), Roy Cullenbine (of). Back row: Joe Hoover (ss), Chuck Hostetler (of), Milton Welch (c), Dr. Raymond Forsyth (trainer). (Courtesy Detroit Tigers.)

son, and 1945 batting champ, Phil Cavarretta (.355 average). Third baseman Stan Hack (.323 average) and centerfielder Andy Pafko (110 RBIs) added considerable punch. The midseason acquisition of Hank Borowy from the Yankees may have been the decisive factor in their drive for the pennant, as he contributed an 11-2 season record to the Bruins' cause. "Oom" Paul Derringer, Claude Passeau, and Hank Wyse rounded out the staff.

In the Series, Tiger ace "Prince" Hal Newhouser contributed two victories against one defeat, along with a record twenty-two strikeouts. Paul "Dizzy" Trout added one win and Trucks the other for the four Detroit wins in the seven-game affair.

In the second game, Passeau threw a one-hitter against the Tigers for the victory. However, Borowy carried most of the pitching burden for the Cubs. He shut out the Bengals, 9 to 0, in the first game, lost the fifth game, won the sixth in relief, and lost the finale after failing to retire a single batter. Cavarretta hit .432 for the Cubs, and Roger Cramer, .379 for the Tigers.

Eddie Mayo, the Detroit second baseman, was picked the junior circuit's MVP by *The Sporting News*. On that newsweekly's 1945 All-Major League Team were Cavarretta and Pafko of the Cubs, and Newhouser and catcher Paul Richards of the Tigers. Earlier in the 1940s, Cub Stan Hack won three such awards. Tigers Trout, Greenberg, and first baseman Rudy York made it once, and outfielder Dick Wakefield, twice. Cubs Bill Nicholson and Thornton Lee were selected once, and Derringer made it playing for the Reds in 1940.

Other outstanding ballplayers in the 1940–1945 period included: William "Bucky" Walters of the Reds, who led the league with twenty-three victories in 1943—he had been the league's MVP in 1939; his teammate Frank McCormick won the same title for the World Champion Reds in 1940; Truett "Rip" Sewell of the Pittsburgh Pirates whose "blooper" pitch reached a height of twenty-five feet before crossing the plate (he won twenty-one games in 1943); young shortstop and manager Lou Boudreau of the Cleveland Indians, American

Two-time MVP, slugger Hank Greenberg. In 1936 and 1940, Hank Greenberg of the Detroit Tigers was MVP of the junior circuit. He hit fifty-eight homers in 1938, tying the major league and AL record for a right-handed batter. (TCMA photo.)

Virgil "Fire" Trucks, whitewash specialist. Trucks tossed two major league no-hitters and a one-hitter in a single year, and had four minor league no-hit games. He pitched for the Tigers from 1941–52 and in 1956. (TCMA photo.)

The 1945 Chicago Cubs, National League champions. Top row: Ed Sauer, *Don Johnson, Frank Secory, Heinz Becker, Paul Derringer, Hy Vandenburg, Ed Hanyzewski, Paul Gillespie, Ray Starr, Bob Chipman, Hank Wyse, and Lotshaw (trainer). Middle row: *Lennie Merullo, Len Rice, Walter Signer, *Andy Pafko, Dewey Williams, *Mickey Livingston, *Peanuts Lowrey, (unidentified), Ray Prim, S. Martin. Front row: Bill Schuster, *Stan Hack, Roy Hughes, R. Johnson, Charlie Grimm (manager), Smith (coach), Stock (coach), *Bill Nicholson, Claude Passeau, *Phil Cavarretta. (*Asterisks denote regulars.*) Cavarretta led the NL in batting with .355. Hack batted .323, Don Johnson, .302; and Pafko, .298. Wyse's 22-10 won-lost record paced the pitching staff, which also included Passeau (17-9), Derringer (16-11), Prim (13-8), and Borowy (11-2). Passeau's five shutouts and Borowy's 2.14 ERA also were NL bests. (Courtesy George Brace, Bra-Mac Card Company, Chicago, Illinois.)

League batting champ in 1944; Tommy Holmes of the Boston Braves, MVP of the older league in 1945 when he hit .354 and led the Nationals in home runs; Joe "Ducky" Medwick, member of the Cardinals' Gas House Gang of the 1930s, leading Series hitter for the Dodgers in 1941, and runner-up in National League batting as a Giant in 1944; veteran shortstop Luke Appling of the Chicago White Sox, who won the American League batting championship in 1943 (to go with his 1936 title); and Bobby Doerr of the Boston Red Sox, young second baseman who was the American League's MVP in 1944 and batting average runner-up. These men would have been outstanding in any era.

In addition, Mel Ott, outstanding player-manager of the New York Giants, was breaking many National League records (RBIs, total bases, walks, runs, hits, and extra-base hits) with his raised-leg stance. Fred "Dixie" Walker of the Dodgers was the NL batting champ in 1944, and his teammates Billy Herman and Pete Reiser were also outstanding.

The pennant-winning 1940 Tigers had some famous players in their lineup: Lynwood "Schoolboy" Rowe (whose record was 16-3 that year), pitcher Freddy Hutchinson (later manager of the Tigers), Louis "Buck" (alias "Bobo") Newsom who won two games for Detroit in the Series (his father died after the opener that Bobo had won), shortstop Dick Bartell, centerfielder Barney McCosky, the great second baseman Charley Gehringer, Hank Greenberg, Rudy York, rightfielder Bruce Campbell, third baseman Pinky Higgins, catcher Birdie Tebbetts, and pitchers Tommy Bridges and Dizzy Trout. McCosky, Campbell, Higgins, and Tebbetts became literally household words for author Young. His brother owned a Pinky Higgins glove, and the others' names were represented on his Cadaco-Ellis All-Star Baseball Game discs. Johnny Mize of the Cardinals and Giants; Harry "the Horse" Danning of the Giants; Goody Rosen, Dolph Camilli, and Whit Wyatt of the Dodgers; Bob Elliott of the Pirates; Cecil Travis of the Senators; and Johnny Pesky, Tex Hughson, and Boo Ferriss of the Red Sox—all have not been mentioned and should be. All were *Sporting News* All-Stars in the 1940–1945 period.

Authors McClure and Young, of course, by the end of the 1945 season were true baseball nuts. Backyard fantasizing of their heroes was being practiced to a fine art. Cadaco-Ellis All-Star Baseball Game spinners were humming. The World Series was a time of great excitement. Young's hometown newspaper, the *Waterloo Daily Courier*,

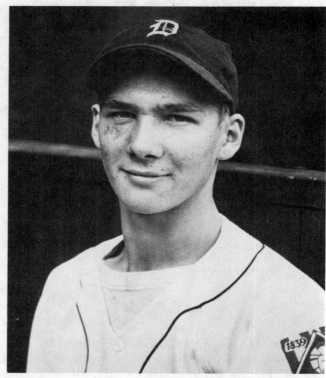

Two-time American League MVP, Hal Newhouser of the Detroit Tigers. "Prince Hal" won twenty-nine and lost nine in 1944, with a 2.22 ERA, and was named MVP. In 1945, he again received that honor after a season with a 25-9 record and a 1.81 ERA. In 1946, Newhouser did not rest on his laurels, winning twenty-six and losing nine. (Courtesy Detroit Tigers.)

White Sox lefty, Thornton Lee. In 1941, Lee led the AL in ERA with 2.37, and in complete games, with thirty. His won-lost record that season was his best, 22-11. "Lefty" Lee pitched eleven years for the White Sox (1937–47) and four for Cleveland (1933–36). (Courtesy Chicago White Sox.)

dutifully published the line scores in bold print on its front pages, since the paper went to press around game time. The newspaper also posted the same news on its large plate-glass windows for pass-ersby. Young's father filled him in on the games' details upon his arrival home from the office, where the radio kept the employers and employees informed. The sports pages of the paper (equally as popular as the comics) were devoured daily for news of the games. Pictures of the stadiums in which the games were played and photographs of Series "heroes," "goats," and key plays were closely examined.

Young's father, Robert A. Young, Sr., was always sympathetic to his son's dedication to sports, and generously aided him in his pursuits by the above-mentioned purchase of equipment, playing catch, and paying for subscriptions to *The Sporting News* and other Spink publications, including the *Baseball Guide* and *Register*. Young vividly and fondly remembers retrieving issues of *The Sporting News* from the porch, the weekly newspaper tightly enclosed in a thin brown wrapper that was often heated by the summer sun or encrusted with the frost of winter. The Willard Mullin cartoons on the cover of the St. Louis-based publication were a highlight for the young reader. The back cover was a source of disillusionment with its Chesterfield ads and photos of players endorsing those cigarettes.

In the postwar period, Young's interest in reading about the sport increased, and books like Harold Kaese's *The Boston Braves*, Frederick Lieb's *The St. Louis Cardinals,* and Frank Graham's *The New York Yankees* were read and took their place on the bookshelf beside the Spink publications. Frank Menke's *The New Encyclopedia of Sports* was a Christmas present and a valued addition to the collection.

Another source of reading materials on sports (as well as the highly desirable comic books of all descriptions) was the Busby-Wing drug store, located a half mile from Young's home adjacent to a small shoe-repair shop, beauty parlor, and corner grocery store—together comprising that era's equivalent of the shopping center. The drugstore was an extremely popular institution for the youth of the 1940s. With its counter service, magazine racks, comic books (usually behind the counter), candy, gum, and spacious concrete steps on the exterior, it was a combination ice-cream parlor, reading room, social hall, and supplier of all the bubble gum and cards and other items avidly sought by nostalgia fanatics today—in addition to its major function of supplying medicine for the ill.

Trips to "Busby's" were frequent, as the Hazen (later Trainor and then Trainor-Keesy) grocery three doors away was the main source of groceries for the Young household; and visits to the shoe repairman, along with such wartime activities as turning in cans of fat for the war effort, and the normal need for items found at a drugstore, brought members of the family frequently to this familiar city block. Bob and Jim Young always hoped they would be recipients of vanilla, chocolate, chocolate "rocky-road," or butter brickle, double-dip ice-cream cones (originally costing a nickel). In later boyhood, with increased freedom and independent but limited financial resources, the array of choices became bewildering for them, with *Captain Marvel* and *Submariner* comic books competing for the purchaser's favor with cherry cokes, salted nut rolls, *Sport* magazine, and an addition to the bubble-gum-card collection. It was here that the youngsters bought their Duncan yo-yos, which were tossed in every possible direction (while "walking the dog," "looping the loop," and "rocking the cradle," for example) on the front steps. Needless to say, the proprietors of the store were often driven to distraction by these and other youthful activities—especially the loitering and long comic-book perusals.

The yo-yo was quite popular in the 1940s for several reasons, including the fact that it was a very cheap form of entertainment. The annual reappearance of the yo-yo was almost as sure a sign of spring as blooming flowers. Neighborhood drugstores were visited occasionally by roving Hawaiian and Filipino experts who could perform "spider webs" and "around the worlds" with amazing agility. These experts were also adept at carving palm trees and initials in the wooden yo-yos of the 1940s. Local contests were fierce in their competition among boys and girls alike.

Sport magazine made its appearance on the newsstand for the first time in 1946, and Young was one of its faithful readers from the beginning. (McClure still has one of his 1947 issues that has Joe and Dom DiMaggio on the cover.) Its beautiful (or so it seemed then) color photos of sports stars ("Sportraits") found their way into Young's burgeoning sports scrapbooks (as well as on to the walls of Paul Hemphill's bedroom—*see below*). This monthly publication was highly valued among Young's youthful colleagues and was avidly read and traded.

One of Young's boyhood dreams was fulfilled in the postwar era when his father took the family to Chicago, and all attended a White Sox game at Comiskey Park. The "Yankee Clipper," Joe Di-

Sports memorabilia from the 1940s. (Baseball and football cards are from collection of Charles Gilbert, Warrensburg, Missouri. Kansas pennant, badges, and book are the authors'.)

Sports literature of the 1940s. (From the collection of the authors.)

Maggio, highlighted the occasion when, with his classically smooth batting style, he stroked a home run for the victorious Yankees. Seeing the Clipper, the venerable Luke Appling, and other Yankee and Sox players; obtaining programs and other souvenirs for the growing collection of baseball memorabilia; hearing the sounds reverberating in the old ball park like the public address announcer with the Eastern accent and crescendos of cheering by the large cosmopolitan crowd; and smelling the beverages, smoke, and industrial exhaust—all were intoxicating to the youthful admirer of the game and its personalities. It was a grand and glorious experience, and future visits to the minor-league (Class B) park of the Waterloo White Hawks, a White Sox farm club, would now always be viewed

Twenty-year White Sox shortstop (1931–50) Luke Appling. Appling was recently voted by fans as the greatest White Sox player of all time. The North Carolina native was AL batting champion in 1936 and 1943. His AL career batting average was .310, and, from 1939–49 (he was in the military in 1944), he batted over .300 in fifteen of sixteen seasons. (TCMA photo.)

with "sophisticated" perspective of one who had seen the best perform. Not that the minor league play was no longer appreciated—on the contrary, it was enjoyed even more—but it was perceived in a broader and more knowledgeable context.

A reading of Paul Hemphill's account of his boyhood, in "I Gotta Let the Kid Go," gives one the impression that Young's experiences recounted above were fairly typical of the era. Hemphill recalls:

And finally, the summer: hitching rides on the hood of Legg's Terraplane Hudson, playing games on rutted city playgrounds, replaying them over ice cream sodas at Hudson's Drug Store; catching the old man's pop flies until dark in the vacant lot across from the house, stumping him with trivia from the *Sporting News* and *Baseball Register* at suppertime, retiring to hear Gabby Bell's imaginative ticker-tape re-creation of Birmingham Baron road games; papering my entire bedroom with full-page color "Sportraits" from Sport magazine. . . .

Hemphill in fact asserts that he was "fairly typical of my generation, I suppose, . . ." and goes on to explain that "I got hooked [on the game of baseball] when I heard Harry Caray's tense description of Enos ("Country") Slaughter of the Cardinals winning the '46 World Series over the Red Sox by scoring all the way from first base on a single."

Hemphill was a Birmingham native. Young was more apt to pick up the Cubs' broadcasts, even though the Cubs were not his favorite team. It seemed to him that *everyone* knew the exploits of Pafko, Cavarretta, Hack, and "Peanuts" Lowrey.

Waterloo, Iowa, however, became a Chicago White Sox farm club, and opened a new (steel, this time) Municipal Stadium in 1946, as minor-league baseball resumed its war-suspended operations in Waterloo and across the land. The *Waterloo Daily Courier* proudly displayed large shots of the new ball park, showed the starting lineup of the White Hawks in photos at their respective positions on the new field, and regularly ran "Know Your White Hawk" columns, introducing the ball players to the fans. Names like Gerry Scala, Buck Behie, and Ken Smith were to roll easily off the tongues of youngsters in Waterloo for some time.

Unknown to youngster and adult alike in that industrial town with its immense John Deere tractor plant (which had made tanks during the war) and Rath Packing Company, minor-league baseball's popularity was to peak only a year later, when the White Hawks averaged over three thousand fans per game. The 1947 season was one to remember for Waterloo residents in many respects. The late Johnny Mostil, former White Sox outfielder with a .301 lifetime major-league batting average, began the year as manager of the White Hawk club, but he was replaced at midseason by Jack Onslow. Onslow took a second-division club and molded them into a smoothly functioning team that went on to finish in the first division and win the playoffs against the Danville Dodgers and other clubs. More excitement was generated by that team in Waterloo than was raised by subsequent *pennant*-winning Waterloo ball clubs.

Young remembers vividly riding his bicycle, taking the bus, or being driven by car to games with his brother Bob and neighbor Phil Gross (son of H.R. Gross, radio newscaster for KXEL at the time and later twenty-six-year veteran of the U.S. Congress). Phil sometimes worked in the press box with his father and Bob (Gene) Elston. On other occasions, he would be employed to "shag" foul balls hit over the grandstand into the parking lot below and return them to the management, or he would sell concessions in the stands. Sometimes the youngsters sat in the bleachers with the YMCA-sponsored Knothole Club, wearing special T-shirts emblazoned with an emblem featuring a white hawk perched on a baseball (Young still has his shirt). Once, while viewing a Waterloo-Danville (Illinois) game from this rightfield perspective, on a row next to the field, Bob and Jim Young were able to talk with the visiting team's bullpen pitcher who was warming up in front of them. Impressed by the man's friendliness and graciousness, the boys asked him his record. "Six-and nothing" was the reply, and the handsome pitcher indicated to the impressed boys that he was scheduled to pitch the next day (Sunday) against Waterloo. Checking the papers for his identity that night, the youngsters learned he was Carl Erskine. The Danville ace was to become a star for the Brooklyn Dodgers and set a World Series single-game strike-out record. Needless to say, he was a hero at the Young household for many years.

That same year Young was to retrieve successfully two baseballs hit in the stands. The economics of minor-league baseball dictated that these be exchanged for two pairs of free passes for future games. The same reward was given to winners of the "lucky-number score card," and the author attended so many games that he won four of those passes too.

In later years, the competition for entertainment time and dollars from the Tunis Speedway (midget auto and stock-car race driving); golf, swimming (two large municipal pools were to be built in postwar Waterloo), and other participant sports; and eventually, of course, television—all were to alter irrevocably and adversely the popularity of minor-league baseball. The Waterloo club would be lucky to draw a thousand fans per game in later decades.

Some of the 1947 White Hawks were to go on to the majors—manager Jack Onslow (with the White Sox as skipper in 1949 and part of 1950), outfielder Jim Busby, and pitcher Howie Judson. To Waterloo-area youth, the Judson-John Perkovich pitching duo was as important as the Spahn and Sain ("and pray for rain") combination of the Braves was to Boston fans of that day. The pitching duels between "herky-jerky" Perkovich and Erskine were classics. One such duel followed the 1947 chance meeting of the Youngs with Erskine, and the Youngs were in attendance.

Paul Hemphill ably describes the colorful atmosphere of minor-league baseball in the postwar era in his "Viewpoint South" column for *Sport*. After describing the modern-day amenities of baseball, he states:

> Yet there is a sadness about all of this if you were teethed in one of those minor-league towns during the late '40s. When World War II let out and everybody came home, it meant the last brief revival of small-town living in America: the towns were full and vibrant and lusting for life again, and because television and other diversions had not yet reached the common man he quenched his thirst at the ballpark. The men he watched perform were just as full and vibrant as the towns they represented, many of them veterans more than willing to play baseball for $200 a month after escaping places like Iwo Jima and Bastogne. Baseball, at that level and at that time, wasn't merely a game; it was a holy war, a celebration, a way of life.

Hemphill laments the passing of the great part of minor-league baseball. He feels that when these bush leagues died, a vibrant form of life went with them.

On the sandlot, the conditions also were much different in the 1940s. In an article entitled "Was Baseball Playing More Fun in the Hot, Dusty '30's?", Roger Swanson of the *Kansas City Star* relates a picture that was very similar to the conditions of the early 1940s as well as during the Depression:

> You went out (no uniform, of course) on the hottest afternoon of the summer. With a few buddies you got the darnest game of scrub under way. Maybe you played all afternoon, even when the temperature was 95. Then you ran home and Mom had a Hires root beer or a big pitcher of lemonade waiting. . . .
> Sounds strange to say, perhaps, but the really best

The 1946 St. Louis Cardinals, World Champions. Front row: Marion, Kurowski, Musial, Brazle, Wares, coach; Dyer, manager; Gonzalez, coach; E Adams, T. Moore, Slaughter, Dickson. Middle row: Sessi, Schmidt, Beazley, Schoendienst, H. Walker, Endicott, Pollet, Dusak, O'Dea, C. Barrett, Grodzicki, Ward, traveling secretary. Back row: Jones, Sisler, Kluttz, Krist, Rice, Burkhart, Weaver, trainer; Wilks, Garagiola, Donnelly, Brecheen, Cross. Batboys Scanlon and Dyer, Jr., in front. (G. S. Gallery photo.)

part of this primitive prehistoric game of the 1930s was the heat. It felt so doggone good to go out when the temperature was near 100 and play and sweat and get dust all over and feel rather exhausted and filthy. But there always was a great remedy—the front lawn sprinkler. You laid under it, drank it up, rolled through it and pranced under it.

Hemphill draws a sharp contrast between that era and the present. He thinks that baseball fails to attract the children of today who were "raised on color television and automobiles and week ends at the lake." Baseball, an innocent game, and hero worship suffer as children become more sophisticated and cynical. Youngsters play baseball today, but it is a highly organized, structured activity with excellent facilities and accoutrements. And all without dust!

As for the major leagues, 1946 marked the transfer of Young's prime baseball loyalty from the St. Louis Cardinals to the Boston Braves, with the transfer of manager Billy Southworth from the former to the latter club. This was a rather foolish change for Young from the standpoint of success,

as the Braves had not won a pennant since the "Miracle Braves" of 1914 swept to the world championship in a great upset over the "A's." And the Cardinals, under Eddie Dyer, were to capture the National League pennant in 1946 after winning the first playoff in major-league history in two games over the Dodgers.

With Harry "the Cat" Brecheen winning three games, and Enos "Country" Slaughter making his famed sprint from first base to home on Harry "the Hat" Walker's single to left-center (while Johnny Pesky, Boston shortstop, held the ball for a split-second too long on the relay), the Cards won the Series in seven games over the talent-laden Red Sox. Boston had led the Series in games three times before bowing. It was the first Boston team to lose a Series up to that time, the Red Sox having won in 1903 (the first time it was held), 1912, 1915, 1916, and 1918. Ted Williams, facing the Cards' shift, was held to five singles and a .200 average in his only Series. Harry Walker batted .416, and Bobby Doerr, missing one game and part of another because of migraine headaches, .409 for the Bosox. Rudy York had two home runs, a triple, and a double for Tom Yawkey's Beantown representative. The papers portrayed Brecheen, who gave up only one run in twenty innings, and Slaughter as the heroes, and Pesky (especially) and Williams (for whom many writers had no love and vice versa), the goats.

Two of Young's sports-loving friends, Dick and Tim Walker, were devoted Yankee and Cardinal fans. They also owned, and played with, an All-Star Baseball Game by Cadaco-Ellis, and were or-

The 1946 Boston Red Sox, American League champions. Front row: Dowd (traveling secretary); Pesky, Doerr, Pellagrini, Woodall, coach; Cronin, manager; D. Baker, coach; Carey, coach; D. DiMaggio, C. Wagner, Gutteridge. Middle row: Green, trainer; M. Brown, Ryba, Campbell, McGah, Lazor, Partee, Moses, H. Wagner, M. Harris, York, Higgins, Culberson, Orlando, clubhouse attendant. Back row: Klinger, McBride, G. Russell, Metkovich, Dreisewerd, Dobson, E. Johnson, Zuber, Bagby, Hughson, Ferriss, Schreiber, Williams. Batboy Kelly seated in front. (G. S. Gallery photo.)

ganizers of, and starters for, the Rosebud Redbirds nine. Occasionally the Young and Walker families would go picnicking together in beautiful, pastoral settings, but the pristine simplicity of the site was always invaded by baseball mitts, baseballs, and a radio bringing in the current baseball encounter. Mixed in with juicy steaks, potatoes fried on a large black skillet over a wood fire, good coffee, milk, and sometimes delicacies like watercress from a nearby stream, were baseball arguments and discussion of baseball lore.

While in fifth grade, Jim Young placed second in the softball throw in his grade school's track and field meet, losing to sixth-grader Dick Bertell. Both qualified for the city track and field meet, which Bertell won for the second consecutive time. The latter was destined to move on to stardom at Iowa State as a catcher, and then played several years for the Chicago Cubs.

It was in 1946 that the authors learned the majors could play rough with outsiders attempting to

Ted Williams of the Boston Red Sox, lifetime .344 hitter. "The Kid" batted .406 in 1941, and was the last person to hit .400 or more. Two times he was the AL's MVP (1946 and 1949). He won the triple crown (leader in average, homers, and RBIs) in 1942 and 1947. The "Splendid Splinter" hit over .300 sixteen times and led the AL in batting six times, including a .388 mark when he was thirty-nine years old. Williams spent nearly five years in the military in World War II and the Korean War, and flew forty missions as a marine pilot in the latter conflict. (TCMA photo.)

establish rival leagues. When the millionaire Jorge Pasquel and his brothers established the Mexican League after the war, it was labeled an "outlaw" by Commissioner A.B. "Happy" Chandler, and major leaguers who disregarded their contractual "reserve clause" and signed and played with these Mexican teams were banned from the major leagues for a number of years. Players who succumbed to the lure of fat contracts included Max Lanier, Fred Martin, Sal "the Barber" Maglie, Mickey Owen, and Ace Adams. Disillusioned with their Mexican experience after a year or so, these men found the doors of the majors closed to them, and Lanier, Martin, and others brought suits. Their action was settled out of court, and suspensions were subsequently lifted.

1947 marked the entry of the first black baseball player in the major leagues. Branch Rickey, general manager of the Brooklyn Dodgers, had surprised the baseball world the year before by signing Jackie Robinson for the Dodgers' top farm club at Montreal. Robinson had previously made a name for himself in football, basketball, and track as well, in his college days at UCLA. With Brooklyn in 1947, Robinson responded admirably not only as a gentleman, but also by leading the NL with thirty-nine stolen bases (he won that crown again in 1949) and was *The Sporting News'* Rookie of the Year. He batted .259 with three RBIs and two doubles in the 1947 World Series. He was the NL's Most Valuable Player in 1949, when he led the circuit in batting with .342.

Also in 1947, Larry Doby became the first black to play in the American League. He was hired by another innovator, Bill Veeck, owner of the Cleveland Indians. Unlike Robinson, Doby did not join his club until July and played only twenty-nine games, batting .156. The following year, however, he hit .301, helping the Indians to the pennant, and he socked a key World Series home run that enabled Steve Gromek to edge Johnny Sain, 2 to 1, before 81,897 fans.

Roy Campanella, another black star, was to join the Dodgers in 1948. He later was to become the only player besides Stan Musial to win the MVP award in the National League three times. Don Newcombe became the third black to win a position with the Dodgers in 1949, when he compiled a 17-8 record and won Rookie-of-the-Year honors.

The legendary Leroy "Satchel" Paige joined Doby on the Indians in 1948, helping Cleveland to the pennant with his 6-1 record. Two hundred thousand fans jammed Municipal Stadium to see him in his first three starts.

In 1974, a reader of Mickey Herskowitz and Steve Perkins' "Sports Hot Line" column in the *St. Louis Globe-Democrat* asked: "Now Cool Papa Bell is in the Baseball Hall of Fame along with Josh Gibson and Satchel Paige and others. I have often wondered, with all these great players available, why was Jackie Robinson picked to break the color line?" The reporters responded: "Robinson was judged to have the correct blend of education, courage and talent—with most of his career still in front of him."

In the 1947 season, Ewell Blackwell won sixteen straight games pitching for the Reds. Burt Shotton managed the Dodgers after the suspension of Leo Durocher for the season, and the Bums eked out a pennant victory over the Cardinals. After reeling off nineteen straight wins in July, the Yankees, with Stanley "Bucky" Harris at the helm, won the AL flag by twelve games over the Tigers. Harris, the "boy wonder," in his first season managing the Senators in 1924 had led the club to the world championship, and now he was duplicating that feat with the Bronx Bombers. The 1947 Series was the first to be telecast, but it would be several years before the average homeowner in Kansas or Iowa would see a game on his own set.

The 1947 Series certainly must rank as one of the most dramatic of all time, and most of its fame

Winner of sixteen consecutive victories in 1947, Ewell "the Whip" Blackwell of the Cincinnati Reds. Blackwell nearly equaled Johnny Vander Meer's record of two consecutive no-hitters. In June of 1947, "the Whip" hurled a no-hitter at the Boston Braves. In his next appearance against the Dodgers, he gave up no hits until the ninth when Eddie Stanky and Jackie Robinson singled. The next three Dodgers were retired in order for a two-hit shutout. Blackwell's 1947 record was 22-8, his career best. (TCMA photo.)

stems from two incidents. In the fourth game, Floyd "Bill" Bevens of the Yankees was one out from pitching the first no-hitter in Series history, although his performance had been somewhat marred by walks and a run stemming from that wildness in the fifth inning. Bevens walked Furillo after one was out in the bottom of the ninth. Johnny "Spider" Jorgensen fouled out, but Al Gionfriddo, running for Furillo, then stole second in an important maneuver. "Pistol" Pete Reiser, who had not started because of a leg injury, pinch-hit for Hugh Casey, the pitcher. Rather than pitching to the ailing Reiser, Manager Harris ordered Bevens to walk him. With the winning run now on base, Eddie Miksis ran for Reiser, and Harry "Cookie" Lavagetto batted for Eddie Stanky. Then, with two outs, two runners on base, and the score 2-1 Yankees, Lavagetto laced the second pitch

Floyd "Bill" Bevens of the Yankees. Bevens was the hard-luck pitcher in one of baseball's most historic games, the fourth game of the 1947 World Series. (Courtesy New York Yankees.)

Stanley "Bucky" Harris, the "Boy Wonder." In his first year as manager, Bucky Harris led the Washington Senators to the 1924 AL pennant, defeating the Yankees, who had won it three straight times. Player-manager Harris batted .333 in the Series, as the Nats edged the Giants in seven games. His Senators also won the 1925 AL title. In 1947 Harris repeated his 1924 feat, this time as a bench manager. In his first year as Yankee pilot, his team won the World Championship. (Courtesy New York Yankees.)

off the rightfield wall to score Gionfriddo and Miksis. The no-hitter was ruined, and the Series was evened at two games apiece.

The other famous 1947 Series event occurred in the sixth game and also involved a substitute player. In the sixth inning, Al Gionfriddo was inserted in the Dodger lineup as a defensive measure. With the Dodgers trailing in the Series, three games to two, but leading in this one, 8 to 5, "Joltin' " Joe DiMaggio came to bat with two Yankees on base and two outs. DiMaggio cracked a long blow that seemed destined for a game-tying home run. But Gionfriddo went "back, back, back, back," as announcer Red Barber put it, and with a miraculous catch hauled down the shot at the bullpen gate, 415 feet from home plate. DiMaggio kicked the dust in disgust. The game was saved for the Dodgers who evened the Series at three apiece.

Veteran sportswriter Furman Bisher of the *Atlanta Journal* in 1971 rated the Lavagetto two-base hit as the "greatest moment of the last 25 years" in responding to an inquiry from *Sport* magazine about the 1946–1971 period—the magazine's first quarter-century. "There have been thrills in bunches since, but nothing to take its place with that one." In a subsequent article for *The Sporting News*, Bisher pointed out some quirks of fate:

In fact, the three names from that autumn carnival that have survived the ravages of time are three guys who never were going to make it back that way again. Bill Bevens threw a few more pitches in relief after Cookie Lavagetto broke up his no-hit game and neither ever made a big league box score again.

As for Gionfriddo, Bisher related:

> The curious still look up Al Gionfriddo in Santa Barbara, California, and ask him about the intelligent catch he made on Joe DiMaggio when the Yankees and the Dodgers played the World Series of 1947. Gionfriddo was only a Dodger about half the season, and the one in the far corner over by the water cooler at that.
> Know what he hit for the season? .175.
> Did you know it was the last game he ever played in the big leagues?

In the finale, Tommy "Old Reliable" Henrich knocked in his third game-winning run of the Series to win it for ace fireman Joe Page (who gave up one hit in the last five innings) and the Yankees. Henrich batted .323 for the Yankees, and Harold "Pee Wee" Reese, .304 for the Flatbush nine, to lead those participating in all seven contests. Furillo batted .353 in six games, and Johnny Lindell in the same number hit an even .500 with nine hits, three doubles, one triple, and seven RBIs. With no pitcher from either team going the route in the Series, Hugh Casey, Page's opposing counterpart, relieved in six games, winning two with no defeats and posting a 0.87 earned-run-average. Rookie pitcher "Spec" Shea was 2-0 for the Yankees, and DiMaggio's home-run blast in the fifth game was the decisive blow in that contest.

The transfer of Young's baseball loyalty from the Cards to the Braves almost made him appear to be clairvoyant to his friends when the Boston Nationals won the league pennant for the first time since 1914. To Young, however, this did not seem an unnatural development with Billy Southworth at the helm. In 1948 he became one of the select group of managers to have won two pennants with more than one club. According to Robert L. Burnes, by 1974 there had been eleven such managers, including Walter Alston who led the Dodgers to championships in two different cities. Of the others—Yogi Berra, Joe Cronin, Leo Durocher, Bucky Harris, Al Lopez, Joe McCarthy, Bill McKechnie, Pat Moran, Billy Southworth, and Dick Williams—most were in baseball in the 1940s in one capacity or another.

Cronin, Harris, and Southworth completed this achievement in 1946, 1947, and 1948, respectively, and Durocher was to follow in 1951. Only McKechnie accomplished this with more than two clubs. He won with the Pirates in 1925, the Cards in 1928, and the Reds in 1939–40.

By 1948 Young's favorite players had switched from Mort Cooper and Stan Musial of the Cardinals to pitchers Johnny Sain and Warren Spahn and third baseman Bob Elliott of the Braves. All had key roles in engineering the Braves' pennant victory. Sain, a tobacco-chewing Arkansas native, led the National League with twenty-four wins (he was to win twenty, three other times), and *The Sporting News* named him Pitcher of the Year. Years later, as a pitching coach, he was to help produce many twenty-game winners and pennants for several major-league clubs, but he often clashed with his managers.

The great Warren Spahn, who later was to become the all-time leader in victories for left-handed pitchers (363) and to win twenty games or more thirteen times (tied with Christy Mathewson for the National League mark in that category), was another important cog in the Braves' 1948 success, with fifteen wins.

Bob Elliott had been an all-major league third baseman for Pittsburgh in 1944 and was the league's MVP in 1947 when he batted .317 and drove in 113 runs. For his efforts in the 1948 championship year, he was picked by *The Sporting*

Warren Spahn, NL's all-time leader in victories for a left-hander. Spahn won 363 games in his career. He won over twenty games thirteen times, breaking the major league record for a left-hander. His first twenty-game season came in 1947, when he led the NL in innings pitched and in ERA. In 1949, he led the league with twenty-one wins, 302 innings pitched, and 151 strikeouts. He threw sixty-three career shutouts (an NL record). (TCMA photo.)

News as the NL's all-star third baseman. Elliott died at age forty-nine in 1966.

In rightfield the Braves had popular and dependable Tommy Holmes, who had set the NL's consecutive-game hitting record of thirty-seven in 1945 when he was the circuit's MVP and an all-star outfielder.

In a nostalgic recollection of old stadiums and the 1948 Braves, Wells Twombly recalls the days when, as a thirteen-year-old New Englander, he considered Tommy Holmes (whose picture adorned Twombly's wall) the greatest ever as a rightfielder. He refers to the jingle "Spahn and Sain, then pray for rain," but correctly notes that rookie Vern Bickford won eleven games for the Beantowners that year. He remembers listening to announcer Jim Britt's broadcasts of Braves games on the same small radio that had recently brought him accounts of the Allies' victories in World War II. The feats of Braves stars Bob Elliott, Earl Torgeson, Tommy Holmes, and Al Dark were exaggerated by the enthusiastic Britt during the late summer heat wave of 1948, if Twombly's poignant recollections are accurate.

In the AL, Cleveland, trailing by four and one half games after Labor Day, put on a stretch drive leading to the top, but their loss on the final day of the season led to the first tie and playoff in league history. A Navy veteran, left-hander Gene Bearden, was a key factor in the Indians' drive to the world championship. In World War II, Bearden suffered injuries when his cruiser was torpedoed, and aluminum plates were imbedded in his head and knee. The naval hero won twenty games while losing seven for the Tribe in 1948, mowed down the Red Sox with a five-hitter (while manager and shortstop Boudreau smacked two homers) in the playoff, won his only Series start by a shutout, and saved the final game.

The Indians' pitching staff also featured twenty-game winner Bob Lemon, "Rapid" Robert Feller, Leroy "Satchel" Paige, and Steve Gromek. Boudreau was *The Sporting News* Player of the Year (Lemon was Pitcher of the Year), in addition to being the majors' all-star shortstop in 1947 and 1948. Larry Doby, Ken Keltner, and Joe Gordon provided offensive punch, and Boudreau, Gordon, and Jim Hegan, defensive strength.

The favored Cleveland team won the "war-of-tribes" Series, four games to two. The most famous incident occurred during the eighth inning of the Braves' victory in Game One, when Feller, a hard-luck loser of a two-hitter, whirled and fired to his manager Boudreau in an attempt to pick off Braves baserunner Phil Masi running for his fellow-catch-

American League MVP in 1948, Lou Boudreau of the Cleveland Indians. In Boudreau's first of twelve seasons with Cleveland (1940), he led the AL in fielding—a feat he accomplished seven more times. He led the league in batting in 1944 with .327, and hit .355 in 1948. (TCMA photo.)

Johnny Sain, NL pitching leader of the 1948 pennant-winning Boston Braves. Favorite pitcher of author Young when the latter was a youngster, Sain led the NL in wins (twenty-four), innings pitched, and complete games in 1948, the first time the Braves had won the NL flag since 1914. (TCMA photo.)

er, Bill Salkeld. Films seemingly indicate that Masi was out, and Boudreau vehemently objected to Umpire Stewart that this was the case. Sain made the second out, and Tommy Holmes promptly drove in Masi with a single, for the only run of the game.

Cleveland pitching proved decisive in the next three games in which Boston scored only two runs. Lemon beat Spahn, 4 to 1, Bearden pitched his shutout (2-0), giving up five hits, and Gromek edged Sain, 2-1, on Doby's long homer. After an 11-5 slugfest and Braves victory, in which Elliott smashed two homers in successive times at bat against the luckless Feller, the Indians edged the Braves, 4-3, with Bearden's help in the clincher. Earl Torgeson and Bob Elliott were the batting stars for the Braves with .389 and .333 averages,

"Rapid Robert" Feller of the Cleveland Indians, strikeout pitcher. Feller pitched three no-hitters in his career, led the AL in strikeouts seven times, and whiffed 348 in 1946 for a disputed AL record (some claim Rube Waddell had one more). "Bullet Bob" had annual marks of 24-9, 27-11, and 25-13 from 1939–41, and then entered military service in which he won eight battle stars. He hurled twelve one-hitters and struck out eighteen, seventeen, and sixteen in single games. Bob Feller was named the Greatest Living All-Time Right-Handed Pitcher in 1969. (TCMA photo.)

while Doby led the Cleveland contingent with .318. Furman Bisher once said: "greater love hath no man than the first big league team he ever worshipped. For Wells Twombly (and converted Cardinal fan Young), "those '48 Braves were the greatest."

As Douglas Wallop put it in his *Baseball: An Informal History*:

> The 1940's ended with another pennant for the New York Yankees, and yet it was more of a beginning than an ending—the beginning of many things, most of them distasteful to that portion of the baseball public that happened to reside and root beyond the west wall of Manhattan Island. For one, it was the beginning of the Casey Stengel era. The 1949 pennant was Stengel's first, and for the New York Yankees he would win nine more.

After the 1948 season Del Webb, co-owner of the Yankees, summoned the much-traveled and colorful Stengel to take over the Yankee managerial reins. The decision was heavily criticized by many Yankee fans at the time, because of Stengel's previous lackluster record as a manager and his zany antics, such as doffing his cap on the field and letting a bird fly out from the top of his head. But Casey was to have unprecedented success with the Yanks.

The closeness of the 1949 pennant races gave no hint of the dominance of the game by the Yankees and Dodgers that was to follow in the 1950s. The Dodgers, with Duke Snider, Gil Hodges, Carl Furillo, Jackie Robinson, "Pee Wee" Reese, Roy Campanella, Don Newcombe, and Carl Erskine, began to resemble the team that would be immortalized in Roger Kahn's *Boys of Summer*. As in 1947, Burt Shotton managed the Dodgers in a tight pennant race that was decided on the last day of the season. Leading the league and Cardinals by a game, "Dem Bums" were forced into extra innings to stop the Phillies, 9 to 7, and to avoid falling back into a season-ending tie for first place.

The Yankees had power and classy fielding with DiMaggio, Henrich, Gene Woodling, Hank Bauer, Johnny Mize (acquired from the Giants in late-season), Gerry Coleman, Phil Rizzuto, and Bobby Brown. One game behind with two games left, the Yankees swept past the Red Sox, 5-4 and 5-3, to cop the flag in a manner similar to the Dodgers—with identical 97-57 records and last-day pennant clinchers.

The most outstanding feature of the 1949 Series was the way it began—with two 1-to-0 pitching gems, a first for the fall classic. Allie "Chief" Reynolds blanked the Dodgers on two hits, and Don

The 1948 Cleveland Indians, World Champions. Front row: Eddie Robinson, Ken Keltner, Al Rosen, Coach Mel Harder, Manager Lou Boudreau, President Bill Veeck, Coach Muddy Ruel, Coach Bill McKechnie, Joe Gordon, and Johnny Berardino. Second row: Harold Goldstein, traveling secretary; Sam Zoldak, Ed Kleiman, Steve Gromek, Russ Christopher, Gene Bearden, Bob Lemon, Satchel Paige, Bob Feller, and Bob Muncrief, and Trainer Lefty Weisman. Third row: Walt Judnich, Allie Clark, Hal Peck, Larry Doby, Hank Edwards, Dale Mitchell, Bob Kennedy, Jim Hegan, Ray Boone, Joe Tipton, and Thurman Tucker. In front is Batboy Bill Sheridan. (G. S. Gallery photo.)

The 1948 Boston Braves, National League champions. Front row: Paul Burris, Bob Sturgeon, Clint Conatser, Batboy Charles Chronopolous, Ballboy Tom Ferguson, Vern Bickford, and John Antonelli. Second row: Phil Masi, Warren Spahn, Jeff Heath, Coaches Bob Keely and Fred Fitzsimmons, Manager Billy Southworth, Coach John Cooney, Al Dark, Tommy Holmes, Sibby Sisti, and George Young, property man. Third row: Charles Lacks, trainer; Si Johnson, Ray Sanders, Al Lyons, Frank McCormick, Bill Voiselle, Earl Torgeson, Johnny Sain, Clyde Shoun, Bob Elliott, and Nelson Potter. Fourth row: Connie Ryan, Bill Salkeld, Eddie Stanky, Mike McCormick, Ernie White, Bob Hogue, Charles Barrett, Glenn Elliott, and John Beazley. (G. S. Gallery photo.)

Newcombe gave up only four while striking out eleven, until the ninth when the Old Reliable, Tommy Henrich, cracked a homer to win for the Yanks. Elwin "Preacher" Roe then proceeded to whitewash the men from Gotham with the aid of Jackie Robinson's double and Gil Hodges' RBI single in the second game. Vic Raschi took the defeat. The third contest was also a pitching duel, between the Yanks' Tommy Byrne and Joe Page and the Dodgers' Ralph Branca, until the ninth when pitch-hitter Johnny Mize knocked in two of three Yankee runs. Solo Dodger homers by Luis Olmo and Roy Campanella were not enough to tie it in the Dodger half of the ninth.

In the fourth game, the Yankees got to Don Newcombe, working with two days' rest, in the fourth inning, scoring three runs. They added three more in the fifth off Joe Hatten when Bobby Brown tripled with the bases loaded. The Dodgers knocked out starter Ed Lopat and cracked out seven singles (to tie a record) and four runs, but Allie Reynolds put out the fire, retiring the last ten batters in succession. The Yankees jumped off to a 10-2 lead in the last game, aided by Joe DiMaggio's circuit clout. The Dodgers rallied for four runs in the seventh, with Gil Hodges hitting a round-tripper. But Joe Page in relief snuffed out the Dodgers' chances. Pee Wee Reese led the hitters with .316 in a pitchers' Series. The Dodgers averaged only .210, while the Yankees, led by Henrich's .263, were little better with .226. Reynolds, Raschi, Page, and Lopat for the Yankees, and Roe for the Dodgers, were credited with the Series victories; the losses went to Yankee Raschi, and Dodgers Newcombe (two), Branca, and Rex Barney.

Thus, the New York Yankees continued their mastery of major league baseball during the 1940s, winning world titles in 1941, 1943, 1947, and 1949, and a pennant in 1942. The Cardinals did the best in holding up the senior league's mantle, winning the World Series in 1942, 1944, and 1946, and the pennant in 1943. Their 1942 title was especially an achievement, as they beat the Yankees four straight after dropping the first game. Those four losses were as many as all the Yankee defeats acquired in participating in eight Series between 1927 and 1941—not since 1915 had a team lost four in a row after opening with a victory. In the 1942 pennant race, the Cardinals had won 106, most since 1909. They trailed by ten and one half games in mid-August, but drove to a close victory over Brooklyn, which won 103 contests.

Cleveland, Detroit, and Cincinnati were the only other teams to win Series titles in the 1940s, giving the American League the edge for the decade, six to four. The Tigers, Browns, and Red Sox were Series losers once, as were the Braves and Cubs. The Dodgers lost their third, fourth, and fifth consecutive World Series in the 1940s, and they were to continue that string in the 1950s. But with their aggressive scouting during World War II, and concomitant building of a strong farm system and their early signing of black ball players, the Dodgers had established themselves as the power of the National League at the decade's end. As mentioned above, author Young admired Carl Erskine; thus, he always cheered for the Dodgers in the classical Yank-Dodger showdowns (the "Subway Series"). Young's loyalties were with the National League, period. McClure, on the other hand, like Young's friend, Dick Walker, was a rabid "Yankee fan." The term was such a common one (and sometimes opprobrious one, depending on one's perspective) that the two words tended to blend together in speech. McClure saw many of the Yankee players (on the way up to, or down from, the majors) play for the AAA farm club, the Kansas City Blues of the American Association.

The decade was a disaster for NL rooters when one considers the results of the All-Star Games. Only in 1940—at Sportsman's Park in St. Louis and in 1944 at Forbes Field in Pittsburgh—were the Nationals victorious.

One of the most dramatic All-Star games occurred in 1941 at Briggs Stadium in Detroit. With two outs in the ninth inning, two on, and the NL leading, 5-4, Red Sox slugger Ted Williams belted a mighty homer into the upper right-field stands to win it for the Americans. Young remembers listening to the 1946 debacle (for him and the Nationals) at the Paul Barger residence next door to his home. It was a Ted Williams power show before the home fans at Fenway, as the Splendid Splinter socked two home runs and two singles and walked once in addition to scoring four runs and driving in five. The future appeared dark to the NL fans as the Americans overwhelmed their opponents, 12 to 0. Young remembers nervously playing the Bargers' upright piano and reading comic books in an attempt to ignore the bad news emanating from the radio. He would not have thought it possible at the time that some day his allegiance would shift to Williams individually and the American League collectively (the AL then began to lose more often).

Other outstanding players in the 1946–49 period that have not been mentioned previously were Ralph Kiner of the Pirates, who won or tied for the NL home run title from 1946 through 1952;

BASEBALL'S FIGHTINGEST CLUB.
NEW YORK YANKEES - 1949 - WORLD CHAMPIONS

The 1949 New York Yankees, World Champions. New York's Vic Raschi (21-10) headed a stellar mound corps, including Allie Reynolds (17-6), Tommy Byrne (15-7), and Ed Lopat (15-10), while fireman Joe Page (13-8) led the league in games and saves. Joe DiMaggio's .346 hitting, after his return to the lineup in June, was also a big factor in the Yanks' success. (TCMA photo.)

BROOKLYN DODGERS - 1949 - NATIONAL LEAGUE CHAMPIONS

The Boys of Summer, Brooklyn's 1949 National League champions. The Dodgers added the 1949 NL flag to those collected in 1941 and 1947 by edging their nemesis, the Cardinals, by a single game. St. Louis contributed to their own demise by losing four in the final week. (TCMA photo.)

George Kell of the Tigers, all-major league third baseman three times in the late 1940s (he added three more in the 1950s); Dom DiMaggio, fine hitter and fielder for the Red Sox, all-major-league outfielder in 1946, and Joe's brother; Mel Parnell and Ellis Kinder, classy pitchers for the Red Sox; and Mickey Vernon, 1946 AL batting champion for the Senators.

One characteristic of the 1940s in baseball, which differentiates it from today, was its stability. There were always sixteen teams in the league. There was no movement of franchises, and the teams played in the same stadia at the major-league level. It is the authors' view that much of the attraction has stemmed from the familiar surroundings of the ball park, its peculiarities, uniqueness, and idiosyncrasies. The teams' uniforms were seldom changed drastically. Recognition of stadia, teams, and players was instantaneous. There are, of course, many things to be said for the modern stadia that are being constructed—roomier seats, better visibility, more restrooms, more water fountains, more concession stands, even escalators—but they seem to lack the character and have less attraction for many fans than the old ball parks (but not for Young's son, Jimmy, who has seen games in Kansas City's old Municipal Stadium, Chicago's venerable Wrigley Field, the more modern Twins' Metropolitan Stadium, and the ultramodern Royals Stadium).

Many writers have bemoaned the passing of the old parks. Perhaps foremost among them has been Detroit sportswriter Joe Falls. In 1970, after stating that ball parks constituted the only hobby of his (at that time) forty-two-year life, Falls wrote:

> These are bad days for me, and sad days, sorrowful days. Crosley Field [in Cincinnati] and Forbes Field [in Pittsburgh] are down, closed forever, and I guess Shibe Park in Philadelphia is next. Call it Connie Mack Stadium if you want, but to me it'll always be Shibe Park.
> And it's Sportsman's Park [St. Louis], not Busch Stadium.
> And Briggs Stadium [Detroit], not Tiger Stadium.
> And Comiskey Park [Chicago], not White Sox Park.
> And Griffith Stadium [Washington], not D.C. Stadium or RFK Stadium or whatever it is they're calling it these days.
> And where have you gone old League Park [Cleveland], as a nation turns its lonely eyes to you?

Falls refers to John Carmichael's *Who's Who in Baseball,* in which the latter showed pictures of all the ball parks, and then to Boston cartoonist Gene Mack's drawings of the same subjects. Those Mack

pictures appeared periodically in *The Sporting News* when Falls was a youngster. All of the places that Falls "loved and dreamed about visiting" were depicted in that series—Crosley Field with its left-field terrace, Forbes Field and its "Greenberg Gardens," Sportsman's Park and its screen in front of the rightfield pavilion, and Comiskey Park with its rooftop light towers.

Home-run hitter, Ralph Kiner of the Pirates. Pittsburgh's Kiner led or tied for the lead in NL home-run production in each of his first seven years in the majors (a record). (TCMA photo.)

59

1949 AL bat champ, George Kell. The Tigers' Kell led AL third basemen in fielding seven times. He hit over .300 eight consecutive years, including his league-leading .343 in 1949. Kell had a lifetime AL average of .306 in 1,795 games. (Courtesy Detroit Tigers.)

Mickey Vernon, two-time AL bat champ. Mickey Vernon led the AL in hitting with .353 in 1946, and .337 in 1953. He set AL first-baseman career records for most games, putouts, and assists. Vernon played for the Washington Senators from 1939–48 and 1950–55). (Courtesy Minnesota Twins.)

Eventually, Falls wrote Mack telling him how much he enjoyed his work, and to Falls' astonishment, a week later he received a four or five-page letter in reply that was hand-printed in India ink; Mack explained to his admirer how he came to do the ball park series and gave details on Fenway Park. The Detroit writer never forgot Mr. Mack and his kindness.

Falls recounts saving his money as a fourteen or fifteen-year-old, buying a round-trip train ticket to Philadelphia, taking photographs of visiting Yankee players, and then using the rest of the film on shots of Shibe Park's rightfield wall (featuring green slats) and the leftfield stands. The latter was done so that he could more readily picture the wall and stands, and the action attendant thereto, while listening to the game on the radio.

In an article about the 1948 Braves, Wells Twombly also refers to the old parks' structural peculiarities: to Twombly, Crosley Field (former home of the Reds) was "an old friend" that had a "slight incline in front of the left field fence." He refers to its foul-line dimensions and the fact that night baseball was first played there in the majors.

Other features of old National League parks noted by Twombly were the "tall, ugly, and concave" rightfield fence in Brooklyn's Ebbets Field (where "courageous" Tommy Holmes was singularly effective); a screen over the rightfield pavilion in Sportsman's Park in St. Louis (he thinks Cardinal fans are snobs to use the high-class name "pavilion" for "what everyone else calls 'bleachers'"); "that oddly named, grotesquely shaped structure called the Polo Grounds," home of the old New York Giants, in which a shortstop who "looked like a case of malnutrition . . . managed to hit seventeen home runs"; and finally Braves Field (in Boston), which had a "steep slope of stands in right field" that resembled and was called a "jury box." There the fans would "drink beer, gamble and love Tommy Holmes."

Twombly ably sums up the appeal of these structures:

Gazing back in fondness through the scattered haze of 22 summers, it doesn't seem as if all those wonderful places where the Braves played were actually architectural horrors, improvised out of bits and pieces of grandstands that were added haphazardly as the population grew.

Surely some mad genius with a taste for drama and an eye for color planned them that way. They lacked beauty and creature comforts, but . . . well . . . sob . . . they had character.

Twombly decries the demise of Crosley Field and the utter sameness of the new stadiums, bemoans that "only Wrigley Field will remain," and half seriously, proposes that it be declared a national shrine. His sentiments are echoed by Falls who mournfully assessed the tearing down of Crosley Field, Forbes Field, and Shibe Park and said: "When Fenway and the green wall go . . . well, I don't even want to think about it, if you don't mind."

Author Young was made to feel his age when Robert L. Burnes, in his weekly sports quiz, asked his readers to identify many of the above-mentioned ballparks. There were even three that Young did not know—League Park in Cleveland, Robison Field (a Cardinals' site twice removed), and Navin Field, which became Detroit's Briggs Stadium and then Tiger Stadium. Burnes points out that of all the parks named in the quiz—Crosley Field, League Park, Navin Field, Robison Field, Shibe Park, Griffith Stadium, Forbes Field, Ebbets Field, the Polo Grounds, and Braves Field—only one is still in existence—the Detroit park twice renamed.

Another ecstatic account of a ballpark came from Art Spander whose "3½ decades of non-living ended" when he saw his first game at Fenway Park in Boston:

It is everything a stadium of the 1970s could never be—pillared, single-decked, natural-turfed, without parking, asymmetrical and even uncomfortable. It has ludicrous dimensions and terrible sight lines. And the scoreboards keep you almost as well informed as a Soviet newspaper.

But it does more for baseball than all the domed stadiums, animated message boards and split-screen TV coverage combined.

To Spander it is not just the "Green Monster" —the thirty-seven-foot leftfield fence only 315 feet away from home plate—that gives the park its character. "It's everything else about the park, and the fans and the tradition—an amalgam that seems to mock the success of a team like the A's, where there is nothing except victories." Spander prefers the old ball parks like Fenway—even in a setting of "urban blight," to the modern multipurpose stadia located along freeway routes. He decries the "antiseptic sameness" of the latter parks with their 330–410–330 feet outfield wall dimensions (distances from home plate). Spander ends his article, "Fenway—A Ballpark To Savor," by stating: "Every other ball park should be so old-fashioned."

Still another famous sportswriter, Bob Broeg of the *St. Louis Post-Dispatch*, speaks fondly of Forbes Field, which he notes was named for a Revolutionary War general:

Forbes Field had a rich-looking brick wall in left, scaled by ivy that was appropriate with Carnegie Museum in the background and the University of Pittsburgh's towering Cathedral of Learning nearby.

For another thing, lush, green Schenley Park loomed in the background over the left field wall. . . .

A baseball reporter's job in those days [after 1947], staying just across the street at the old Schenley Hotel, was in sitting around the ball park press room or Frank Gustine's restaurant, polishing off those splits of ice-cold Rolling Rock beer with Bill Schragen's Western Union crew or Pie Traynor.

And so it goes.

Another colorful aspect of baseball in the 1940s were the nicknames with which the players were tagged to the extent that their real, given names became obscured. These were nicknames with *character*. Schoolboy Rowe, Duke Snider, Rube Walker, Dutch Leonard, Preacher Roe, Spider Jorgensen, Satchel Paige, Connie Ryan, Sibby Sisti, Cookie Lavagetto, Lefty or Goofy Gomez, Lefty Grove, Bucky Harris, Dixie Walker, Bobo or Buck Newsom, Bucky Walters, Dizzy Dean, Daffy Dean, Gabby Hartnett, Peanuts Lowrey, Tex Hughson, Boo Ferriss, Red Rolfe, Red Ruffing, Yogi Berra, Birdie Tebbetts, Pee Wee Reese, Red Schoendienst, Stubby Overmire, Buddy Rosar, Pinky Higgins, Goody Rosen, Barney McCoskey, Dizzy Trout, Snuffy Stirnweiss, Arky Vaughn, Casey Stengel, Ducky Medwick, Mickey Owen, Rip Sewell, Spud Chandler, Whitey Kurowski, and Spec Shea—all are illustrative of those involved in the game in the 1940s. Other players' first names were remembered by fans who also knew their nicknames. This was true of "Joltin'" Joe DiMaggio, the "Yankee Clipper"; Ted Williams, the "Splendid Splinter" or "the Kid"; Harry "the Hat" Walker, Harry "the Cat" Brecheen, Leo "the Lip" Durocher, Paul "Big Poison" Waner, Lloyd "Little Poison" Waner, Enos "Country" Slaughter, Joe "Flash" Gordon, Stan "the Man" Musial, "Pistol" Pete Reiser, Allie "Chief" Reynolds, and Sal "the Barber" Maglie, for example.

Nicknames sometimes stemmed from the color of one's hair, other physical characteristics, or talkativeness The animal kingdom and geographical

The 1950 Philadelphia Phillies, National League champions. The "Whiz Kids" had many players from the 1940s, including the 1948 Rookie of the Year, Richie Ashburn, who also led the league in stolen bases and batted .333 in the latter year. Hall of Fame pitcher Robin Roberts was with the Phils from 1948–61, and won twenty or more games six years in succession. Seated: Bloodworth, Donnelly, Ashburn, Caballero, Bengough, coach; Sawyer, manager; Perkins, coach; Cooke, coach; Ennis, Sisler, Jones. Middle row: Wiechec, Church, Miller, Heintzelman, Silvestri, Lopata, Hollmig, Roberts, Whitman, Meyer, Hamner, Thompson, Powell, traveling secretary. Back row: Nicholson, Johnson, Ridzik, Waitkus, Candini, Mayo, Konstanty, Seminick, Goliat, Brittin, Stuffel, McDonnell, Simmons. Batboy: Kenny Bush. (G. S. Gallery photo.)

locations provided some nicknames, as did certain occupations. Other monickers were affectionate appellations given by parents or childhood friends. Some players were labeled later by teammates in the minor or major leagues. Of course, the 1940s had no monopoly on nicknames, although, as Sid Bordman of the *Kansas City Star* has said, "Nicknames no longer flow in baseball as they did in the past."

In some ways, baseball reached a peak in the late 1940s. Although Commissioner Bowie Kuhn quotes figures showing that baseball has achieved unprecedented popularity today, the statistics are normally based on total attendance over a 162-game schedule for twenty-four teams. (In the 1940s, 154 games were played by each of sixteen teams.) Red Smith

pointed out in a 1974 column that Kuhn is "ignoring the fact that attendance per game in the majors has been down for 25 years." Many of the single-game attendance records by club were set in the 1940s, especially in 1947 and 1948. Increasing competition from football and other spectator sports, and other leisure-time pursuits have eroded baseball's popularity considerably, *relative to other activities.* This is not intended to detract from the fact that there are obvious advantages to be derived from a measured, mild, relaxing, and entertaining sport that is baseball, in an era in which these qualities are at a premium.

Joseph Durso has noted that money that formerly would have been spent on baseball is now being spent on participant activities such as jogging, fishing, and golf. Affluence, the sophistication of youth, and an increasing number of leisure-time diversions have detracted from a passionate interest in baseball and other "old-time spectator sports."

But in the 1940s, even if a boy did not play baseball on a team, he imagined that he did, and many times he did both. Richard Schickel has described his activities in this regard. If there were no game after school, he would take his tennis ball and baseball glove into his backyard and throw the ball high against the house. He could make the ball rebound so that in order to catch it he would have to run into a fence, like the famous Pete Reiser. All of this was accompanied by Schickel's play-by-play imaginary radio commentary on his own feats.

And Bil Gilbert described how he engaged in similar activity with a tennis ball, a two-dollar baseball glove, a sloping porch roof, and the side yard.

As Swinburne said, "time remembered is grief forgotten," and youngsters today are not without imagination and devotion to heroes. But somehow it seems that the average youngster's dedication to the game today is not as it once was in the 1940s.

Early Wynn, 300-game winner. Wynn pitched most of the 1940s for the Senators (1939, 1941–44, and 1946–48). He was with the Indians from 1949–57. Altogether, Wynn played in four decades, and he holds the major-league record for most years pitched in the majors. He won twenty or more games five times. (TCMA photo.)

3

TRACK AND FIELD

The sport of track and field is one of the few that the authors followed more closely after the 1940s than during that decade. In part this is due to the fact that Young proved to be more proficient at that sport than any other in the 1950s and has been involved in the coaching and officiating of it since. The fact that McClure matriculated in the 1950s at the University of Kansas, site of the famed Kansas Relays and a collegiate track power, is another reason. Both were intensely interested in the sport during the 1940s, but that intensity has increased, whereas the attention given detail in many other sports has declined since boyhood. Conversations with the authors' contemporaries indicate that this relative decline of interest in sports like baseball and football is not an isolated phenomenon.

Because of McClure and Young's tender age, many of the top performances and performers of the early 1940s in track and field escaped their notice and attention. Both became familiar with the courage and exploits of the Kansas Ironman, Glenn Cunningham, from their parents who had been impressed by him in the Depression decade. Those exploits included a world mile record (4:06.7) in 1934, several national championships, and a silver medal in the 1936 Olympic Games in the 1,500 meters. Cunningham's running career ended in 1940.

There were many athletes who were of Olympic gold medal calibre, but were unable to participate in an Olympiad because of the cancellation of the Games in 1940 (originally scheduled for Tokyo and then reassigned to Helsinki) and 1944 (awarded to London). One such athlete was the vaulter Cornelius "Dutch" Warmerdam whom Reid Hanley, author of *Who's Who in Track and Field*, called "probably [the] greatest vaulter of all time

considering [the] type of pole used." He was the world's first vaulter to clear fifteen feet, a height that he eventually cleared forty-three times. He won or tied for seven national AAU (NAAU) championships, including those held from 1940 through 1944. He broke the world record with his first fifteen-foot vault and proceeded to better his own record repeatedly.

Warmerdam's 15 feet 7¾ inches outdoor world record set in 1942 (he went 15 feet 8½ inches indoors) was not broken until 1957. His indoor record stood for sixteen years and his outdoor record, fifteen years. No other person was able to clear fifteen feet until 1951. Cordner Nelson, in *Track and Field: The Great Ones*, said: "In the entire history of track and field, no athlete's superiority has been so unquestioned as Warmerdam's. . . . He would have been everyone's favorite for Olympic champion in 1944, as well as in 1940. . . . No athlete ever had so many marks so far ahead of the next best man of all time, in any event." Nelson quotes 1904 double silver medalist sprinter Nat Cartmell: "Warmerdam is the only all-time, indisputable, supreme champion the athletic world has ever known." Bob Richards, who became the second person to vault fifteen feet, said that Cornelius "wasn't human."

Warmerdam was the son of a Dutch immigrant (thus the nickname, used affectionately). Nelson reports that he was "unassuming to an unusually pleasant degree" and "had a quiet maturity which put pole vaulting in its place, but he also had some pride." This may have been due in part to the fact that he worked hard on his father's ranch from the age of ten (when he also had built his first uprights on the fruit drying field). In high school he had tied for third in the California state meet (his best mark was 12 feet 3 inches). He did not go on to college for one and one half years (although he graduated before he was seventeen), but then he attended Fresno State. A year later he had tied for first with Earle Meadows, Bill Sefton, and three others in the West Coast Relays, and in 1936 he tied for the title at the Drake Relays. He won the 1937 Pan American Games in Dallas, defeating Meadows while still a collegian. Most of his fine marks were made after college when he was a member of the San Francisco Olympic Club. Warmerdam's name was a familiar one to Young and McClure because he held the world record throughout their boyhood, although they were too young to appreciate fully his exploits when they took place.

The "Heavenly Twins," Earle Meadows and Bill Sefton, were teammates at Southern California in the late 1930s who tied or nearly tied for several national championships. Meadows was Olympic gold medalist in the vault in 1936, and Sefton was fourth. Sefton retired in 1937, but Meadows stayed active and won the 1940 and 1941 NAAU indoor titles.

In addition to Warmerdam, there were other American athletes who set world marks in the early 1940s, but did not compete in the Olympic Games because of their cancellation. One was Les Steers who set the world high jump record at 6 feet 11 inches in June of 1941. In fact, he had the five highest jumps of all time that year. Using the straddle style, Steers won an NCAA title for Oregon in 1941 and NAAU titles in 1939 and 1940. He jumped over 6 feet 10 inches six times in 1941 and might have been the world's first seven-foot jumper (he did make it in practice) if war had not intervened.

The late Archie Harris, competing for Indiana, broke the world discus record with 174 feet 9 inches at the 1941 NCAA championships. He was the first American to hold the record since 1934 and the only black to hold the mark. The NCAA (but not world) record lasted twelve years. Harris was 1940 NCAA champion also and won the 1941 NAAU discus title.

In 1941 Fred Wolcott of Houston and Rice Institute tied the world record of :13.7 set by Forrest "Spec" Towns in the 110 meter hurdles. The record lasted until 1948 when Harrison Dillard broke it at the Kansas Relays. In 1940 Wolcott broke Jesse Owens' 220 yard hurdle record with a :22.5 time. He won that race in the 1938, 1939, and 1940 NCAA meets and the 120 yard high hurdles in the 1938 and 1939 meets. In addition he was the victor in the 1938–41 NAAU low hurdles and 1938, 1940, and 1941 AAU highs. Cordner Nelson called him "the greatest hurdler of all time before Dillard."

Yrjo Nikkanen of Finland set a world javelin record of 258 feet 2⅜ inches in 1938; the mark lasted fifteen years. A silver medalist in the 1936 Olympics, Nikkanen was second in the European Championships of 1938 and 1946.

Shotputter Hans Woellke had achieved fame in the 1936 Berlin Olympics as the first person to win a gold medal for Germany. He was the German champion from 1934 through 1938 and in 1941 and 1942.

Al Blozis won three NCAA shot put championships for Georgetown in 1940, 1941, and 1942, his 1940 mark lasting nine years. He also won several NAAU championships, hitting over 57 feet indoors in 1942. He played pro football briefly for the New York Giants. Blozis was killed in combat on the Western Front in World War II.

Another track star killed in the war was Pole Janusz Kusocinski who had been world record holder in the 3,000 meters and gold medalist and record breaker in the 10,000 meters at the 1932 Los Angeles Olympics. A knee injury bothered him after that until 1939 when he broke a Polish 5,000 meters record. He appeared to be a contender for another Olympic title in 1940. Seriously wounded in the defense of Warsaw, he recovered and joined the Polish underground but was arrested and executed in 1940.

On the other side, Rudolph Harbig of Dresden, Germany, set a world record in the 800 meters (1:48.6) at Milan in July of 1939, a second world mark at Frankfurt in the 400 meters (:46) in August of that war year, and a third at Dresden in the 1,000 meters (2:21.5) in May of 1941. One of the first to use interval training, Harbig died in the war on the Eastern Front.

Donald Finlay of Great Britain won the bronze medal at the 1932 Olympics and the silver medal at the 1936 Games in the 110 meter hurdles. He won the 1938 European Championships. In 1948, as Wing Commander, he took the Olympic Oath for the athletes of all nations at the London Games, but in the 110 meter hurdle race later, he fell. The following year, at age forty, he won a meet against France in :14.4 seconds.

Sprinters who did not receive the recognition due to them because of World War II include Harold Davis, premier American dash man from 1940 through 1943. He won the AAU 100 meter dash in 1940, 1942, and 1943, and the 200 meter event in 1940 through 1943. Only a defeat by Barney Ewell in the 1941 100 meters kept him from winning a sprint double all four years. He added the 100 and 220 yard dash NCAA championships in 1942 and

1948 Olympic gold medalist, Norwood "Barney" Ewell. (Courtesy Pennsylvania State University.)

Mozel Ellerbe of Tuskegee Institute is shown successfully defending his title in the 100 yard dash at the Penn Relays in 1940. (Acme Photo, Courtesy Tuskegee Institute.)

1943, running for California. After high school, he was undefeated in the 220 and was defeated only twice in the 100 during the same period. He was not a good starter but was known for an extremely strong finish. He would have been favored for Olympic golds in both the 100 and 200 meters in 1940 and 1944 had the Games been held.

Mozel Ellerbe of Tuskegee Institute was another great sprinter who might have won medals for the United States if the 1940 Games had been held. He won the NCAA 100 in 1938 and 1939, and won many important races against top competition in 1940, including the NAAU Indoor 60 yard dash.

Grover Klemmer from San Francisco tied the world records in the 440 yard and 400 meter dashes in the same race in 1941 (his times were :46.4 and :46.0, respectively), winning the NAAU title in the latter event. He also had tied the 440 mark in the previous month. Klemmer was also the 1940 AAU titleholder in the quarter-mile.

John Woodruff of Connellsville, Pennsylvania achieved fame as the Olympic gold medalist in the 800 meters at Berlin in 1936, and he might have succeeded in defending his crown in 1940. He won the 1937 AAU title at that distance, and, running for Pitt, annexed the 1937, 1938, and 1939 NCAA crowns in the 880. In 1940 he broke the American record in the 800 meters.

In the distances, Britain's Sydney Wooderson was a world-class runner in races from 800 to 5,000 meters. He set the world mile record in 1937 with 4:06.4. The following year Wooderson won the 1,500 meters at the European Championships, and he broke the world records for 800 meters and 880 yards. After the war in 1945 he lost to Arne Andersson of Sweden in a close mile race and won the European Championships in the 5,000 in 1946. Only Gunder Hägg had run it faster.

Don Lash of Indiana may not have been a favorite for a 1940 Olympic gold medal, but he was a top-flight American distance runner, having broken Paavo Nurmi's world record in the two-mile in 1936. He also won the 1936 NCAA 5,000 meter run and AAU six-mile in 1936 and 1940. He won the AAU three-mile in 1936 and every NAAU cross country title from 1934 through 1940. The 1938 Sullivan Award winner had been a favorite in the 1936 Olympics, but only placed fourteenth in the 5,000 and eighth in the 10,000.

In the 1941 indoor circuit, Greg Rice, Notre Dame graduate of 1939, set a world record in the two-mile on 15 February, broke the world's three-mile record on 22 February at the AAU Indoor, and in the Chicago Daily News Relays, the last big invitational meet of the indoor season, ran two miles in 8:51.1, the fastest ever run inside or out. Four days later, he was declared unfit for service in the U.S. Army because of a triple hernia. In 1940, Rice received the Sullivan Award, given to the nation's Outstanding Amateur Athlete. (Other trackmen receiving the Sullivan Award in the 1940s were Les MacMitchell in 1941, Cornelius Warmerdam in 1942, and Gil Dodds in 1943; Felix "Doc" Blanchard was selected for both football and track in 1945, Arnold Tucker, as an all-around athlete in 1946, and Bob Mathias, as an all-around athlete in 1948.)

In 1940, Chuck Fenske had brought the fabled Glenn Cunningham's career to an end, beating him six consecutive times in the indoor season (Cunningham had beaten him seventeen times in a row prior to that). Fenske also equalled Cunningham's indoor record of 4:07.4 and won the 1940 AAU Indoor mile. Only a year before, in 1939, Cunningham had broken two world records.

Also during the 1940 indoor season, at Madison Square Garden, Greg Rice broke his own world indoor record for three miles with 13:52.3. Don Lash, one-time record holder, was second, and Finland's Taisto Mäki was third. Rice's time was only ten seconds slower than the world mark Mäki had set in the event *outdoors* in 1939. In that year, Mäki had also set four other world records in the two-mile, three-mile, 5,000 meters, six-mile, and 10,000, all at Helsinki. These records had previously been held by Mäki's idol, coach, and traveling companion, Paavo Nurmi.

Among the women athletes, Stella Walsh, 1932 Olympic gold medalist and 1936 silver medalist in the 100 meters, was winning championships well into the 1940s. Her record of longevity and success in track and field may well be unequalled by any other man or woman. Born in Poland (her Polish name was Stanislawa Walasiewicz), she was raised in the United States but ran for her native Poland in the Olympics. She won American AAU titles in the: 100 meters in 1930, 1943, 1944, and 1948; 200 meter titles in 1930, 1931, 1939, 1940, and 1942 through 1948; and long jump championships in 1930, 1939 through 1946, 1948, and 1951! She also won many indoor NAAU titles during this span of years. During the 1930s she set women's world records at 60 meters, 100 meters, 200 meters, and 220 yards.

Young first became aware of track and field during World War II when two Swedish distance aces, Gunder Hägg and Arne Andersson began lowering world distance records on a wholesale basis. Gunder "the Wunder," a self-coached runner, broke fifteen world records from the mile to the three-mile during the 1940s. Having trained for several years with the unstructured method now called "fartlek," he set his first world mark in the 1,500 meters in 1941. After suspension from Swedish amateur ranks, he returned in 1942 to crack ten world records at seven distances from the mile to the three-mile in eighty-two days. The first was a 4:06.2 mile at Goteborg, Sweden.

In 1943 Hägg made a hazardous voyage to the United States and proceeded to win all of his races in this country. He beat Greg Rice in the process, but did not set any world records. Meanwhile, back in Sweden, his arch rival, Arne Andersson, lowered Hägg's 1,500 meter world mark to 3:45 and mile record to 4:02.6.

Back in Sweden, in 1944, Hägg defeated Andersson in 3:43 in the metric mile, but Andersson then achieved his only victory over Hägg with Arne running the mile in 4:01.6. Gunder then lowered the two-mile record twice, his second race time of 8:42.8 standing for eight years as a world record. In 1945 Hägg made another trip to the United States and, on his return, defeated Andersson in a 4:01.3 mile, which was to be the world's best time for the next nine years. In late 1945 he and Andersson were barred from amateur competition because of financial irregularities. Were it not for this, Gunder Hägg, rather than Roger Bannister, might well have been the first sub-four-minute miler, and the mark might have been achieved in the 1940s rather than in 1954. The fact that Hägg and Andersson were nationals of one of the few neutral and unoccupied nations of Europe escaped the notice of the authors.

In 1942 Young won his first prize—war savings stamps that when purchased in sufficient numbers and denominations were used to buy United States "war" or "victory" bonds—in track competition by winning a dash event at the Rotary Club picnic. An article in the *Waterloo Daily Courier* reporting that "Jimmy" Young had won the event, pasted in the baby book, was proudly referred to on many occasions by that youngster!

In 1946 Young won his first ribbons in track and field. At a cub scout pack picnic, he won his den's ball throw competition and placed second in the 50 yard dash. Then in competition against all dens—the whole pack—he won the Grand Prize of the meet—a large blue ribbon—by narrowly winning the 50 yard dash. That was to be the highest award he would ever receive in the individual sprints, as his forte was to be the shot put and discus throw.

Persuaded by a friend to watch a local high school meet, Young biked to Sloane Wallace Stadium in Waterloo for the West Waterloo-East Waterloo-Dubuque high school triangular track meet. This was his first experience as a spectator in a track and field activity, and it was to be followed soon by actual participation in the long jump, sprints, and ball throw in grade school gym classes on the Kingsley school playground. The latter was located across the street from his home, and in the spring, when the playground was empty, he would try his hand at high jumping over the bamboo pole suspended between wooden standards or, from the embedded take-off board, broad jumping into the sand pit. A highlight of the year at Kingsley School was the school track meet. Top placers qualified for the City Meet. When Young was in fifth grade, Kingsley won the boys' division of the City Meet held at the West High (Sloane Wallace) Track.

In 1947 and 1948 Young organized track meets for younger children of the neighborhood—Nancy and Linda Barger and Robby Dotson, primarily. This involved setting out running courses around his yard, using makeshift high jump standards and crossbars, finding large rocks for shots, and cutting and typing on ribbons for awards. A year later he competed in track meets sponsored by the Northey Athletic Club. David and Edward Northey, who lived nearly a mile away, had run off meets (much like Young did for his neighbors) for their younger brothers, Harry and John, and others; Young, a contemporary of Harry, was eventually drawn into that circle of competition. The Northey brothers even awarded medals and ribbons to the winners. Soon, Jim was pulled into the orbit of school-sponsored athletics, and in 1948 and 1949, this was at the junior high level.

The *Des Moines Register,* which was a second (morning) paper for many Iowa households at the time, has consistently covered track and field events in competent fashion. This coverage, plus the fact that one of the nation's finest track meets, the Drake Relays, is held in Des Moines, have made many Iowans track-conscious. The high schools and colleges of the state have produced their share of excellent track teams, individuals, and coaches.

Similarly, the Kansas Relays have been one of the great spring track "carnivals" along with Texas, Drake, and Penn, and the state of Kansas and it fine universities have excelled in track and produced many national and Olympic champions in addition to top-flight programs at collegiate, secondary school, and club levels.

Young became interested in the Drake Relays by reading the full accounts and viewing the action photographs in the *Register* and then prevailed on his father (it did not take much urging

Olympic champion in the 800 meters, John Woodruff of Pitt. In 1940, he broke the American record for 800 meters in 1:48.6, and also ran 1:47.7 indoors. War prevented him from defending his Olympic title. (Courtesy University of Pittsburgh.)

Baldwin-Wallace's Harrison Dillard, winner of four gold medals in the 1948 and 1952 Olympic Games. (Courtesy Baldwin-Wallace College.)

to take the family to the 1947 version of that classic spring athletic carnival. The Saturday afternoon events, the best-attended of the (then) two-day meet, exceeded the fondest expectations of the Young family, and Robert Young was to take his family back to the Relays year after year. Jim became a high school and collegiate participant in the late-April Relays from 1953 through 1958.

At their first Drake Relays, the Youngs saw several world-class athletes, but undoubtedly the most famous was Harrison Dillard of Baldwin-Wallace, who flashed brilliantly to a Drake record of :14.1 in the 120 yard high hurdles. Bill Porter of Northwestern was second. Willie Steele of San Diego State captured the broad jump with 24 feet 6½ inches. Arthur Harnden, a Texas A. & M. quartermiler, also participated. All four athletes were to become gold medalists in the 1948 Olympic Games. Fortune Gordien of Minnesota won the shot put with a Drake record of 51 feet 6⅞ inches. Dwight "Dike" Eddleman, all-around athlete from Illinois, competed in the high jump. Clyde "Smackover" Scott, All-American football player from Arkansas, finished third behind Dillard and Porter in the

highs. Scott, Gordien (in the discus), and Eddleman were to be Olympic placers in 1948. Fortune Gordien was third in the 1948 London Olympiad, fourth at Helsinki in 1952, and second in 1960 at age thirty-eight in Rome. Another entrant, Verne McGrew of Rice was to be one of the United States' high jumpers at the 1948 Games while he was only eighteen-years-old.

Other famous athletes at the 1947 Relays were Dick Ault, hurdler from Missouri; Augie Erfurth of Rice (defending high hurdles champ who was fourth this time); Don Gehrmann, miler from Wisconsin; Leo Nomellini, All-American and later all-time all-pro tackle from Minnesota; Herbert Wilkinson, All-American basketball guard from Iowa (his brother Clayton, an outstanding Iowa player, was also there); Paul Unruh, All-American cager from Bradley; and Dick Hoerner, all-Big Ten and later Los Angeles Rams fullback from Iowa.

Other fine trackmen included Bill Martineson of Baylor, who defended his 100 yard dash crown successfully; Fred Feiler, two-time Drake Relays two-mile champ from the host school; Mel Sheehan from Missouri, who won the discus (and later was to be athletic director at his alma mater); Don Pettie, sprinter from Drake; Bob Karnes of Kansas, later to be coach at Drake and Relays Director; and Dick Maxwell of Ohio State, a hurdler who became coach at Central Missouri State and friend of the authors at that institution.

University and college coaches at the 1947 Drake Relays included, among others, M.E. "Bill" Easton of Drake University (Relays Director), Gordon

Winner of a record eleven letters at Illinois, Dwight "Dike" Eddleman. He was ranked as one of the most versatile and brilliant athletes of the 1940s. After winning four state high-school high-jump titles, Eddleman captured his specialty three times in the Penn Relays and Big Nine Indoor, two times in the Big Nine Outdoor, and once in the 1948 NCAA Championships, when he tied Irv "Moon" Mondschein. Dike was fourth at the 1948 London Olympics in the high jump. In football he set the Big Nine punting record and played for the victorious Illini in the 1947 Rose Bowl. In basketball he was all-state three times, and in his senior year paced his state champion team. At Illinois, he was All-Big Nine, MVP in the Big Nine, and All-American. As a pro, he starred for the Tri-Cities Blackhawks and the Fort Wayne Pistons in the NBA. (Courtesy Dwight Eddleman.)

Clyde "Smackover" Scott, Olympic silver-medalist hurdler and All-American football player. Scott starred in four sports for Smackover (Arkansas) High School. He scored the only TD for Navy in a 23-7 loss to Army in 1944. In the 1945 rematch, Scott caught a pass from Bruce Smith and eluded Glenn Davis to score one of the Middies' two TDs in their 32-13 loss to the Cadets. Playing for Arkansas in 1946, "Smackover" led the Razorbacks to the Southwest Conference championship. He became the first Arkansas player to be All-Conference three consecutive years, and in 1948 was a Consensus All-American. In one of his few attempts at the sprints, Scott tied the world record in the 100 yard dash (then 9.4 seconds). He was second in the 110 meter hurdles at the 1948 Olympics, and he starred professionally for the Philadelphia Eagles and Detroit Lions from 1949–52. (Courtesy Clyde "Smackover" Scott.)

70

Minnesota's Fortune Gordien, holder of the world discus mark for ten years. Bob Fitch of Minnesota and Archie Harris of Indiana were other Big Ten athletes to hold the world discus record in the 1940s. (Courtesy Fortune Gordien.)

Fisher of Indiana, Leo Johnson of Illinois, George Bresnahan of Iowa, Ray Kanehl of Kansas, Karl Schlademan of Michigan State (Relays Referee), Jim Kelly of Minnesota, Tom Botts of Missouri, Ed Weir of Nebraska, Frank Hill of Northwestern, Larry Snyder of Ohio State, Ralph Higgins of Oklahoma A.&M., Dave Rankin of Purdue, Clyde Littlefield of Texas, Tom Jones of Wisconsin, Art Dickinson of Iowa State Teachers College, Alex Wilson of Loyola, Payton Jordan of Occidental, and Eddie Weems of Pepperdine. Francis X. Cretzmeyer, later to be Young's coach at Iowa, was coaching North Des Moines' high school team that included the "flying four" of Gary Scott, Conrad Jones, Reginald Kaiser, and George Nichols, a sprint relay team that set national prep records. Kelly, Snyder, and Jordan were to become head coaches of the 1956, 1960, and 1968 U.S. Olympic track teams, respectively.

Bill Stern, the dean of sports broadcasters and sports director of NBC, broadcast the Relays nationwide from a platform on the infield. It was his fifth appearance in that role.

Ohio State annexed crowns in the 480 yard shuttle hurdle, two-mile, and mile relays. Texas with Charlie Parker won the 440 and 880 relays, and Jerry Thompson of the Longhorns won the two-mile. Host Drake captured the four-mile relay, and Michigan State and Indiana won the sprint and distance medleys. Ault took the 440 yard hurdles. Cretzmeyer's North Des Moines sprint quartet, destined for greatness, won the 440 and 880 high school relays in record time. Athletes from Davenport High School (the alma mater of Young's mother) won four events, and Grinnell, with John Bonyata anchoring, won the 880 and mile relays for Iowa colleges. Bradley, Pepperdine, Baldwin-Wallace, and Southwest Texas State were college division relay winners.

Two-time National Collegiate champion, Fred Feiler of Drake. Feiler won the NCAA cross-country races in 1944 and 1945, and was Drake Relays champion in the two-mile run in 1945 and 1946. (Courtesy Drake University.)

1948 was a memorable year in many respects. It was Leap Year, Election Year, and Olympic Year. It was the year in which the Sultan of Swat, George Herman "Babe" Ruth died. It was the year that Citation, the pride of Calumet Farms, won the Triple Crown of horse racing—the Kentucky Derby, Preakness, and Belmont Stakes· (that feat was not to be repeated for twenty-five years when Secretariat accomplished it). It was also the year the Boston Braves won the pennant (first time since 1914).

The fact that it was an Olympic year took on greater significance because the war had forced cancellation of the Olympiads scheduled for 1940 and 1944. London, site of the games forty years ago and awarded them in 1944, had been given another chance to be the host. This was a large assignment for a war-torn nation beset by rationing, shortages, and housing and other building problems. The British thus made use of the facilities extant, but, as Kieran and Daley said, gave them "a bit of spit and polish."

As Britain prepared for the Summer Games, the

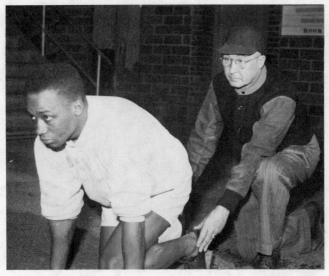

George Bresnahan, Iowa track coach during most of the 1940s and co-author of the book *Track and Field Athletics*. He is shown helping one of his sprinters. (Courtesy University of Iowa.)

Michigan State track coach, Karl Schlademan. Founder of the Kansas Relays, Schlademan also coached at Washington State, where his squads won nine straight North Division Pacific Coast titles. He became head coach of the Spartans in 1940. Under his direction, Michigan State won the NCAA cross-country team championships in 1948 and 1949. (Courtesy Michigan State University.)

The late Jim Kelly, track coach at Minnesota from 1937–63. Kelly's Golden Gophers won the 1948 NCAA team title and the 1949 Big Ten crown. He was coach of the 1956 U.S. Olympic track team, which won fifteen gold medals. In 1936 he had been the first American Olympic basketball coach. (Courtesy University of Minnesota.)

Sprinter Payton Jordan of Southern California. Representing USC, Jordan ran on a world record-breaking 440 yard relay team, and helped USC win two NCAA and conference crowns. He ran on winning sprint relay teams at the 1941 NAAU meet, and had :09.4 and :20.5 times to his credit in his career. As coach at Occidental from 1946–56, Jordan won two NAIA team titles. He was the coach of the highly successful U.S. Olympic track team in 1968. (Courtesy Stanford University.)

Highest scorer in the University of Iowa's track and field history, Francis X. Cretzmeyer. "Cretz" coached record-breaking relay teams at North Des Moines High School, and for over twenty-five years has been a successful mentor at his collegiate alma mater. (Courtesy University of Iowa.)

Crack sprinter for the Texas Longhorns in the late 1940s, Charlie Parker. He was the 1950 NCAA 220 yard dash champion. (Courtesy University of Texas.)

North Des Moines High School's sprint relay team, once holder of three national interscholastic sprint relay records (l to r): Gary Scott, Conrad Jones, Reginald Kaiser, and George Nichols. Francis X. Cretzmeyer coached this unit when they were juniors. He coached Grinnell College the following year (1948), and started his successful head coaching career at Iowa in 1949. (Courtesy Francis X. Cretzmeyer.)

Three-time NCAA titlist, Jerry Thompson of Texas. Thompson also was the Drake Relays two-mile victor in 1943 and 1947. He was the outstanding athlete of the 1947 Relays. (Courtesy University of Texas.)

Winter Olympics resumed operations, after their twelve-year lapse, in St. Moritz, Switzerland. After the usual hassles and difficulties, including balky weather and a credentials dispute over which of two hockey teams would represent the United States, the Games got underway. The United States achieved its best showing ever, taking its first gold medals in history in skiing and figure skating and picking up a third first-place in bobsledding. Mrs. Gretchen Fraser won the women's slalom ski race, Dick Button won in men's figure skating, and Frank Tyler steered the bobsledders to victory after charging that someone had tried to sabotage the Americans' sleds.

Closer to home, author Young attended his first Teachers College (now Art Dickinson) Relays in a town adjacent to Waterloo—Cedar Falls. The "lawn city" was the location of Iowa State Teachers College (now the University of Northern Iowa), the only state institution designed primarily for teacher training in Iowa. The Silver Anniversary of the Teachers College Relays held in 1948 featured the world record holder in the discus, Bob Fitch of Minnesota, who threw in exhibition. His throws did not better his world mark of 180 feet 2¾ inches, but they sailed far beyond the flag set at the Relays record of 138 feet.

A few years later, Young's friend, Dick Walker (the Yankee fan) was to travel to Iowa City, where Fitch was an assistant football coach for the University of Iowa. There Fitch taught Walker his Minnesota or jump-style discus spin. Walker passed on this information to West Waterloo High School track coaches Lyle Anderson and Don Blue, and Walker and Young were to use this style to win state high school discus titles for West High from 1952 through 1954.

The referee of the Teachers College Relays was Gordon Meeter, former Grinnell College football and track star and Waterloo school administrator for many years. Meeter also was to be of assistance to Young in later years, helping him with his shot put form. One of the best-known visiting coaches at the Relays was the 1943 Sullivan Award winner, Gil Dodds. The "flying parson" had been the nation's premier miler for a time.

A week later at the Drake Relays the weather was sunny and in the seventies for both Friday and Saturday sessions. A fine crowd of 15,500 watched the Saturday afternoon events. A new addition in the 1948 field was Mal Whitfield of Ohio State, who was to become a gold medal winner in both the 1948 and 1952 Olympics in the 800 meters. Returning were future Olympic gold medalists Harrison Dillard, Bill Porter, and Arthur Harn-

Gil Dodds, former Ashland College running great, makes an acceptance speech after being inducted into that school's Athletic Hall of Fame. Dodds won the NCAA cross-country championship in East Lansing, Michigan, in 1940, with a record time. He also won three NAAU Outdoor 1,500 meters titles and three NAAU Indoor mile races in the 1940s. (Courtesy Ashland College.)

den. Future Olympians Dike Eddleman, Fortune Gordien, Clyde Scott, Verne McGrew, Dick Ault, and Don Gehrmann were back. Lee Hofacre, Augie Erfurth, and Leo Nomellini were entered as well as Dick Schnittker and Paul Unruh, basketball All-Americans at Ohio State and Bradley, respectively.

Dillard, Porter, and Scott were one-two-three, respectively, in the 120 yard highs with the victor Dillard repeating his record :14.1 clocking. Gordien won his specialty, this time with a record discus heave of 164 feet 5 inches. McGrew and Eddleman tied for first in the high jump with 6 feet 6 inches, two inches off Pete Watkins' record. Hofacre led defending champ Ault to the tape in the 440 yard hurdle event in a record :52.7. With sprinter Charlie Parker and miler Jerry Thompson, the Texas Longhorns captured four relays— the 440, 880, distance medley, and two-mile. The Ault-led Missourians won the 480 shuttle hurdle relay, and the Texas Aggies took the prestigious John L. Griffith one-mile relay, the last event of the exciting and spectacular Relays.

Indiana's Charlie Peters bested Paul Bienz of Tulane and Charlie Parker of Texas in the 100 in

1948 and 1952 Olympic champion at 800 meters, Mal Whitfield. The Ohio State star is now a member of the Citizens Savings Hall of Fame, and is a charter member of the new (1974) National Track and Field Hall of Fame at Charleston, West Virginia. (Courtesy Ohio State University.)

star, was now Drake coach and Relays Director. Drake's Jerry Jefchak took first in the two-mile. Bill Easton had moved south to take the Kansas coaching and Relays-directing posts. Jim Kelly's Minnesota squad, led by Gordien's discus victory, was to win the 1948 NCAA team championship.

In 1948 Young competed in the West Junior High Relays in Waterloo against seventh graders from junior highs in Waterloo and nearby towns. He won a second place in the shot put and a third place in a relay.

Seeing an ad for a 1948 London Olympic Games program, Young sent for and received it. During the Summer Games he methodically filled in the spaces provided in the program for the names of event winners. From this he was to learn new words such as "tandem" (bicycling) and "Greco-Roman wrestling" and that track and field was called "athletics" in Europe. He also realized that Olympic coverage in newspapers was not sufficiently comprehensive, and some blanks in the program were thus left unfilled.

In the final Olympic Trials at Evanston, Harrison Dillard hit the first hurdle, lost his stride, and hit more hurdles, finally coming to a stop before the seventh one. The sports world was shocked by his failure to make the team in the highs. He had won eighty-two consecutive races before bowing to Porter the week before in the NAAU. But in the Trials he displayed his sportsmanship by jogging to the finish line and embracing Porter who had

Indiana's Charley Peters winning the 220 yard dash in the 1949 Pacific Coast-Big Ten Dual Meet of Champions. Peters defeated Charlie Parker of Texas and Paul Bienz of Tulane to win the Drake Relays century in 1948. (Courtesy Indiana University.)

a time of ten seconds flat. Pepperdine, East Texas, Baldwin-Wallace, and Loyola took college division relays. The star in the East-West-Dubuque high triangular that was Young's first meet as a spectator (see above)—Ralph Richman of the Dubuque Rams—won the high school century, and North Des Moines' national record holders blasted the 440 and 880 relay records. Ocie Trimble of Roosevelt Cedar Rapids won the high school mile. Jim Robertson of Ames won a double in the weights. Francis "Cretz" Cretzmeyer was now coaching at Grinnell, and his forces won the two Iowa college events, the 880 and mile relays.

Tom Deckard, former Indiana middle distance

Paul Bienz of Tulane was 1949 and 1950 Drake Relays champion in the 100 yard dash. (Courtesy Tulane University.)

won again. "I can run some too," Dillard said to consolers.

Dillard had qualified for the American team by finishing third behind Barney Ewell and Mel Patton in the 100 meters. In that event, he had won his heats, but in the finals he got a bad start.

At London in the 100 finals, Dillard was first out of the blocks, and he never trailed in the race, winning by a foot over the fast-closing, thirty-one-year-old Barney Ewell. World record holder Mel Patton, Lloyd LaBeach, a Panamanian who ran for Wisconsin in college; and Ewell were in the middle lanes, and at the end of the race Ewell danced in jubilation over what he thought was a victory. But he had not noticed Dillard on the outside lane. Dillard equalled the Olympic record of :10.3 into a wind of five miles an hour. It was the most stunning upset of the Games. After the race, Dillard said: "Just imagine, dreaming about the Olympics for all these years and then winning an Olympic championship in another event." Dillard's coach, Eddie Finnegan of Baldwin-Wallace reiterated:

This was the day we waited for so long. To think it came not in the hurdles but in the event we [Finnegan and Jack Clowser] thought Dillard couldn't win. Fate is strange and wonderful. I'm going out to find a church somewhere. My heart is bursting.

Ewell was second, and La Beach, third; both were timed at :10.4. Patton was fifth.

As a youngster in Cleveland, Dillard had been befriended by his hero, Jesse Owens, winner of four gold medals in the 1936 Berlin Games. His junior high teammates laughed at his scrawniness and called him "Bones." His coach said he was not sufficiently strong to sprint. But Owens gave the track shoes he wore at Berlin to Dillard and taught him to love hurdling. Dillard wore the shoes Owens gave him and won both hurdle races in the 1941 Ohio state high school track meet. He became the only man ever to win Olympic golds in both the hurdles and the sprints when he edged Jack Davis in the 110 meter high hurdles at the 1952 Helsinki Games. His time was 13.7 seconds. He also ran on the winning 400 meter relay teams at both London and Helsinki for a total of four Olympic golds. He won crowns in both the highs and the lows at the 1946 and 1947 NCAA and NAAU meets, and he held the world record in both races (:13.6 and :22.3, respectively).

Mel Patton had been regarded as "the world's fastest human" in 1948 because of his :09.3 world record in the 100 yard dash (although tied ten times, the record lasted thirteen years). Patton came back after his 100 meter defeat to win the 200 meter dash at London. Facing 400 meter favorite Herb McKenley (of Jamaica and Illinois University) on the pole, LaBeach in lane three, Ewell in lane four, Cliff Bourland of Southern California in lane five, and Jamaica's Les Laing in six, Patton got a good start and soon was in a two-man race with Ewell. The latter made a bid for the lead, but "Pell Mell" held him off to win by a foot in :21.1 seconds. LaBeach was again third. After the 100, Patton figured that Olympic glory had evaded him, but, like Dillard, he salvaged an individual gold in another event.

In the 400 meter relay, Ewell, Lorenzo Wright, Dillard, and Patton raced to a six-yard win over host Britain, but an official ruled the pass from Ewell to Wright had been outside the zone. The Jury of Appeal studied the J. Arthur Rank films, however, and four days later ruled the judge was wrong, and the Americans were declared winners. Barney Ewell had won *his* gold medal also, after two close defeats and almost a third disappointment.

Mel Patton won five NCAA sprint crowns for Southern California from 1947 through 1949—the

1948 Olympic champion at 200 meters, "Pell" Mel Patton of USC. (Courtesy University of Southern California.)

sprint double the last two years and the 100 in 1947. He did not run in AAU meets. He also broke Jesse Owens' 200 meter and 220 yard world marks in 1949. On the same day, Patton ran the 100 in :09.1 with a 6.5 mile per hour wind. He had five of the ten fastest 220 times ever run.

Norwood "Barney" Ewell had an especially long career for a sprinter, starting with a 100 meter victory in the Junior NAAU in 1936. He won six NAAU Outdoor championships from 1939–48, and NCAA 100 and 220 titles in 1940 and 1941.

The finals of the 400 and steeplechase and the first day of the decathlon were held on 5 August. Rain poured down all morning, and mist prevailed in the afternoon. Herb McKenley of Jamaica was rated the best quarter-miler in the world, having run the 440 in a world record forty-six seconds flat, and the 400 meters in :45.9. Heavily favored at London in the 400, he was caught by the stretch drive of fellow Jamaican, Arthur Wint, who went on to win by two yards in :46.2 on the soggy track. America's Mal Whitfield was third.

In the 800 meters, Army sergeant Mal Whitfield of Ohio State had the fastest time in the preliminary round with 1:52.8. Marcel Hansenne of France had the fastest time in the world before the Games. In the finals Whitfield took the lead after the first 400 meters and held off the late bid of Arthur Wint to win by two yards in Olympic record time of 1:49.2. Wint was second and Hansenne third.

In the 1,600 meter relay, on the last day of track and field competition (7 August, the day of the relays, women's high jump, 10,000 meter walk, and marathon), the American team of Art Harnden of Texas A&M, Cliff Bourland of Southern California, Roy Cochran, and Whitfield was leading the Jamaican team by fifteen yards during Cochran's leg. Jamaica's Wint then suffered a leg cramp that forced him off the track. The United States team went on to win easily, with France and Sweden taking the silver and bronze medals.

Mal Whitfield was rated by Cordner Nelson as "one of the greatest competitors of all time and probably the fastest doubler among middle distance runners." In the half-mile from 1948 through 1954, he won two NCAA and five NAAU titles, two Olympic Trials, and two Olympic 800 meter golds—he won at Helsinki in 1952, also in 1:49.2. The Ohio State star won a gold medal in the 1,600 meter relay in 1948 and a silver in that event at the 1952 Games. He held the world record in the 880 with 1:49.2 and 1:48.6.

Arthur Wint of Jamaica had won the 800 meters at the Fourth Central American and Carribbean Games in 1938. During the war he joined the Royal Air Force and then became a medical student at the University of London. He was twenty-six-years-old when he won the 400 and took second in the 800 at London. In 1952 Wint again was runner-up to Whitfield in the 800 and was fifth in the 400. He also ran the lead leg on the Jamaican 1,600 meter relay team. Their time of 3:03.9 was a world and Olympic record.

Herb McKenley of Jamaica attended Boston College and Illinois for five years. He won NAAU 400 titles in 1945, 1947, and 1948, and (for Illinois) NCAA 220 and 440 championships in 1946 and 1947. At London he was fourth in the 200 meters in addition to his second in the 400. At the 1952 Helsinki Games he was second in the 100 and 400 and finally won an Olympic gold medal in the 1,600 meter relay in which he ran a :44.6 leg.

Cliff Bourland, member of the 1948 American 1,600 meter relay team that won at London, was a NCAA and NAAU champion in the quarter-mile in 1942 and 1943. He was fifth in the 200 meters at London in addition to his winning relay leg.

In the prestigious 1,500 meter race, held on 6 August, with the second day of the decathlon and women's 200 meters, Lennart Strand of Sweden, and the Swedes generally, were favored. But the track was soaked with rain (which persisted throughout the day), and sticky from the wet clay, and Strand was upset by fellow countryman, Henri Eriksson. Eriksson, the third-ranking Swede in the event, had never defeated Strand. Hansenne of France led for 1,000 meters; then Eriksson passed Strand and Hansenne. Strand, ordinarily a better finisher, could not overtake his stronger teammate. Eriksson won in 3:49.8, Strand placing second, and fast-closing Willie Slijkhuis of the Netherlands, third.

The Swedes were to take four other firsts for a harvest of five golds in the Games. Thore Sjoestrand won the 3,000 meter steeplechase in 9:04.6. John Mikaelsson captured the 10,000 meter walk (45:13.2), and John Ljunggren the longer walking race—50,000 meters—in 4:41:52.0. Arne Ahman copped the top prize in the hop, step, and jump (with 50 feet 6¼ inches) for the Swedes' only field event victory. Sweden swept the steeplechase with Erik Elmsaeter taking the silver medal, and Gote Hagstroem, the bronze medal. Mikaelsson repeated his victory at Helsinki in 1952, breaking his own record.

The 1948 Olympic 5,000 meter race is more understandable with knowledge of the 10,000 that preceded it. London was experiencing its worst heat wave in eighty years when the Olympic competition began on 30 July with the latter distance event. The 10,000 had been won by the Finns—including Hannes Kolehmainen and Paavo Nurmi—in five of the last six Olympics. Their world record holder Viljo Heino was a heavy favorite that day. If he faltered, it was thought that one of the other Finns would win.

Heino took the lead, but in the tenth lap a red-jerseyed Czech named Emil Zatopek assumed the first position. Zatopek, a barrel-chested, fun-loving blonde with a receding hairline, had been guided in the race by a fellow national in the crowd who held up a white sock for the first eight laps to indicate that the pace was satisfactory. But after the eighth lap, the aide held up a red vest, and Emil responded by going from twenty-seventh place to the lead at 4,000 meters.

Zatopek was a relative unknown at the time, even though he had defeated Heino by a yard in the 5,000 at Helsinki in 1947 and run the 10,000 in May of 1948 in a time that was less than two seconds slower than Heino's world record.

It was difficult for a spectator to take him seriously because of his running form. Nelson described him as an "awkward, scrawny little man" who "seemed to be in pain." Everything from his hair to his head, tongue, shoulders, hands, and breathing gave the impression that he was about to have a fit and was "about to drop out." But

Nelson added: "Never has a runner been so deceiving."

Kieran and Daley gave a similar account:

[Zatopek] ran like a contortionist with the itch. He twisted and jerked and strained. His head was thrown back. His shoulders were hunched. Occasionally he'd clutch his side as though some wayward javelin thrower had inadvertently speared him in the ribs. Students of footracing style covered their eyes in dismay at the sight of him.

In another description they said:

If any of the American coaches noticed him, he'd grab the arm of his nearest pupil and exclaim, "There's a perfect example of how not to run a race. That's the most atrocious form I ever saw in my life." One press box tenant looked at him, shuddered and remarked, "He runs like a man who'd just been stabbed in the heart."

Zatopek had begun his career at age eighteen in German-occupied Czechoslovakia in 1941. The regime singled him out for training the following year, and in 1943 he began a form of interval work. The Russians took over, and he became a soldier after the war. In the winter of 1946–47, he trained on a path in a wood, running in all types of weather conditions, and wearing military *boots*. He ranked first in the world at 5,000 meters in 1947, the year he beat Heino.

Viljo Heino was thirty-four-years-old in 1948. He had broken several world records, including the six-mile and 10,000 meters in a 1944 race, Nurmi's ten-mile record in 1945, and the one-hour run mark in 1946. These and other world records made Heino the heavy favorite for the 10,000 gold medal at London.

Czechs in Wembley Stadium were chanting "Zato-pek," and when Emil burst past Heino, many others joined in shouting his name. The awkward Czech had become the crowd favorite. Zatopek and Heino dueled for the next six laps of the twenty-five-lap race, but then Emil burst into a lead of thirty yards in less than a lap. He became confused after lapping some runners, as he could not locate Heino. An official informed him that the famous Finn was out of the race. He had dropped out!

In stifling heat the Czech incredibly sped up the pace. Another Finn, Evert Heinstrom, was led off the track after near-collapse, and two Americans, Eddie O'Toole and Fred Wilt, even passed the third Finn. Zatopek finished the race forty-seven seconds ahead of Alain Mimoun of France and won in a new Olympic record of 29:59.6—the first Czech Olympic victory. Bertil Albertsson of Sweden was third.

The next day Zatopek ran much faster than necessary in his 5,000 meter qualifying heat. Two days after that, the same day that Whitfield and Wint dueled in the 800 final, Zatopek tried for the "Woolworth double"—victories in both the 5,000 and 10,000 meter races. He led for nine laps, followed by Gaston Reiff of Belgium, Willie Slijkhuis of Holland, and Erik Ahlden of Sweden. Everyone else was well off the pace.

Reiff, a twenty-six-year-old clerk, sensed Emil was tiring and took the lead which he increased in the next two and one half laps to thirty yards. On the last lap, Zatopek responded to the bell and took off after Reiff and Slijkhuis. He passed the Dutchman (who finished third) before the last turn and made a desperate attempt to overtake Reiff. But he ran out of space, and Reiff won by two yards. Gaston had a new Olympic record of 14:17.6, and Emil had also broken the old record. Zatopek's mad pursuit on the soggy track in the 5,000 seemed even more impressive to some than his great victory in the 10,000.

Zatopek was to go on to win three more gold medals at the 1952 Olympic Games—in the 5,000, 10,000, and marathon. He set eighteen world records from 5,000 to 30,000 meters. He placed sixth in the marathon in the 1956 Olympics, a year in which he had undergone a hernia operation and lost three months of racing in the summer. Reid Hanley called him "One of [the] greatest to run on [a] track."

Alain Mimoun of France, second to Zatopek in the 10,000, went on to win the 1956 Olympic marathon after copping two silver medals in the 5,000 and 10,000 at Helsinki. He was to win thirty-two French national titles.

The longest race (26 miles 385 yards) and last one of the track and field program, is the marathon. A Belgian,, Etienne Gailly, led for seventeen miles. Then a Korean took over until the twenty-five-mile mark when Gailly, an exparatrooper, regained the lead. Gailly entered the stadium first, but he was exhausted and bewildered. Then another runner burst from the tunnel to take the last lap around the Wembley track. It was Delfo Cabrera, a twenty-seven-year-old fireman from Argentina, who had been regarded as that country's third best in the event and was not even mentioned as a contender. He soon overtook Gailly and captured the gold medal. Thomas Richards of Great Britain was second, and Gailly, third.

In the 110 meter highs, Bill Porter of Northwestern and the USA was favored. He had beaten Dillard at the 1948 AAU and at the Final Trials, while winning both races. Porter was six feet, three

inches in height and weighed 160 pounds. Like Craig Dixon from UCLA, he had excellent hurdling form. Clyde "Smackover" Scott, All-American football player from Arkansas, relied more on speed and determination.

The 110 meter hurdles were held on 4 August, the Queen's birthday, and the King and Queen were in attendance. The javelin and women's hurdles, shot put, and broad jump were also conducted that day. The men's hurdle race turned out to be a sweep for the United States, even without Dillard. Porter broke the record in :13.9, and Scott, the silver medalist, and Dixon, who received the bronze, were timed in :14.1.

In the 400 meter intermediate hurdles the Americans were also victorious. In the semi-finals, Rune Larsson, a Swedish schoolmaster, broke Glenn Hardin's Olympic record of :52.0 with a :51.9, and the USA's Roy Cochran equalled the latter time in his heat. The next day in the finals, Cochran raced to a five-yard victory, lowering the record to :51.1. Ceylon's Duncan White had :51.8 for second, and Larsson, :52.2 for third.

Roy Cochran had won the 400 meter hurdles in the 1939 NAAU meet in :51.9, only one-tenth of a second off the world record. After winning at Drake for Indiana in 1940, he broke the Drake Relays 440 yard hurdle record in 1942, running for the Navy by way of Great Lakes. He was picked the most outstanding 440 yard hurdler in the Drake Relays' first fifty years. Cochran was twenty-nine-years-old and living in Los Angeles with his wife and two children in the year of his Olympic triumphs.

Americans were victorious in three field events. One of these was the shot put in which Wilbur "Moose" Thompson led a United States sweep. At the Trials, Thompson finished behind James Delaney, a Notre Dame graduate and member of the San Francisco Olympic Club, and ahead of Jim Fuchs of Yale. Charley Fonville of Michigan had broken the world record in April at the Kansas Relays with a put of 58 feet 1/4 inch to become the only black shot-putter to hold the global mark. Capable of ten flat in the 100 yard dash, Fonville hurt his spine before the Trials and missed the team, although he was fourth with a very creditable 54 feet 1⅜ inches.

Although he was just a bit over six feet and weighed only 195 pounds, Wilbur Thompson had been nicknamed "Moose." He had been a fine Southern California shot-putter, and in 1948 represented the Los Angeles Athletic Club. The Olympic record of 53 feet 1¾ inches had been set by Hans Woellke of Germany. Thompson, a twenty-

World recordholder in the shot put, Jim Fuchs of Yale. Fuchs was a Yale football star and excellent discus thrower as well. (Courtesy Yale University.)

seven-year-old staff sergeant, smashed that mark by more than three feet with a 56 feet 2 inches put—his personal best. Delaney took the silver with 54 feet 8¾ inches, and Fuchs, the football and track star, copped the bronze with 53 feet 10½ inches.

Fuchs broke the world shot put record four times in 1949 and 1950, his best of the four being 58 feet 10¾ inches. He was a bronze medalist again in the 1952 Games in another USA sweep, and he won the 1949 and 1950 NCAA shot titles for Yale. He also placed first at the NAAU Indoor in 1950–52, and NAAU Outdoor in 1949 and 1950.

The discus throw was conducted on the same wet, cold day (2 August) as the 800 and 5,000 races and pole vault. Fortune Gordien had been undefeated that year and was the main American hope. A member of the NCAA champion Minnesota team, Gordien won three NCAA crowns in a row and (ultimately) six NAAU championships. He broke the world mark in the discus twice in 1949 and once in 1953 (194 feet 6 inches); the latter mark stood for ten years. Jim Young met him at the Sigma Alpha Epsilon fraternity house in Iowa City. Gordien, a member of that fraternity at Minnesota, was putting on a magic show when Young, a youngster visiting the house with his father, met him. Later, in an article, Gordien claimed there

was a "trick" one had to learn in throwing the discus, which if mastered, was not easily forgotten.

Gordien had not been throwing as well in the summer as he had earlier, and two Italians were improving. Born in 1917, Adolpho Consolini had been a world-class competitor since 1938, and was to enjoy amazing longevity in the sport. He broke Archie Harris' world mark in October of 1941, bettered it in 1946, lost the record to Bob Fitch in 1946, and regained it with 181 feet 6 inches in October of 1948.

The other "hot" Italian was Giuseppe Tosi. At London, Consolini and Tosi broke the American Ken Carpenter's Olympic record of 165 feet 7 inches, which had been set at Berlin. Vic Frank and Bill Burton of the United States were hampered by morning rains and did not qualify. When it was all over, Consolini emerged with the gold medal and a new record of 173 feet 2 inches; Tosi was second with 169 feet 10½ inches; and Gordien, third with 166 feet 7 inches. Consolini, an Italian hero of large proportions, was second in the 1952 Olympics, sixth in 1956, and seventeenth in 1960.

In the hammer throw, the United States and Ireland dominated until 1936, when Karl Hein of Germany won with 185 feet 4 inches. The United States was not shut out in 1948, as Robert Bennett took third with 176 feet 3½ inches; but the gold medal went to Hungary's Imre Nemeth, and the silver, to Ivan Gubijan of Yugoslavia.

Nemeth was not a "whale," as the Irish-Americans of yesteryear had been called. He weighed only 184 pounds, but his form was excellent. His winning throw of 183 feet 11½ inches, however, was short of the record. Gubijan's runner-up heave was 178 feet ½ inch.

Born in 1917 in Czechoslovakia, Hungary's Nemeth tied the world record of 193 feet 7 inches just before the Games on 14 July 1948. He broke this record with 195 feet 5 inches in 1949 and upped it to 196 feet 5 inches in 1950. He placed third in the 1952 Olympics. The winner was Jozef Csermak of Hungary, a student of Nemeth.

The javelin throw had been the province of the Swedes and Finns since 1906, when the event was first adopted in the Olympics. In 1936 Gerhard Stoeck of Germany broke the Scandinavian dominance.

The United States' hopes in 1948 were with Dr. Steve Seymour, an osteopath and a Temple graduate. He held the American record of 248 feet 1 inches, set in 1947. The favorite had been Sven Daleflod of Sweden, but illness kept him from participating.

Finland's Kaj Rautavaara, an actor, returned the championship to Finland with a throw of 228 feet 10½ inches. Seymour took second with 221 feet 7½ inches, and Jozsef Varszegi of Hungary was third with 219 feet 11 inches.

In the opening day of competition, 30 July, Americans were dealt a surprising blow when they failed to capture first place in the high jump. Americans had dominated the event in past Olympiads, and this one was not expected to be an exception. The three American jumpers—Dwight Eddleman of Illinois, Verne McGrew of Rice, and George Stanich of UCLA—had all gone 6 feet 8 inches and were regarded as the best in the world. But McGrew went out at 6 feet 2¾ inches. Five men, including Eddleman and Stanich, cleared 6 feet 4 inches. The others were John Winter, a twenty-two-year-old Australian bank clerk from Perth, Bjorn Paulsen from Norway, and G.E. Damito from Morocco.

Winter hurt his back clearing that height, however. He felt that he had only one good jump left in him, and with an all-out effort he cleared 6 feet 6 inches. None of the others could clear that height as Winter sat and watched, nursing his painful back.

Eddleman was to be an eleven-letter man at Illinois. Winter's personal best was 6 feet 7¼ inches. He was an Australian champion three times and national record-setter three times.

The United States' Willie Steele, from San Diego State College, captured the long-jump championship on the same day (31 July) that Dillard, Cochran, Nemeth, and Ljunggren won their events. Steele was one of the first five twenty-six footers in the history of track and field. His winning Olympic leap in warm and sunny conditions was 25 feet 8 inches. An Aussie, Theodore Bruce, jumped 24 feet 9½ inches for second, and the Americans' Herbert Douglas was a quarter-inch behind Bruce in third.

Willie Steele was "probably the top long jumper of the 1940s," according to Reid Hanley. He had a jump of 25 feet 7¼ inches before his World War II stint in the Army. He won the 1946 and 1947 NAAU broad jump and the 1947 and 1948 NCAA titles. His winning leap was 26 feet 6 inches in the 1947 NCAA meet. Steele won in the 1948 Olympics despite injuries.

George Stanich of UCLA, basketball and track star. Stanich placed third in the 1948 Olympic high jump. He also was named an All-American basketball player for his performance in the 1949–50 season. (Courtesy UCLA.)

1948 Olympic broad-jump gold medalist, Willie Steele of San Diego State. (Courtesy San Diego State University.)

The triple jump, won by Sweden's Arne Ahman, with a distance of 50 feet 6¼ inches, was held on 3 August, the same misty day as the 200 meters and shot put. Gordon Avery of Australia and Ruhi Sarialp of Turkey were second and third with marks of 50 feet 5 inches and 49 feet 3½ inches, respectively. None of the American triple jumpers qualified for the finals.

The foul, rainy weather of 2 August hampered the pole vault more than any other event. The United States' best hope, A. Richmond Morcom, an ex-New Hampshire athlete, was bothered by an old injury that flared up in the competition, and he only finished sixth. But University of California graduate Guinn Smith outlasted his competitors and the elements to win the vault after most had left the stadium. His winning height was 14

New Hampshire's A. Richmond "Boo" Morcom, NAAU pole-vault titlist in 1947. Morcom also was co-champion in the NCAA pole vault that year. He won the Final U.S. Olympic Trials in 1948 with a vault of 14 feet, 8⅛ inches. (Courtesy University of New Hampshire.)

feet 1¼ inches. Erkki Kataja of Finland went 13 feet 9½ inches for the silver, and Bob Richards of the USA, the same for third.

Born in Texas, Owen Guinn Smith was twenty-eight at the time of the Olympics. He had served eighteen months in the Army Air Force and had a torn knee cartilage. Doctors had advised him to quit vaulting. Prior to his war service he tied for first in the 1941 NCAA vault while at California.

Bob Richards, the "vaulting vicar," went on to win the 1952 and 1956 Olympic vault titles. He is the only person to win two Olympic vault gold medals.

The decathlon winner, Robert Bruce "Bob" Mathias of Tulare, California, was selected by *Sport* as the Top Performer in Track and Field in the twenty-five-year, 1946–1971, period. The seventeen-year-old high school sophomore in 1948 was the youngest trackman ever to make a United States Olympic squad.

Mathias had not even competed in a decathlon until eight weeks before the Olympic competition. He had won his first ten-event contest in the Southern Pacific Association AAU meet with 7,094 points and then had won the NAAU at Bloomfield, New Jersey, sixteen days later.

At the end of the first day of 1948 Olympic competition (5 August, when it rained), Enrique Kistenmacher of Argentina was the leader, but Ignace Heinrich, a twenty-year-old Frenchman, was a close second. The three Americans—Mathias, Floyd Simmons of the Los Angeles Athletic Club, and Irving "Moon" Mondschein—were next. Kistenmacher had won the 100, 400, and broad jump.

On the second day, in the worst weather of the Games, if not in all of Olympic history, Mathias began competing at 10:30 A.M. and did not finish until twelve hours later. All of his main rivals were in another flight that finished before dark. Mathias huddled under a blanket to escape the rain and ate only two box lunches throughout the day. His winning discus flag was knocked over and misplaced short of the actual mark; the vault took place in the dark with only poor light from the stands, the pole was slippery, and he could hardly see the crossbar; he could not see the restraining line in his first javelin toss, which caused him to foul, and a flashlight was needed to see the line on his other throws. With three events left (the vault, javelin, and 1,500 meters), Mathias learned that Heinrich had finished his ten events and was leading with 6,974 points.

Mathias accomplished his victory with only one undisputed first in a single event—the discus, but he tied for first in the high jump and pole vault

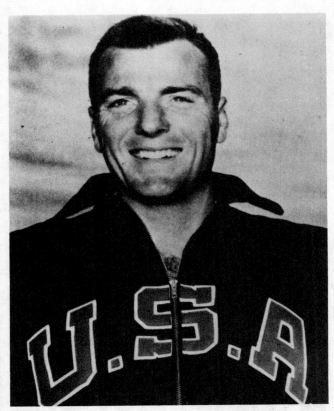

The only man to win the Olympic decathlon twice, Bob Mathias. As a seventeen-year-old from Tulare high school in California, he won the 1948 Olympic decathlon title, and, in 1952, he repeated at Helsinki as the world's greatest athlete. World record holder, four-time national decathlon titlist, and Sullivan Award recipient, Mathias also was an excellent fullback at Stanford and played in the Rose Bowl. (Courtesy Bob Mathias.)

and scored well in all ten events. Bob's 7,139 point total was the only one over 7,000 in the competition. His ten performances were: 100 meters, :11.2; 400 meters, :51.7; high jump, 6 feet 1¼ inches; shot put, 42 feet 9¼ inches; broad jump, 21 feet 8½ inches; 110 meter hurdles, :15.7 seconds; discus, 144 feet 4 inches; pole vault, 11 feet 5¾ inches; javelin, 165 feet 1 inch; and 1,500 meters, 5:11. Ignace Heinrich was second, and Floyd Simmons, third. Under the subsequently revised scoring tables, Mathias's point total was 6,826.

After stupendous celebrations in his home state and town, Bob Mathias was voted the Sullivan Award as the nation's top amateur athlete in 1948. In 1950 he set the world decathlon record. After playing in the 1952 Rose Bowl for Stanford, he reset the world decathlon mark in the 1952 Olympic Trials. Mathias went on to win the 1952 Olympic decathlon championship. His total of 7,887 points was both a world and an Olympic decathlon record. He thereby became the only man to win two Olympic gold medals in that grueling event. The four-time national decathlon champ was to serve in Congress from 1967 to 1975 as a Republican.

Among the women athletes, the heroine of the Games was Fanny Blankers-Koen of Holland. Fanny had been a talented athlete as a child. When she was sixteen in 1935, triple jumper Jan Blankers saw her win her first major race and soon became her coach. Twice a week she bicycled eighteen miles to train under his supervision. Soon Fanny was the best woman runner in the Netherlands. She won every major Dutch sprinting event in 1939. By 1948 she had married her coach and had two children. She also held four world records.

In the 1948 Olympics, Fanny dispelled the doubts of English reporters who thought she was too old (nearly thirty) to be a serious contender. She easily won the 100 meters in 11.9 seconds. She became the first woman to be a double winner since Mildred "Babe" Didrickson in 1932 by winning the 80 meter hurdles after a poor start. The time was :11.2, a world and Olympic record. On 6 August, she became the first woman to win three golds in an Olympics by taking the 200 meters, a new Olympic event for women, with a :24.4 clocking. Two Audreys won the silver and bronze medals—Audrey Williamson of Britain and Audrey Patterson of the USA.

The Dutch were not favored in the women's 400 meter relay. By the time the "Flying Dutchwoman" took the baton in her anchor leg, her team was in fourth place. Fanny proved her mettle by overtaking the leader, Joyce King of Australia, in the last stride of the race. The Dutch team had won, and Fanny had her fourth gold medal!

Shirley Strickland of Australia won bronze medals in the 100 meters and in the 80 meter hurdles. She won a silver as a member of the Aussie 400 meter relay team. At the 1952 Games, she won the 80 meter hurdles and was third in the 100. In the 1956 Melbourne Olympics she won two golds, for a career total of seven Olympic medals.

Great Britain also did well in the 1948 races. In addition to Williamson's 200 meter silver medal, Britishers Dorothy Manley and the late Maureen Gardner were silver medalists in the 100 and hurdles, respectively. The Commonwealth picked up another medal with Canada's bronze in the relay.

Mrs. Olga Gyarmati of Hungary copped the broad jump title on 4 August, with a leap of 18 feet 8¼ inches. Simonetto de Portela of Argentina was second with 18 feet 4½ inches; and Anne Leyman of Sweden, third with 18 feet 3⅜ inches.

The other jumping event was the only women's track and field event won by an American. Alice Coachman of the USA broke the Olympic high jump record with her jump of 5 feet 6⅛ inches. Mrs. Dorothy Tyler of Great Britain jumped that height too, but was second because of more misses.

The third-place winner in the high jump easily was the second most dominant woman performer in the athletics portion of the Games. Micheline Ostermeyer of France jumped 5 feet 3¼ inches for the bronze. On 4 August, she had joined the "Marvelous Mama," Fanny Blankers-Koen, as a double winner by capturing the shot put. Her 45 feet 1½ inches put was comfortably ahead of those by Amelia Piccinini of Italy (42 feet 11¼ inches) and Ina Schäffer of Austria (42 feet 10¾ inches). In Olympic competition, the event was held for the first time in 1948.

Micheline's first victory was achieved on the first day of competition in the discus. She won on her last throw with 137 feet 6½ inches. Italy also had the runner-up in this weight event, as Cordiale Gentile flipped the platter 135 feet ½ inch, and Micheline's teammate, Jacqueline Mazeas, was third with 132 feet 9 inches. Micheline Ostermeyer also has won the *Grand Prix du Conservatoire de Musique* in the piano.

The other throwing event, the javelin, was won by Herma Bauma of Austria. Her 149 feet 6 inches heave was nearly six feet farther than the 143 feet 8 inches throw of Finland's Kaisa Parviäinen, and Lily Carlstedt of Denmark was next with 140 feet 6½ inches.

The coach of the American track and field team at the 1948 Olympics was Dean Cromwell of Southern California. "The Dean" coached track there for thirty-nine years and won twelve NCAA team titles, nine of those consecutively.

At the end of the spectacular track and field portion of the 1948 Olympics, the United States men had won eleven gold, four silver, and nine bronze medals. Sweden had won five gold, three silver, and four bronze. The men had broken eight Olympic records and tied two under miserable conditions.

Since the 1936 Olympics took place during the year of their birth, the 1948 London Games were the first that Young and McClure followed as youngsters, and it made a great impact on them, increasing their already considerable interest in track and field, especially, and other Olympic sports.

Young had the worst year in his career as a track competitor the next spring, adding only one yel-

Dean Cromwell, coach of champions. Cromwell (1879–1962) was head track coach of Southern California from 1910–48. He was head coach of the 1948 Olympic team, which won eleven gold medals. (Courtesy University of Southern California.)

low fourth-place ribbon to his valued collection, and that was attained in a 440 yard *relay* at the West Junior High Relays. But his enthusiasm for track and field was unflagging and was intensified by the Fortieth Annual Drake Relays, 1949 edition.

The list of entries was impressive and included, *inter alia,* jumper Jerome Biffle of Denver and discus thrower Sim Iness of Compton College. Biffle won the broad jump with 23 feet 11½ inches and tied for third in the high jump. Iness did not place in the discus. They were to become gold medalists in the broad jump and discus, respectively, at the 1952 Olympic Games.

Olympians Dike Eddleman and Verne McGrew were at Drake again in 1949, Eddleman tying for the high jump title at 6 feet 6⅝ inches with Len nertson of Washington University of St. Louis Don Laz of Illinois tied for the pole vault crown at 14 feet with Bennett of Wisconsin and Harry Cooper of Minnesota. Laz was to win a silver med al at Helsinki.

Competing for the University of Denver, Jerome Biffle won the broad jump, took second in the 100, and tied for third in the high jump in the 1949 Drake Relays. He repeated as broad-jump winner in 1950 (and is now a member of the Drake Relays Hall of Fame). Biffle was NCAA champion in that event in 1950, and became Olympic champion in 1952 at Helsinki. (Courtesy University of Denver.)

better than his 1948 mark. Augie Erfurth, Lee Hofacre, Charlie Parker, and Don Gehrmann were back. Roy Griak, future Gopher track coach, was competing for Minnesota. Football stars Tobin Rote of Rice, Jim Doran of Iowa State, Ed Tunnicliff of Northwestern, John Helwig of Notre Dame, and Ray Renfro of North Texas State were also entered.

Famous miler Gil Dodds was present as coach of Wheaton College. F.X. "Cretz" Cretzmeyer had moved on from North Des Moines in 1947 to Grinnell College in 1948, and now was head coach at Iowa, replacing retiring George Bresnahan. Cretz (who broke the all-time scoring record for Iowa trackmen in the 1930s, developed North's "flying four," and led Grinnell to the Iowa College relay titles in 1948) was to be at Iowa for more than a quarter-century. He later coauthored a famous book on track and field with Bresnahan and W.W.

Byrl Thompson, winner of the Drake Relays discus crown in 1946 representing Camp Grant, was back wearing Minnesota's colors, and he proceeded to shatter the record of another Golden Gopher, Fortune Gordien, in winning the discus at 170 feet 3 inches. The *Des Moines Register* published sequential photos of Thompson's throwing. Young later posted these "machine gun photos" on his bedroom bulletin board and studied them as an aid in mastering discus technique. In 1956 Young, competing for Iowa, was to throw *against* Thompson who was then completing his collegiate work at Minnesota! Thompson was Big Ten champion in the latter year.

Olympian Dick Ault of Missouri was back, and he won the 220 low hurdles in :24.1. Paul Bienz of Tulane won his first of two century titles in :09.8. Norm Wasser of Illinois successfully defended his shot put title with 52 feet 9⅞ inches, ⅛ inch

Olympic discus champion and record breaker Sim Iness. Iness hailed from the same town—Tulare, California—as did Bob Mathias at the time of his ultimate triumph in 1952. He held the world record (as the first to reach 190 feet) and was a two-time NCAA champion and recordholder. Iness was an entrant in the 1949 Drake Relays, representing Compton College. (Courtesy Sim Iness.)

Tuttle, and led Iowa to several Big Ten titles.

Coaching the University of California contingent was Brutus Hamilton. He later became the head coach of the 1952 Olympic track team, which won thirteen gold medals. Hamilton (born in Peculiar, Missouri) was coach at California from 1932 to 1965 during which his teams were second six times in NCAA championships.

Coach of the Denver University team at Drake in 1949 was Jesse Mortensen. He coached at Southern California from 1951 to 1961 when USC won seven NCAA team titles.

Leo Johnson, Illinois coach, was Drake Relays Referee, and J. Eddie Weems of Pepperdine was Assistant Referee. Laz and Eddleman were Johnson-coached athletes, and Pepperdine won the College two-mile relay. Weems-coached teams at Abilene Christian and Pepperdine had not failed to win a first at Drake since 1930. Johnson's Illini had won NCAA team titles in 1944, 1946, and 1947.

In other competition, Wisconsin, Michigan State, and Oklahoma A.&M. (440 and 880) won two relays each. The meet-ending John L. Griffith one-mile relay was won by Rice, and Kansas took the University two-mile relay. Hampton of Texas A.&M. won the two-mile run, Christiansen of Michigan State copped the highs, and Pickarts of Santa Barbara captured the javelin.

Compton took the College 880 and sprint medley relays, and Loyola, the mile relay. In high school events Ocie Trimble repeated in the mile, and Jim Robertson (setting the record) did the same in the shot put. Hugh Hines of Burlington, later Young's teammate at Iowa, won the broad jump, and Clyde Gardner of Newton broke the discus record. Gardner broke the national high school discus record in 1949, and the mark lasted until Al Oerter, to be a four-time Olympic gold medalist, broke it in 1954. Young was to shoot for Gardner's high school records and his Iowa University school record in the 1950s (and compete against the invincible Oerter).

Ames won two relays in addition to the shot put, and West Waterloo, Young's future alma mater, won the sprint medley, Jim Pilkington, later to be a Drake star and coach at Central Missouri State, was running for Red Oak high school.

Many of the top performers of the 1940s were to contribute significantly to track news of the 1950s. This has already been noted in connection with athletes Biffle, Consolini, Dillard, Gordien, Iness, Mathias, Mimoun, Reiff, Richards, Whitfield, Wint, and Zatopek; and coaches Hamilton, Kelly, Snyder, Jordan, and Mortensen; and others.

In addition, Parry O'Brien, future two-time Olympic champ, world record holder, first sixty-footer, four-time Olympian, and revolutionizer of shot put form, was putting the twelve-pound high school shot 57 feet 9½ inches in 1949. Charley Moore, 400 meter hurdles champion in the 1952 Olympics, was winning his first NAAU title in 1949. (His father had been reserve 110 meter hurdler on the 1924 Olympic team. Young met Charley's parents on a European trip in 1957.) Horace "Nip" Ashenfelter became the only American to win a gold medal in the 3,000 meter steeplechase, in the 1952 Olympics. He won the NCAA two-mile for Penn State in 1949.

Ferreira Adhemar Da Silva of Brazil was eleventh in the 1948 Olympics in the triple jump. He was to become the 1952 and 1956 Olympic champion and world record holder. Hanley called him the "greatest athlete in South American history." George Rhoden of Jamaica, competing for Morgan State, won the 1949 NAAU 400 meters for his first national title He was to become a world record holder and a gold medalist (defeating McKenley) in the 400 at the 1952 Olympics. He also an-

Coach of three NCAA team track champions, Leo Johnson of Illinois. Johnson's Illini captured the NCAA crown in 1944, 1946, and 1947. The Illinois coach from 1938–65, he guided his teams to ten Big Ten titles outdoors and seven indoors. Among the most famous Illinois track athletes in the 1940s were national champions Herb McKenley, Bob Richards, Dike Eddleman, and Buddy Young. (Courtesy University of Illinois.)

qualify for the 200 meter finals in the 1948 Olympics, but at the Helsinki Games in 1952 she won a gold medal as a member of the United States' 400 meter relay team that broke the world record. She won a bronze in the 1956 Olympics as a member of the American 400 meter team.

On 30 August 1974, at Charleston, West Virginia, twenty-six charter members were inducted into the National Track and Field Hall of Fame. The members were chosen by representatives of seven major governing bodies of amateur athletics

Olympic 400 meter hurdle champion and record-holder, Charles Moore, Jr. (shown winning an indoor middle-distance race in 1949). Running for Cornell, Moore won the NCAA 440 in 1949. His winning time in the 1949 NAAU 440 yard hurdles (:51.9) lasted as a record until 1956. He also won the next three national meets in the intermediate hurdles. Charlie's Olympic record in 1952 was run on a slow track, and he also ran an exceptional leg on the United States' second place 1,600 meter relay team. (Courtesy Cornell University.)

chored the winning Jamaica 1,600 meter relay team to world and Olympic records.

Andy Stanfield of Seton Hall won the 100 and 200 in the 1949 NAAU meet. He went on to many more national titles, world records, and a gold medal in the 200 meters at the 1952 Olympics. He also anchored the USA's 400 meter relay team to a first place. In the 1956 Games he was second in the 200 behind Bobby Morrow.

Mae Faggs won an indoor NAAU 220 with a meet record :25.9 in 1949. The record stood until Wilma Rudolph broke it in 1960. Faggs failed to

1949 NCAA two-mile champion, Horace "Nip" Ashenfelter. He became America's only Olympic gold-medal winner ever in the 3,000 meter steeplechase at Helsinki in 1952. (Courtesy Pennsylvania State University.)

Seton Hall's Andy Stanfield won the 100 meters and 200 meters in the 1949 NAAU meet and captured the NAAU 200 in 1952, and 220 in 1953. At the Helsinki Olympics he won two gold medals by winning the 200 meters (tying Jesse Owens' record), and anchoring the 400 meter relay to a four-yard victory. At the 1956 Olympics, he finished second in the 200 meters, a yard behind Bobby Morrow. (Courtesy Seton Hall University.)

in the United States. The competitors chosen were: Ralph Boston, Lee Calhoun, Glenn Cunningham, Glenn Davis, Hal Davis, Babe Didrickson Zaharias, Harrison Dillard, Ray Ewry, Rafer Johnson, Alvin Kraenzlein, Bob Mathias, Lon Myers, Parry O'Brien, Al Oerter, Harold Osborn, Jesse Owens, Wilma Rudolph, Bob Simpson, Les Steers, Cornelius Warmerdam, and Mal Whitfield. Also named were three coaches, Dean Cromwell, Brutus Hamilton, and Mike Murphy; and two administrators, Avery Brundage and Dan Ferris. The decade of the 1940s was well represented in this group: Hal Davis, Dillard, Mathias, Steers, Warmerdam, and Whitfield among the athletes, and all the coaches and officials

except Murphy were prominent in their track and field specialities during a substantial portion of the 1940s. Cunningham also participated in 1940, his last year as a competitor.

A second group of ten athletes, two coaches, and one track club founder were inducted into the National Track and Field Hall of Fame in June of 1975. The selectees were athletes Horace Ashenfelter, Alice Coachman Davis, John B. Flanagan, Ralph Metcalfe, Bobby Joe Morrow, Bob Richards, Helen Stephens, Jim Thorpe, Bill Toomey, and Stella Walsh; coaches M.E. "Bill" Easton and Edward P. Hurt; and University of Chicago Track Club founder, Edward M. "Ted" Hayden. Ashenfelter, Coachman, Richards, and Walsh, were among the very prominent athletes in the world of track and field during the 1940s.

Ashenfelter, Brundage, Cromwell, Cunningham, and Mathias, along with Don Canham, Don Lash, Bill Schroeder, and Kenneth L. "Tug" Wilson were athletes and administrators from the 1940s named to the United States Track and Field Hall of Fame at Angola, Indiana—another shrine for the sport—in August of 1974, along with twenty-eight other track and field greats.

As the 1940s drew to a close, the sport of track and field was coming into more and more prominence in Young's life, as it was to be his best participation sport. The cumulative impact of the Drake Relays and Olympic Games had stirred his enthusiasm for the sport. In the 1950s this was to develop into high school and college competition, and eventually into extensive instructional and officiating activities.

In retrospect, the 1940s in track and field began with some outstanding performances by excellent athletes who often did not receive the publicity due them, because their fleeting moments of glory coincided or overlapped with an era in which two consecutive Olympic Games were cancelled. 1945 seemed to be a demarcation line as far as Young and McClure's direct perception of personalities and activities in the sport was concerned, basically because this was the time in which they learned to read. Nearly all of the athletes who starred after that time were noticed and read about at the time, and most were admired by these growing, impressionable boys. In the late 1940s many of these personalities and events were observed directly by the authors. Because of their growing participation in the sport, relationships or connections were beginning to develop between the authors and sports figures, institutions, and events.

Track and field is generally considered an "individual" sport even though team competition is also involved. The notion of *citius, altius, fortius* (faster, higher, stronger) is an appealing one to the athlete, coach, spectator, and reader, to young and old alike. Track is a sport in which individual heroes abound because of its inherent nature. From the authors' standpoint, in recent years the use of drugs such as amphetamines and anabolic steroids by track athletes, growing professionalism (and conversely the decline of the amateur code or ideal typified by the late and much maligned Avery Brundage), college recruitment evils on a greater scale, increased injection of politics into the competitive scene as in the Olympic Games, and other developments have combined to detract sadly from the appeal of the sport. But at the individual and local levels, these can be stripped away, and the pursuit of excellence, the respect for achievement, and the values of heroic participation remain, making the sport of track and field an eternally worthwhile activity.

NCAA TRACK AND FIELD CHAMPIONS OF THE 1940s

Claude "Buddy" Young demonstrating his national championship sprinting form. Young paced Illinois to the NCAA track championship at Marquette in 1944, when he broke the tape first in both the 100 and 220. In football he tied Red Grange's mark by scoring thirteen touchdowns in 1944, a year he averaged 8.9 yards per carry. In 1947, he ran for 103 yards in twenty carries and scored twice in the Rose Bowl. Young was the MVP in the College All-Star Game in 1947, and then starred in the pros for nine years. (Courtesy University of Illinois.)

100 Yard Dash

1940	Barney Ewell	Penn State	:09.6
1941	Barney Ewell	Penn State	:09.6
1942	Hal Davis	California	:09.6
1943	Hal Davis	California	:10.0
1944	Buddy Young	Illinois	:09.7
1945	John Van Velzer	Navy	:10.1
1946	William Mathis	Illinois	:09.6
1947	Mel Patton	Southern California	:09.7
1948	Mel Patton	Southern California	:10.4*
1949	Mel Patton	Southern California	:09.7

*100 meters

220 Yard Dash

1940	Barney Ewell	Penn State	:21.1
1941	Barney Ewell	Penn State	:21.1
1942	Hal Davis	California	:21.2
1943	Hal Davis	California	:21.4
1944	Buddy Young	Illinois	:21.6
1945	Earl Collins	Texas	:22.4
1946	Herb McKenley	Illinois	:21.3
1947	Herb McKenley	Illinois	:20.7
1948	Mel Patton	Southern California	:20.7*
1949	Mel Patton	Southern California	:20.4
1950	Charlie Parker	Texas	:21.5

*200 meters

440 Yard Dash

1940	Lee Orr	Washington State	:47.3
1941	Hubert Kerns	Southern California	:46.6
1942	Cliff Bourland	Southern California	:48.2
1943	Cliff Bourland	Southern California	:48.5
1944	Elmore Harris	Morgan State	:47.9
1945	Bill Kash	Navy	:49.8
1946	Herb McKenley	Illinois	:47.5
1947	Herb McKenley	Illinois	:46.2
1948	Norman Rucks	South Carolina	:47.2*
1949	Charley Moore	Cornell (New York)	:47.0

*400 meters

1945 NCAA 220 yard dash champion, Earl Collins of Texas. (Courtesy University of Texas.)

1948 National Collegiate champion in the 400 meter dash, Norman "Scooter" Rucks of South Carolina. (Courtesy University of South Carolina.)

880 Yard Run

1937	John Woodruff	Pittsburgh	1:5▢3
1938	John Woodruff	Pittsburgh	1:5▢3
1939	John Woodruff	Pittsburgh	1:5▢3
1940	Campbell Kane	Indiana	1:5▢5
1941	Campbell Kane	Indiana	1:5▢2
1942	Bill Lyda	Oklahoma	1:5▢8
1943	Joe Nowicki	Fordham	1:5▢2
1944	Robert L. Kelley	Illinois	1:5▢1
1945	Ross Hume	Michigan	1:5▢7
1946	Lewis Smith	Virginia Union	1:5▢6
1947	Bill Clifford	Ohio State	1:5▢8
1948	Mal Whitfield	Ohio State	1:5▢1*
1949	Mal Whitfield	Ohio State	1:5▢3

*800 meters

One Mile Run

1940	John Munski	Missouri	4:1▢7
1941	Leslie MacMitchell	NYU	4:1▢4
1942	Bob Ginn	Nebraska	4:1▢1
1943	Don Burnham	Dartmouth	4:1▢1
1944	Robert & Ross Hume	Michigan	4:1▢5
1945	Ross Hume	Michigan	4:1▢5
1946	Robert Rehberg	Illinois	4:1▢2
1947	Gerry Karver	Penn State	4:17▢
1948	Don Gehrmann	Wisconsin	3:54▢*
1949	Don Gehrmann	Wisconsin	4:09▢

*1,500 meters

Two Mile Run

1940	Roy Fehr	Michigan State	9:18▢
1941	Fred Wilt	Indiana	9:14▢
1942	Art Cazares	Fresno	9:10▢
1943	Jerry Thompson	Texas	9:29▢
1944	Francis Martin	Notre Dame	9:38▢
1945	Francis Martin	NYU	9:25▢
1946	Francis Martin	NYU	9:38▢
1947	Jerry Thompson	Texas	9:22▢
1948	Jerry Thompson	Texas	15:04▢*
1949	Horace Ashenfelter	Penn State	9:03▢

*5,000 meters

10,000 Meter Run

| 1948 | Robert Black | Rhode Island | 32:13▢ |

120 Yard High Hurdles

1940	Ed Dugger	Tufts	:13▢
1941	Robert Wright	Ohio State	:14▢
1942	Robert Wright	Ohio State	:14▢
1943	Bill Cummins	Rice	:14▢
1944	David Nichols	Illinois	:15▢
1945	George Walker	Illinois	:14▢
1946	Harrison Dillard	Baldwin-Wallace	:14▢
1947	Harrison Dillard	Baldwin-Wallace	:14▢
1948	Clyde Scott	Arkansas	:13▢*
1949	Craig Dixon	UCLA	:13▢

*110 meters

90

Indiana middle-distance star, Campbell Kane. The long-striding Kane won the 880 yard run in both the 1940 and 1941 NCAA meets. He was the Big Ten champion in 1941 and 1942. (Courtesy Indiana University.)

1947 NCAA 880 yard dash champion, William Clifford of Ohio State. Clifford's victory launched a three-year Buckeye dominance of the NCAA half-mile event. In 1948, Clifford won the 880 in the Big Ten Indoor and Outdoor meets, helping the Buckeyes to team championships in both. (Courtesy Ohio State University Photo Archives.)

Penn State's Gerry Karver, 1947 NCAA mile-run champion. (Courtesy Pennsylvania State University.)

Two-time NCAA cross-country champion, Bob Black of the University of Rhode Island. (Courtesy University of Rhode Island.)

1940 NCAA 120 yard high hurdles champion, Ed Dugger of Tufts. Dugger is shown in a Tufts-Northeastern indoor dual meet in 1940. In this race, he broke the Tufts record for the 300 yard dash with his :33.4 time. (Courtesy Tufts University.)

Ohio State's Robert Wright, top collegiate hurdler in 1941 and 1942. (Courtesy Ohio State University Photo archives.)

Illinois' Dave Nichols, 1944 NCAA champion in the 120 yard high hurdles. Illinois won the team title by a wide margin, and thus broke USC's NCAA team victory skein at nine. (Courtesy University of Illinois.)

George Walker, winner of three NCAA hurdling championships for Illinois. (Courtesy University of Illinois.)

220 Yard Low Hurdles

1940	Fred Wolcott	Rice	:23.1
1941	Robert Wright	Ohio State	:23.4
1942	Robert Wright	Ohio State	:23.7
1943	Bill Cummins	Rice	:23.9
1944	Elmore Harris	Morgan State	:23.9
1945	George Walker	Illinois	:24.0
1946	Harrison Dillard	Baldwin-Wallace	:23.0
1947	Harrison Dillard	Baldwin-Wallace	:22.3
1948	Event not run		
1949	Craig Dixon	UCLA	:22.7
1951	Charley Moore	Cornell (New York)	:22.7

400 Meter Hurdles

| 1948 | George Walker | Illinois | :52.4 |

3,000 Meter Steeplechase

| 1948 | Browning Ross | Villanova | 9:25.7 |

Hop, Step, and Jump

| 1948 | Lloyd Lamois | Minnesota | 45–10 |

Pole Vault

1940	Kenneth Dills	Southern California	13–10
1941	Guinn Smith	California	
	Harold Hunt	Nebraska	14–2
1942	Jack DeField	Minnesota	14–1
1943	Jack DeField	Minnesota	14–1
1944	John Schmidt	Ohio State	
	William Blackwell	Oberlin	
	Phillip Anderson	Notre Dame	
	Robert Phelps	Illinois	13–6
1945	Robert Phelps	Illinois	11–6
1946	Bill Moore	Northwestern	13–8
1947	Robert Hart	Southern California	
	Ray Maggard	UCLA	
	Bill Moore	Northwestern	
	George Rasmussen	Oregon	
	Richard Morcom	New Hampshire	
	Bob Richards	Illinois	14–0
1948	Warren Bateman	Colorado	
	George Rasmussen	Oregon	14–0
1949	Bob Smith	San Diego	14–3

Broad Jump

1940	Jackie Robinson	UCLA	24–10¼
1941	Billy Brown	LSU	24– 7⅜
1942	Dallas Dupre	Ohio State	24– 2¼
1943	William Christopher	Rice	24– 7¼
1944	Ralph Tyler	Ohio State	23– 4½
1945	Henry Aihara	Illinois	23– 1⅝
1946	John Robertson	Texas	24–10½
1947	Willie Steele	San Diego	26– 6
1948	Willie Steele	San Diego	24–11¼
1949	Fred Johnson	Michigan State	25– 2½
1950	Jerome Biffle	Denver	25– 4¾

Double victor in the 1949 NCAA meet, Craig Dixon of UCLA. Dixon also won the bronze medal in the 1948 Olympics in the 110 meter hurdles. (Courtesy UCLA.)

John Schmidt, NCAA pole-vault co-champion in 1944. (Courtesy Ohio State University Photo Archives.)

Northwestern's Bill Moore, national champion pole vaulter. (Courtesy Northwestern University.)

1947 NCAA pole-vault co-champion, Ray Maggard of UCLA. (Courtesy UCLA.)

Oregon's George Rasmussen, NCAA co-champion in the pole vault in 1947 and 1948. (Courtesy University of Oregon.)

One of the nation's most versatile athletes, Jackie Robinson of UCLA. In 1940 Robinson was the NCAA broad-jump champion. He also starred in football, basketball, and baseball. (Courtesy UCLA.)

Dallas Dupre (second from right) of Ohio State, winner of the 1942 NCAA broad jump. Buckeye mile-relay team members Porter, Collins, Hammond, and Owens are also pictured (l to r). (Courtesy Ohio State University Photo Archives.)

John Robertson of the Texas Longhorns, 1946 NCAA broad-jump winner. (Courtesy University of Texas.)

National champion broad jumper, Fred Johnson of Michigan State. The Spartan star leaped 25 feet 4½ inches to capture first place in the 1948 NAAU meet. That distance was two inches more than his winning jump in the 1949 NCAA championships. (Courtesy Michigan State University.)

Don Canham of Michigan, 1940 NCAA high-jump co-champion. Canham later became track coach and athletic director for the Wolverines. (Courtesy University of Michigan.)

High Jump

Year	Name	School	Mark
1940	John Wilson	Southern California	
	Don Canham	Michigan	6– 6⅜
1941	Les Steers	Oregon	6–10⅞
1942	Adam Berry	Southern	6– 7¾
1943	Fred Sheffield	Utah	6– 8
1944	Ken Wiesner	Marquette	6–7³⁄₁₆
1945	Fred Sheffield	Utah	
	Ken Wiesner	Marquette	6– 6⅝
1946	Ken Wiesner	Marquette	6– 8⅜
1947	Irv Mondschein	NYU	6–6¹³⁄₁₆
1948	Irv Mondschein	NYU	
	Dike Eddleman	Illinois	6– 7
1949	Dick Phillips	Brown	6– 7

Javelin Throw

Year	Name	School	Mark
1940	Martin Biles	California	204–10
1941	Martin Biles	California	220– 1
1942	Robert Biles	California	213– 9¾
1943	George Gast	Iowa State	202– 1½
1944	Bob Ray	Wisconsin	174– ⅝
1945	Robert Patton	Navy	191– 1
1946	Robert Likins	San Jose	198–10½
1947	Robert Likins	San Jose	209– 1
1948	Bud Held	Stanford	209– 8
1949	Bud Held	Stanford	224– 8¼
1950	Bud Held	Stanford	216– 8⅝

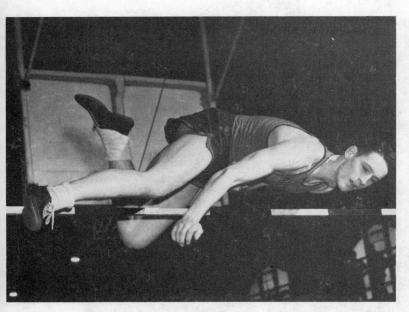

Three-time NCAA high-jump champion, Ken Wiesner of Marquette. (Courtesy Marquette University.)

NCAA winner in the javelin in 1948, 1949, and 1950, Franklin "Bud" Held of Stanford. Held was the first thrower in the world to reach 260 feet and eight meters. He won the 1955 Pan American Games event and five NAAU titles. He is perhaps best known for his development of an improved javelin. (Courtesy Stanford University.)

Dick Phillips of Brown, national champion high jumper. Phillips leaped six feet seven inches to win the NCAA meet in 1949, and captured the NAAU Indoor high-jump crown that year with the same height. (Courtesy Brown University.)

1945 NCAA shot-put champion, Ed Quirk of Missouri. Quirk was one of three national-class weightmen for the Tigers during the war years. He also starred for the Tigers in football at fullback in 1944 and 1947. (Courtesy University of Missouri.)

Bill Bangert of Missouri, 1944 and 1945 NCAA discus-throw champion. (Courtesy University of Missouri.)

Hammer Throw

1948	Sam Felton	Harvard	170– 9¼

Discus Throw

1940	Archie Harris	Indiana	162– 4½
1941	Archie Harris	Indiana	174– 8¾
1942	Bob Fitch	Minnesota	164– 8¼
1943	Howard Debus	Nebraska	144– 4¾
1944	Bill Bangert	Missouri	149– 5
1945	Bill Bangert	Missouri	151– 9⅛
1946	Fortune Gordien	Minnesota	153–10¾
1947	Fortune Gordien	Minnesota	173– 3
1948	Fortune Gordien	Minnesota	164– 6½
1949	Vic Frank	Yale	168– 9½
1952	Sim Iness	Southern California	173–2⅜
1953	Sim Iness	Southern California	190– ⅞

Shot Put

1940	Al Blozis	Georgetown	56– ½		1945	Ed Quirk	Missouri	53– 1⅛
1941	Al Blozis	Georgetown	54–10½		1946	Bernard Mayer	NYU	52–10½
1942	Al Blozis	Georgetown	54– 9⅝		1947	Charles Fonville	Michigan	54–10⅞
1943	Elmer Aussieker	Missouri	52– 3¾		1948	Charles Fonville	Michigan	54– 7
1944	Norm Wasser	NYU	49– 1		1949	Jim Fuchs	Yale	56– 1½
					1950	Jim Fuchs	Yale	56–11³⁄₁₆

NCAA TEAM CHAMPIONS OF THE 1940s

Year	Site	Champion	Coach of Team Champion
1940	Minnesota	Southern California	Dean Cromwell
1941	Stanford	Southern California	Dean Cromwell
1942	Nebraska	Southern California	Dean Cromwell
1943	Northwestern	Southern California	Dean Cromwell*
1944	Marquette	Illinois	Leo Johnson
1945	Marquette	Navy	E. J. Thomson
1946	Minnesota	Illinois	Leo Johnson
1947	Utah	Illinois	Leo Johnson
1948	Minnesota	Minnesota	Jim Kelly
1949	Southern California	Southern California	Jess Hill**

* His USC teams also won in 1926, 1930–31, 1935–39.
** His USC team also won in 1950.

Navy's 1945 NCAA champion track team. The Middies won individual titles in the 100 yard dash (John Van Velzer), 440 yard dash (William Kash), and javelin (Robert Patton). E. J. Thomson, a 1920 Olympic hurdling champion for Canada, was the Midshipmen's coach. (Courtesy of the Naval Academy Athletic Association.)

NCAA CROSS COUNTRY CHAMPIONS OF THE 1940s

Year	Site	Individual Winner	School	Time
1940	Michigan State	Gil Dodds	Ashland	20:30.2
1941	Michigan State	Fred Wilt	Indiana	20:32.1
1942	Michigan State	Oliver Hunter	Notre Dame	20:32.3
1943	No meet held			
1944	Michigan State	Fred Feiler	Drake	21:04.2
1945	Michigan State	Fred Feiler	Drake	21:14.2
1946	Michigan State	Quentin Brelsford	Ohio Wesleyan	20:22.9
1947	Michigan State	Jack Milne	North Carolina	20:41.1
1948	Michigan State	Bob Black	Rhode Island	19:52.3
1949	Michigan State	Bob Black	Rhode Island	20:25.7

	Team Champion	Points	Coach of Team Champion
1940	Indiana	65	Earle "Billy" Hayes
1941	Rhode Island	83	Fred Tootell
1942	Indiana, Penn State	57	Earle "Billy" Hayes and C. D. Werner
1943	No Meet		
1944	Drake	25	Bill Easton
1945	Drake	50	Bill Easton
1946	Drake	42	Bill Easton
1947	Penn State	60	C. D. Werner
1948	Michigan State	41	Karl Schlademan
1949	Michigan State	59	Karl Schlademan

4

FOOTBALL

FOOTBALL

Perhaps I'm over-featured
In the headline's stirring plea
Perhaps I'm more important
Than a mere game ought to be;
But with all the sins they speak of,
And the list is quite a span,
I'm the soul of college spirit,
And the maker of a man.

from "Football's Answer" by Grantland Rice

During the 1940s, this verse, from the pen of the acknowledged dean of American sportswriters, did not seem hypocritical or unrealistic to two Midwestern boys who were imbued from childhood with the lore of the Great Game of Football. Although they had never seen Jim Thorpe, Red Grange, the Four Horsemen, the Seven Blocks of Granite, or Nile Kinnick and the Iron Men play, "Jimmy" Young of Iowa and "Bud" McClure of Kansas certainly knew about the exploits of those past heroes. But the football greats of the 1940s were sufficient to occupy their impressionable young minds.

There were men like Suffridge of Tennessee; Sinkwich and Trippi of Georgia; Davis and Blanchard of Army; Whitmire and Dick Scott of Navy; Clyde Scott of Navy and Arkansas; Agase of Purdue and Illinois; Evans of Kansas; Wedemeyer of St. Mary's; Fenimore of Oklahoma A.&M.; Bertelli, Lujack, Connor, Hart, and Sitko of Notre Dame; Harmon, Chappuis, the Wisterts, and the Elliotts of Michigan; Nomellini and Tonnemaker of Minnesota; Walker and Rote of SMU; Albert of Stanford; Layne of Texas; and Justice of North Carolina in the college ranks. There were also Baugh

of the Redskins; Hutson of the Packers; Turner, Fortmann, Kavanaugh, Stydahar, McAfee, and Luckman of the Bears, Dudley of the Steelers and Lions; Pihos and Van Buren of the Eagles; Waterfield of the Rams; Graham, Groza, Speedie, Lavelli, Motley, and Jones of the Browns; and Harder of the Cardinals in the pro ranks, among others.

Iowa and Kansas Universities have had a few years of national football prominence and have turned out great players such as Kinnick and Evans. Iowa also produced Duke Slater, Gordon Locke, Calvin Jones, Alex Karras, Randy Duncan, and John Niland; and Kansas, Otto Schnellbacher, Mike McCormack, John Hadl, Gale Sayers, Bobby Douglass, and John Zook. But it is not an exaggeration to say that overall those two institutions have not been the Titans of American Football. Hence, Young and McClure focused not only on the Hawkeye and Jayhawk gridiron heroes, but also on the stars of other pigskin elevens.

For example, during the early 1940s, Young proudly wore a maize and blue jersey with number "98" and the name "Tom Harmon" emblazoned on it. A gift from his parents, that football shirt was worn proudly by the asthmatic Iowan as he played his imaginary games on the Kingsley School playground. The author, under a hot Iowa sun, would fend off imaginary tacklers, even without Michigan back Forrest Evashevski (of whom Young knew nothing as yet) clearing the way.

Young's earliest memories of his role as a spectator date back to his attendance at West High of Waterloo's football encounters with city-rival East High and traditional foes like Mason City, Fort Dodge, and Dubuque. His father, Robert Young, an alumnus of West Waterloo, taught the game of football to him while they watched the West High

Nile Kinnick of Iowa, scoring the winning touchdown against Notre Dame in 1939. Before the snap from center, Kinnick had shifted from left to right halfback. He took a direct pass from center and then bolted forward between his guard and tackle. As the photograph indicates, his blockers opened the hole, but Milt Piepul of the Irish (shown about to meet Kinnick) made contact on the two. Kinnick drove him back into the end zone. (Photo by Bruce Palmer of the *Waterloo Daily Courier*. Courtesy University of Iowa.)

All-American Dick Scott of Navy. Grantland Rice picked Scott on *Colliers'* 1947 All-America Team at the center position. (Courtesy of the Naval Academy Athletic Association.)

Nile Kinnick of Iowa, 1939 winner of the Heisman and Walter Camp trophies and Maxwell Award. The great Hawkeye halfback played in the 1940 College All-Star Game. He was killed in an air crash in World War II. (Courtesy University of Iowa.)

Dante Lavelli of the Cleveland Browns played one season for Coach Paul Brown in 1942 at Ohio State, and then entered the service. After surviving the Battle of the Bulge, Lavelli (and other Ohio State players with more collegiate eligibility, including Lou Groza and Bill Willis) followed Coach Brown to the AAFC Cleveland Browns, much to the chagrin of the Buckeyes. Along with opposite end Mac Speedie, Lavelli was a target for Otto Graham passes. He was All-NFL twice and set the league career record for receptions in championship games. (Courtesy Cleveland Browns.)

games and played together in the back yard—that is, when Jimmy was able to overcome the effects of the ragweed pollen that "laid him low" during the late summer and fall. Occasionally Bob and Edith Young took their children to Iowa City to see the war-depleted Hawkeyes succumb to some powerful opponent such as the Iowa Seahawks, the navy preflight team based in Iowa City that featured great coaches and players from all over the nation. McClure saw his first Kansas game in 1946 when all-American Ray Evans led KU to victory

Star Cleveland Browns back, William "Dub" Jones, played on several of the Browns' title teams and once scored six TDs in a game against the Chicago Bears. His son now stars in the pros as a quarterback. (Courtesy Cleveland Browns.)

over Oklahoma A.&M. with Bob Fenimore.

Most of the details of professional and collegiate football activity of the early 1940s escaped the notice of Young and McClure, however, because of their tender age and inability to read as yet.

1940

The Chicago Tribune's All-Star Game in 1940 was won by the 1939 NFL champion Packers over the College All-Stars, 45 to 28. Nile Kinnick, Iowa's Consensus All-America and winner of the coveted Heisman, Maxwell, and Walter Camp trophies, played for the All-Stars and scored three points-after-touchdowns (PATs). Young was to win a Nile Kinnick scholarship at the University of Iowa from 1954 to 1958. He was required to maintain at least a 3.0 grade average and participate in a sport to retain the grant, based as it was on the high standards of scholarship and athletics adhered to by Kinnick. In 1970 Nile Kinnick was selected as the greatest player ever to perform for the Hawkeyes.

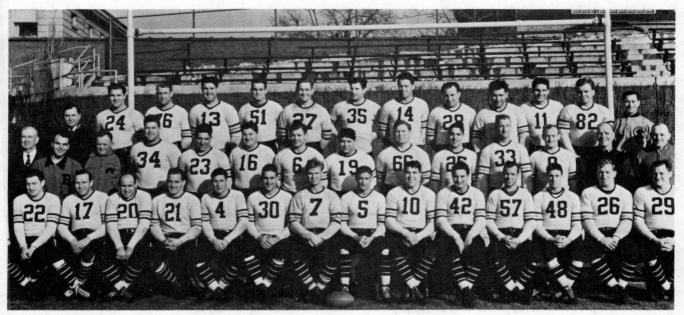

The 1940 Chicago Bears, NFL champions. (Courtesy Chicago Bears Football Club.)

In 1940 the Chicago Bears and Washington Redskins battled to divisional titles in the National Football League (NFL). In the regular season, the Redskins had compiled a 9-2 won-loss record, while the Bears were 8 and 3. Three weeks before the championship game, Washington edged the Chicago team, 7 to 3. The 'Skins, whose Sammy Baugh had had his best season, were thus favorites in the NFL title game.

The 1940 Bears-Redskins championship game turned into one of the most shocking events in sports history. *Time* reported:

> . . . what happened was a walking nightmare to the Washington fans. The Bears began to roll—like the German Army rolling through France. Dazed onlookers waited for the defenders to make a stand—in Belgium, at the Somme, at Dunkirk—but the juggernaut kept rolling, rolling, rolling. They chalked up 21 points in the first quarter, seven in the second. Radio fans, tuning in at half time, thought they were listening to a basketball game. By sixes and sevens, the score jumped: 35, 41, 48, 54.

Bears coach George Halas was introducing revolutionary changes in the T-formation and was using quick openers counter to the flow of play. Sid Luckman, who has been called by at least two experts "one of the first, and surely the best, of the T-formation quarterbacks," directed the Bear attack, calling the plays like a clairvoyant. When it was all over, the Bears had shellacked the Redskins, 73 to 0! Ten different Bears scored eleven

Rhodes Scholar Byron "Whizzer" White of the Detroit Lions. White has been an Associate Justice of the Supreme Court since 1962. (Courtesy Detroit Lions.)

touchdowns (TDs), and the seven conversions were made by six different players. Of the Bears scoring six-pointers, the most famous were fullback Bill Osmanski (who went 68 yards on the second play from scrimmage for the first score), Luckman, end Ken Kavanaugh, halfback George McAfee, and rookie center Clyde "Bulldog" Turner (he also recovered a Frank Filchock fumble setting up another TD). Tackle Joe Stydahar was one of the Bears who added a PAT. All of these Bears were all-pro at least once in their careers, as was left guard Danny Fortmann. All of them except Osmanski were ultimately hall of fame (college and/or pro) selectees.

The 1940 All-Pro Team was as follows:

LE	Don Hutson	Green Bay Packers
LT	Joe Stydahar	Chicago Bears
LG	Danny Fortmann	Chicago Bears
C	Mel Hein	New York Giants
RG	John Wiethe	Detroit Lions
RT	Frank "Bruiser" Kinard	Brooklyn Dodgers
RE	Perry Schwartz	Brooklyn Dodgers
QB	Clarence "Ace" Parker	Brooklyn Dodgers
LHB	Sammy Baugh	Washington Redskins
RHB	Byron "Whizzer" White	Detroit Lions
FB	John Drake	Cleveland Rams

Season statistical leaders included:

Scoring	Don Hutson	Green Bay	57 points
Rushing	Byron White	Detroit	514 yards
Passing	Sam Baugh	Washington	
Pass Receiving	Don Looney	Philadelphia	58 catches
Field Goals	Clark Hinkle	Green Bay	9
Punting	Sam Baugh	Washington	51 yards (league record)

The coaches of the 1940 NFL·teams also read like a hall of fame listing:

Western Division	W	L	T	Pct.
Chicago Bears	8	3	0	.727
Creen Bay Packers	6	4	1	.600
Detroit Lions	5	5	1	.500
Cleveland Rams	4	6	1	.400
Chicago Cardinals	2	7	2	.222

Coach	Year of Hall of Fame Selection
George Halas	1963
Earl "Curly" Lambeau	1963
George "Potsy" Clark	
Earl "Dutch" Clark	1963
Jim Conzelman	1964

Eastern Division	W	L	T	Pct.
Washington Redskins	9	2	0	.818
Brooklyn Dodgers	8	3	0	.727
New York Giants	6	4	1	.600
Pittsburgh Steelers	2	7	2	.222
Philadelphia Eagles	1	10	0	.091

Coach	Year of Hall of Fame Selection
Ray Flaherty	1976
John "Jock" Sutherland	1951 (College Hall)
Steve Owen	1966
Walt Kiesling	1966
Bert Bell	1963

Indeed, all but Potsy Clark had been named to the Pro Football Hall of Fame at Canton, Ohio, or the College Football Hall of Fame at New Brunswick, New Jersey, by 1976.

In 1972 Sid Luckman was quoted as saying: "Those old Monsters of the Midway probably would crown me, but I think the Miami Dolphins conceivably could beat our Chicago Bears of 1940, called the greatest professional team of all time." (The Dolphins later broke the NFL record for consecutive victories.) George Halas, owner of the Bears, always has regarded the 1934 Bears (led by Beattie Feathers and Bronko Nagurski) and the 1940, 1941, and 1942 Bears teams as peerless. Luckman, a plastics firm executive in 1972, remarked that Don Shula, coach of the Dolphins, reminded him of George Halas when Sid was playing. When asked to compare the Dolphins and his Bears, Luckman said:

Well, it's like saying who would win between Jack Dempsey and Joe Louis. . . . It would be a meeting of two super teams, but because of size and speed, I'd have to go for the Dolphins. And that's a brash thing for me to say with Bulldog Turner, Joe Stydahar, George Musso, George McAfee, Ken Kavanaugh, Bill Osmanski among others of those great 1940 Bears still alive and kicking.

He did note that the 1940 Bears had a twenty-eight-man squad and that the regulars played both on offense and defense. "It might be a horse of a different color if the Dolphins had to match us with their best twenty-eight guys and they had to play

The 1939 Tennessee Volunteers went through the regular season with their goal line uncrossed. In the 1940 Rose Bowl, however, they lost to Coach Howard Jones' Southern California Trojans, 14 to 0. Ace Tennessee tailback George Cafego played, but was far below form because of an injured knee. All-time All-American Bob Suffridge and Ed Molinski gave the Vols one of the best guard combinations in history. (Courtesy University of Tennessee.)

Sugar Bowl	New Orleans	Texas A.&M. 14 Tulane 13
Orange Bowl	Miami	Georgia Tech 21 Missouri 7
Cotton Bowl	Dallas	Clemson 6 Boston College 3
Shrine East-West Game	San Francisco	West 28 East 11
Blue-Gray Game	Montgomery, Alabama	North 14 South 2

both offense and defense." Luckman remained impressed, however, by the size and speed of the modern pros:

> But the modern football players have so much going for them, skilled coaching from the kid level, bigger bodies and greater speed. I look and shudder when I see those 270–280 pound men moving with the speed and agility they do today.
> I'll tell you one thing, though, Kavanaugh would be a superstar receiver in any era. So would McAfee as a runner and Turner, Stydahar and Musso as linemen.

He added: "I guess we didn't have the vitamins they build up on these days."

In collegiate football the decade of the 1940s was ushered in by the New Year's Day bowl games. There were not as many of them in those days, and the scores were:

| Tournament of Roses | Pasadena, California | Southern California 14 Tennessee 0 |

Other bowls included the Sun Bowl at El Paso, Texas; the Prairie View A.&M. Bowl at Prairie View, Texas; and the Orange Bowl Classic at Miami.

The national leaders in the 1940 collegiate football season, according to the late Joseph Sheehan of the *New York Times,* John McCallum, and Charles Pearson, were Minnesota, Stanford, Michigan, Tennessee, and Boston College. Minnesota's Golden Gophers, victors in the Big Ten, were regarded as the "national champions." They were coached by Bernie Bierman. The most important game of the year featured undefeated Michigan and Minnesota (five wins apiece). Minnesota, led by halfbacks George Franck and Bruce Smith, edged Michigan, coached by Fritz Crisler and featuring Tom Harmon, by a 7-to-6 score. In 1971, *Sports Illustrated* listed this game as one of the "25 college football games, played over the past 65 years" which "were perhaps the most publicized in the history of the sport, both before and after they were played." The article by Dan Jenkins

This is the backfield on Clemson's 1940 Cotton Bowl team—the school's first in a postseason classic. Clemson defeated Boston College, 6-3. Left to right are: Joe Payne, Bru Trexler, Banks McFadden, and Shad Bryant. McFadden was a football and basketball All-American, and has been considered the greatest all-around track athlete in the history of South Carolina. He was voted the nation's most versatile athlete in 1940. (Courtesy Clemson University.)

The Minnesota Golden Gophers of 1940, national champions. The squad included an unusually large number of All-Americans: tackle Urban Odson, tackle Dick Wildung, halfback George Franck, halfback Bruce Smith, and fullback Bill Daley. Bob Fitch, later a world recordholder and NCAA champion in the discus, also played for this great team. (Courtesy University of Minnesota.)

Stanford's undefeated and untied 1940 football team. Clark Shaughnessy had been the University of Chicago coach from 1933 to 1939 and, with little talent, compiled a 17-37-4 record. After the 1939 season, when Chicago had a 0-8 record, President Robert Hutchins ordered the school to drop football. While in California for a NCAA convention, Shaughnessy was hired by Stanford, who had lost all of its conference games in 1939. With most of that losing squad back, Coach Shaughnessy's 1940 Stanford team rolled over all opponents, including Nebraska in the 1941 Rose Bowl by a 21-13 score. The Indians' backfield of Frankie Albert, Hugh Gallarneau, Pete Kmetovic, and Norm Standlee has been regarded as one of football's best. In one year, Shaughnessy, using his modernized T-formation, had gone from an unemployed football coach and a 1940 Rose Bowl spectator to the summit of football fame. (Courtesy Stanford University.)

noted that "each one stimulated interest and excitement far beyond its region and in most instances a national championship rested on the outcome."

Tom Harmon of Michigan won the Heisman Memorial Trophy, presented to the "outstanding Intercollegiate Football Player of the United States," as determined by a vote of sportswriters and sportscasters. He also won the Walter Camp Memorial Trophy given to the "College Back of the Year," and the Maxwell Award. The Knute Rockne Memorial Trophy, awarded by Washing-

ton D.C.'s Touchdown Club (as is the Walter Camp Trophy) to the "College Lineman of the Year," was won by the late Bob Suffridge of Tennessee who in 1969 was picked to the Modern (1919–1969) All-Time All-American Team. Clark Shaughnessy of Stanford's 1941 Rose Bowl champions was picked Coach of the Year. Along with George Halas of the Chicago Bears (with whom he had formed a close association while coaching at the University of Chicago) and Ralph Jones, former Bears coach, Shaughnessy is credited with revolutionizing the T-formation and popularizing it.

The Consensus All-American Team—its collegiate players receiving more All-America selections from organizations like the AP, UP, INS, NEA, *Colliers,* and *The Sporting News,* etc., than any others at their respective positions—for 1940 was as follows:

E	Gene Goodreault	Boston College
E	Dave Rankin	Purdue
T	Nick Drahos	Cornell
T	Urban Odson	Minnesota
T	Alf Bauman	Northwestern
*G	Bob Suffridge	Tennessee
G	Marshall Robinet	Teaxs A.&M.
C	Rudy Mucha	Washington
*B	Tom Harmon	Michigan
*B	John Kimbrough	Texas A.&M.
B	Frank Albert	Stanford
B	George Franck	Minnesota

* Unanimous selection

107

"Old 98," Tom Harmon of Michigan. A slashing runner, Harmon broke several records held by Red Grange, with whom he was often compared. He won the 1940 Heisman, Maxwell, and Walter Camp awards. (Courtesy National Football Foundation and Hall of Fame.)

1940 Consensus All-American center, Rudy Mucha of the University of Washington. (Courtesy University of Washington.)

PURDUE

Purdue's 1940 Consensus All-American end, Dave Rankin. Rankin once shared the world record in the 60 yard low hurdles. He captained the Boilermakers in 1940, and the College All-Star team in 1941. After his return from service as a war hero, he was installed as Purdue's track coach in 1946, a position he held until 1973. (Courtesy Purdue University.)

Time described Tom Harmon this way:

His speed, and his uncanny sense of anticipation, a formidable straight arm, powerful leg drive that shakes off tacklers like tenpins, a confounding change of pace and rumba hips, make a Harmon touchdown a memorable performance. In addition to his ball-carrying talents, he is a better-than average blocker, passer, punter, place-kicker, quick kicker, and kickoff man.

Illinois had ganged up on Harmon and had upset Michigan in 1939, 16 to 7. Harmon had been termed "better than Grange" by Wolverine coach Herbert "Fritz" Crisler before that game. Prior to the 1940 Michigan-Illinois contest, Harmon had scored sixty-nine points as Michigan mowed down California, Michigan State, and Harvard. Despite the Illini's attempt to "do or die for the ghost of old Red Grange" and to gang up on Harmon, Tom scored once and kicked a field goal as Michigan trounced Illinois, 28 to 0.

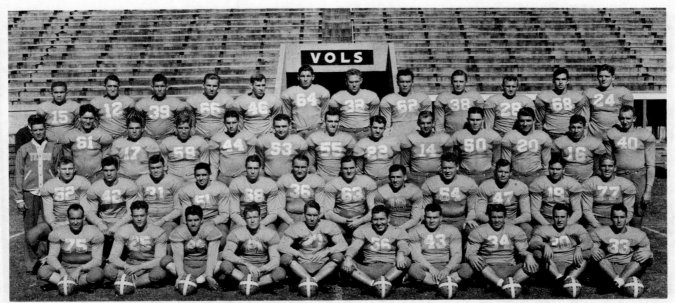

The unbeaten and untied **Tennessee Volunteers** of 1940. In the 1941 Sugar Bowl, however, Boston College downed the Vols, 19 to 13. (Courtesy University of Tennessee.)

In the Wolverines' 1940 finale, he scored twenty-two of his team's forty points while Ohio State was held scoreless. During his twenty-four-game career, Harmon scored thirty-three TDs and kicked thirty-three PATs and two field goals for a total of 237 points, better than Red Grange's and the best scoring record in Big Ten history. Harmon averaged almost six yards a carry in his collegiate career, totaling 2,338 yards on the ground. He completed 101 of 233 passes, sixteen of them for TDs. His scores against the Golden Bears were on runs of 94, 72, 86, and 80 yards. Amos Alonzo Stagg considered Harmon "superior to Grange in everything but running."

Harmon was picked by the Associated Press as Athlete of the Year in 1940. While in California for the East-West Shrine Game in 1941, he met actress Elyse Knox who was to be his future wife. In World War II, he bailed out of wrecked planes twice and made it back to safety after being given up as lost. Harmon's son, Mark, was an outstanding quarterback for UCLA in 1973.

In the 1950s, author Young was a member of the football squad at the University of Iowa, coached at the time by Forrest Evashevski. "Evy" was regarded as Harmon's best blocker.

Results of the 1941 bowl games were:

Rose	Stanford 21 Nebraska 13 (This triumph by Shaughnessy's Indians plus the Chicago Bears' 73–0 NFL title victory precipitated a wholesale adoption of the T-formation by teams in the 1940s.)
Orange	Mississippi State 14 Georgetown 7
Sugar	Boston College 19 Tennessee 13
Cotton	Texas A. & M. 13 Fordham 12
Shrine	West 20 East 14
Blue-Gray	South 16 North 0

1941

The Bears had no trouble with the College All-Stars, 1941 version, crushing them, 37 to 13, in Chicago's Soldier Field before 98,203 spectators. In a year that saw Elmer Layden elected NFL president and Earl "Greasy" Neale take the coaching reins at Philadelphia, the Bears rolled on to a 10-1 won-lost record only to tie for the Western title with Green Bay. In a game between the Eastern Division leaders on 7 December, the New York Giants were tangling with the rival Brooklyn Dodgers at the Polo Grounds. The WOR play-by-play account went like this:

The Dodgers are ready to kick off now. They've just scored. Ace Parker did it. Jock Sutherland's boys lead the Giants, seven to nothing.

Here's the whistle. Merle Condit comes up. He boots it. It's a long one. Down to around the three yard line. Ward Cuff takes it. He's cutting up to his left. He's over the ten. Nice block there by Leemans. Cuff's still going. He's up to the 25. And now he's hit and hit hard about the 27 yard line. Bruiser Kinard made the tack—.

We interrupt this broadcast to bring you this

The 1941 Chicago Bears, NFL champions. Among the many Bears stars pictured are: Danny Fortmann (21), Bill Osmanski (9), George McAfee (5), Sid Luckman (42), Clyde "Bulldog" Turner (66), Ken Kavanaugh (51), and Joe Stydahar (13). Two backs on the 1941 Rose Bowl-winning Stanford team are also shown—Hugh Gallarneau (8) and Norm Standlee (22). (Courtesy Chicago Bears Football Club.)

The 1941 New York Giants, Eastern Division champions. (Courtesy New York Giants.)

important bulletin from the United Press. Flash! Washington: The White House announces Japanese attack on Pearl Harbor. Stay tuned to WOR for further developments which will be broadcast immediately as received.

A week later, the Bears won the Western Division playoff game by trimming the Packers, 33 to 14. Two weeks after Pearl Harbor, the effects of war were already being felt on the sporting scene, when only 13,341 fans showed up to watch the championship game at Chicago between the Bears and the Giants. The Giants made a game of it for a while, as the score was tied early in the third quarter, 9 to 9. But then Norm Standlee bolted over for two Bear touchdowns, George McAfee added a third, and end Ken Kavanaugh fulfilled a lineman's dream when he intercepted a Giant lateral and ran 42 yards for a score. Bob Snyder kicked three field goals for the Bears in the first half, and Tuffy Leemans booted one for New York, whose only TD came in the first quarter on a four-yard pass from Leemans to George Franck (of Davenport, Iowa). The Bears won their fifth NFL championship that day, by a 37 to 9 margin.

Statistical leaders during the regular season included Cecil Isbell of the Packers in passing; his target, Hutson, in scoring (ninety-five points) and pass receiving (fifty-eight catches); Clarence "Pug" Manders of the Dodgers in rushing; and Hinkle and Baugh repeating in field goals and punting. Marshall Goldberg of the Cardinals led in interceptions with seven.

Hutson, Fortmann, and Schwartz again made the All-League Team. Bruiser Kinard of the Dodgers and Wilbur Wilkin of the Redskins were the tackles honored: Joe Kuharich of the Cardinals was the other guard; and second-year Bear, Bulldog Turner held down the center spot. Sid Luckman, Cecil Isbell, George McAfee, and Clark Hinkle made up the dream backfield. The Bears thus dominated the All-NFL Team with four selections.

On the college scene, Bernie Bierman's Minnesota team repeated as national champions. Duke, Notre Dame, Texas, and Michigan were the other powers. Bill Dudley of Virginia won the Maxwell Award and the Walter Camp Trophy, while Bruce Smith of Minnesota copped the coveted Heisman statue. Endicott "Chub" Peabody was College Lineman of the Year (Knute Rockne Memorial Trophy winner). The 1941 Consensus All-American Team was as follows:

E	Holt Rast	Alabama
E	Bob Dove	Notre Dame
T	Ernie Blandin	Tulane
T	Dick Wildung	Minnesota
G	Ray Frankowski	Washington
G	Endicott Peabody	Harvard
C	Darold Jenkins	Missouri
B	Frank Sinkwich	Georgia
B	Bill Dudley	Virginia
B	Bob Westfall	Michigan
B	Bruce Smith	Minnesota
B	Frank Albert	Stanford

In addition to the poor attendance at the NFL title game, an unusual event in the aftermath of the Pearl Harbor attack was the scheduling of the Rose Bowl at Durham, North Carolina, at which Duke, the hometown team, was defeated by its rude guest Oregon State, 20 to 16. Fordham edged Missouri in the Sugar Bowl, 2 to 0; Georgia outlasted Texas Christian in the Orange Bowl, 40 to 26; and Alabama defeated Texas A. & M., 29 to 21, in the Cotton Bowl. The South shut out the North, scoring 24 points in the Blue-Gray contest, while on 3 January, the East and West played to a 6-6 tie in the Shrine Game.

With the United States now officially involved in the war, the pro and college football squads began to be depleted by the manpower needs of the military. The NFL eventually sent 638 men into the service. Young Bussey, substitute Bear quarterback, was to be killed in action, and end John Lummus of the Giants would lose his life on Iwo Jima. Iowa's All-American and Iron Man, Nile Kinnick, winner of the 1939 Heisman, Walter Camp, and Maxwell trophies, died when his naval plane crashed at sea. Al Blozis, Georgetown football All-American and national shot put champion, also lost his life in World War II.

Professional football possessed an advantage over pro baseball in that the former's games were played only on week ends. Thus players could hold down jobs in a defense plant (and thereby gain a deferment) on week days, practice after working hours, and play pro games on the week end. Servicemen like the great Sid Luckman even played while on weekend passes.

There were problems, however. The Cleveland Rams' owner and coach went into the service. The Rams thus sought and received permission to suspend operations during the 1943 season. Also in that year, the Philadelphia Eagles and Pittsburgh Steelers, suffering from similar problems, combined forces to play as the Phil-Pitt Eagles (or

Minnesota's 1941 national champions. In addition to Bruce Smith (captain, number 54) and Urban Odson (74), the Golden Gophers squad included Herb Hein (third row, extreme left), who was a 1943 Grantland Rice All-American selection. But in 1943 Hein was playing for *Northwestern* (which also had All-American Otto Graham at quarterback). And the 1943 unanimous All-American fullback was Bill Daley (45), who was then playing for *Michigan!* Tackle Dick Wildung (second row, extreme right) was Consensus All-America in 1940 and 1941. (Courtesy University of Minnesota.)

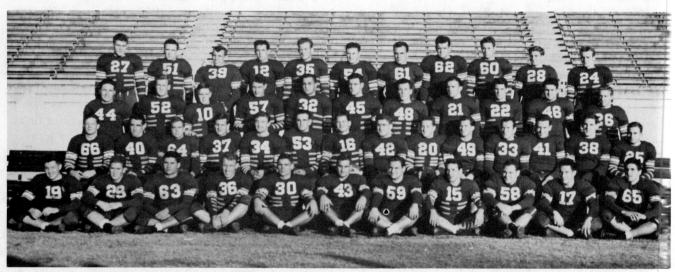

1941 Duke football team, Southern Conference champions. Duke lost to Oregon State, 20 to 16, in the Rose Bowl game, which was played at Durham because of wartime restrictions on the West Coast. (Courtesy Duke University.)

112

The incomparable Don Hutson, All-NFL end nine times. A Consensus All-American at Alabama (1934), where he combined with Dixie Howell as a potent passing combination, Hutson was with the Green Bay Packers from 1935–45. His honors include membership in the National Football Foundation Hall of Fame, the Citizens Savings Hall of Fame, and the Pro Football Hall of Fame and placement on the Modern All-Time All-American Team and the All-Century Team. (Courtesy Green Bay Packers.)

Danny Fortmann, rugged Chicago Bears left guard, was All-NFL six times in a row from 1938 to 1943. (Courtesy Chicago Bears.)

1941 Heisman Trophy winner, Bruce Smith of Minnesota. Smith was captain of the East team in the Shrine Game and MVP of the College All-Stars in their game against the Chicago Bears. (Courtesy University of Minnesota.)

"Bullet Bill" Dudley of Virginia achieved a unique status by receiving MVP football honors as a collegian, in the armed services, and in the NFL. Despite his small size, Dudley was All-American in 1941, and All-Pro in 1946, for the Steelers. In 1975, Art Rooney, the only owner that the Steelers have had, called Dudley "the best all-around player I've ever seen." (Courtesy University of Virginia.)

Ernie Blandin of Tulane, 1941 Consensus All-American tackle. (Courtesy Tulane University.)

Stanford's Frankie Albert, Consensus All-American in 1940 and 1941. Albert passed the undefeated Indians to victory in the 1941 Rose Bowl, and, as quarterback for the San Francisco 49ers, he was second (to Otto Graham) in all-time All-American Conference passing statistics. (Courtesy Stanford University.)

Missouri's 1941 Consensus All-American center, Darold Jenkins. Jenkins captained the Tigers during what may have been their most impressive season. Fordham edged Missouri, 2-0, on a slippery field at the 1942 Sugar Bowl. Later, "Jack Hammer" Jenkins, a B-17 pilot during World War II, was shot down over Germany. In a POW camp, he often took walks with a Fordham end from Missouri's Sugar Bowl opponents, and the two "replayed" the game many times in their conversations. (Courtesy University of Missouri.)

Ray Frankowski of Washington, 1941 Consensus All-American guard. (Courtesy University of Washington.)

114

Steagles). The following year the Steelers paired up with the Chicago Cardinals. As in baseball, 4-Fs and older players helped complete pro rosters (sixteen-year-olds were playing for some college teams). A prime example of the older players making a comeback was Bronko Nagurski, who came out of a six-year retirement to help the Bears win the 1943 NFL championship. By 1943 all of the NFL teams had lost most of their star players to the war effort, but a few famous players like Baugh, Hutson, and Luckman remained with their teams (at least on Sundays). Their teams, incidentally, each won an NFL title during the war years. Attendance remained good although not as high as prewar totals.

At the amateur level, the war had three main effects: (1) With no college deferments available, the campus populations were decimated, forcing many schools to drop the sport and others to field weak teams or play informal schedules; (2) Navy service teams, in the form of preflight training or V-5 and V-12 programs located in campus communities, playing college schedules with former college and pro stars, and guided by top coaches, became football powers; and (3) West Point became a football super-power, considered by most sports writers as "not only the best college eleven, but also superior to any other service or professional teams then in action." The Naval Academy also fielded very strong teams.

Many colleges saw the fate of their football teams depend on whether Army or Navy training programs were located on their campuses. In the 1943 and 1944 seasons, the Navy allowed its V-5 and V-12 cadets to play college football, but the Army barred its trainees on campuses from intercollegiate competition (on the theory they would not be diverted from their studies). Lingeman noted the consequences of these different policies:

> As a result, schools with Navy training units were able to mount strong teams, while those with Army training programs gave up the sport [in 1943]. Among the latter were Alabama, Tennessee, Florida, Mississippi State, Fordham, Syracuse, Stanford, Oregon, and Washington State. Most of these schools managed to return to action in 1944 with teams composed of 4-f's and freshmen, the latter having been made eligible under a special dispensation.

Sometimes players were switched from one college to another by military orders. For example, Minnesota fullback Bill Daley became a V-12 trainee at the University of Michigan in 1943. He helped the Wolverines smash his former Gopher teammates, 49 to 6, Michigan's first win over Min-

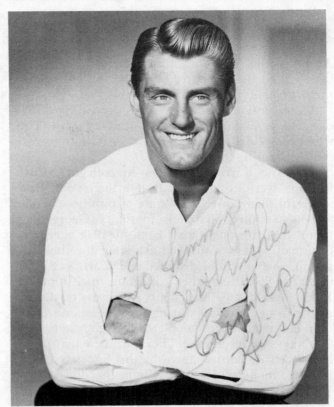

Elroy "Crazy Legs" Hirsch, the only athlete in modern Michigan history to win four letters in a single academic year. Originally enrolled at Wisconsin, Hirsch enlisted in the Marines, and in 1943 was one of eleven Badgers on "lend-lease" to Michigan. There he was trained in the Navy V-12 program, and he participated in football, basketball, baseball, and track. He ran sixty-one yards for a TD on the first play of the game against Minnesota, and scored twice more in Michigan's 49-6 victory, its first over the Golden Gophers in eleven years. After service in World War II, Hirsch was the MVP for the winning collegians in the 1946 College All-Star Game (they defeated the Rams, 16 to 0). He played for the Chicago Rockets in the AAFC until fracturing his skull in 1948. He went on to star for the Rams from 1949–57, when he broke and tied Don Hutson's records. As a youngster, co-author Young heard Hirsch speak at a YMCA banquet, after which the gracious football star wrote an appropriate message on the youngster's scrapbook color photo (clipped from *Sport*) of "Crazy Legs."

nesota since 1932. Daley was a unanimous 1943 All-American, even though he left for the service after the next (sixth) game, a 42-6 rout of Illinois. Another member of that team was Elroy "Crazy Legs" Hirsch, on "lend-lease" to Michigan from the University of Wisconsin. He became the only Wolverine in modern athletic history to win four letters in a single academic year. Thus, V-12 trainees at Michigan played *for* the University's team.

At Iowa, the preflight trainees fielded a separate team called the "Seahawks," which played *against* the University eleven.

A variation of the above pattern was the transfer of a college player to a service academy team. This was exemplified by Doc Blanchard's move from North Carolina to West Point.

Dramatic wartime changes in college football fortunes were exemplified by Fordham's fall from an established power to a "state of puniness." Some schools adopted six-man football. Georgetown found that not one player from its 1942 varsity or freshman squads would be available for the 1943 season, so the school dropped the sport, as did almost two hundred other collegiate institutions in 1943. Penn State lost twenty-four varsity players to the armed services during a single season.

In contrast with the depleted college rosters were the Navy service teams. The Top Ten list of college football teams, as rated by the Associated Press in 1943, included Iowa Pre-Flight (second), Navy (fourth), Great Lakes Naval Training Center (sixth), Del Monte Pre-Flight (eighth), and March Field (tenth). In 1944 the Top Ten included Army (1), Randolph Field (2), Navy (4), Bainbridge Naval Training Center (5), Iowa Pre-Flight (6), and the Fourth Air Force (10).

Bernie Bierman, director of athletics at Iowa Pre-Flight, had other football coaching greats Don Faurot, Bud Wilkinson (who had played for Bierman at Minnesota), and Jim Tatum to assist him. Bierman required every cadet to participate in football. Another wartime power, the Great Lakes Navy Training Center, was coached by Paul Brown. Service team coaches also included such notables as Jim Crowley, Wallace Wade, and Dick Hanley. Einstein concluded that "except for West Point, the thrust of all wartime football, both collegiate and service, was Navy . . ."

Even though the Navy service teams were powerhouses, they were plagued by turnovers in their ranks and were still a cut or two below the two service academies at West Point and Annapolis. Army and Navy could attract the most promising young players and retain them long enough to develop incomparable football elevens.

Army coach Colonel Earl "Red" Blaik was able to field two units and obtain revenge from schools that had regularly beaten the Academy in prewar times. Blaik's highly successful use of the T-formation made it even more popular among colleges during the war.

Notre Dame had not been defeated by Army since 1931, and had not allowed the Black Knights even to score a point against them since 1938. But in 1944 Army obtained retribution, smashing the Irish to the tune of an unbelievable 59-to-0 score! Penn, who had defeated West Point four consecutive times, went under, 62 to 7. The Army juggernaut, with its linemen blocking like scythes, rolled over Pitt, 69 to 7, and destroyed Villanova, 83 to 0. The only teams that could stay reasonably close to the cadets were Navy, who lost 23 to 7, and Duke (which had a Navy program), defeated by a 27-to-7 score. Army was led by its superb running combination of Felix "Doc" Blanchard ("Mr. In-

Don Faurot of Missouri, originator of the split-T formation. The handsome Missourian believed in recruiting mainly within his own state (all forty-eight of his players on the 1948 Gator Bowl team were from Missouri). With his unique formation, Faurot was known for making the most of his players' talents. Faurot also coached at Northeast Missouri State, as well as at Iowa Pre-Flight and Jacksonville during World War II. All-Americans Paul Christman, Bob Steuber, and Darold Jenkins were his best-known stars. The stadium at the University of Missouri is named for him. (Courtesy University of Missouri.)

side") and Glenn "Junior" Davis ("Mr. Outside").

Blanchard was a bruising, 205-pound fullback with speed and tremendous drive, and Davis was a skittering, breakaway runner capable of sudden accelerations that left would-be tacklers stumbling in his wake.

Along with this famed duo, Army in the 1943–46 era had All-Americans Doug Kenna and Arnold Tucker at quarterback, Barney Poole at end, Tex Coulter at tackle, and Cas Myslinski at center. Other fine players included Dale Hall and Max Miner. (Navy had All-Americans Don Whitmire at tackle, Bob Jenkins at halfback, and Richard Duden at end in the 1944–45 period.) Many football experts, including their coach Red Blaik and Michigan's Fritz Crisler, rated the 1946 Army backfield of Blanchard, Davis, Tucker, and Tom "Shorty" Mc-Williams as the "Greatest Backfield of All Time." Even the 1939 Chicago Bears backfield of Osmanski, Luckman, McAfee, and Ray Nolting was not rated as high by these observers. Army won all eighteen of its games during the 1944–45 period by lopsided margins and was national champion both years.

The relationship between football and the attributes of a successful member of the armed services was alluded to by General Douglas MacArthur in his high evaluation of Red Blaik:

"Just as football will remain a leading competitive sport in college athletics, so will Earl Blaik be remembered as an outstanding architect on the gridiron. . . . For apart from his innate grasp of successful strategic and tactical concepts, he possesses those essential attributes of leadership which mold men into a cohesive fighting team and inspire in them an invincible will to victory."

Charles Einstein similarly quotes a former Navy coach and director of athletics:

"Football! Navy! War!" wrote Coach Tom Hamilton. "At no time in history have these words been more entwined and intermeshed than they are now." From a former director of athletics at Annapolis, Admiral Jonas H. Ingram, came the observation that "the closest thing to war in time of peace is football!"

Einstein adds that Coach Lou Little of Columbia doubted football's relevance to the sinews of war, but notes that this was decidedly a minority view. More typical, he thought, was Field Marshal Montgomery's compliment that America had the "foresight to punt and bide time for a scoring opportunity."

The Bears extended the pros' winning streak in the Chicago Tribune's annual College All-Star Game by shutting out the collegians, 21 to 0, as the sportsman's attention began to turn to football in 1942. The remnants of the great Bears team were coached by Hunk Anderson, Luke Johnson, and Paddy Driscoll after George Halas was called into Navy duty at midseason. These men led the Bears to their best regular season record in history, as they were undefeated in eleven games. In the Eastern Division the Washington Redskins also put together their club's best seasonal won-lost record,

Regarded by many as the Dean of American football coaches, Coach Lou Little of Columbia University. Little's teams included All-Americans Sid Luckman, Paul Governali, and Bill Swiacki, and the "Goal Dust Twins," Lou Kusserow and Gene Rossides. Although he lost more than he won at Columbia from 1930–56 (his *overall* coaching record was slightly over .500), Little's ability to utilize available material and his sportsmanship and teaching ability earned him places in the Citizens Savings Hall of Fame and the National Football Foundation Hall of Fame, and the affection of his players. (Manny Warman, Columbia University.)

attaining a 10-1 mark. The NFL championship game in Washington on 13 December was played before 36,000 fans. The Redskins, led by Sammy Baugh in his halfback position and using the familiar single-wing formation, were motivated by thoughts of revenge for their 73-0 humiliation in 1940. The other top passer of the era, Sid Luckman, again was on hand to lead the Bears in their T formation.

In the second quarter Bear tackle Lee Artoe scooped up a fumbled pass from center and dashed fifty yards for a score, but the PAT attempt was unsuccessful. A Baugh-to-Wilbur Moore aerial connected for a 25-yard Redskin touchdown, and Bob Masterson's extra-point kick was good. The only other TD came in the third period when the Redskins drove eighty yards, Andy Farkas carrying on ten of the twelve plays in the series and bowling over from the one for the TD. Masterson's successful PAT made it Redskins 14 Bears 6, and the game ended with that score on the board.

The Packer passing combination of Isbell and Hutson repeated as NFL leaders in the passing, and scoring and receiving categories, respectively. Isbell became the first man in NFL history to reach the two thousand yard mark in passing yardage, and Hutson set a scoring record of 138 points that was not to be broken until 1960. Hutson also had seventy-four receptions for a record seventeen TDs. Sammy Baugh was the other statistical leader who repeated, with his 46.6 yard punting average. The Steelers' Bill Dudley, the league's first draft choice, justified Pittsburgh's faith in him by winning the rushing title in his rookie year. Bill Daddio's five field goals for the Cardinals led the league (compare that mark with more recent years!), and Bulldog Turner was tops in interceptions with eight.

On the All-League Team, Hutson landed an end spot for the fifth consecutive year and the sixth time in seven years. Fortmann also made it for the fifth straight year at left guard. Turner was selected for the second consecutive time at center; Mel Hein of the Giants had won the spot the previous eight years. Wilkin of the Redskins at tackle and Luckman and Isbell were chosen for the second consecutive year. Bill Edwards of the Giants at right guard, Lee Artoe of the Bears at right tackle, Bob Masterson of the Redskins at right end, and Gary Famiglietti of the Bears at fullback rounded out the team. "Official" league selection of the All-NFL Team was discontinued after 1942, and the wire services were to make their own choices in subsequent years.

In the college ranks the mythical national championship was won by Ohio State. Duke, Notre Dame, Texas, and Michigan were also regarded as powers.

On 31 October, 1942, unbeaten Georgia (6-0) was pitted against undefeated Alabama (5-0) at Atlanta. The Bulldogs were coached by Wally Butts and were led by All-American Frank Sink-

Member of the Modern (1919–69) All-Time Football Team, "Slingin'" Sammy Baugh. Consensus All-American for Texas Christian in 1936, Baugh went on to become the NFL's career recordholder in passes, completions, TD passes, and passing-completion percentage. He led the Washington Redskins to five Eastern Division titles and two NFL championships. (Courtesy Pro Football Hall of Fame)

The 1942 Chicago Bears, Western Division champions. (Courtesy Chicago Bears Football Club.)

wich at halfback. The Frank Thomas-coached Crimson Tide featured All-American Joe Domnanovich at center. In a contest that was rated by *Sports Illustrated* in 1971 as one of the top twenty-five college football games in sixty-five years, Georgia defeated Alabama, 21 to 10.

Sinkwich went on to win the Heisman and Walter Camp Memorial Trophies, while Paul Governali of Columbia received the Maxwell Award. Bob Dove of Notre Dame was the recipient of the Knute Rockne Memorial Trophy. The 1942 Consensus All-American Team was as follows:

*E	Dave Schreiner	Wisconsin
E	Bob Dove	Notre Dame
T	Albert Wistert	Michigan
T	Dick Wildung	Minnesota
G	Julius Franks	Michigan
G	Harvey Hardy	Georgia
G	Chuck Taylor	Stanford
C	Joe Domnanovich	Alabama
B	Mike Holovak	Boston College
B	Paul Governali	Columbia
B	Frank Sinkwich	Georgia
B	Billy Hillenbrand	Indiana
* Unanimous selection		

1943 bowl game scores included:

Rose	Georgia 9 UCLA 0
Sugar	Tennessee 14 Tulsa 7

Frankie Sinkwich of the Detroit Lions, Most Valuable Player of the NFL in 1944. He was also a two-time All-American and the 1942 Heisman Trophy winner for Georgia. (Courtesy Detroit Lions.)

119

Orange	Alabama 37 Boston College 21
Cotton	Texas 14 Georgia Tech 7
Shrine	East 13 West 12
Blue-Gray	Boys High 13 Meridian 0 (A high school game was substituted as a wartime measure.)

Columbia's star back Paul Governali was a Consensus All-American and Maxwell Award winner in 1942. (Columbia University Photo.)

1943

The 1943 season began with the traditional College All-Star Game, and the collegians proceeded to snap their four-game losing streak by routing the Redskins, 27 to 7. The Redskins acquired the "distinction" of losing both their appearances in the ten-year history of the classic; they had been beaten by the All-Stars, 28 to 16 in 1938.

With the Phil-Pitt entry in the Eastern Division and the loss of the Rams for a season, the number of NFL teams in 1943 was down from the usual ten to eight. The defending champion Redskins were led by Sammy Baugh to a tie for the divisional title with the Giants and then a playoff victory (28 to 0) over them. The Luckman-led Bears repeated in the West, setting up another championship clash between the Redskins and Bears. Luckman threw seven touchdown passes against the Giants in a regular season game. Roger Treat summed up title game action this way:

> The Bears, beaten previously by the Redskins during a season game, had lured the aged [35 years] Bronko Nagurski out of retirement, but it was Luckman's passing that saved the title for the Bears. Baugh received a concussion late in the game which put the Redskins out of contention.

Luckman threw five passes for touchdowns, two of them to Harry Clark, two to Dante Magnani, and one to Jim Benton. Nagurski plunged for the other Bear TD. The Redskins' scores came on a

Billy Hillenbrand of Indiana, Consensus All-American back in 1942. Hillenbrand led the nation in punt returns and had sixty-eight pass catches in two years of college competition. (Courtesy Indiana University.)

120

Star quarterback for the mighty Chicago Bears teams of the 1940s, Sid Luckman. A 1938 All-American at Columbia, Luckman led the Bears to four NFL championships. He was All-Pro five times in the 1940s. (Columbia University Photo.)

line buck by Andy Farkas and passes from Baugh to Farkas (who ran nine yards after the catch) and to Joe Aguirre. Baugh suffered his injury in the fourth quarter after the latter pass. The Bears were victorious, 41 to 21. It was their sixth title.

Don Hutson added the field goal leadership (he had three and was tied with Ward Cuff of New York) to his traditional winning of the scoring (117 points this time) and pass receiving (47 catches) "titles." Bill Paschal of the Giants led the league in rushing with 572 yards. "Slinging" Sammy Baugh led in passing and punting again and also in interceptions (eleven).

Hutson and Fortmann made the All-NFL Team for the sixth consecutive year. Turner made it three in a row, and Luckman, three. Bruiser Kinard added the 1943 Associated Press (AP) honor as a tackle to all-league awards achieved in 1940 and 1941, while Baugh nailed down a halfback position as he had done in 1937 and 1940. Al Blozis of the Giants, a three-time national shotput champion

from Georgetown, was picked at right tackle. He died in combat on the Western Front in 1945. Others selected were Vic Sears of Phil-Pitt (United Press—UP—pick) at left tackle, Dick Farman of the Redskins at left guard, Ed Rucinski of the Cardinals at right end, Harry Clark of the Bears at right half, Tony Canadeo (AP) of the Packers at fullback, and Ward Cuff of the Giants at fullback.

Bronko Nagurski told a *New York Times* reporter in 1972 that his greatest thrill was returning after his six years' retirement to lead the Bears to their 41-21 championship victory over the Redskins in 1943. The *Times* account of his reaction to today's football was as follows:

"I sometimes think there's less enjoyment in the game now," he mused, "the quarterback always handles the ball. The games all seem so much alike. Only the faces and numbers change. And, of course, the platoons. We had 18 men on a team and you played 60 minutes, sometimes twice a week."

The Irish of Notre Dame were recognized as the national champions of collegiate football. Iowa Pre-Flight, Michigan, Navy, Purdue, and Duke were leading contenders for the honor.

Angelo Bertelli of Notre Dame won the Heisman and Walter Camp trophies. One of author Young's oldest memories of football concerns a radio broadcast of one of Notre Dame's victories and Bertelli's role in that triumph. Robert Odell of Penn received the Maxwell Award, and Casimir Myslinski of Army, the Knute Rockne Memorial Trophy. Members of the 1943 Consensus All-American Team were:

E	John Yonakor	Notre Dame
E	Ralph Heywood	Southern California
T	Don Whitmire	Navy
T	Jim White	Notre Dame
G	Alex Agase	Purdue
G	Pat Filley	Notre Dame
*C	Casimir Myslinski	Army
*B	Bill Daley	Michigan
B	Angelo Bertelli	Notre Dame
B	Creighton Miller	Notre Dame
B	Bob Odell	Pennsylvania

* Unanimous

Results of the major 1944 bowl games were:

Rose	Southern California 29 Washington 0
Sugar	Georgia Tech 20 Tulsa 18
Orange	LSU 19 Texas A. & M. 14
Cotton	Texas 7 Randolph Field 7
Shrine	East 13 West 13
Blue-Gray	South 24 North 7

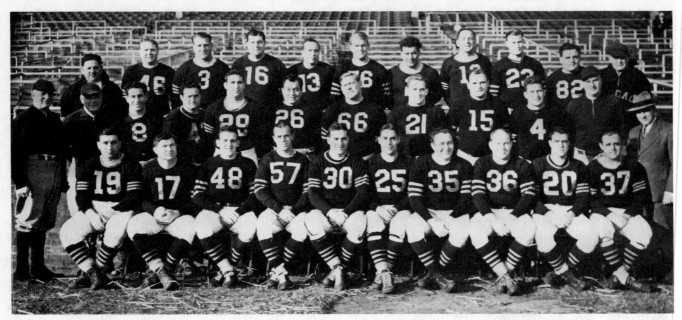

The 1943 Chicago Bears, NFL champions. (Courtesy Chicago Bears Football Club.)

Tony Canadeo, All-Pro back for Green Bay in 1943 and 1949. A fine runner, receiver, and punter, Canadeo was one of the leaders of the NFL champion Green Bay Packers in 1944. A member of the All-Pro Squad of the 1940s, picked by the Pro Football Hall of Fame, he was inducted into the latter shrine in 1974. (Courtesy Pro Football Hall of Fame.)

1944 Knute Rockne Memorial Trophy winner, Don Whitmire of Navy. The College Lineman of the Year was a Consensus All-American tackle in 1943 and 1944 (he was a unanimous selection in the latter year). Whitmire played for Alabama in 1941 and 1942. A solid blocker and tackler, he was named to the all-time Cotton Bowl team and the all-time Orange Bowl team. He attained the highest rank available at Annapolis, and later became a submarine officer. (Courtesy Naval Academy Athletic Association.)

122

1943 Consensus All-American, Bill Daley of Michigan. Daley also starred for Minnesota. (Courtesy University of Minnesota.)

Rugged guard Alex Agase won Consensus All-American honors at both Purdue (1943) and Illinois (1946). The Big Ten's MVP in 1946, and a star of the Illini's victory over UCLA in the 1947 Rose Bowl, Agase played for several pro clubs. (Courtesy Purdue University.)

Southern Cal's Gray hauls in a pass that leads to a score for the Trojans in their 29-0 Rose Bowl victory over Washington in 1944. (Courtesy University of Washington.)

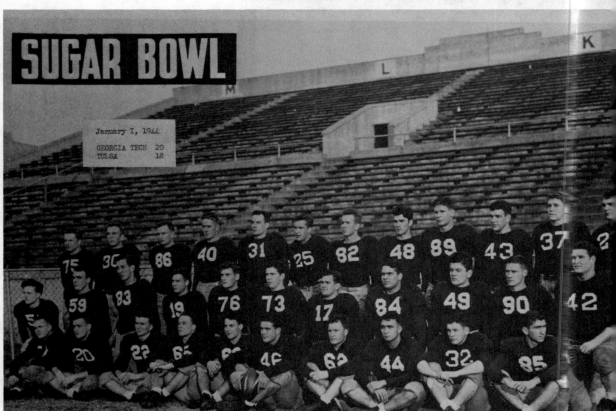

Georgia Tech Sugar Bowl team, 1943 Southeastern Conference champions. The Yellowjackets' Phil Tinsley, 1944 Consensus All-American end, is sixth from left in back row. Freshman Frank Broyles, first on left in second row, is the University of Arkansas football coach. (Courtesy Georgia Institute of Technology.)

1944

The Chicago Bears' momentum barely carried over into the 1944 season, but it was enough to eke out a 24-to-21 victory over the College All-Stars at Chicago. The Green Bay Packers dropped the Bears to second in the 1944 Western Division race, as the New York Giants captured the Eastern Division title. Curly Lambeau then went on to win his sixth and last NFL championship when his Packers held on for a 14-7 victory over the Giants in the title game before 46,000 at New York. Both of Green Bay's touchdowns came in the first half on a plunge by Ted Fritsch and a pass from Irv Comp to Fritsch. Don Hutson added the conversion both times. The Giants' Ward Cuff bolted into the end zone from the one on the first play of the fourth quarter, and Ken Strong made the PAT to bring the Giants within seven points, but there was no more scoring.

The NFL was back to ten teams with the addition of a new franchise, the Boston Yanks (they were 2-8-0 for the year), and the Cleveland Rams were back in operation. As mentioned, the Cards and Steelers combined operations as the "Card-Pitt" entry.

Don Hutson repeated as scoring (85 points) and pass receiving (58 receptions) leader, and Bill Paschal of the Giants did the same in rushing (737 yards). Sammy Baugh's teammate, Frankie Filchock, took the passing honors this time; Ken Strong of the Giants led in field goals with six; Frank Sinkwich of the Lions had the best punting average with 41.0 yards, and Howard Livingston of the Giants, the most interceptions with nine.

Hutson added his seventh straight All-NFL honors as an end in 1944, and Bulldog Turner made it four straight at center. Bruiser Kinard of the Dodgers repeated as the AP choice at right tackle, and Luckman was the quarterback (AP) for the fourth straight year. Otherwise the dream team had a new look to it:

LE	Don Hutson	Green Bay	AP, UP
LT	Albert Wistert	Philadelphia	AP, UP
LG	Leonard Younce	New York	AP, UP

The 1944 New York Giants, Eastern Division champions. (Courtesy New York Football Giants.)

125

C	Bulldog Turner	Chicago Bears	AP, UP
RG	Riley Matheson	Cleveland	AP, UP
RT	Bruiser Kinard	Brooklyn	AP
	Frank Cope	New York	UP
RE	Joe Aguirre	Washington	AP, UP
QB	Sid Luckman	Chicago Bears	AP
	Leroy Zimmerman	Philadelphia	UP
LHB	Frank Sinkwich	Detroit	AP, UP
RHB	Steve Van Buren	Philadelphia	AP
	Ward Cuff	New York	UP
FB	Bill Paschal	New York	AP, UP

Army won the AP poll as the national champion in the collegiate ranks, and Ohio State, the undefeated Big Ten champion, was the leading contender.

"Mr. Outside," Glenn Davis of Army, received the Walter Camp and Maxwell trophies, and Leslie Horvath of Ohio State won the Heisman award. The other major individual honor, the Knute Rockne Trophy, went to Don Whitmire of Navy. The 1944 Consensus All-America selections were:

E	Jack Dugger	Ohio State
E	Phil Tinsley	Georgia Tech
E	Paul Walker	Yale
*T	Don Whitmire	Navy
T	John Ferraro	USC
G	Ben Chase	Navy
G	Bill Hackett	Ohio State
C	John Tavener	Indiana
B	Glenn Davis	Army
B	Doc Blanchard	Army
B	Bob Jenkins	Navy
*B	Les Horvath	Ohio State
* Unanimous selection		

The authors, by this time were very much aware of All-America selections. Young had clippings of Ohio State's All-Americans Bill Hackett and Les Horvath in his scrapbook. Although Young liked Horvath, as a representative of his beloved Big Ten Conference, he was surprised that he beat out Glenn Davis for the Heisman Trophy.

Les Horvath gained high school honors in Cleveland before going on to play for Ohio State in 1940–42 and 1944 (he skipped a year because of military service). The 1942 Buckeyes were national champions. The circumstances in which he was notified of his Heisman Trophy selection by the Downtown Athletic Club were retold by Horvath in 1971 in a *New York Times* article:

"I was in chemistry class when the dean called to announce the award. I must say the professor was something less than impressed. In fact, he was pretty upset because the class had been interrupted."

Horvath said he was about as upset as the professor, but in an opposite manner.

Mississippi's Frank "Bruiser" Kinard, tackle on the Modern All-Time College Football Team. In the pros he was All-NFL for the Brooklyn Dodgers four times, and he served in the Navy during World War II. He was one of four brothers to play for Ole Miss, and his son was a star fullback there. (Courtesy Pro Football Hall of Fame.)

One of the best centers of all time, the Chicago Bears' Clyde "Bulldog" Turner. Six times All-Pro, the speedy Turner was a powerful blocker and crushing tackler, and led the league in pass interceptions in 1942. (Courtesy Chicago Bears Football Club.)

Four-time All-Pro halfback, Steve Van Buren. As a collegian for Louisiana State, Van Buren scored all three Tiger TDs in their winning 1944 Orange Bowl effort (18-14 over Texas A.&M.). He established LSU's season TD record. With the Philadelphia Eagles from 1944–51, Van Buren led the league in rushing four times. He was named on the All-Pro Squad of the 1940s by the Pro Football Hall of Fame. (Courtesy Pro Football Hall of Fame.)

1944 All-American end, Jack Dugger of Ohio State. In addition to winning Consensus All-American honors, he was awarded the 1945 Conference Medal of Honor for Scholarship and Athletics. (Courtesy Ohio State University Photo Archives.)

1944 Consensus All-American end, Paul Walker of Yale. (Courtesy Yale University.)

Southern California's John "the Wrecker" Ferraro, 1944 Consensus All-American. (Courtesy University of Southern California.)

Ben Chase of Navy, 1944 Consensus All-American guard. (Courtesy of the Naval Academy Athletic Association.)

Rugged Buckeye guard, Bill Hackett. (Courtesy Ohio State University Photo Archives.)

Ohio State's Les Horvath, 1944 Heisman Trophy winner. The Buckeye star had to receive more votes than Glenn Davis and Doc Blanchard for that honor. Horvath led Ohio State to the national championship in 1942, and an undefeated and untied season in 1944 (as a dental-school senior). (Courtesy Ohio State University.)

Navy's Bob Jenkins, 1944 Consensus All-American back. (Courtesy of the Naval Academy Athletic Association.)

"Honestly," he recalled, "I didn't know I was even in the running for the trophy."

"The students were enthusiastic and so was the dean and most of the professors," said Horvath. "They shut the school for a 'Les Horvath Day,' the band turned out and the players chipped in a buck apiece to buy me a set of luggage and a topcoat for my trip to New York for the Heisman presentation."

Bowl game scores in 1945 were:

Rose	Southern California 25 Tennessee 0
Sugar	Duke 29 Alabama 26
Orange	Tulsa 26 Georgia Tech 12
Cotton	Oklahoma A. & M. 34 Texas Christian 0
Shrine	West 13 East 7
Blue-Gray	North 26 South 0

Glenn Davis was only five feet nine inches tall and weighed only 172 pounds, but he was the only football player ever to win any one of the major player-of-the-year honors as a sophomore. He won the 1944 Maxwell Award and Walter Camp Memorial Trophy, the 1946 Heisman Trophy, and, along with Mr. Inside (so named by *New York Sun* football editor George Trevor), Doc Blanchard, was a Consensus All-American three times. He was runner-up in the Heisman balloting in 1944 and 1945. Army's 59-0 and 48-0 victories over Notre Dame in 1944 and 1945 tell a great deal about how Army's national champions dominated the game during those two years. A 9.8 second sprinter in a California high school, Davis went on to score twenty touchdowns in 1944 for Army, most of them with dashes of thirty or more yards. In 1944 and 1945 he gained a phenomenal average of 11.5 yards per carry, a national record (he also set several others). He scored fifty-nine TDs in his college career and was named Player of the Year by the Helms Foundation in 1944 and 1946.

Tom Lombardo, football star at West Point and captain of the 1944 national champion Army team, was killed in action in Korea in 1950. Lombardo was a football star at St. Louis' Soldan High School. Robert L. Burnes, in his column for the *St. Louis Globe-Democrat*, said that "Every coach for whom Tom Lombardo played, every friend in school characterized him in the same way—'quiet, hardworking, excellent athlete, splendid gentleman and a leader'. . . . In the halls of Soldan High School there is a plaque in his memory." Lombardo spent a year at St. Louis University where he was an outstanding student and freshman player until obtaining his appointment to West Point. He was captain and quarterback of a First Cavalry Division football team in Japan in 1945–46, and a teammate of his there, Lee Laird of Casper, Wyoming later stated: "Your [Burnes'] remarks about Lt. Lombardo as an outstanding athlete, gentleman, and leader would never be faulted by those who knew him in service."

1944 Southern Conference champion, Duke. The Blue Devils were victorious over Alabama in the Sugar Bowl, 29-26. (Courtesy Duke University.)

Three-time All-American halfback, Glenn Davis of Army. "Mr. Outside" formed one-half of probably the most famous duo in football history. "Junior" Davis was a Consensus All-American in 1944, when he also won the Walter Camp Memorial Trophy, the Maxwell Award, and Helms Foundation Player of the Year honors. He led the nation in scoring, TDs accounted for, and average yards rushing (11.5) that year. In 1945, he again paced the NCAA in the latter two categories (he had an identical 11.5 yards-per-carry average). He was unanimous All-American in 1945 and 1946. In the latter year he won the Heisman Trophy (he had been second in the balloting for that award in 1944 and 1945) and was again named the Helms Foundation's Player of the Year. Davis was also an excellent passer, receiver, and defensive player. Moreover, he was a star in track and baseball. Glenn Davis, director of special events for the *Los Angeles Times,* is a member of the Citizens Savings Hall of Fame and the National Football Foundation Hall of Fame. (Courtesy National Football Foundation and Hall of Fame.)

1945

The Green Bay Packers upheld the prestige of the NFL by downing the College All-Stars, 19 to 7, in the annual Tribune charity game. V-E and V-J days occurred prior to the beginning of the 1945 NFL season. Of the 638 men that the NFL had sent into World War II, twenty-one would never return from the field of battle. 355 had served as commissioned officers, and sixty-six were decorated.

Surprisingly, in 1945 the Bears lost more (seven) than they won (three), finishing fourth in the Western Division. Bob Waterfield, rookie quarterback from UCLA, who used the bootleg play with adeptness, led the Cleveland Rams to that division's title. Cleveland, who was not represented in the league in 1943, lost only one of ten games. Once again, the Washington Redskins, led by the veteran Sammy Baugh, captured the Eastern Division championship, this time by one game over the Eagles.

In 1974 this rhetorical question was asked in a sports column: "Did you know that a National Football League title was once decided because a star player scored the winning points for the opposing team!" Yes, it happened in 1945 when the Rams edged the Redskins, 15 to 14, for the NFL championship. Sam Baugh tried a pass from his end zone in the first period. The wind, which had been strong and erratic, blew the ball into the goal post, and under the rules at that time, it was an automatic safety and two points for the Rams. It was so cold that day in Cleveland that the musical instruments of the famous Redskin band froze even before the game began, and could not be used. Workers had covered the field with straw, but the footing was still slippery.

The 'Skins scored the first TD in the second quarter on a pass from Frank Filchock to Steve Bagarus, but the Rams countered by a Waterfield-to-Jim Benton aerial to put Cleveland in the lead by 9 to 7 at the half. (Aguirre had added the PAT for the Redskins, and Waterfield, for the Rams.) In the third quarter, Bob Waterfield clicked on another TD pass, this one to Jim Gillette, but Bob missed the conversion attempt. Filchock passed successfully to Bob Seymour in the end zone to close the gap to one point (15-14), but both teams were scoreless for the remainder of the game.

Don Hutson, playing his last season, was dislodged from his scoring leadership position by the Eagles' Steve Van Buren who tallied 110 points and also ran for 632 yards, more than anyone else in the league. Hutson did retain his pass receiving leadership with forty-seven. Sam Baugh was the passing leader again, and this time he smashed the completion percentage record with 70.3. Teammate Joe Aguirre led in field goals (seven), Roy McKay of Green Bay was the best punter with a 41.2 yard average, and Leroy Zimmerman of Philadelphia was the best pass-theft artist with seven. The Chicago Cardinals, who chose Pat Harder of

Bob Waterfield, quarterback for the Cleveland and Los Angeles Rams. In his rookie year with the Rams (1945), he won NFL honors as MVP, All-Pro, and Rookie of the Year, as Cleveland won the league title. (Courtesy Los Angeles Rams.)

Wisconsin as the league's first draft pick in 1944, had the same opportunity in 1945 and selected Charlie Trippi of Georgia. The "dream backfield" was forming for the last-place Cards.

Don Hutson made the All-NFL Team for the eighth straight year and the ninth time in his eleven-year career. Wistert, Matheson, Cope, and Van Buren repeated, and Baugh made one of his frequent appearances on the team. The picks:

LE	Don Hutson	Green Bay	AP, UP
LT	Albert Wistert	Philadelphia	AP, UP
LG	Riley Matheson	Cleveland	AP, UP
C	Charles Brock	Green Bay	AP, UP
RG	Bill Radovich	Detroit	AP, UP
RT	Frank Cope	New York	AP
	Emil Uremovich	Detroit	UP
RE	Jim Benton	Cleveland	AP
	Steve Pritko	Cleveland	UP
QB	Bob Waterfield	Cleveland	AP
	Sam Baugh	Washington	UP
LHB	Steve Van Buren	Philadelphia	AP, UP
RHB	Steve Bagarus	Washington	AP
	Bob Waterfield	Cleveland	UP
FB	Bob Westfall	Detroit	AP
	Ted Fritsch	Green Bay	UP

In their monumental work for the National Football Foundation, *College Football U.S.A. 1869–1971*, John McCallum and Charles Pearson called Don Hutson, of University of Alabama and Green Bay Packers fame, "the most dangerous end on attack football has ever seen. . . . It surprised no one when he was named on the All-Century Team." Hutson caught passes in heavily defended areas, ran the end-around with expertness, and used multiple faking. After Alabama's Rose Bowl victory over Stanford in 1935, he was called "the world's greatest pass-catching, speed merchant end," and, McCallum and Pearson add, "no one has tried to put anyone ahead of him since." For the Packers, he led the league in scoring five times, in touchdowns eight times, and in pass catching eight times. Fourteen of his nineteen records were still in the record books fifteen years after he retired.

Hutson led the Packers to the NFL championship in 1937, 1939, and 1944. Dave Anderson in *Great Receivers of the NFL* notes:

. . . he was more than a pass-catching specialist. He was an effective blocker, a sharp tackler as a defensive back and an almost perfect place kicker.

He adds that Hutson's decision to sign with Green Bay after finishing his college days at Alabama "may have saved Green Bay from losing its franchise," as the financial going had been rough for the small northern Wisconsin city during the Depression before Hutson arrived and changed things. He scored on his first play from scrimmage on an eighty-three-yard play, eluding Bear defender Beattie Feathers, one of the fastest defensive backs. The fleet Packer end once snagged a touchdown pass against defensive back Dante Magnani, who was covering him well, by grabbing one of the goal posts, swinging around, and catching the ball. Playing without shoulder pads to enable him to have greater freedom of movement, Hutson was setting his records in an era when most NFL teams relied mainly on a running game. Anderson points out that "For all his records and honors, Don Hutson never boasted about them. He usually smiled shyly and said nothing. His actions spoke louder than words, anyway." He was one of the charter members of the Pro Football Hall of Fame.

Army's Black Knights of the Hudson repeated as the collegiate national champions, as determined by the AP poll. There was nobody who was even close to them this time. Bo McMillan's Indiana Hoosiers won the Big Ten title, and Missouri, the Big Six; Georgia Tech, TCU, and Southern California won the Southeastern, Southwest, and Pacific Coast Conferences, respectively.

Felix "Doc" Blanchard swept the Heisman, Walter Camp, and Maxwell awards, while Richard Duden of Navy took the Knute Rockne Trophy for linemen. By this time, Young and McClure knew the All-American teams "by heart." The 1945 Consensus All-America selections were:

E	Hubert Bechtol	Texas
E	Dick Duden	Navy
E	Bob Ravensburg	Indiana
E	Max Morris	Northwestern
T	George Savitsky	Penn
T	Tex Coulter	Army
*G	Warren Amling	Ohio State
G	John Green	Army
C	Vaughn Mancha	Alabama
*B	Glenn Davis	Army
*B	Doc Blanchard	Army
B	Bob Fenimore	Oklahoma A.&M.
*B	Herman Wedemeyer	St. Mary's
* Unanimous		

This backfield, along with the dream backfields of 1946–49, included players who were more revered as heroes by American youth than perhaps any others in history (in the humble opinion of the authors!).

Harry Gilmer, a *Colliers* All-America pick, led the Alabama Crimson Tide to a 34 to 14 rout of Southern California in the 1946 Rose Bowl, the first Tournament of Roses classic that both Young and McClure can remember listening to on the radio (complete with visions of Gilmer's jump passes). The 1946 Sugar Bowl is the best remembered of all such New Orleans classics so far as Young is concerned. It pitted St. Mary's Herman "Hula Hips" Wedemeyer against the Oklahoma Aggies' Bob "Blond Blizzard" Fenimore, two All-American, explosive, triple-threat backs. Oklahoma A.&M. won it, 33 to 13. Miami edged Holy Cross in the Orange Bowl, 13 to 6; and Texas, with Hub Bechtol and Bobby Layne, won the Cotton Bowl game, 40 to 27, over Missouri. The Shrine Game ended in the third tie (7-7) in the last five years. The South beat the North in the Blue-Gray Game, 20 to 13. Harry Gilmer was the outstanding player in the game (not played on New Year's Day).

Doc Blanchard, the college player of the year and eventual three-time Consensus All-American, just ran over opponents who got in his way. His punting, kicking, blocking, tackling, and pass receiving also can only be described in superlatives. The scout who first spotted him playing for the fresh-

Consensus All-American for Ohio State in 1945 and 1946, Warren Amling. The fast and aggressive guard was the Buckeye recipient of the Big Ten Medal of Honor for Scholarship and Athletics in 1947. (Courtesy Ohio State University Photo Archives.)

Triple-threat star of the St. Mary's Gaels and All-American in 1945 and 1946, Herman "Hula Hips" Wedemeyer. (Courtesy St. Mary's College of California.)

Hubert "Hub" Bechtol, Consensus All-American end for Texas in 1945 and 1946. (Courtesy University of Texas.)

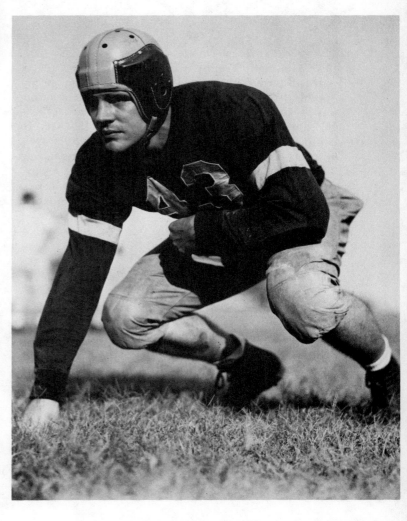

men at the University of North Carolina said, "Compared to Blanchard, Paul Bunyan was a bum." A man who had scouted for Notre Dame for years called Blanchard "the best football player I ever saw." Ironically, Blanchard's first football game for Army was *against* North Carolina, and the Tarheels were crushed. Army was unbeaten in Blanchard and Davis' three seasons there (1944–46). The powerful Blanchard had the ten-flat speed of a sprinter and often boomed punts fifty to sixty yards. He survived tours of duty as a fighter pilot in the Korean and Vietnamese conflicts, and today he is a retired colonel living in Texas.

1945 Consensus All-American end, Dick Duden of Navy. (Courtesy of the Naval Academy Athletic Association.)

1945 Heisman Trophy winner, Felix "Doc" Blanchard of Army. "Mr. Inside," one-half of the incomparable Blanchard-Davis backfield combination, was a Consensus All-American three times (1944–46), and was a unanimous selection in 1945–46. In addition to winning the Heisman Trophy in 1945, he swept the other individual awards—Walter Camp Trophy, Maxwell Award, and Sullivan Award. There probably has been no better football performer. (Courtesy National Football Foundation and Hall of Fame.)

1946

In the thirteenth annual College All-Star Game at Soldier Field, the All-Stars gained their fourth victory, this time at the expense of the Rams, who were crushed 16 to 0. But it was the Los Angeles rather than the Cleveland Rams who were shut out by the collegians, for Dan Reeves had moved the NFL championship club to greener pastures, climatically and financially. Rejected initially in

his bid to move the club, Reeves claimed $50,000 losses with the top NFL team. In the Rams' first 1946 season game at Los Angeles, played against the Redskins in a rematch, attendance was 95,000.

Bert Bell became commissioner after the resignation of Elmer Layden and was met by a new rival league, the All-America Football Conference (AAFC). Black players Kenny Washington and Woody Strode played for the Rams, and Marion Motley and Bill Willis, for the AAFC Cleveland Browns, who won that conference's championship. Blacks such as Fritz Pollard and Duke Slater had played for NFL teams in the 1920s (Slater finishing with the Chicago Cardinals in 1931), and black Joe Lillard was with the Cards in 1932–33. However, an unofficial color line was imposed after that until 1946, the year that Jackie Robinson broke in with Montreal in the baseball world.

The 1946 version of the Chicago Bears, with George Halas back at the helm, took the Western Division title, and the New York Giants won in the Eastern Division. Before the championship

UCLA's all-time rushing leader and first All-American (1939), Kenny Washington. Just as backfield mate Jackie Robinson was the first black to play major-league baseball, Washington and another UCLA teammate, Woody Strode, were the first of that race to play in the NFL since the early 1930s. (Courtesy Los Angeles Rams.)

Powerful fullback for the Cleveland Browns, Marion Motley. Motley's Canton, Ohio high-school team was beaten only three times in three years, and each time it was by Paul Brown's legendary Massillon team. Motley played for Brown at Great Lakes and helped the Naval Training Station wallop Notre Dame in 1945. He was the all-time leading rusher of the AAFC, and he led the NFL in that category in 1951. Not only strong but also fast, he played for the Browns' four AAFC winners and two of their NFL title teams. (Courtesy Cleveland Browns.)

The list of statistical leaders was notable for the absence of the names of Don Hutson, now retired, and Sammy Baugh. In 1946 Ted Fritsch of the Packers led in scoring with one hundred points and in field goals with nine. "Bullet" Bill Dudley of the Steelers was also a double leader, in rushing with 604 yards and interceptions with ten. Bob Waterfield of the Rams led in passing, and his partner, Jim Benton, took the pass receiving crown with sixty-three catches. The Packers' Roy McKay had the best punting percentage with 42.7 yards. In the rival AAFC, the champion Browns, coached by Paul Brown, had two leaders, their passing combination of quarterback Otto Graham and end Mac Speedie, in passing and receiving, respectively.

Statistical leaders Benton, Waterfield, Dudley, and Fritsch made the United Press All-NFL Team at left end, quarterback, left halfback, and full-

game it was learned that Giant halfback Merle Hapes had been offered a bribe. He did not take it but did not report it either and was immediately suspended by Bell. Frankie Filchock, Giant quarterback, who was not involved but knew of the bribe, was allowed to play. He was suspended after the game (the suspension was lifted in 1950).

In the NFL title game, the Bears struck for two first quarter touchdowns on a Luckman to Kavanaugh pass and a pass interception by Magnani. A Filchock to Frank Liebel aerial connected for a Giant TD, and the score read 14-7, Bears, at the end of the first quarter and at halftime. The Giants tied it on a Filchock pass to Steve Filipowicz in the third period. But the veteran Sid Luckman fooled the Giants on a quarterback "keeper" play in the last quarter and scored on a nineteen-yard run. Frank Maznicki, who made all three Bear PATs, kicked a field goal to put the game beyond reach, and the Bears had another NFL crown, 24 to 14. Ken Strong made both extra points for the Giants.

Four-sport star, Jackie Robinson of UCLA. Robinson and All-American Kenny Washington led the Bruins to an undefeated season (6-0-4) in 1939. (Courtesy UCLA.)

137

The 1946 Chicago Bears, NFL champions. (Courtesy
Chicago Bears Football Club.)

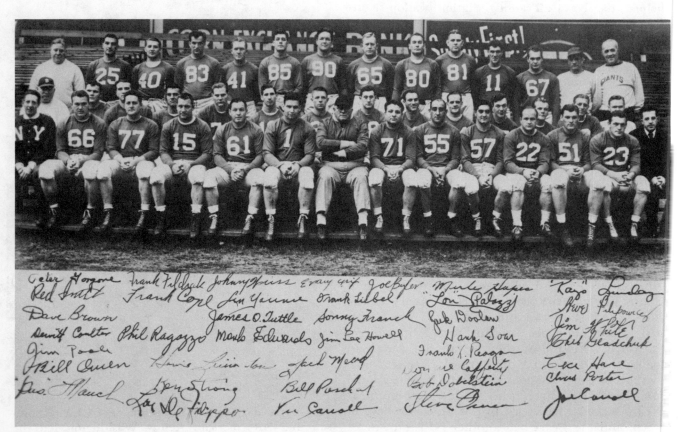

The 1946 New York Giants, Eastern Division champions. The Giants were "always a bridesmaid" in the
1940s. (Courtesy New York Football Giants.)

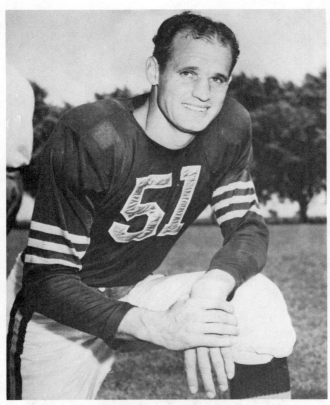

Ken Kavanaugh of LSU and the Chicago Bears, the first recipient of the Knute Rockne Trophy. The 1939 Consensus All-American end scored TDs in three NFL title games won by the Bears. Decorated as a war hero during World War II, he returned to the pro ranks and became All-NFL in 1946 and 1947. (Courtesy Chicago Bears Football Club.)

Coach of Ohio State's national champions in 1942, Paul Brown. The incomparable Brown had been a great success at Massillon High School in Ohio during the 1930s. After coaching the Buckeyes (1941–43), he was the head coach of the most powerful service team (other than the academies) during the war, Great Lakes. He then guided the Cleveland Browns to four (of four possible) AAFC titles from 1946–49. (Courtesy Cleveland Browns.)

Northwestern's Otto Graham, All-American in football and basketball. Graham, also talented in music and other sports (he was an eight-letter man at Northwestern), led the College All-Stars to victory over the Redskins in 1943. A pro cager and All-NFL five times, he played for ten divisional and seven league champions in ten seasons with the Cleveland Browns. (Courtesy Cleveland Browns.)

back, respectively. In addition to Benton, Waterfield, and Fritsch, repeaters from the previous (1945) season were Al Wistert of the Eagles and Riley Matheson of the Rams. Bulldog Turner was back at his center spot after a year's absence. Augie Lio of the Eagles at left guard, Jim White of the Giants at right tackle, Ken Kavanaugh of the Bears at right end, and the suspended Filchock at right half rounded out the squad.

The 1946 collegiate football season amounted to a return to near-normalcy, with football stars such as Charlie Trippi, "Choo Choo" Justice, and Johnny Lujack back from the service. Notre Dame was back at full strength, and they bounced right back to the top of the national rankings. Led by Lujack and George Connor, the Irish were named as national champions by the Associated Press. More accurate, however, was the assessment of McCallum, Sheehan, and Pearson for the National Football Foundation. They selected Notre Dame and Army as tied for first place. This reflects the fact that both teams were undefeated (Army with nine wins and the Fighting Irish with eight) with one blemish— a scoreless tie when they played each other. That battle, fought at New York City on 9 November when Army had won seven games and Notre Dame five, was one of those twenty-five top games of a sixty-five-year period, as picked by *Sports Illustrated*. The game would have gone to Army had not Lujack (playing sixty minutes despite an injury) tackled Doc Blanchard in the open field to prevent a touchdown. Charlie Trippi led Georgia to an undefeated ten-game season and the Southeastern Conference championship. Buddy Young, Burr Baldwin, Charlie Justice, Weldon Humble, and Ray Evans led Illinois, UCLA, North Carolina, Rice, and Kansas (respectively) to titles in the other major conferences. McCallum and Pearson (in *College Football U.S.A. 1869–1971*) note that some call the late 1940s the age of the "strongest football." Authors Young and McClure agree and assert that it was a high point in athletics generally, in part because it was a period of great national athletic heroes.

The Outland Trophy was awarded by the Football Writers Association of America for the first time in 1946. It goes to the nation's outstanding guard or tackle as selected by the writers. They chose George Connor of Notre Dame, the only player from that football power to make the All-Century Team. Triple-threat Charlie Trippi of Georgia won the Walter Camp Trophy and the Maxwell Award (unanimous pick) and later signed with the Chicago Cardinals for the most money paid to a player since Red Grange. McCal-

Called by some the greatest player from the South, Charlie Trippi played for three bowl-winning Georgia teams and was unanimous All-American, and Maxwell Award and Walter Camp Trophy winner, in 1946. An All-Time Rose Bowl Team choice, Trippi was a member of the Chicago Cardinals' "Dream Backfield," and played for the Cards' NFL title team of 1947. (University of Georgia photo.)

lum and Pearson called him "the greatest thing to come out of the South since the invention of the cotton gin" and "the best all-around halfback ever to play in Dixie." Trippi, playing as a substitute for the injured Frankie Sinkwich in the 1943 Rose Bowl, had been named the outstanding player of the game and subsequently was picked on the All-time Rose Bowl First Team. He captained Georgia's undefeated and untied 1946 team, and a year later led the Chicago Cardinals to the NFL title. Glenn Davis won the Heisman Trophy, and Burr Baldwin of UCLA, the Knute Rockne Memorial Trophy. The 1946 Consensus All-America:

E	Hank Foldberg	Army
E	Hubert Bechtol	Texas
•E	Burr Baldwin	UCLA
T	George Connor	Notre Dame

Notre Dame's only member of the First All-Century Team, tackle George Connor. A Consensus All-American in 1946 and 1947 for the Irish, Connor also played two years for Holy Cross (1942–43). He was the first recipient of the Outland Trophy, awarded to the nation's outstanding guard or tackle by the Football Writers Association of America. With the Chicago Bears from 1948–55, Connor was All-Pro five different seasons, and in three of those years was named to both the offensive and defensive units. (Courtesy National Football Foundation and Hall of Fame.)

Notre Dame's Johnny Lujack, unanimous All-American quarterback in 1946 and 1947. Probably the most famous T-formation college quarterback of that decade, Lujack won the 1947 Heisman Memorial Trophy, the 1947 Walter Camp Memorial Trophy, and the 1948 William M. Coffman Trophy as the outstanding offensive player in the East-West Game. Notre Dame was ranked first by the AP in 1943, 1946, and 1947—the years Lujack played for the varsity. Lujack played both offense and defense for the Chicago Bears from 1948–51. He is a member of the Citizens Savings Hall of Fame and the National Football Foundation Hall of Fame. (Courtesy John Lujack.)

1948 Consensus All-American and Walter Camp Memorial Trophy winner, Charlie "Choo Choo" Justice of North Carolina. Along with Doak Walker, Justice was one of the most publicized and genuine football heroes of all time. The Tarheel back was runnerup in Heisman Trophy voting in both 1948 and 1949, and was named to All-American teams both years. As a senior in high school in Asheville, North Carolina, he compiled one of the most amazing football records of all time when he averaged twenty-five yards every time he carried the ball. He did everything well on defense, too. Charlie Justice led North Carolina to the Sugar Bowl in 1947 and 1949, and the Cotton Bowl in 1950. (Courtesy National Football Foundation and Hall of Fame.)

Illinois, 1947 Rose Bowl champions. Coached by Ray Eliot (first row, fifth from right), the Big Ten champions overpowered a highly touted UCLA eleven, 45-14. The Indians featured All-American guard Alex Agase (front row, sixth from left); Buddy Young (front row, extreme right), an NCAA track champion who was just as fleet on the gridiron; Dike Eddleman (first row, fourth from left), the best punter in Big Ten history and one of the outstanding athletes of the decade; and hard-driving back Julie Rykovich, who had played on Notre Dame's national champions in 1943. Quarterback Perry Moss (front row, second from right) was an outstanding passer and field general, and ends Ike Owens and Jim Valek contained the opposition effectively. (Courtesy University of Illinois.)

Unanimous 1946 All-American end, Burr Baldwin of the UCLA Bruins. Co-captain Baldwin was one of his school's all-time greats. He won the 1946 Knute Rockne Memorial Trophy as College Lineman of the Year. (Courtesy UCLA.)

Dick Huffman of Tennessee, 1946 Consensus All-American tackle. (Courtesy University of Tennessee.)

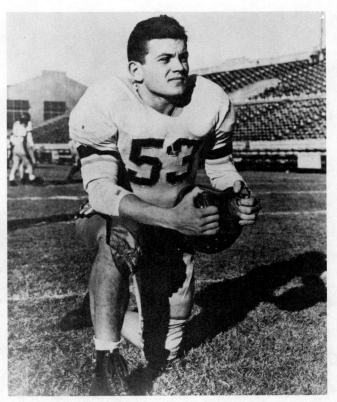

Georgia Tech's 1946 Consensus All-American center, Paul Duke. (Courtesy Georgia Institute of Technology.)

T	Warren Amling	Ohio State
T	Dick Huffman	Tennessee
G	Weldon Humble	Rice
G	Alex Agase	Illinois
C	Paul Duke	Georgia Tech
*B	Glenn Davis	Army
*B	Doc Blanchard	Army
*B	Charlie Trippi	Georgia
*B	Johnny Lujack	Notre Dame

* Unanimous selection

In 1946 an important event for young sports fans was the initial publication of a quality monthly magazine called *Sport*. Featuring beautiful photography and articles by well-known sportswriters, *Sport* included a preseason All-America team in its first issue. *Sport*'s picks, selected by George Trevor, were Doc Blanchard, Glenn Davis, Charlie Trippi, and Herman Wedemeyer in the backfield and Hub Bechtol, Hank Foldberg, George Connor, John Ferraro, Alex Agase, Warren Amling, and Vaughn Mancha in the line. (In October of 1971, *Sport*, celebrating its twenty-fifth anniversary, published a "follow-up" article entitled *"Sport*'s First All-America Team . . . Where Have You Gone?"*)

Trevor had done his homework well in preparing his 1946 pigskin prognostications: All of his choices were truly All-Americans.

In the first Rose Bowl game played under the arrangement between the Big Ten and the Pacific Coast Conference, Illinois, led by Buddy Young and Alex Agase, punished UCLA, 45 to 14. In a battle between great triple-threat halfbacks (Trippi and Justice), Georgia defeated North Carolina in the Sugar Bowl, 20 to 10. In a game featuring two All-America linemen (Humble and Huffman), Rice turned back Tennessee, 8 to 0, in the Orange Bowl, and Arkansas and LSU battled to a 0-0 tie in the Cotton Bowl. The West won the Shrine Game, 13 to 9, and the South, the Blue-Gray contest, 33 to 6.

1947

The 1947 pro football season was unusual in several respects. Not least among these was the order of finish in the two divisions: Chicago's Cardinals and Bears were one-two in the West, and the Eagles and Steelers tied for first in the East with the

Eagles winning the playoff, 21 to 0. Cleveland and New York were divisional champions in the rival AAFC, with Paul Brown's Browns winning the league title, 14 to 3.

The owner of the Cardinals, Charles Bidwill, died in April, 1947, and did not live to see his team win its first NFL championship since 1925. The Cardinals were the oldest franchise in pro football in terms of continuous operations. A member of the Cardinals' "Million Dollar Backfield," Paul Christman of Missouri passed for more than two thousand yards and seventeen TDs in regular season play. Pat Harder of Wisconsin, Elmer Angsman of Notre Dame, and Charlie Trippi held down the other spots in that "dream" backfield.

The NFL title game was played on a frozen turf. It featured the explosive quick openers of the Cardinals and grinding ground game of the Eagles. Greasy Neale's eight-man line could not stop the quick bursts of Trippi and Angsman. Trippi scored on a forty-four yard quick opener and again

"Pitchin' Paul" Christman of the Chicago Football Cardinals' "Dream Backfield." All-American for Missouri from 1938–40, quarterback Christman excelled in passing. He helped the Cardinals to an NFL title in 1947, and a divisional title in 1948. (Courtesy St. Louis Football Cardinals.)

Mal Kutner of Texas, All-American end in 1941. After serving in the military, he was an All-NFL end twice for the Chicago Cardinals and played for their NFL championship team in 1947. (Courtesy University of Texas.)

on a seventy-five yard punt return, and Angsman added six-pointers with two seventy-yard runs. Pat Harder successfully booted four PATs. The Eagles made it close by a Tommy Thompson to Pat Mc-Hugh scoring pass and two one-yard TD plunges by Van Buren and Russ Craft. Cliff Patton kicked all three of his extra-point attempts through the uprights, but the Eagles never led in their 28-21 defeat.

Two seasonal statistical honors went to Harder —scoring (102 points) and field goals (seven— tied with Cuff and Waterfield). Van Buren's 1,008 yards topped the rushers, and Sam Baugh again led in passing. Jim Keane of the Bears led in reception with sixty-four. Jack Jacobs of Green Bay won the punting crown with a 43.5 yard average, and Frank Reagen of the Giants was first in interceptions with ten. In the All-America Conference, Brown stars dominated—Otto Graham in passing; one of his favorite targets, Mac Speedie in receiving (fifty-eight catches); and Marion Motley in rushing (964 yards).

Six Chicago players made the United Press All-NFL Team—Kavanaugh at left end, Mal Kutner of the Cardinals at right end, Vince Banonis of the Cards at center, Fred Davis of the Bears at right tackle, Luckman at quarterback, and Harder at fullback. Albert Wistert, Van Buren, and Baugh again held down positions as did Leonard Younce of the Giants at left guard and Bill Moore of the Steelers at right guard.

Michigan won the Associated Press poll (a special one held after their 1948 Rose Bowl victory)

The University of Detroit's Vince Banonis, a Grantland Rice All-American selection in 1941. Banonis joined the Chicago Cardinals in 1942; but in 1943, he played for the Iowa Seahawks, the Navy Pre-Flight Training Center in Iowa City. Coached by Lieutenant Don Faurot of Missouri, the Seahawks lost only once, to Notre Dame, and were ranked second to the Irish in the final AP poll. The Seahawks included many other pros in their lineup. In 1947 Banonis was All-Pro center for the NFL champion Cardinals. (Courtesy University of Detroit.)

Coach of Michigan's 1947 national champions, Herbert "Fritz" Crisler. Crisler's Wolverines overpowered USC in the 1948 Rose Bowl, 49 to 0. He was Michigan's athletic director and athletic board chairman for many years after his coaching career. (Courtesy University of Michigan.)

The first great T-formation quarterback of the Southwest Conference, Bobby Layne, was a 1947 Consensus All-American. He smashed many Texas (and later NFL) passing records. (Courtesy University of Texas.)

Chappuis, an aerial gunner, had been shot down over Italy during the war. All-American Bump Elliott was backfield coach at Iowa when the author was on the squad there in 1955 (in the 1970s, Bump was athletic director for the Hawkeyes).

Michigan, Southern California, Kansas (tied with Oklahoma), SMU, Mississippi, and Penn were major conference champions that year. McCallum, Pearson, and Sheehan picked Notre Dame as coholder of the mythical championship. The regular season-end AP poll had them in sole possession of first. The Irish featured unanimous All-America Johnny Lujack and Consensus All-Americas George Connor and Bill Fischer. Paul Cleary of the Trojans, Doak Walker of the Mustangs, Charley Conerly of Ole Miss, and Chuck Bednarik of the Quakers were also Consensus All-Americans for the above-mentioned conference championship teams, and the Jayhawkers' Ray Evans and Mississippi's Barney Poole garnered several All-America picks.

Ray Evans, who wore jersey number "42" for Kansas, established a national passing record in 1942 with 101 completions. He sparked the Jayhawkers to their second successive Big Six cochampionship in 1947, and scored two touchdowns in the Orange Bowl game on 1 January 1948 against Georgia Tech. He was named to the 1947 AP All-American backfield along with Lujack, Chappuis, and Doak Walker. The *New York Sun* called Evans the "outstanding back in the nation" during 1947. Evans was also named to the Helms Foundation All-American basketball squads in 1942 and 1943.

The 1 November clash between undefeated Texas and SMU is listed as one of the twenty-five most-publicized college football games of a sixty-five-year period, as picked by *Sports Illustrated*. Blair Cherry's Longhorns, featuring Bobby Layne, were edged by Matty Bell's Mustangs, with their star Doak Walker, by a 14 to 13 score. Layne and Walker had been teammates at Highland Park High School in Dallas, and they double-dated after the historic 1947 game.

Also in 1947 an amazing horizontal catch by Bill Swiacki enabled Columbia to edge Army and break the Black Knights' twenty-five-game winning streak.

Unanimous All-America Johnny Lujack received the Heisman and Walter Camp Trophies, and Doak Walker, the Maxwell Award. Linemen Chuck Bednarik of Penn and Joe Steffy of Army won the Knute Rockne and Outland Trophies. Lujack later was awarded the William M. Coffman Trophy as the outstanding offensive player in the 1948 East-West Game.

and accolades as the national champion collegiate football team of 1947. The Wolverines, coached by Fritz Crisler, featured a sparkling single-wing backfield with Howard Yerges, Chalmers "Bump" Elliott, Jack Weisenburger, and Bob Chappuis. Line play was spearheaded by end Dick Rifenburg and tackle Alvin Wistert, who was to become (in 1948) the third All-American from the same family. With the exception of the Hawkeyes, the Wolverines were Young's favorite team (he had always liked them since Harmon's days), and Chappuis, unanimous All-American, was his favorite player.

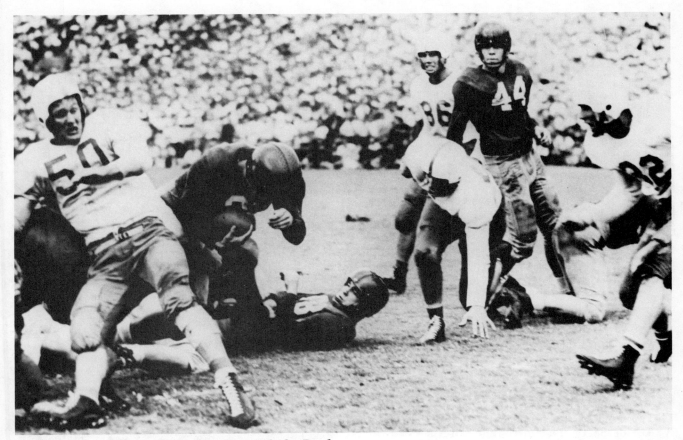

In the 1948 Southern Methodist-Texas clash, Doak Walker of the Mustangs crashes through the Longhorn line to score as Harris (50) of Texas is spun out of the way. Number 44, Kyle Rote of SMU, looks on. SMU defeated Texas, 21 to 6. (Courtesy Southern Methodist University.)

The 1947 Consensus All-America Team was studded with all-time greats:

E	Bill Swiacki	Columbia
E	Paul Cleary	USC
T	George Connor	Notre Dame
T	Bob Davis	Georgia Tech
G	Joe Steffy	Army
G	Bill Fischer	Notre Dame
C	Chuck Bednarik	Penn
B	Bob Chappuis	Michigan
B	Johnny Lujack	Notre Dame
B	Doak Walker	SMU
B	Bobby Layne	Texas
B	Charley Conerly	Mississippi

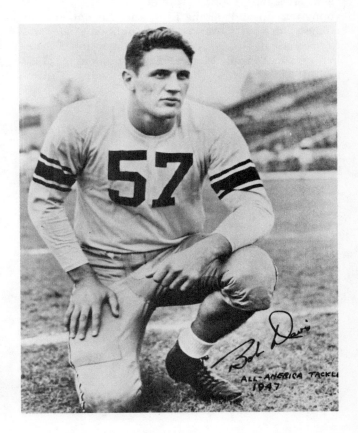

Bob Davis of Georgia Tech, 1947 Consensus All-American tackle. (Courtesy Georgia Institute of Technology.)

147

The epitome of the sports hero of the 1940s, Doak Walker of SMU. The three-time All-American, and 1948 Heisman Trophy winner, was a model for youngsters on and off the field, and did not lose his modesty despite unprecedented publicity. He was to become an All-NFL player four times and a member of the Detroit Lions' NFL champions of 1952 and 1953. (Courtesy Southern Methodist University.)

Kansas' first football All-American, Ray Evans, achieved the honor more than once in each of two sports—football and basketball. (Courtesy University of Kansas.)

Two-time Consensus All-American center, Chuck Bednarik of Penn. Bednarik flew thirty combat missions as an aerial gunner in World War II. The decorated war hero entered Penn in 1946, at age twenty. He received the Knute Rockne Memorial Trophy in 1947, and the Maxwell Award in 1948, the two years he was named a Consensus All-American. He was also the Helms Foundation Player of the Year in 1948. He won the last two awards over some of the most highly touted backs in football history. The "Bethlehem Bomber," son of an immigrant steelworker from Czechoslovakia, was NFL Rookie of the Year in 1949, playing for the world-champion Eagles. Chuck Bednarik was named the greatest center of all time by a prestigious panel in 1969. (Courtesy National Football Foundation and Hall of Fame.)

Otto Schnellbacher of Kansas starred in football and basketball in 1943, 1946, 1947, and 1948, and played on the undefeated (8-0-2) 1947 Jayhawk team that went to the Orange Bowl. The "Claw" (so named because of his strong hands) was a defensive standout with the New York Giants. (Courtesy University of Kansas.)

Michigan, which had beaten Stanford, 49 to 0, in the first Rose Bowl (Tournament of Roses) game in 1902, returned for its second appearance in 1948, and with an identical score, smashed Southern California. It was the first televised Rose Bowl game. Texas' Bobby Layne and Tom Landry outdid Alabama's best as the Longhorns defeated the Crimson Tide, 27 to 7, in the Sugar Bowl. In the Orange Bowl, Georgia Tech with All-America tackle, Bob Davis, edged the Kansas Jayhawks, despite Ray Evans and Otto Schnellbacher, 20 to 14. Hometown favorite, Southern Methodist, with

Doak Walker, tied Penn State, 13 to 13, in the 1948 Cotton Bowl. The East slaughtered the West, 40 to 9, in the Shrine Game, and the North beat the South, 19 to 13, in the Blue-Gray contest.

1948

The Chicago Cardinals shut out the College All-Stars in Chicago, 28-0, as Young watched with his parents and brother at Soldier Field. The awesome pillars and brightly illuminated stadium combined with the spotlighted, individual introduction of the starters and the immense crowd to dazzle the youngsters who had read about all of the players in the newspaper and sports magazines.

The Cardinals (11-1) and the Bears (10-2) again were one-two in the Western Division NFL standings in 1948, as the Eagles (9-2-1) coasted to the Eastern Division title. The Cleveland Browns won fourteen games without a loss in the Western Division of the AAFC, while Buffalo won only one more game than it lost (8-7) in leading the Eastern Division.

The NFL title game was a rematch of the 1947 contestants. It was played in Philadelphia's Shibe Park in a blinding snow storm. 36,309 fans braved blizzard conditions to watch the Cardinals and Eagles struggle through three scoreless quarters. The line markers were covered with deep snow, as was the rest of the field, and the snow fell relentlessly throughout the game in one of Philly's worst storms. The officials and players did remarkably well under the conditions. Rugged Eagle tackle Frank "Bucko" Kilroy recovered a Cardinal fumble by quarterback Ray Mallouf on the Cardinal seventeen. Steve Van Buren bolted over from the five yard line to score, and Cliff Patton kicked the PAT for the only points of the game. The Browns rolled over the Buffalo Bills in the AAFC title game, 49 to 7.

Cardinal Pat Harder won the NFL season scoring crown with 110 points, but the Eagles took most of the other statistical honors. Van Buren rushed for 945 yards and the league leadership in that department. Tommy Thompson (and Baugh) won passing honors, Patton led in field goals (eight), and Joe Muha, in punting with 47.2 yards. Tom Fears of the Rams was first in pass receptions with fifty-one, and Redskin Dan Sandifer's record thirteen interceptions was tops in that category.

Record-setting statistical leaders in the AAFC were Spec Sanders of the New York Yankees in scoring (114 points) and rushing (1,432 yards),

1947 Penn State football team. The Nittany Lions, sparked by *Colliers* All-American guard Steve Suhey and end Sam Tamburo (a 1948 All-American), held opponents to seventeen yards per game on the ground during the regular season. In the 1948 Cotton Bowl, Penn State and SMU battled to a 13-13 tie. After trailing 13-0 at the half, Coach Bob Higgins put reserve quarterback Elwood Petchel in charge. The Lions' offense roared back to knot the score, while their defense checked Doak Walker (who had spearheaded the successful Mustang attack in the first half). A substitute Penn State end dropped a pass in the end zone on the last play of the game. (Courtesy Pennsylvania State University.)

End Tom Fears, outstanding pass receiver for the Los Angeles Rams. Fears was an All-American for UCLA in 1947. He led NFL receivers in 1948, 1949, and 1950. (Courtesy Los Angeles Rams.)

Tom Landry, famous Dallas Cowboys coach, was an All-Southwest Conference back for Texas as a junior. He co-captained the Longhorns the following year (1948), and played on two bowl-winning teams. (Courtesy University of Texas.)

Mac Speedie in receiving (sixty-seven catches), and Ben Agajanian of the Los Angeles Dons in field goals (fifteen). Otto Graham and Y.A. Tittle (of the Baltimore Colts) led the passers.

On the United Press 1948 All-NFL Team there were three repeaters in the backfield—Van Buren, Baugh, and Harder. Charlie Trippi took the other backfield honor slot. Kutner and Albert Wistert were the only line repeaters from 1947, but Clyde "Bulldog" Turner was back at his center position. Pete Pihos of the Eagles, whom Young had seen play for the Big Ten Champion Indiana Hoosiers against Iowa in 1945, was the all-pro left end. Raymond Bray of the Bears was at left guard, Garrard Ramsey of the Cards, at right guard, and Dick Huffman of the Rams, at right tackle to round out the team.

Appearing in 1948 to assist Young, McClure, and other youthful fans in following their collegiate and professional football heroes were the

Five-time All-Pro end, Pete Pihos of the Philadelphia Eagles. With the Philadelphia Eagles from 1947-55, he played on the NFL title teams of 1948 and 1949. The three-time NFL receiving leader and Indiana star (1942–43, 1945–46) was named to the All-Pro Squad of the 1940s by the Pro Football Hall of Fame. (Courtesy Pro Football Hall of Fame.)

Leaf bubble gum cards. Young acquired a stack of the cards, eventually held together by stout rubber bands, at the Busby-Wing drugstore, and trading of the duplicates was fast and furious on the commodious concrete steps outside the store. The players of the 1948 and 1949 period were perhaps the best "known" of all pros in these youngsters' lifetime partly because of the pictorial assistance of these "All-Star Football Gum" cards.

Undefeated and untied Michigan was the collegiate mythical national champion in 1948. Once-tied Notre Dame and Army were also powers, and California (10-0-0), Oklahoma (9-1-0), Georgia (9-1-0), and SMU (8-1-1) won the major conference championships.

Southern Methodist's famed number "37," Doak Walker, won the coveted Heisman Trophy, "Choo Choo" Justice of North Carolina received the Walter Camp Trophy, and a lineman, Chuck Bednarik, the Maxwell Award. Bill Fischer of Notre Dame won both the Outland and Knute Rockne awards.

The 1948 Consensus All-America Football Team:

E	Leon Hart	Notre Dame
E	Dick Rifenburg	Michigan
T	Leo Nomellini	Minnesota
T	Alvin Wistert	Michigan
G	Bill Fischer	Notre Dame
G	Buddy Burris	Oklahoma
C	Chuck Bednarik	Penn
*B	Doak Walker	SMU
B	Clyde Scott	Arkansas
B	Charlie Justice	North Carolina
B	Jackie Jensen	California
B	Emil Sitko	Notre Dame

* Unanimous selection

In the opinion of the authors, no All-America Team has surpassed the 1946, 1947, and 1948 squads in ability, fame, and truly All-American characteristics. Sport hero worship was seemingly at its peak during the 1945–49 period.

Michigan was barred from appearing in the Rose Bowl by the Big Nine-Pacific Coast pact, but twice-beaten Northwestern managed to blemish California's record by downing the Golden Bears, 20 to 14. Cal's Golden Boy, Jackie Jensen, scored a touchdown. In subsequent years he played in a World Series (1950) and was named the American League's MVP (1958)! Jensen married national diving champion Zoe Ann Olsen, whose name was well known to Young, as she had grown up in La-Porte City, fifteen miles from the author's hometown.

Oklahoma, rising to national prominence under

1948 bubble-gum cards, a product of the Leaf Gum Company, Chicago, Illinois. (From the collection of Charles Gilbert, Warrensburg, Missouri.)

Last lineman to win the Heisman Trophy, Leon Hart of Notre Dame. Hart was a Consensus All-American end in 1948 and 1949, and was a unanimous choice in the latter year, when he won both the Maxwell Award and Heisman Trophy. The only other lineman to win the latter was end Larry Kelley of Yale in 1936. Hart also was the recipient of the Knute Rockne Memorial Trophy in 1949. He played with Notre Dame's national champions of 1947 and 1949, and with the Detroit Lions' NFL title teams of 1952, 1953, and 1957. (Courtesy National Football Foundation and Hall of Fame.)

1948 Consensus All-American back and Rose Bowl star, Jackie Jensen of California. Jensen went from the Golden Bears to the New York Yankees with whom he appeared in the 1950 World Series. (TCMA photo.)

Two-time Consensus All-American, Leo Nomellini of Minnesota. Born in Italy and raised in Chicago, Nomellini was a marine veteran of the Saipan and Okinawa battles in World War II. After gaining All-American recognition in 1948 and 1949, he went on to become one of the best pro tackles of all time. He was also a shot-putter and wrestler as a collegian and a pro wrestler in later years. (Courtesy University of Minnesota.)

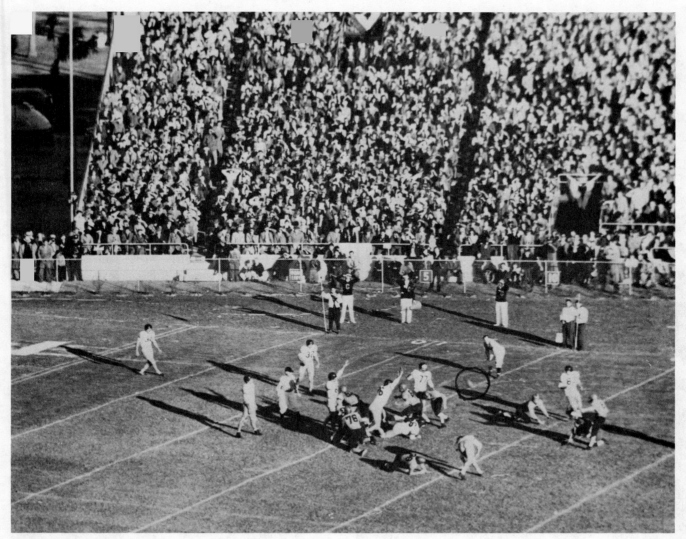

Jack Miller kicks a field goal in the 1949 Gator Bowl, enabling Clemson to defeat Missouri, 24 to 23. Clemson was undefeated that season with an 11-0 record. (Courtesy Clemson University.)

Bud Wilkinson, defeated North Carolina's Tarheels and Charlie Justice in the Sugar Bowl, 14 to 6. Texas outraced Georgia in the Orange Bowl, 41 to 28. Southern Methodist and "the Doaker" defeated Oregon, 21-13, in the Cotton Bowl, which had to have another deck added to accommodate fans attracted by the Mustangs' great All-American. Clemson nipped Missouri, 24-23, in the Gator Bowl. The East edged the West, 14 to 12, in the Shrine Game, and the South began a five-game victory streak over the North by winning, 27 to 13, in the Blue-Gray classic.

1949

The Young family was back at Soldier Field to see the 1949 College All-Star Game, won that year by the Eagles in a rout, 38 to 0. The All-Stars were coached by Oklahoma's Bud Wilkinson, and their roster included Norm Van Brocklin of Oregon, Pete Elliott of Michigan, and Chuck Bednarik of Pennsylvania. The Eagles were also loaded with stars, including backs Joe Muha, Bosh Pritchard, Frank Szymanski, Tommy Thompson, and Steve Van Buren; and linemen Bucko Kilroy, Cliff Patton, Pete Pihos, George Savitsky, Vic Sears, Albert Wistert, and Alex Wojciechowski (one of the "Seven Blocks of Granite," along with Vince Lombardi).

In the regular season, Bob Smith of the Lions, whom Young had seen play for Iowa, ran an intercepted pass 102 yards for a touchdown and record. The Bears' Johnny Lujack passed for 468 yards against the Cardinals. And Steeler Bob Gage ran ninety-seven yards from scrimmage, tying a record.

The AAFC was down to one division in 1949, and the "playoff" game was between the first-place Browns and second-place 49ers. The league folded after the season, with Cleveland (winner in all

NFL title game, played in drenching rain in Los Angeles, the Eagles scored on a pass from Tommy Thompson to Pete Pihos that covered thirty-one yards in the second period. Cliff Patton added the PAT for a 7–0 halftime lead. The game's only other touchdown came in the third period when the Rams' Bob Waterfield slipped while attempting to punt from his own five. Eagle Ed Skladany blocked the kick and then retrieved the ball, running it into the end zone for six points. Patton's extra point attempt was good, and the 14-0 score held up as the final count.

Familiar names among the statistical leaders were Pat Harder (scoring—102 points, tied with Gene Roberts of the Giants), Steve Van Buren (rushing—1,146 yards, a record), Sammy Baugh (passing), Tom Fears (receiving—seventy-seven

Oregon passing ace, Norm Van Brocklin. Switched from a reserve tailback spot to a starting position when Oregon turned to the T-formation, Van Brocklin led the Ducks to an undefeated conference record and a berth in the 1949 Cotton Bowl. He went on to a creditable professional career with the Rams and Eagles. (Courtesy University of Oregon.)

four years of the AAFC's existence), San Francisco, and Baltimore going into the NFL.

The Eagles (11-1-0) romped to the championship in the NFL East, and the Rams, with one less win and one less loss than the Bears (but with two ties) eked out a victory in the West. In the

Lou "the Toe" Groza, six-time All-NFL tackle. He was one of football's greatest kickers. His pro career with the Cleveland Browns spanned the years 1946 to 1967. (Courtesy Cleveland Browns.)

catches), and Bob Waterfield (field goals—nine, tied with Cliff Patton of the Eagles). Mike Boyda of the New York Bulldogs (an entry made up of players from the old Boston Yanks [1944–48], which lasted only one year) was the best punter, and Bob Nussbaumer of the Cardinals led in interceptions with twelve. The Browns had four league-leading performances in the AAFC in Lou Groza (scoring and field goals), Otto Graham (tied with Glenn Dobbs of Los Angeles in passing), and Mac Speedie (pass receiving). Spec Sanders repeated as leader in rushing.

The final All-NFL Team of the 1940s had Waterfield, Van Buren, and Harder in the backfield along with Tony Canadeo of the Packers who had made it back in 1943. Pihos, Bray, Ramsey, Huffman, and Fears were picked in the line as were Fred Naumetz of the Rams at center and the Eagles' Vic Sears at left tackle.

In the last collegiate football season of the 1940s, Notre Dame captured its third undisputed AP poll national championship. Led by powerful end Leon Hart and backs Bob Williams and Emil Sitko, Frank Leahy's Irish rolled over ten opponents. Ohio State and Michigan tied for the Big Nine title, and Oklahoma, undefeated in ten games, copped the Big Seven championship and went on to romp in the Sugar Bowl over LSU, 35 to 0. California had a perfect ten-win record, only to lose in the Rose Bowl, 17 to 14, to Ohio State. SMU captured the Southwest Conference, and Tulane, the Southeastern Conference. Army was 8-0-1.

Leon Hart of Notre Dame won the Heisman Trophy in 1949. He is the last lineman to win that award. Hart also received the Maxwell Award and Knute Rockne Memorial Trophy, and teammate Emil Sitko, the Walter Camp Memorial Trophy. Ed Bagdon of Michigan State was the recipient of the Outland Trophy.

The Midwest dominated the Consensus All-America in 1949:

*E	Leon Hart	Notre Dame
E	Jim Williams	Rice
T	Alvin Wistert	Michigan
T	Leo Nomellini	Minnesota
G	Ed Bagdon	Michigan State
*G	Rod Franz	California
*C	Clayton Tonnemaker	Minnesota
B	Arnold Galiffa	Army
*B	Emil Sitko	Notre Dame
B	Bob Williams	Notre Dame
B	Doak Walker	SMU

* Unanimous selection

Doak thus became a three-time Consensus All-America. *Sport* said that Walker was "perhaps the

Michigan State's Ed Bagdon, 1949 Consensus All-American guard and Outland Trophy winner. (Courtesy Michigan State University.)

Clayton Tonnemaker, unanimous All-American center for Minnesota in 1949. (Courtesy University of Minnesota.)

155

SMU's Kyle Rote, 1950 Consensus All-American. A teammate of Doak Walker on the Mustangs, Rote starred in the famous 27-20 SMU loss to Notre Dame in 1949. He played in four NFL title games with the Giants before launching a successful television career in sportscasting. (Courtesy Southern Methodist University.)

greatest all-around player ever." That magazine in 1971 picked him as the top college football performer of the 1946–71 period, and it said:

Walker was perhaps the last incarnation of the All-American boy. He was boyishly handsome, he was appealingly modest and his deeds matched his appearance. And he came to flower when the country was still full of idealism. We had just won a great war, we still respected the old-fashioned virtues and we danced to the lyrics of "Isn't It Romantic?" and believed that life *was* romantic. . . . Doak Walker was the right man in the right place at the right time. He was the ultimate All-American.

SUMMARY

In sum, the Chicago Bears dominated the pro ranks, and Notre Dame, the college scene in the 1940s. The Bears won NFL championships in 1940, 1941, 1943, and 1946. The Eagles won the last two titles of the decade, in 1948 and 1949, and the Redskins (1942), Green Bay Packers (1944), Cleveland Rams (1945), and Chicago Cardinals (1947) each won one title. Losers in the league championship games but division winners included the Redskins in 1940, 1943, and 1945; the New York Giants in 1941, 1944, and 1946; and the Bears (1942), Eagles (1947), Cardinals (1948), and Los Angeles Rams (1949). Cleveland won four titles in the AAFC, and, as the 1950 season showed (when they won the NFL), they ranked with the best of the older league. Among the backs, the greatest stars were Sammy Baugh, Sid Luckman, Steve Van Buren, Bob Waterfield, and Pat Harder. The class of the linemen were Bulldog Turner, Danny Fortmann, Bruiser Kinard, and Don Hutson. Coaches George Halas and Earl "Greasy" Neale won three and two NFL crowns, respectively.

In college competition, Bernie Bierman's Minnesota opened the decade with two national championships, as determined by the AP poll, in 1940 and 1941. Ohio State, with Paul Brown as coach, was first in 1942, followed by Frank Leahy's first mythical title as coach of Notre Dame in 1943. His Irish squad also won in 1946 and 1949. Earl "Red" Blaik's Army team also won two, in 1944 and 1945. Finally, Michigan won a pair under Fritz Crisler and Benny Oosterbaan in 1947 (the final AP poll; Notre Dame won an earlier one) and 1948. Impressive winning streaks of the decade were topped by Michigan (1946–49) and Army (1944–47) with twenty-five and Notre Dame (1946–48) with twenty-one. Oklahoma won twenty-one straight in 1948 and 1949 and extended their string to thirty-one in 1950 before tasting defeat.

Frankie Albert, Tom Harmon, Frankie Sinkwich, Doc Blanchard, Glenn Davis, Bob Fenimore, Herman Wedemeyer, Johnny Lujack, Doak Walker, Charlie Trippi, "Choo Choo" Justice, and Emil Sitko were the most heralded of the college backs. Bob Suffridge, Alex Agase, Warren Amling, George Connor, Hub Bechtol, Chuck Bednarik, Alvin Wistert, Bill Fischer, Leo Nomellini, and Leon Hart topped the linemen.

Youthful enthusiasm for football was also manifested in ways other than reading about pro and college games, teams, and players. As mentioned, Young was a spectator at high school and college football games in the early 1940s. This football-watching continued throughout the decade. Hardly a home high school game played by Bob Young's alma mater, West High of Waterloo, was missed. From 1947 to 1949 the author sat on the opposite stands from his parents, with the junior high root-

Ohio State, 1942 national champions. The only loss (17-7) in Ohio State's 9-1 record was administered by Wisconsin, which featured All-American end Dave Schreiner (killed in World War II), fullback Pat Harder, and halfback Elroy "Crazy Legs" Hirsch. But Iowa edged Wisconsin, 6-0, the following week, and Auburn dumped previously unbeaten Georgia to enable the Bucks to win the mythical national title. (Courtesy Ohio State University Photo Archives.)

Michigan's Bennie Oosterbaan guided the Wolverines to a perfect season and national championship in 1948, his "rookie" year as head coach. He was named Coach of the Year. (Courtesy University of Michigan.)

Oklahoma State backfield great, Bob Fenimore. The "Blond Blizzard" was an All-American for Oklahoma A.&M. in 1944 and 1945 (a Consensus choice in the latter year), when he became the only player to average more than two hundred yards per game over two seasons. Fenimore paced the Cowboys to a 1945 Cotton Bowl win over TCU (34-0) and a 33-13 victory over St. Mary's and Herman Wedemeyer in the famous 1946 Sugar Bowl contest. (Courtesy National Football Foundation and Hall of Fame.)

Tennessee's guard on the Modern All-Time All-America Team, the late Bob Suffridge. Suffridge helped Tennessee to a 31-2 record from 1938–40, and berths in the Orange, Rose, and Sugar Bowls. In 1940, he was a unanimous All-American selection and winner of the Knute Rockne Memorial Trophy. (Courtesy University of Tennessee.)

ers. He paid much less attention to the game in those years.

West High's Wahawks, coached by Glenn Strobridge, had only a fair record in the early 1940s ("Stro" was a highly successful basketball coach at West for over twenty-five years), but even a losing season could be salvaged if East Waterloo's Trojans could be beaten in the last and ninth game of the season, traditionally played on the first weekend of November. Unfortunately, West suffered five defeats in a row at the hands of its city rival, which was coached by the late Leonard Raffensperger. Raff's record at East was so good that he was hired as head coach by the University of Iowa at the end of the decade.

Raff utilized the T-formation to good advantage at East in the period just after it was popularized by Clark Shaughnessy and George Halas. One of East's speedy backs, Don Commack, who excelled on the quick openers that characterized the T, went on to star for several years at Iowa.

Strobridge at West, on the other hand, utilized a formation called the "Y," which in some respects was a forerunner of the wishbone except that the quarterback, adjacent to the center, *faced* his other backs and away from the center, with his hands back through his legs. This curious stance facetiously came to be called "butt-to-butt." College coach Ossie Solem (once at Iowa) was credited as being the Y-formation's originator.

In the last part of the decade, the tables were turned, as West, under Coach Lou Breitbach, switched to the single-wing formation. In 1949 the Wahawks won the mythical state championship and defeated in the process a powerful Mooseheart, Illinois team that had compiled an impressive record. The clash was one of the best high school games ever witnessed by the writer. Lowell Sisson, one of the fine backs on that 1949 West team, went on to star as an end for four straight seasons at Army and was voted the most valuable athlete of both his high school and West Point classes.

Bob Young also took his family regularly to the home games of the University of Iowa at Iowa City. The Hawkeyes only had two winning seasons during the 1940s (1942 and 1946), but they were 4-4-0 in 1940 (the year after Kinnick and the Iron Men) and won four of nine in 1948 and 1949. They were 3-5-0 in 1941 and 3-5-1 in 1947, and never were winless. The late Dr. Eddie Anderson, one of college football's winningest coaches, was at Iowa from 1939–42 and 1946–49. Slip Madigan was at the helm in 1943–44, and Clem Crowe, in 1945.

One of Young's favorite Hawkeyes was Dick Hoerner, 1946 All-Big Ten fullback from Dubuque. Hoerner held the shot put record at Iowa when Young was participating there in that event from 1955–58. Hoerner went on to star for the Los Angeles Rams. Other All-Big Ten performers at Iowa in the 1940s were: Mike Enich (tackle, 1940 —also picked on *The Sporting News* and *New York News* All-America first teams), Tom Farmer (quarterback, 1942), Earl Banks (guard, 1946), and Bill Kay (tackle, 1948, also picked on the AP All-America, second team). Other sparkling performers were the diminutive quarterback Al DiMarco, ends Hal and Herb Shoener and Jack Dittmer (DiMarco's targets), Bob Smith, and Emlen Tunnell, who went on to stardom and All-Pro status as a defensive back for the New York Giants. The Youngs, of course, saw many of the great All-Americas and national championship teams of the era—from Notre Dame, Minnesota, Michigan, Ohio State, and other schools.

Another football activity from age nine on was entering the *Waterloo Daily Courier*'s "Major Hoople contest." Each Wednesday during the foot-

Dick Hoerner of Iowa, All-Big Ten fullback in 1946. Hoerner held the Iowa record for the shot put for many years. He went on to stardom as fullback for the Los Angeles Rams. (Courtesy Los Angeles Rams.)

The All-Big Ten quarterback and Drake Relays 100 yard dash champion in 1942, Tom Farmer of Iowa. Farmer went on to play with the Los Angeles Rams (1946) and Washington Redskins (1947–48). (Courtesy University of Iowa.)

Mike Enich of Iowa, 1940 All-American tackle and member of the "Iron Men." (Courtesy University of Iowa.)

Rugged All-Big Ten guard (1946), Earl Banks of the University of Iowa. Banks became athletic director for Morgan State University. (Courtesy University of Iowa.)

159

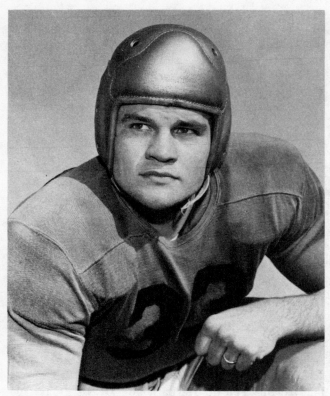

Stalwart tackle of the Iowa Hawkeyes, Bill Kay was All-Big Ten and second-team All-American in 1948. Iowa's MVP in 1946, Kay played in the 1948 North-South and 1949 College All-Star games. (Courtesy University of Iowa.)

Another manifestation of football mania was the playing of the Cadaco-Ellis game, Foto-Electric Football. The game is played with offensive cards (used by one player) and defensive sheets (used by the other player), the latter being placed over the former on top of a box illuminated from below with a light bulb. A cardboard piece just below the offensive card and defensive sheet is pulled toward the player, revealing a lighted line that progressively lengthens and snakes inside and outside potential tacklers (appearing on the defensive sheet on top in the form of dots). The cards and sheets are designed to represent the different plays

ball season the sports editor of the paper (Al Ney throughout much of the period) would list fifteen college games on the sports page. Contestants mailed in their picks of winners of those games by Friday, and in that evening's edition, the Major's predicted winners would be published. Contestants anxiously awaited the scores of games on Saturday, which could be anything from a contest involving Iowa State Teachers College (in nearby Cedar Falls) to Slippery Rock Teachers, Pennsylvania, to Southern Cal. Winners were those who picked more victors than Major Hoople (ties were losses for the contestants, and many times the author's picks were unfortunately the same as the Major's). Winners were announced in the following Monday's paper and were entitled to two free passes to a local movie theatre. Jimmy Young averaged about two victories a season over the Major, and once he even picked all fifteen winners (along with Hoople and a few hundred others), which entitled him to a free banquet. Oh, those were the days, my friend . . . (Actually, the *Courier* has continued to hold the contest.)

The late Emlen Tunnell, the Pro Football Hall of Fame's selection as the All-Time Best Safety. Tunnell broke his neck playing football for the University of Toledo, but later helped his school gain a NIT berth in basketball. After service in the Coast Guard, he resumed his collegiate career at Iowa. The first black to play for the New York Giants (1948-58), Tunnell broke NFL marks for interceptions, interception yardage, punt returns, and punt-return yardage. He was named All-Pro four times. (Courtesy University of Iowa Photo Service.)

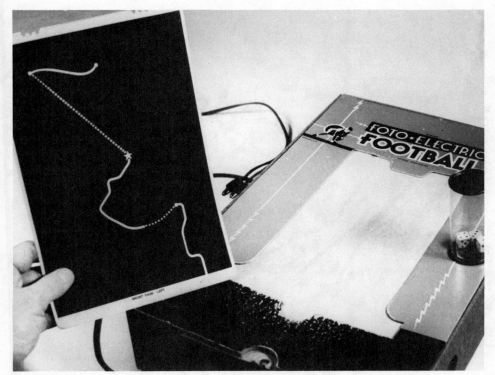

Foto-Electric Football. The offensive play (Short Pass—Left) is selected by one player and is not shown to the other player. (Copyright, Cadaco, Inc., Chicago, Illinois. Game is from collections of authors.)

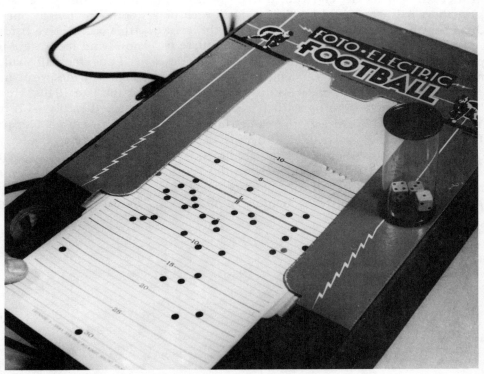

The defensive play (Very Strong Against Short Passes) is inserted face up into the Play Viewer. (From the collections of the authors.)

Modern (1975) edition of Foto-Electric Football Game. (Courtesy Cadaco, Inc.)

in football—off tackle, end run, line plunge, long pass, short pass, etc., (and "strong against" each of these for the defense). The choosing of the card and sheet, and the placing of them in different positions over the cardboard sliding piece, provides many variables and great excitement.

As in the case of the Cadaco-Ellis All-Star Baseball game, leagues were organized by solo player Young who also "broadcast" the games much like Bob Elston would re-create the details of away games from the bare-bones teletype accounts.

Finally in the late 1940s there were the beginnings of organized football for youngsters then in junior high. Here the fundamentals of blocking and tackling were learned, and the first permanent tooth was lost as one of the costs of participation (this was the age before the face mask, and broken noses and teeth were more common).

Thus football had a pervasive influence and made a widespread impact on the maturing child of the late 1940s. He read about it, listened to it, watched it, played it in organized and unorganized fashion, engaged in parlor games representing the sport, entered contests, bought and traded bubble gum football cards, and modeled his life after the Nile Kinnicks, the Tom Harmons, the Bob Chappuises, the Doak Walkers, and the other football heroes and All-Americans of the day.

162

5

BASKETBALL

As might be expected of boys in two Midwestern states, basketball was the sport of greatest interest in the winter months for authors McClure and Young. Wrestling occasionally rivaled it in importance in Waterloo, Iowa for Young, as that community has been a hotbed for the sport. But that is another story (see chapter 6). Although hockey was established as a professional sport, it did not appeal greatly to the writers, whose main exposure to hockey came from reading about it in magazines or newspapers. Measured by hours spent practicing, watching, and reading about the respective winter sports, basketball was certainly "number one."

Unlike the situations in football, baseball, and hockey, the current major professional league in basketball (the National Basketball Association—NBA) was not in existence in the early 1940s. There were professional leagues and teams prior to and during that time, but it was the college game that was the center of attraction. Even college basketball was young, relatively speaking, since the game itself had been invented as late as 1891. Twenty points per game was still an unusual point production for an individual player, and team scores in the thirties and forties were common. The jump shot was rarely used, and most set shots were of the two-hand variety. Underhand free throws were orthodox; dribbling and ball handling were emphasized more; and the "key" really looked like a keyhole, with its narrower width beyond the circle.

Madison Square Garden was the mecca of basketball, with its National Invitation Tournament (NIT) enjoying more prestige, vis-a-vis the NCAA tourney, than it does today. Ned Irish's college basketball doubleheaders at the Garden drew large

Author Young dribbling in his basement during the 1947–48 season.

Author McClure dribbling on an outdoor court as a youngster.

and enthusiastic crowds. New York City, with St. John's, Long Island University (LIU), and City College of New York (CCNY), was also a center of collegiate basketball power.

The national tournaments of college basketball were also in their infancy. The NCAA championships had only begun the previous year (Oregon won), and the NIT and National Association for Intercollegiate Basketball (NAIB and, since 1951, the NAIA) tourney were only two years old. Temple and LIU had won the first two NIT titles, and Central Missouri State and Southwestern (Kansas) were the initial victors in the NAIB, based in Kansas City.

1939–40

The first season overlapping into the decade of the 1940s was noteworthy for the fact that Dr. James Naismith, basketball's inventor, died in Lawrence, Kansas at age seventy-eight. Dr. Naismith had devised the game at (now) Springfield College in Massachusetts as a pleasurable means of indoor exercise and recreation during the winter months. He coached basketball at Kansas (1899–1907), and headed the physical-education department from 1899–1925. A physician and minister in addition to being a physical educator, Naismith was honored at the 1936 Olympics, and, there, tossed the ball at the first Olympic basketball game ever played. The Basketball Hall of Fame is named in his honor, and he was inducted posthumously as a member there in its first year (1961). He was also elected to the Helms Hall of Fame and the NAIA Hall of Fame.

Alexander Weyand, in his excellent history of basketball, thought that Indiana, the NCAA champion, "seemed most deserving of first place in the nation" in 1939–40. The "Laughing Boys"—as Coach Branch McCracken's Hoosiers were called —lost only three (all in the Western Conference or Big Ten) of their twenty-three games. In the NCAA Tournament, they disposed of Springfield (fittingly, New England's representative and best team in the season of Naismith's death), Duquesne, and then Kansas in the final game, 60-42, at the Kansas City Auditorium. Weyand called Indiana a "fast-breaking, hard-fighting team," which, while "roaring all over the court . . . dazzled spectators and opponents alike." Captain Marvin Huffman became the first recipient of the NCAA Tourney's Most Valuable Player (MVP) award. Bill Menke and Bob Dro were also Hoosier team leaders.

Weyand notes that the University of Southern

Coach of the 1940 NCAA basketball champions Branch McCracken of Indiana. (Courtesy Indiana University.)

California (USC), under Coach Justin "Sam" Barry, was acclaimed as the nation's best by "almost everybody" before the 1940 tournaments and the Helms Foundation and a "group of associated basketball authorities" thought they were the "U.S.A. champion" afterward, as well. Kansas nipped the Pacific Coast Conference champion Trojans by one point in the NCAA tourney. Ralph Vaughn led USC and was named an All-American. His nine field goals before 18,425 fans in Madison Square Garden, as USC broke LIU's forty-three-game winning streak, helped him obtain that honor.

The NIT champion in 1940 was Colorado, winner of the Mountain Big Seven Conference. The Buffaloes, coached by Forrest "Frosty" Cox, defeated De Paul and then Duquesne in the title game at Madison Square Garden. The championship victory avenged an earlier defeat by Duquesne. Missouri Valley champion Oklahoma A.&M. was third.

Bob Doll was a leader for Colorado as a sophomore. And the Buff's Jack Harvey was named a 1940 All-American. He had played for three conference champions under Coach Cox. Colorado was second in the NIT during his sophomore year.

A successful coach for Iowa and Southern California, Justin "Sam" Barry. Barry coached the Hawkeyes to shares of two Big Ten basketball titles in 1923 and 1926. His Trojan cagers won 260 and lost 130, and his 1948 USC baseball team won the NCAA title. (Courtesy University of Iowa.)

A third collegiate tournament champion was Tarkio College of Missouri in the NAIB at Kansas City. San Diego State with Milky Phelps took second after falling to Tarkio's Owls in the final game, 52-42. Melford Waits captained Tarkio and led the team in scoring. He won the tournament MVP and sportsmanship awards.

Another top-flight team was Kansas' Jayhawkers who were second in the NCAA tourney. Coach Phog Allen's Big Six champions defeated the Missouri Valley titlists Oklahoma A.&M. (who had split with Kansas in the regular season) to win their NCAA district. At the national tourney, Kansas defeated Rice and USC before bowing to Indiana. KU's Howard Engleman led the tourney scorers. Phog Allen's son, Bobby, was high scorer in the Indiana game. Ralph Miller was another Jayhawk star. He was to become a successful coach

at Wichita State, Iowa, and Oregon State. His teammate, Dick Harp, also became a major college coach. Because the Kansas players were small and spirited, they were called the "Pony Express."

The national scoring leader was Stanley Modzelewski with 509 points. His team, Rhode Island State, averaged seventy-five points per game. Gus Broberg of Dartmouth again broke the Eastern League's scoring record, and Illinois' forward and captain, Bill Hapac, took the season scoring honors in the Big Ten. UCLA's Jackie Robinson led Pacific Coast Conference scoring.

George Glamack of Southern Conference champion North Carolina was named by Helms as Player of the Year. The 1940 Helms Foundation All-American Team was as follows:

F	Ralph Vaughn	Southern California
F	Gus Broberg	Dartmouth
F	John Dick	Oregon
F	William Hapac	Illinois
C	George Glamack	North Carolina
C	Stanley Modzelewski	Rhode Island
G	Jesse Renick	Oklahoma A.&M.
G	Bobby Moers	Texas
G	John Lobsinger	Missouri
G	Fred Beretta	Purdue

Mentor of championship teams and coaches, Dr. Forrest "Phog" Allen of Kansas. In the forties, Allen's Jayhawks shared three conference championships (1940, 1941, and 1942) and won two others outright (1943 and 1946). The 1940 team reached the NCAA finals. Allen was once basketball's winningest coach, and he was succeeded in that honor by one of his former students, Adolph Rupp. (Courtesy University of Kansas.)

Wisconsin rose from rags to riches in the 1940–41 season—from near the bottom of the Big Ten the year before to the NCAA crown. The Badgers were also picked by the Helms Foundation as the national champion. Paced by All-American Gene Englund and John Kotz, Wisconsin won the Big Ten en route to a 20-3 season record. By the end of the NCAA tournament, it had avenged all three defeats. Coach Harold "Bud" Foster used a combination of short passing, the fast break, and deliberate ball handling with a shifting man-to-man defense. Wisconsin defeated Washington State in the final game of the NCAA tournament with spring-legged Englund scoring thirteen points and John Kotz, twelve. Kotz was named the tourney's

Kansas' Howard Engleman, 1941 All-American forward, paced the Jayhawks in 1940 to a runner-up finish in the NCAA Tournament. (Courtesy University of Kansas.)

Broberg, Renick, Lobsinger, and Moers were repeaters from Helms' 1939 All-America team.

Players picked on other All-America teams included outstanding dribbler Chet Aubuchon, diminutive guard from Michigan State; and James McNatt of Oklahoma, who set the single-game scoring record in the Big Six Conference.

The Amateur Athletic Union (AAU) Men's Tournament champions were the Phillips 66ers of Bartlesville, Oklahoma. They were led by All-American Grady Lewis, formerly of Southwestern Oklahoma State and Oklahoma. The AAU Women's Tourney was won by the Lewis-Norwood Flyers of Little Rock, Arkansas.

For the first time, a basketball game was televised. The telecast took place in Madison Square Garden on 28 February 1940, in a college basketball doubleheader.

Four-sport star, Jackie Robinson of UCLA. Robinson was the Pacific Coast Conference basketball scoring leader in 1939–40. He paced the Southern Division of the PCC in points the following year. (Courtesy UCLA.)

166

MVP. Charles Epperson, Fred Rehm, and Ted Strain rounded out the Badgers' lineup.

The author was to see Englund play many games for Oshkosh in the National Basketball League and later in the NBA—against the Waterloo Hawks. Coach Foster, who became professor of athletics at Wisconsin, starred for Mason City (Iowa) high school, Mason City Junior College, and Wisconsin, where he was named All-American. He also played pro ball with Oshkosh and other teams, and was named to the Helms and Naismith halls of fame.

Clair Bee's Long Island University team won the NIT; in the process, breaking Seton Hall's forty-three game winning streak. 1941 All-American Ossie Schechtman, Hank Beenders, and Si Lo-

Fred Beretta of Purdue, 1940 Helms Foundation All-American guard. (Courtesy Purdue University.)

The Phillips 66ers, 1939–40. Phillips' first NAAU championship team defeated the Denver Nuggets, 39 to 36, in the final tournament game. Coached by Chuck Hyatt, the team's record was 48-5. This was the thirteenth season for an Oilers team and their sixth NAAU tournament entry. Joe Fortenberry, Grady Lewis, and Don Lockard were 1940 AAU All-Americans. Shown are (l to r, front): Lloyd Tucker, Fred Pralle, Ray Ebling, Don Lockard, and Bill Martin; (back) Coach Chuck Hyatt, Grady Lewis, Joe Fortenberry, Fred Troutwin, Frank Groves, and Don Shields. (Courtesy Phillips Petroleum Company.)

The 1940–41 Wisconsin team, eating hearty breakfasts. After Coach Foster's first Wisconsin team won the Big Ten championship in 1935, his Badgers fell upon hard times, and the 1939–40 squad placed ninth in the conference. The 1940–41 season started inauspiciously with Wisconsin dropping nonconference games to Pittsburgh and Marquette, and losing their league opener with arch-rival Minnesota. Part of the team is shown here, on the morning of their 40-30 loss to Marquette, in Milwaukee's Blankinton Hotel coffee shop (21 December 1940). Left to right are: Ray Lenheiser (right arm and face partially visible), Fred Rehm, Warren Schrage, Charles Epperson, Ted Schiewe, Coach Foster, and John Kotz.

After their loss to the Gophers, the Badgers caught fire and won twelve consecutive games (including a nonconference victory over Butler) to win the Big Ten. (Courtesy University of Wisconsin and Coach Bud Foster.)

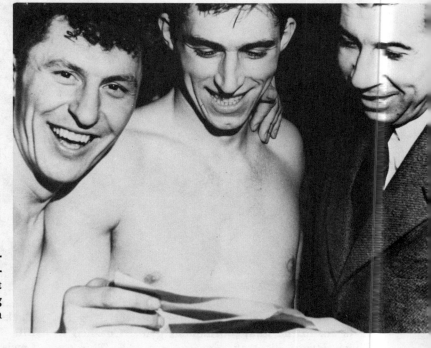

Jubilant John Kotz (left) and Gene Englund (center) with Wisconsin Coach Bud Foster (right), reading congratulatory telegrams. The Badgers had just clinched the 1941 Big Ten championship by tripping Illinois, 38 to 30. (Courtesy University of Wisconsin and Coach Bud Foster.)

Wisconsin's NCAA and Big Ten basketball champions (1941). Left to right are: Ted Strain, Bob Alwin, Gene Englund, Ted Schiewe, Charles Epperson, Warren Schrage, and Fred Rehm. Englund broke the Big Ten and Wisconsin season scoring records. (Courtesy Bud Foster and University of Wisconsin.)

Wisconsin Coach Foster and reserve center Don Timmerman during 1941 NCAA victory celebration. Approximately twenty thousand enthusiastic rooters at the Chicago North Western railroad station at Madison greeted the victorious Badgers upon their return from the NCAA finals at Kansas City. An old red Kissel fire engine ironically caught on fire during the festivities, when at least fifty people crowded on it for a ride. (The rear brake band smoked and then burst into a tiny flame because of the pressure on the rear of the vehicle.) One eager coed climbed the wall of the station to the platform top for a better look at her heroes. The Badgers' All-American center, Gene Englund, was not with the squad, as he was appearing before his local draft board in hometown Kenosha, and visiting his wife, who was teaching there. (Courtesy Bud Foster and University of Wisconsin.)

Northwestern Louisiana State was the NAIB Tourney's MVP and was his school's first All-American.

Twentieth-Century Fox of Hollywood, California won the Men's National AAU Tournament. Frank Lubin, one of five UCLA players to play for the 1936 U.S. Olympic team—the nation's first —led the movie studio club and was named a 1941 AAU All-American. His team had to defeat Phillips 66 and the San Francisco Olympic Club (which was led by the great Hank Luisetti) to win the 1941 championship. Helms picked Lubin as the greatest player in Southern California for the first half-century. Lubin played Frankenstein among other roles in the movies. The Lewis-Norwood Flyers of Little Rock defended their Women's AAU title successfully in 1941.

The 1941 Helms Foundation All-American Team was as follows:

Coach Bud Foster and Mrs. Foster at the 1941 NCAA victory celebration in Madison. Coach Foster, a member of the Naismith Hall of Fame and the Citizens Savings Hall of Fame, had been a 1930 All-American for Wisconsin. He replaced Dr. Walter Meanwell (a member of the same two halls of fame) as coach of the Badgers in 1934, and held that position through 1959. In addition to his 1941 NCAA and Big Ten titlists, his first Badger team (1935) and his 1947 squad won conference championships. (Courtesy Bud Foster and University of Wisconsin.)

bello led the Blackbirds to a 26-2 season record. They defeated Ohio University, 56 to 42, in the NIT final game before 18,377 spectators. LIU thereby became the first team to win the NIT twice.

Frank Baumholtz of runner-up Ohio University led the NIT scoring and was picked the MVP. He was named a 1941 All-American and went on to a brief professional basketball career (1946–47) and a longer professional *baseball* career (1947–57) with the Reds, Cubs, and Phillies. (The authors remember him as a baseball player only.)

San Diego State moved up from their 1940 second-place finish to the NAIB title in 1941. All-American Milton "Milky" Phelps again paced the California quintet. Charles "Red" Thomas of

Ohio University's Frankie Baumholtz, MVP and high scorer of the 1941 NIT. (Courtesy Ohio University.)

Most Valuable Player in the 1941 NAIB Tourney, Charles "Red" Thomas of Northwestern Louisiana. (Courtesy Northwestern State University of Louisiana.)

F	Gus Broberg	Dartmouth
F	John Adams	Arkansas
F	Howard Engleman	Kansas
F	Gene Englund	Wisconsin
C	George Glamack	North Carolina
C	Stanley Modzelewski	Rhode Island
G	Lee Huber	Kentucky
G	Milton Phelps	San Diego State
G	Walter O'Connor	Drake
G	Ray Sundquist	Washington State

George Glamack of North Carolina closed out his career in 1940–41 with a three-year total of 1,336 points. Called the "Blind Bomber" because of his weak eyes (it is said he "shot from memory"), Glamack scored forty-five points against Clemson and thirty-one in an NCAA game with Dartmouth. For the second time in a row, he was selected as Player of the Year by Helms. He was named to their All-American team again and to

the Helms All-Time All-American Team. Glamack, a tall forward, shot a "hook" with either hand.

Gus Broberg, a three-time All-American (1939–41) for Dartmouth led the Eastern League in scoring for an unprecedented third time. The Indians won their conference each of those years. Broberg made fifty-six consecutive free throws in games spanning two seasons, and was also a baseball star for Dartmouth.

Stan Modzelewski of Rhode Island State made the Helms All-America team for the second time. 1941 NCAA runner-up Washington State placed Ray Sundquist on the Helms honor team.

John Adams, a forward for Southwest Conference champ Arkansas, was the top scorer in the NCAA tourney (forty-eight points in three games). Lee Huber of Kentucky was Coach Adolph Rupp's seventh All-American. Huber relied on a long-range two-hand set shot. With basketball greats Bob Cousy, Bob Davies, Paul Arizin, and Ed Macauley, he was to be selected on the All-Time Sugar Bowl Team.

Howard Englemen was a forward for Kansas' Big Six co-champs (they tied with Iowa State) in 1941, after playing for the 1940 NCAA runner-up

A 1941 All-American guard, Walter O'Connor of Drake. (Courtesy Drake University.)

171

Three-time All-American, Gus Broberg of Dartmouth. (Courtesy Dartmouth University.)

Seton Hall's Bob Davies, 1941 All-American guard. As a star player for the Rochester Royals, he was All-Pro first team four times, and second team once. (Courtesy Seton Hall University.)

team. Engleman led the team in (season) scoring twice. In 1942 he played for the Phillips 66ers, who also placed second in the nation, but finished the season as coach of his collegiate alma mater after Phog Allen was injured.

Players selected on other All-American teams include Bob Davies of Seton Hall. An all-around star and excellent dribbler, Davies was a big factor in Seton Hall's forty-three consecutive victories from 1939 to 1941.

Other noteworthy players were William "Red" Holzman, member of CCNY's two NIT teams in 1941 and 1942, and future pro player and coach; and Charles "Buzz" Ridl of Westminster, who captained his Pennsylvania team to a position in the 1941 NIT. A member of Wyoming's 1941 NCAA Tournament entry later was to become famous as a television sports announcer. His name is Curt Gowdy.

1941–42

The 1941–42 basketball season had barely begun when Japanese air squadrons rained down bombs on Pearl Harbor. As was the case with other sports, war considerably altered the usual patterns of collegiate basketball. Many schools had to rely on seventeen-year-olds and/or freshmen (witness the Utah NCAA champions of 1944), 4-Fs, and others in deferred classifications. Colonel Weyand reported that thirty-eight conferences suspended operations in 1944, but many of the individual schools in those conferences were playing schedules, and some were strengthened in 1944 and 1945 by naval trainees based in university towns. Weyand thought the standard of play remained high during the war, despite the circumstances.

The 1942 NCAA championship went to the Stanford Indians, coached by Everett Dean. The Helms Foundation also picked Stanford (27-4 for the season) as the "U.S.A. Champion." Coach Dean had had successful records at Carleton College and Indiana (three Big Ten titles) before moving on to Palo Alto. There he won four Pacific Coast titles in his first four years and added the NCAA title in the fourth year. As a player for Indiana he had been an All-American in 1921. Ron Mendell notes that Dean has been acclaimed as "one of [the] game's finest gentlemen."

The NCAA title game pitted two teams nicknamed the "Indians" from opposite coasts at a site in the Heartland of America—the Kansas City Auditorium—before 6,000 fans. Stanford had defeated Rice and Colorado to reach the finals against

Curt Gowdy and the 1941 University of Wyoming basketball team. Everett Shelton's Cowboys won thirteen and lost six. They were champions of the Mountain Big Seven conference and participated in the NCAA tournament. Front row (l-r): Bill Strannigan, Charles Bentson, Curtis Gowdy; back row: Wilmer Rothman, Nick Krpan, James Smith, Karl Kerback. (Courtesy University of Wyoming.)

Dartmouth. Stanford's 1942 All-American Jim Pollard, the "Kangaroo Kid," had scored forty-three points (high for the tourney), but flu kept him out of the championship tilt. Sophomore Howie Dallmar picked up the slack admirably, scoring fifteen points (he was named the Tourney's MVP), and Stanford decisively turned back Dartmouth, 53 to 38. Co-captain Bill Cowden, a rebounding and defensive star, co-captain Donald Burness, and Edward Voss rounded out the starting five—called the "Iron Men" because they did most of the playing for Stanford.

Pollard went on to greatness in the pros. He played on five NBA championship teams with the Minneapolis Lakers and was named to the All-

Everett S. Dean of Stanford, coach of the 1942 NCAA champions. (Courtesy Stanford University.)

173

The "Kangaroo Kid," All-American, Jim Pollard. Pollard was a member of Stanford's 1942 NCAA champions, and was high scorer of the tournament. He was All-NBA twice for the Minneapolis Lakers, who dominated the league while he and George Mikan played for them. (Courtesy Stanford University.)

Howie Dallmar, one of Stanford's NCAA champion "Iron Men" of 1942. He was All-Pro for the Philadelphia Warriors in 1948. (Courtesy Stanford University.)

NBA first team twice. Young saw Pollard play for Minneapolis against the Waterloo Hawks before a record crowd at the Waterloo Hippodrome on New Year's Eve (1949). Player of the half-century George Mikan, Vern Mikkelson, Arnie Ferrin, Slater Martin, and Pollard made the Lakers overwhelming in the NBA that year and in succeeding seasons.

Dartmouth, again the champion of the Eastern League, downed Penn State and Kentucky to reach the NCAA finals. The runner-up team was coached by Osborne "Ozzie" Cowles, who, like Dean, had coached at Carleton. (Cowles went to college there, too.) All-American George Munroe led the 1942 Dartmouth club as well as the Eastern League in scoring. All-league Indian guard, Charles "Stubby" Pearson, never returned from a flight mission in World War II.

Big Ten champion Illinois was one of the most colorful teams of all time in the 1941–43 seasons. Guided by the 1941 Coach of the Year, Doug Mills, the Illini featured an all-sophomore starting lineup: Andy Phillip, Gene Vance, Ken Menke, Jack Smiley, and Art Mathiesen. This unit became famous as the "Whiz Kids." Andy Phillip was selected an All-American in 1942 and 1943, and was all-conference in 1942, 1943, and 1947. Young read about him in *Sport* and saw him play for Chicago in the NBA in later years. Jack Smiley became the player-coach of the Waterloo Hawks in the NBA in 1949–50, a season in which the author saw many of his boyhood basketball heroes play for the Hawks' opponents. Phillip was named to the Associated Press's All-Time All-American Team and to the Helms and Naismith halls of fame.

Doug Mills, former basketball team captain at Illinois, coached his "Whiz Kids" to Big Ten titles in 1942 and 1943, and enjoyed many other successful seasons as coach and athletic director at Illinois before retiring in 1967. One of the 1942 team's defeats was administered by the Iowa Hawkeyes, 46-32. Iowa, coached by the late Rollie Williams, tied for second in the Big Ten.

West Virginia (19-4), coached by Richard "Dyke" Raese, surprised the field and nation by capturing the NIT championship. Seeded last, the Mountaineers, led by All-American Floyd "Scotty" Hamilton, upset first-seeded LIU in the first round and then toppled Toledo and Western Kentucky State (47-45) for the title. West Virginia trailed during most of the final game, but pulled ahead on free throws by Roger Hicks and Hamilton to win. Captain Rudy Baric, who scored forty-eight points and played well defensively, was selected as the tourney's MVP.

Rhode Island's Stan (Modzelewski) Stutz (standing), Helms Foundation All-American center in 1940, 1941, and 1942. Playing for Coach Frank Keaney's racehorse Rhode Island State teams, Stutz was the nation's leading scorer twice. He broke the four-year major college scoring record with 1,730 points in eighty-one games. That accomplishment occurred during an era when twenty points in a game by an individual was unusual. Stutz is shown at a 1972 banquet during which he was inducted into the University of Rhode Island Hall of Fame. (Courtesy University of Rhode Island.)

Two-sport All-American, Ray Evans of Kansas. Evans was selected by the Helms Foundation as an All-American basketball guard in 1942 and 1943. In football, he received All-American commendations in 1942, 1946, and 1947. (Courtesy University of Kansas.)

NIT runner-up, Western Kentucky, was coached by Ed Diddle. Diddle's basketball teams used the fast break, while the coach threw and waved his red towel on the sidelines. He was the first to coach one thousand games at one college.

Another NIT entrant was Rhode Island State, which had a 78.9 scoring average for the year and featured Stanley Modzelewski, the nation's leading scorer again with 21.4 points per game. Modzelewski finished his career with 1,730 points, a four-year major college record. Helms picked him to their All-American team three times (1940–42).

The 1942 NAIB crown was won by Hamline of St. Paul, Minnesota. Junior John Norlander led the Pipers in scoring, as he did in three other seasons. Another member of the 1942 Hamline champs was Howie Schultz, who later played on major-league basketball and baseball teams. Young saw him as a member of the Anderson Packers in the NBL and NBA.

An old collegiate scoring record fell in 1942 when John "Broom" Abramovic of Salem College (West Virginia) totaled 777 points for a 29.2 points-per-game average. The latter figure broke Chris Steinmetz's record, which was set in 1905.

All-American Price Brookfield of West Texas scored 520 points in twenty-five games. Two years later he paced Iowa State to a Big Six title.

John Kotz, who had helped Wisconsin win first place in the 1941 NCAA Tournament, scored 242

First University of Evansville All-American, Wilfred "Gus" Doerner. (Courtesy University of Evansville.)

points in fifteen games to break the Big Ten scoring record. He was selected as a 1942 All-American by Helms, Converse, and *Pic*.

Kansas was co-champion of the Big Six with Oklahoma in 1942, and competed in the NCAA tourney. The Jayhawks were paced by Ray Evans, who was one of the few to be named as an All-American in both football and basketball. Author McClure's brother later went to the high school from which Evans graduated (Wyandotte in Kansas City, Kansas), and idolized this Kansas athletic hero. Evans was selected as a basketball All-American by Helms in 1942 and 1943.

The 1942 Helms Foundation All-American Team:

F	John Kotz	Wisconsin
F	Price Brookfield	West Texas State
F	James Pollard	Stanford
F	George Munroe	Dartmouth
C	Stanley Modzelewski	Rhode Island
C	Bob Kinney	Rice
G	Scott Hamilton	West Virginia
G	Ray Evans	Kansas
G	Bud Millikan	Oklahoma A.&M.
G	Andrew Phillip	Illinois

Another 1942 All-American was Wilfred "Gus" Doerner of Evansville, the first person chosen for that honor from that school. Doerner led his college team in scoring for three years. (He had 8.2 points per game as a sixteen-year-old freshman!)

The Denver American Legion team won the 1942 Men's AAU Basketball Tournament. Jack Harvey was a Denver star. The Davenport, Iowa, American Institute of Commerce team won the Women's National AAU Tournament.

1942-43

The 1943 NCAA champion was the first one of which the writer was aware at the time it was playing; that is, his knowledge of previous tourney winners has come *ex post facto*, usually from reading historical accounts. A *Life* magazine article about the Wyoming Cowboys caught the attention of the writer as a youngster learning to read. Wyoming's All-American player, Kenny Sailors, was featured in the magazine's pictorial account. The Cowboys (30-2), winners of the Mountain States Conference, turned back the bids of Texas and Oklahoma in the first two rounds of the NCAA, and then they defeated Georgetown in the final game, 46-34, at Madison Square Garden before 13,300 people. Captain Sailors was brilliant,

scoring sixteen points, and he was named the MVP. Teammate Milo Komenich scored forty-eight points in Wyoming's three games to lead tourney scoring.

In an American Red Cross benefit game, Wyoming won over St. John's, 52 to 47 in an overtime, with Cowboy James Weir scoring five of Wyoming's six points in the extra period and Komenich netting twenty in the whole contest. Wyoming also placed third in the National AAU tournament, losing in the semifinals to the Denver Legion team. The Cowboys defeated the Phillips Oilers twice in polio benefit games. Everett Shelton coached the 1943 Wyoming team.

St. John's Redmen (21-3), coached by one of the famous Original Celtics, Joe Lapchick, won the NIT by beating Rice, Fordham, and Toledo, in that order. Harry Boykoff of the Redmen was the high scorer of the NIT with fifty-six points. Young saw the rugged Boykoff play for the Waterloo Hawks in the NBA in 1949–50.

Andrew "Fuzzy" Levane also starred for St. John's in 1942–43. Sportswriters elected him the Metropolitan player of the year. Levane became a member of the champion Rochester Royals in 1946. He played with the football and basketball great, Otto Graham; pro basketball and baseball player, Del Rice; Bob Davies, Al Cervi, George Glamack, and Red Holzman.

Another excellent guard on the 1943 St. John's club was Richard "Tricky Dick" McGuire. McGuire was named All-Metropolitan four times with the Redmen. He also played with Dartmouth under the V-12 program and went on to an eleven-year career in professional basketball, mostly with the Knicks.

Coach Joe Lapchick did not receive a high school or college education, but went on to fame as a center with the Celtics and other pro clubs and as a coach of St. John's and the New York Knicks. His Redmen won four NIT titles.

Illinois' Whiz Kids were a year older and stronger in 1942–43. Alexander Weyand described them as "one of those superteams that appear now and then and elicit comparisons with the great teams of history." He added that they had "one of the smoothest and fastest attacks imaginable." Coach Doug Mills' Illini won all twelve games in the Big Ten en route to a 17-1 season record, their only loss at the hands of Camp Grant, a service club. In twelve games (rather than the fifteen in which previous conference records had been made) they broke the Big Ten team scoring record with 75 points; and Andy Phillip, an All-American for the

To the winners. Coming from behind in the last few minutes of play, a scrappy team from the University of Wyoming captured the 1943 NCAA basketball title by swamping Georgetown, 46 to 34, at Madison Square Garden. Here, Coach Everett Shelton (standing, center of group) receives the championship trophy from Professor Phillip O. Badger (standing, far right), president of the NCAA, as members of the team look on. First row (l to r): Don Waite, Earl "Shadow" Ray, and Jim Reese. Back row: Jim Collins, Floyd Volker, Milo Komenich, Coach Shelton, Lou Roney, Kenny Sailors, Jim Weir, and Professor Badger. (Courtesy University of Wyoming, Acme photo.)

second straight year, cracked the individual season mark with 225. Andy Phillip, Art Mathiesen, Jack Smiley, and Gene Vance were first-team All-Big Ten selections, and Ken Menke made the second-honor team. Never before had four from the same school made the first unit. The Whiz Kids did not participate in the NCAA tournament.

One of the entrants in the NIT was Rice, co-champion of the Southwest Conference. Their captain and conference scoring leader was Bill Closs. In addition to being selected All-League for the third time, Closs was picked as a 1943 All-American. He played on a fleet championship team in the Marines and went on to the pros. Young saw him when he played for the Anderson Packers in the NBL and NBA.

Ray Evans led Kansas to another Big Six championship. The Jayhawks won all ten conference

1943 All-American Ken Sailors of Wyoming. Sailors was MVP of the 1943 Tournament, won by the Cowboys. An AAU All-American, he also played pro ball for seven clubs from 1946–51. (Courtesy University of Wyoming.)

Princeton basketball star, John "Bud" Palmer. After naval duty, he played (from 1946–49) for the New York Knickerbockers in the BAA, averaging 11.7 points per game in his three seasons of pro ball. Palmer became a famous television sports announcer. (Courtesy Princeton University.)

Member of the AP's All-Time All-American Team, Andy Phillip of Illinois. The Granite City, Illinois flash was named to the Helms Foundation's All-American team in 1942 and 1943. Leader of the Illini's famous "Whiz Kids," Phillip sparked that unit to back-to-back Big Ten titles in 1942 and 1943. (Courtesy University of Illinois.)

games. The versatile Evans was named All-Big Six and All-American for the second consecutive year.

Oklahoma's NCAA entry was led by another all-around athlete and individual, Gerald Tucker. He was to repeat as an All-American after the war.

John Abramovic of Salem College scored 630 points, best in the nation for the second consecutive year, for a career total of 2,170 points in ninety-six games, a national record. His fifty-seven points in one game was also a national mark.

George Senesky of St. Joseph's of Philadelphia was the leading scorer in total points (515) and average (23.4) for major colleges. Senesky was picked as the Helms Foundation Player of the Year.

One 1943 basketball star was to succeed as a television sports announcer—that was John "Bud" Palmer of Princeton, who broke the Eastern League record with seventy-three field goals in twelve games.

Gale Bishop of Washington State led the Pacific Coast Conference in scoring and was named to All-Conference and All-American teams. Bishop became a two-time AAU All-American, and was selected on the All-Time Pacific Coast Conference team.

The 1943 Helms Foundation All-American Team:

F	Robert Gale Bishop	Washington State
F	Kenneth Sailors	Wyoming
F	George Senesky	St. Joseph's
F	Andy Phillip	Illinois
C	Gerald Tucker	Oklahoma
C	Bill Tom Closs	Rice
G	Raymond Evans	Kansas
G	William Morris	Washington
G	Robert Rensberger	Notre Dame
G	John Mahnken	Georgetown

Southeast Missouri State won the 1943 NAIB Tournament, and the Davenport A.I.C. successfully defended its Women's AAU National Championship. Phillips 66 took their second Men's National AAU crown. James McNatt of the champions was picked as an AAU All-American. The player-coach for Phillips was John "Jumpin' Jack" McCracken. McCracken had played high-school basketball for Hank Iba in Oklahoma City, and led his team to second in a national tournament. He followed his mentor to Northwest Missouri State and played center for the Bearcats, who won forty-three consecutive games and compiled a 31-0 season record in 1930. McCracken played for Phillips and Denver in the AAU circuit and was named AAU All-American eight times.

1 9 4 3 – 4 4

1940 had its "Laughing Boys"; 1942, its "Iron Men"; 1942 and 1943, its "Whiz Kids"; and 1944 had its "Cinderella Kids." The latter was Coach Vadal Peterson's Utah quintet, which averaged 18½ years of age per player. The Redskins were

Washington's Bill Morris, 1943 All-American guard selection of the Helms Foundation. (Courtesy University of Washington.)

the only team in the Mountain Big Seven to play a full schedule. After losing only three of twenty-two season games, all to service teams, Utah was knocked out of the NIT in the first round by Kentucky. When the Arkansas team was involved in an auto accident, Utah received a last-minute invitation to take the Razorbacks' place in the NCAA tourney at Madison Square Garden.

The Cinderella Kids fulfilled the impossible dream when they clipped Missouri and Iowa State and then, in the tourney finals, nipped perennial Eastern League champion, Dartmouth, 42-40, before 15,000 spectators. Freshman captain Herb Wilkinson (who transferred to Iowa the following year) sank a set shot with three seconds left in an overtime to win the crown for Utah. Arnie Ferrin, freshman All-American, scored twenty-two points in the game and received the MVP award.

Later, the Redskins defeated the Redmen of St. John's in a benefit game before 18,125 at the Garden by a 43-36 score. A player of Japanese ancestry, little Wat Misaka, sparked Utah with his exciting play.

The NCAA runnerup, Dartmouth, captured their seventh straight Eastern League championship, and toppled Ohio State and Catholic University in the NCAA tourney before bowing to Utah. Their only other loss in twenty-one games was to a service team, Mitchell Air Field. All-American Audley Brindley, a junior and captain of the Dartmouth Indians, led the Eastern League in scoring, and took the total point honors in the NCAA Tournament.

Joe Lapchick coached the St. John's Redmen to a successful defense of their NIT title, as the inexperienced team defeated Kentucky, Bowling Green, and DePaul (47-39). Bill Katsores received the MVP award. De Paul's George Mikan led NIT scoring with forty-nine points. "Big Number 99" had never played high school basketball, yet he was an All-American in this sophomore year of his college career. The Helms Foundation picked him as Player of the Year.

Kentucky, led by All-American Bob Brannum, won third place in the talent-laden NIT by topping Oklahoma A.&M. Kentucky was Southeastern Conference champion, and the Aggies were regarded as the best in the Missouri Valley Conference, which was temporarily defunct because of the war. Oklahoma A.&M. was led by another sophomore All-American, Bob "Foothills" Kurland, who was seven feet in height. Kurland, like Mikan, was to be a three-time All-American, and both were picked on the Helms All-Time All-American Team.

The Phillips 66ers, 1942–43. "Jumpin" Jack Mc-Cracken guided the 1943 Phillips team to its second NAAU crown in four years. The Oilers won four-teen of eighteen games in this war year, and turned back the defending champion Denver Legion team, 57-40, in the tourney finals. Jimmy McNatt and Fred Pralle were AAU All-Americans. Team members were (l to r, front): R. C. Pitts, Fred Pralle, player-coach Jack McCracken, Howard Engleman, and Gene Clark; (back) Don Shields, Bud Browning, Willie Rothman, and Jimmy McNatt. (Courtesy Phillips Petroleum Company.)

Army (undefeated in fifteen games and not en-tered in the post-season tourneys) was picked by the Helms Foundation as the 1944 national cham-pion. After coaching at Fordham for sixteen seasons, Edward Kelleher won this national honor and at-tained his only undefeated season in his first year as coach of West Point. He lost only once the fol-lowing year for a 29-1 two-year record at Army. Coach Kelleher died in 1945 while teaching basket-ball to officers in Germany.

Two football players from the backfield with Glenn Davis and Doc Blanchard paced the Army basketball team. One was All-American basketball star, Dale Hall, who led the team in scoring.

Doug Kenna, who was picked by Grantland Rice as the 1944 All-American quarterback, topped the Black Knights' basketball scorers in their win over Navy. The inspirational captain and center of the 1944 Army cagers was Edward Christl. Less than a year after graduation, Christl won a Distin-guished Service Cross and was killed in the war. John Hennessey, another gridder, and Robert Faas completed the first cadet unit.

The 1943–44 season was the first one in which the author regularly followed the Iowa Hawkeyes. The star of the Hawkeye quintet that year was deadeye Dick Ives, Young's first basketball hero. Ives scored forty-three points against Chicago for an all-time Iowa single-game scoring record, and paced the Big Ten scorers for the season. In Pops Harrison's first year as Iowa coach, the Hawkeyes tied for second in the Big Ten (won by Ohio State) with a 9-3 record and 14-4 overall. Dave Danner was selected as an All-Big Ten first-team choice and as a forward on *The Sporting News* All-American, second team. Ives was named to third-team units by coaches and writers for *Pic* and by Chuck Taylor for Converse.

The nation's team scoring leader again was Rhode Island State, and the latter's Ernie Calverley topped the nation's individual scorers with a 26.7 average. Young remembers Calverley as being well publicized in *Sport* in subsequent years.

The 1944 Helms Foundation All-American Team:

F	Dale Hall	Army
F	Bob Dille	Valparaiso
F	Arnold Ferrin	Utah
F	Otto Graham	Northwestern, Colgate
C	Audley Brindley	Dartmouth
C	Robert Brannum	Kentucky
G	George Mikan	DePaul
G	Alva Paine	Oklahoma
G	Robert Kurland	Oklahoma A.&M.
G	Bill Henry	Rice

The NAIB Tournament was not held in 1944 because of the war. Phillips 66, led by All-American James McNatt, took the Men's National AAU title again, and the Vultee Aircraft team of Nashville won the Women's AAU crown.

1944-45

The NCAA champion was Oklahoma A.&M., coached by the famed Hank Iba. The Helms Foundation also picked the Aggies as 1945 U.S.A. champions. In his second All-American season, Bob Kurland tallied 529 points and led the Aggies to a 27-4 record. In the NCAA Tourney they eliminated Utah and Arkansas and then turned back New York University by a 49-45 score. Kurland scored 65 points in the three games, and was named the Most Valuable Player.

The 1945 national champs were typical of Iba-coached teams, with emphasis on ball handling, defense, and passing. Kurland provided the scoring and rebounding punch in the pivot. Football star Cecil Hankins, Weldon Kern, Doyle Parrack, and Blake Williams rounded out the starting lineup. In an American Red Cross charity game after the NCAA tournament, Oklahoma A.&M. avenged a

regular-season defeat at the hands of De Paul by downing Coach Ray Meyer's crew, 52-44, before 18,158. Hankins scored twenty for the Cowpokes in that contest between basketball titans.

The De Paul Blue Demons were sparked again by big George Mikan, the 1944 and 1945 Helms Foundation Player of the Year. De Paul rolled over all of its regular season opponents except Illinois (with whom they split) and Great Lakes. In the NIT, De Paul conquered West Virginia, Rhode Island State, and, in the title game, Bowling Green, 71-54. After pouring through the nets a fantastic 120 points (53 against Rhode Island State!), Mikan was named the Tourney's Most Valuable Player. His 23.3 points per game led the major colleges. The NIT champs ran into their usual troubles with the NCAA titlist in the post-tourney charity game. De Paul was hurt against the Aggies when Mikan fouled out in the first half.

In addition to the mighty Oklahoma A.&M. and De Paul champions, there were "three formidable teams, each of which lost but once, [that] did not exhibit their wares at either tournament," to quote Alexander Weyand's description. One was Rice,

Kentucky's 1944 All-American center, Bob Brannum. (Courtesy University of Kentucky.)

The Phillips 66ers, 1943–44. The first Bud Browning-coached Phillips 66 team won the NAAU championship in 1944. They won thirty-four, while losing only three, and downed the Denver Legion again in the finals of the tourney. Gordon Carpenter, Fred Pralle, and Jimmy McNatt were AAU All-Americans. Members of the champion 1943–44 Oilers were (l to r, front): John Boerner, Fred Pralle, John Freiberger, Gordon Carpenter, and Martin Nash; (back) Jimmy McNatt, Dave Perkins, Willie Rothman, and player-coach Bud Browning. (Courtesy Phillips Petroleum Company.)

Coach of 1945 and 1946 NCAA champion Oklahoma A.&M., Henry Iba. Famous in more recent years for molding Olympic champion teams, Iba's squads employed outstanding defense and deliberate offense. They featured All-Americans Jack McCracken at Northwest Missouri State and Bob Kurland at Oklahoma A.&M. (Courtesy Northwest Missouri State University and Naismith Hall of Fame.)

The 1944–45 Bowling Green basketball team. Bowling Green's Falcons were second in the 1945 NIT. DePaul, with George Mikan, defeated them in the final game, 71 to 54. 1945 All-American Wyndol Gray was held to nine points in that game, but Don Whitehead and Johnny Payak took up the slack somewhat with seventeen and twelve, respectively. Seated (l to r) are: Tom Inman, Don Whitehead, Wyndol Gray, Don Otten, John Payak, and Jim Knierin. Standing are George Muellich (assistant coach) at the left and Harold Anderson (head coach) at the right. Number 5 is Leo Kubiak. (Courtesy Bowling Green State University.)

which won the Southwest Conference crown. All-American Bill Henry raised his own conference scoring record to 288 points. Coach Joe Davis' Owls lost only to the Oklahoma Aggies.

Army under Edward Kelleher won fourteen of fifteen, its only loss at the hands of Penn. Cadet Dale Hall had another All-American season for a team that beat Navy and NYU, among others. Navy lost only two games, the other at the hands of Bainbridge Naval Training Station, and the Midshipmen downed Penn.

The Iowa Hawkeyes were the other unit described by Weyand as formidable. Coach Lawrence "Pops" Harrison's crew won seventeen of eighteen games during the season, losing only to Illinois (which Iowa also defeated), and captured the Big Ten championship, the first undisputed Western Conference basketball title in Iowa's history.

There will never be another team like this one so far as Young is concerned, as it was his favorite as a youngster. His hero, forward Dick Ives, led the

team in scoring for the season and in its Big Ten games. Ives was picked as a first-team All-American by *Argosy* magazine (chosen by coaches and writers). Converse (Chuck Taylor) named him to their second team. Herb Wilkinson, who had sunk the winning goal for Utah in overtime to win the 1944 NCAA final game, was now playing for the Hawkeyes. The stellar guard and playmaker was named on the first Helms All-American team, second *Sporting News* unit, and third *Argosy* honor squad. Herb also was first-team All-Big Ten in 1945, 1946, and 1947. His brother Clayton also was selected on the All-Big Ten first team. Jack Spencer, Ned Postels, Dave Danner, and Murray Wier were the other members of that Iowa squad who did most of the playing.

Young listened to all of the Iowa games on WSUI, the university's radio station. Dick Yocum and Bob Brooks were the student broadcasters that year, and Young remembers their accounts as always exciting. Bob Brooks, now KCRG (television

Iowa, 1944–45 Big Ten champions. The Hawkeyes won seventeen and lost one (a single-point defeat at the hands of Illinois, whom Iowa beat later). Iowa was a contender for national honors, but did not participate in either postseason tournament.

Left to right are: Lawrence "Pops" Harrison, coach; Clayton Wilkinson, center; All-American Herb Wilkinson, guard; Jack Spencer, guard; All-American Dick Ives, forward; and Ned Postels, forward. (Courtesy University of Iowa.)

and radio) sports director in Cedar Rapids, also remembers that team warmly. It was his first of many years of broadcasting Iowa games.

The games were sponsored by the Iowa Dairy Association. Young remembers sending to WSUI for free press guides about the Hawkeyes. Often he listened to the games as he dribbled his basketball all over the basement recreation-room floor. "Games" would be played on that "court" with shots aimed at two blue dots on the white concrete wall near the ceiling. If the ball hit the ceiling and wall simultaneously and covered the blue dots, it was a basket. There was a free-throw line, of course, and a scorer's table, complete with a score sheet for

the game. With one person serving in several roles —as players, referees, scorer, fans, and broadcaster —whole conference schedules were played, and statistics carefully kept. All of this could be accomplished, of course, while the WSUI radio accounts of Iowa's games were being digested by the listener.

Illinois, who split with Iowa and De Paul, placed Walton "Junior" Kirk on the Helms Foundation's first All-American team. It was the Illini's first such choice since the Whiz Kids. Kirk was Illinois' captain in 1945 and the team's MVP in 1946.

Howie Schultz, member of Hamline's NAIB titlist in 1942, was back with the Pipers in 1944–45. He was picked on the Helms first team also.

Arnie Risen, Ohio State basketball star. Risen and Don "the Great" Grate led Ohio State to the 1944 Big Ten championship with a 10-2 record. They were two of the first outstanding "big" men of basketball. (Courtesy Ohio State University Photo Archives.)

Vince Hanson, All-American from Washington State, led the nation's scorers among the major colleges with 592 points in thirty-four games. The Rhode Island State Rams again topped the nation's scoring as a team, and their individual leaders, All-American Ernie Calverley and Dick Hole, scored 549 and 525 points, respectively.

The 1945 Helms Athletic Foundation All-American Team:

F	Bill Henry	Rice
F	Dale Hall	Army
F	Howie Schultz	Hamline
F	Max Morris	Northwestern
F	George Mikan	De Paul
F	Vince Hanson	Washington State
*D	Robert Kurland	Oklahoma A.&M.
D	Adrian Back, Jr.	Navy
D	Walton Kirk, Jr.	Illinois
D	Herb Wilkinson	Iowa

* In 1945 the Helms Athletic Foundation began selecting players for "forward" and "defense" positions. Centers could be named to either position.

Loyola University of New Orleans won the NAIB; Phillips 66, the Men's National AAU; and Vultee Aircraft of Nashville, the Women's National AAU championships. It was the third consecutive victory for the Oilers and fourth of the decade. Vultee's crown was their second in a row.

1945–46

Oklahoma A.&M. (31-2) became the first team to win the NCAA tourney twice, and they did it in consecutive years. In Bob Kurland's senior year, he scored 245 points for the Aggies in the conference, a new record. The Helms Foundation named him player of the year, and his team, the national champions. Weldon Kern, Samuel Aubrey, J. L. Parks, and Blake Williams were the other starters for Coach Hank Iba's 1945–46 squad. The Aggies lost only to De Paul (which also fell to the Aggies) and Bowling Green. Mendell states that Kurland's "one-on-one confrontations with George Mikan [were] a highlight of [the] pre-1950 era."

The Cowpokes downed Kansas in a regional playoff game, and defeated Baylor and California

Helms All-American in 1945, Adrian Back, Jr., of Navy. (Courtesy of the Naval Academy Athletic Association.)

185

The Phillips 66ers, 1944–45. Bud Browning's champions (36-7) had a narrow escape in the NAAU Tourney finals, winning by a single point over the Denver Ambrose, 47-46. Gordon Carpenter, Paul Lindemann, Jimmy McNatt, and Fred Pralle received AAU All-American honors. The team (l to r, front): Vernon Yates, Gordon Carpenter, Paul Lindemann, Charlie Halbert, Frank Schwarzer, Fred Pralle; (back) Allie Paine, Frank Stockman, Willie Rothman, Martin Nash, Bud Browning. (Courtesy Phillips Petroleum Company.)

in the first two rounds of the NCAA tournament. The final game between Oklahoma A.&M. and North Carolina was played before 18,479 at Madison Square Garden. The Aggies won the exciting game and the championship, 43 to 40, with Kurland scoring twenty-three and putting on an awesome all-around performance. Kurland was again named the tourney's Most Valuable Player.

Three-time All-American Kurland rejected professional basketball offers and played for the AAU Phillips 66ers from 1947–52. He played on two U.S. Olympic squads, in 1948 and 1952, the first American to do so.

As mentioned, one of the two conquerors of the

Three-time All-American, Bob Kurland. The Oklahoma A.&M. star paced the Aggies to NCAA tournament titles in 1945 and 1946, and he was tourney MVP both years. (Courtesy Phillips Petroleum Company.)

Charlie Black of Kansas, 1946 Helms Foundation All-American forward. He was known as "the Hawk" for his ability to steal the ball from opponents. (Courtesy University of Kansas.)

Aggies was Bowling Green. The latter school was paced by center Don Otten, who was named as an All-American. Young saw Otten star with Tri-Cities in the NBA. The Bowling Green ace played pro ball with five clubs from 1947 to 1953.

Kansas, vanquished by Oklahoma A.&M. in the NCAA regional playoffs, was Big Six champion. Charlie Black, a slender forward and center, was the Jayhawks' star. Black was named All-Big Six (as he was in 1942 and 1947) and All-American.

North Carolina, NCAA runnerup, defeated Ohio State and NYU in the tourney. Jim Jordan of the Tarheels was named as an All-American. He later transferred to Kentucky and played for the NCAA championship team of 1948.

Horace "Bones" McKinney was another star of that Tarheels team. Young saw him play in the NBA too.

Ben Carnevale, North Carolina coach, had a 51-11 two-year record there in 1945 and 1946, before going on to the Naval Academy. There he was named National Coach of he Year (1947).

One of North Carolina's 1946 NCAA victims was New York University. NYU featured the lean All-American guard, Sid Tanenbaum.

The Kentucky Wildcats (28-2) won the NIT in 1946 on a free throw by Ralph Beard in the final seconds. Their victim, by a 46 to 45 score, was traditionally high-scoring Rhode Island State. Captain Jack Parkinson led the Wildcats in scoring during the season with only an 11.3 average. Kentucky's points were well distributed among its starting five. That quintet also included All-Conference selections Beard, Jack Tingle, and Wallace Jones. Coach Adolph Rupp's crew swept through the Southeastern Conference (SEC) and the conference tourney without a defeat. They downed Arizona and West Virginia in the NIT before winning the finale. Weyand says that Kentucky was "generally rated second in the nation" in 1945–46. Jack Parkinson was All-SEC three times and was All-American in 1946.

Wallace Jones, since the fifth grade called "Wah Wah"—his younger sister's pronunciation of his first name—was All-Conference in basketball (four times!) and in football (twice). He was also All-American twice and played with the "Fabulous Five," as the Kentucky team by then was called, and on the professional Indianapolis Olympians. The Olympians frequently played the Waterloo Hawks in the 1949–50 NBA season, and the games were always well attended and exciting.

To the author, Ralph Beard will always be the epitome of the All-American basketball guard. The well-muscled Wildcat was a three-time All-American from 1947–49. A 1948 Olympian, he played for two years with the Indianapolis professional team of that name and was All-Pro both years.

One of the conquerors of the Wildcats during the season was Notre Dame. All-American "Crystal" Klier was the key to the Irish attack, as he had been in two previous seasons.

The NIT runner-up, Rhode Island State, was the New England Conference champion. Again the nation's leader in team scoring, the Rams featured the slightly built Ernie Calverley. He had helped win the NIT semifinal game over Bowling Green by sinking a fifty-five footer with two seconds remaining. That shot sent the game into overtime. He garnered MVP honors by his fifty-one tourney points and all-around play against Bowling Green and Kentucky.

De Paul declined to participate in the tournaments in 1946. In his senior year George Mikan scored 555 points in twenty-four games for a 23.1 points-per-game average, the latter figure being the nation's best among major colleges. A three-time All-American, Mikan was to be named by the Associated Press as Basketball Player of the First Half

The 1944–45 Rhode Island State basketball team, semifinalists in the NIT. Left to right are: Coach Frank Keaney, Mike Santoro, Dick Hole, Ernie Calverley, Al Nichols, and Bob Shay. DePaul wrecked the Rams' tourney chances, 97 to 53, as George Mikan's fifty-three points equaled Rhode Island's entire output.

In 1946, Rhode Island, with Calverley, Hole, Nichols, and Shay returning, was nipped by Kentucky, 46 to 45, in the thrilling NIT finals. The versatile Keaney and his wife, Winifred, coached and taught most sports (Frank was even a chemistry teacher) at Rhode Island State. (Courtesy University of Rhode Island.)

Century. The Helms Foundation selected him as player of the year twice. Whereas Kurland helped bring about a ban on goal-tending because of his shot blocking, Mikan's dominance around the basket provided a catalyst for widening the lane.

The 1946 Helms Athletic Foundation All-American Team:

F	Max Morris	Northwestern
F	Charles Black	Kansas
F	Leo Klier	Notre Dame
F	Tony Lavelli	Yale
F	Robert Kurland	Oklahoma A.&M.
F	George Mikan	De Paul
D	Sid Tanenbaum	NYU
D	Jack Parkinson	Kentucky
D	Paul Huston	Ohio State
D	James Jordan	North Carolina

Southern Illinois State Teachers (now Southern Illinois University) won the NAIB tourney. One NAIB school, Hamline, was paced by guard Rolland Seltz who earned All-American honors in 1946. Seltz later played with the Anderson Packers and Waterloo Hawks.

The author met some of his basketball heroes when his father took him to the dressing room of the Iowa Hawkeyes after an exciting victory over Purdue at Iowa City in 1946. Young met and obtained the autographs of Dick Ives, Clayton and Herbert Wilkinson, Jack Spencer, Murray Wier, and Coach "Pops" Harrison, among others.

Herb Wilkinson was picked by The Sporting News and the Helms Foundation on their second All-America teams, and Ives was on True magazine's third team (picked by coaches and writers). Both had been first team choices in 1945.

George Mikan of DePaul, the AP's Basketball Player of the First Half Century. "Big Number Ninety-nine" was a three-time All-American for the Blue Demons from 1944–46. Mikan was All-Pro six times, and the leading scorer and player for the dominant team in the NBA's early years—the Minneapolis Lakers. Here he is shown rebounding, in a 1942 game against Camp Grant in Chicago Stadium. (Courtesy DePaul University.)

The Phillips 66ers with star James McNatt won the Men's National AAU crown for the fourth consecutive year. The Nashville Goldblumes won the Women's AAU championship.

1 9 4 6 – 4 7

An important development in *professional* basketball occurred in 1946, when the predecessor of the current National Basketball Association (NBA) was formed. The Basketball Association of America (BAA) was organized in June of 1946, and league play began that November. The teams were controlled by Eastern arena owners, most of whom had had experience in running pro hockey franchises. The original teams numbered eleven: the Boston Celtics, Chicago Stags, Cleveland Reb-

Ohio State's Paul Huston, 1946 All-American. (Courtesy Ohio State University Photo Archives.)

189

The Phillips 66ers, 1945–46. AAU All-Americans Gordon Carpenter, Jimmy McNatt, Bill Martin, and Martin Nash paced the Phillips crew to a fourth consecutive NAAU title in 1946. The Oilers (43-5) checked the San Diego Dons in the final game of the tournament, 45 to 34. Members of the squad were (l to r, front): R. C. Pitts, Kenny Jastrow, Jimmy McNatt, Lonnie Eggleston, Martin Nash, Bill Martin, and Cab Renick; (back) Trainer "Doc" Johnston, Manager R. H. Lynn, Paul Lindemann, Gordon Carpenter, Grady Lewis, and Coach Bud Browning. (Courtesy Phillips Petroleum Company.

els, Detroit Falcons, New York Knickerbockers, Philadelphia Warriors, Pittsburgh Ironmen, Providence Steamrollers, St. Louis Bombers, Toronto Huskies, and Washington Capitols.

A sports editor of the *New York Journal-American,* Max Kase, had been one of the early leaders in organizing the league. Walter Brown, president of the Boston Garden, Al Sutphin of the Cleveland Arena, and Kase sold their idea to Ned Irish, Madison Square Garden promoter, and other influential people. Maurice Podoloff of New Haven, then head of the American Hockey League, became the first president.

Professional basketball, of course, was not new in 1946. In 1898, seven years after Naismith's in-vention of the game, a professional circuit called the National League was formed. It was short-lived, as were other professional associations established in small geographic areas. The best teams were actually independents like New York's Original Celtics and Tex Rickard's Whirlwinds who thrived on tours and barnstorming, although they would also enter, and win, leagues.

An attempt to establish a truly major association was made in the 1920s when the American Basketball League was formed. In the initial 1925 season, it had teams in Washington, Detroit, Rochester, Brooklyn, Chicago, Cleveland, and Fort Wayne. New York and Philadelphia were admitted after the 1925–26 season.

The league did not operate in the Depression years of 1932 and 1933. When it resumed activities, the South Philadelphia Hebrew Association (the Sphas), coached by Eddie Gottlieb, won the 1934 title and six of the next twelve championships. The Celtics, owned by singer Kate Smith, were one of the other better-known teams in the ABL. The American League survived the BAA but was relegated to minor status. Most of the American League's stars went into the BAA when the latter was formed.

The National Basketball League (NBL) was formed in 1937, with teams in Anderson (Indiana), Chicago, Detroit, Fort Wayne, Indianapolis, Moline, Oshkosh, Rochester (New York), Sheboygan, Syracuse, Toledo, and Youngstown. Most of the teams were sponsored by businessmen or industries indicated by the teams' nicknames (e.g. the Anderson Duffey Packers, Fort Wayne Zollner Pistons, and the Chicago Gears).

The founder of the Oshkosh All Stars, Lonnie Darling, was also a prime mover behind the organization of the NBL. The winners of the National League before 1947 were:

1938	Akron Goodyear Tires
1939	Akron Firestones
1940	Akron Firestones
1941	Oshkosh All Stars
1942	Oshkosh All Stars
1943	Fort Wayne Zollners
1944	Fort Wayne Zollners
1945	Fort Wayne Zollners
1946	Rochester Royals

The 1945 Zollner Pistons defeated the College All-Stars, 63 to 55, at the Chicago Stadium before 23,912 people. In 1946 Ward "Piggy" Lambert became commissioner of the league after stepping down from his position at Purdue. Most of the NBL players stayed with their clubs when the BAA was formed.

The arrival of George Mikan in the National League in 1946 was comparable to the signing of Red Grange with the Bears in terms of the stimulus it gave to the professional sport. The Chicago Gears, with Mikan, won the 1947 playoffs after tying for third in the Western Division. Fort Wayne player-coach, Bob McDermott, had transferred to Chicago at midseason. But league rules provided that the champion was the team with the best record for the entire season. Coach Les Harrison's Rochester Royals fit that description. Al Cervi of the Royals, one of the few pros who had not gone to college, led NBL scorers with 632 points. Cervi and teammate Bob Davies, Mikan,

McDermott, and Fred Lewis of the Sheboygan Redskins made the All-League team.

The first BAA season (1946–47) featured a runaway in the Eastern Division by the Washington Capitols. Coach Arnold "Red" Auerbach, a twenty-nine-year-old with only high school coaching experience, guided the team (recruited from fellow ex-servicemen) to a 49–11 season. That record was not bettered for twenty years. The Capitols' guards were Bob Feerick, Freddie Scolari, and Irv Torgoff. Bones McKinney, John Norlander, and John Mahnken were in the front court.

Feerick, from Santa Clara, was the BAA's second leading scorer that year and was named to the first All-League Team. He led the league twice in free-throw and field-goal percentage. Freddie Scolari was All-BAA second team. North Carolina All-American McKinney was a first-team choice.

Runnersup to Washington in the regular season, but playoff (and thus official 1947 BAA) champions were the Philadelphia Warriors, coached by Eddie Gottlieb. Joe Fulks of the Warriors led the league with 23.2 points per game, nearly seven points (per game) more than second-place Feerick, who had 16.8. Fulks' scoring was a product of a jump shot that he pioneered, and he was the only unanimous All-League selection. Young saw him play for the Warriors against Waterloo in a later year.

1943 College Player of the Year and St. Joseph's All-American George Senesky was in the Warriors' backcourt. Angelo Musi, Art Hillhouse, and Jerry Fleischman also played for Philadelphia.

The Chicago Stags and St. Louis Bombers tied in the Western Division, and the Stags won a one-game playoff in overtime. Coached by Harold Olson, who had just left behind a successful career at Ohio State, the Stags eliminated the Capitols four straight in the playoffs and ultimately finished second to the Warriors. Chicago's Max Zaslofsky of St. John's University was first team All-League that year and for the next three seasons as well. Using a two-hand set shot, he averaged 14.8 points in 540 pro games. Chuck Halbert, Don Carlson, Tony Jaros, Marv Rottner, and Jim Seminoff were the others who did most of the playing for the Stags.

The first All-BAA Team for 1946–47 was:

Joe Fulks	Philadelphia
Bob Feerick	Washington
Bones McKinney	Washington
Max Zaslofsky	Chicago
Stan Miasek	Detroit

An intent crowd watched 1949–50 NBA action between the Philadelphia Warriors and the Tri-Cities Blackhawks. At right (10) is the late "Jumping Joe" Fulks. He was the scoring leader in the first season of the BAA, one of the two leagues that merged into the NBA. The Philadelphia Warriors won the BAA championship that year. In 1949, he scored sixty-three points in one game against the Indianapolis Jets. Fulks was first team All-Pro in 1947, 1948, and 1949. (Courtesy Murray Wier.)

The second honor unit included:

Ernie Calverley	Providence
Frank Baumholtz	Cleveland
John Logan	St. Louis
Chuck Halbert	Chicago
Fred Scolari	Washington

Feerick led the league in field goal percentage (40.1), and Scolari, in free throw percentage (81.1). Calverley had the most assists.

Four of the league's eleven teams permanently disbanded after the 1946–47 season. The third, fourth, and fifth place teams in the Western Division—the Cleveland Rebels, Detroit Falcons, and Pittsburgh Ironmen—plus one of the teams tied for fifth (last) in the Eastern Division—the Toronto Huskies—folded up shop.

The NCAA title was won by a school east of the Mississippi for the first time in 1947, when Coach Alvin "Doggie" Julian's Holy Cross Crusaders (27-3) turned the trick. And the New England school, also named the national champion by the Helms Foundation, did not even have a court of its own and had to play all of its games away from home.

Holy Cross' losses were suffered during Christmas break at the hands of Duquesne, Wyoming, and North Carolina State. In the NCAA tourney at Madison Square Garden, the Crusaders downed Navy, City College of New York (CCNY), and, in the final, Oklahoma, by a 58-47 score before 18,445. In all three NCAA games Holy Cross came from behind to win. The Oklahoma contest was tied eleven times. The winners' switch to a fast break in the second half helped change the game in their favor. All-American George Kaftan scored 63 points and rebounded well for Holy Cross in the three games and was named MVP. Co-captains Joe Mullaney and Kenneth Haggerty, Dermott O'Connell, and Frank Oftring were the other regulars. Bob Curran and a freshman guard named Bob Cousy were also members of the Crusaders team.

Coach Julian's Holy Cross players were experts at ball handling, and most became college coaches. Julian moved on to Dartmouth where he won three Ivy League championships.

Oklahoma, the NCAA runnerup, was paced by Gerald Tucker, Helms Foundation Player of the Year and All-American. Like Tony Lavelli and Otto Graham, Tucker was skilled in athletics and music. He was Big Six tennis champion in 1942, and sang with a university quartet and choir. Later he played for three years with Phillips 66 and made the AAU All-American team. He also coached the 66ers for four years, and his 1958 team was national champion. In 1956 Tucker coached the Olympic gold-medal team.

Utah, with Coach Vadal Peterson and All-Americans Arnie Ferrin (member of the 1944 "Cinderella Kids") and Vern Gardner, was the 1947 NIT champion. The Indians did not even win the Big Seven Conference (Wyoming did), and lost five regular-season games. But in the NIT they defeated West Virginia, avenged an earlier loss by downing Duquesne, and, using ball-control tactics, upset top-rated Kentucky, 49 to 45, before 18,467 in the final. Little Wat Misaka was another returnee from the Cinderella Kids, and he helped oust Duquesne in the semifinal with a last-minute basket. Vern Gardner, who led tournament scoring with 51 and rebounded well, was named MVP.

Kentucky's Wildcats won the SEC title and sported a 34-3 record for the season before placing second in the NIT. Ralph Beard and Alex Groza were selected as All-Americans in 1947. Groza—brother of Lou "the Toe," famous kicker for the Cleveland Browns—was the top scorer and rebounder for the "Fabulous Five" (Beard, Groza, "Wah Wah" Jones, Kenny Rollins, and Cliff Barker). Cliff Barker had been a B-17 gunner in the war and was shot down over, and imprisoned in, Germany for sixteen months. He polished his passing skills in the prison camp. Mendell points out that ten years separated his first and last year at Kentucky. An All-American transfer from North Carolina's 1946 NCAA runner-up team, Jim Jordan, also played for the Wildcats.

Texas' third place NCAA finishers were led by All-American guard John Hargis. He went on to play for Anderson, Tri-Cities, and Fort Wayne from 1948–51.

Lew Beck teamed with All-American Red Rocha on the Pacific Coast Conference champion Oregon State team. Beck went on to be captain of the 1948 Olympic team. Three-time all-conference Rocha played and coached in both collegiate and pro ranks.

The 1947 Helms Athletic Foundation All-American Team:

F	Gerald Tucker	Oklahoma
F	John Hargis	Texas
F	George Kaftan	Holy Cross
F	Ralph Hamilton	Indiana
F	Don Barksdale	UCLA
F	Ed Koffenberger	Duke
D	Sid Tanenbaum	NYU
D	Arnold Ferrin	Utah
D	Ralph Beard	Kentucky
D	Leland Byrd	West Virginia

Marshall College of Huntington, West Virginia, ousted favored Hamline and went on to the championship in the grueling thirty-two team NAIB tournament at Kansas City. The National AAU Men's Tournament was won by the Phillips 66ers for the fifth straight time and the sixth of the decade. Atlanta Sports Arena won the Women's title.

1 9 4 7 – 4 8

In professional basketball, the Minneapolis Lakers took over the franchise of Detroit and were admitted into the National Basketball League. Flint also came into the NBL, while Chicago and Youngstown folded. The Lakers dominated the Western Division and won the playoffs for the 1948 league championship. George Mikan, who had moved to the Lakers from the defunct Chicago Gears, led the league in scoring with 1,195 points. He and his teammate, Jim Pollard, made the All-League Team with Marko Todorovich of Sheboygan and Red Holzman and Al Cervi of Rochester.

The coach of the Lakers was former Minnesota All-Big Ten star, Johnny Kundla. Kundla had played for the Gophers' conference cochampions of 1937.

In the 1948 BAA season, another newcomer to a professional league "took all the marbles" when the Baltimore Bullets defeated the Philadelphia Warriors, defending champions, in the final play-

1947 UCLA All-American Don Barksdale. Barksdale, a 1948 Olympian, played AAU ball and then became one of the first blacks in the NBA. (Courtesy UCLA.)

Ed Koffenberger, 1947 All-American forward for Duke. (Courtesy Duke University.)

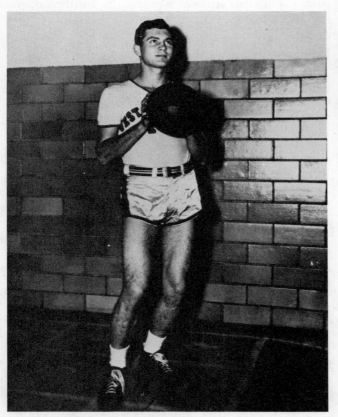

Leland Byrd, All-American in 1947, for the West Virginia Mountaineers. (Courtesy University of West Virginia.)

The Phillips 66ers, 1946–47. The 1947 version of the Phillips 66ers made it five national titles in a row by overpowering the Oakland Bittners, 62 to 41, in the tournament finals. Bob Kurland, in his first year with the Oilers, led the team in scoring (as he was to do for the next five seasons) and was named AAU All-American, along with Gordon Carpenter, Martin Nash, and Cab Renick. With Kurland in the lineup, the Oilers compiled a 52-2 record. (L to r, front): R. C. Pitts, Ed Beisser, Bob Kurland, Gordon Carpenter, Cab Renick, Coach Bud Browning; (back) Lonnie Eggleston, Martin Nash, Frank Stockman, Buddy York, Jack Perrault, Weldon Kern. (Courtesy Phillips Petroleum Company.)

1947 NAIB champions, Marshall University. In the front row (l to r) are: Bill Hall, Bill Toothman, Andy Tonkovich, Gene James, and Mervin Gutshall; in the second row: Coach Cam Henderson, Dick Erickson, Jim Bakalis, Bob Wright, and manager John Wellman. In the rigorous NAIB tourney at Kansas City, the Thundering Herd (32-5) defeated Wisconsin State in the opener, 113-80, setting a tournament scoring record and winning the hearts of the fans. In the second round, Marshall edged by one point the NAIB favorite, Hamline University. Hamline's Pipers featured Vern Mikkelsen (later of Laker fame). A basket by Tonkovich won it with eight seconds left. Marshall then defeated Eastern Washington (56-48) and Emporia State (56-55)—Toothman scored with twenty seconds remaining in the latter game. A final-game victory over Mankato State (73-59) gave Marshall the championship. The Marshall players were given a dollar a day for meals during the tournament. (Courtesy Marshall University.)

off series. Harry "Buddy" Jeannette was player-coach for the Bullets. He teamed with veteran pros and Purdue's Paul Hoffman to help Baltimore take second in the Western Division before winning the league title via the playoffs route.

Red Rocha, All-American center from Oregon State, had joined the Bombers of St. Louis and was an immediate star. St. Louis won the Western Division by one game; the other three teams were tied for second. Baltimore eventually won the second spot, Chicago was awarded third, and Washington fourth, after divisional playoffs of the tie. The Chicago Stags had added two of the Whiz Kids, All-American Andy Phillip and Gene Vance. All-League Stan Miasek from the defunct Detroit team was another valuable addition. Chuck Halbert, 1947 second team All-BAA center, had been sent by the Stags to the Warriors.

In the East, the Warriors nosed out the Knicks by one game. The only noncompetitive team in both divisions was Providence (6-42) in the East.

The Knicks obtained Bud Palmer of Princeton and Helms three-time All-American Stan (Modzelewski) Stutz from the fast-breaking Rhode Island Rams. Another Knick find was Colgate's Carl Braun, a fine shooting guard. He broke a league record by scoring forty-seven in a game against Providence. Another "name" ballplayer added to the Knicks roster was Sid Tanenbaum of NYU.

Max Zaslofsky led the BAA in total points with 1,007 for a 21.0 average. The Warriors' Joe Fulks led in points-per-game with 22.1. Bob Feerick of the Capitols had the highest field-goal and free-throw percentages, and Howie Dallmar of the Warriors was first in assists.

Zaslofsky, Fulks, Feerick, Dallmar, and Ed Sadowski of Boston made the first All-BAA Team. Braun, Miasek, and Jeannette were on the second team, along with John Logan of St. Louis and Fred Scolari of Washington.

The season had been exciting, but with competition from the NBL (which had the better players), and from the AAU, the NIT, and NCAA tourneys; the Olympic Games, and the collegiate basketball doubleheaders in large cities—the financial situation of the BAA (unlike the NBL) was not sound. Rejecting Ned Irish's advice to be patient, Maurice Podoloff engineered a coup during the summer of 1948 by first luring into the BAA the Indianapolis Kautskys (owned by a florist) and the Fort Wayne Zollner Pistons, and then the cream of NBL teams—the Minneapolis Lakers and Rochester Royals. As Leonard Koppett so candidly stated: "In effect, the National League was dead, then and there, although it went on with eight teams. . . ." One of those was the Waterloo Hawks.

The "Fabulous Five" of Kentucky University was the dominant team of the 1947–48 collegiate season, winning the SEC without a loss and rolling over Columbia, Holy Cross, and Baylor to win the NCAA championship. In the Olympic playoffs, they defeated Louisville and Baylor, but lost to the Phillips 66ers, 53 to 49, in the final game. In the NCAA title game with Baylor, Kentucky won, 58 to 42. Alex Groza was voted the MVP of the NCAA Tourney in which he scored 54 points. Captain Ken Rollins, Groza, Ralph Beard, "Wah Wah" Jones, and Cliff Barker made the Olympic team, and Adolph Rupp was chosen assistant coach. Groza led Wildcat scorers in all games with 488, and Beard was a close second with 476. Bill Schroeder, the Helms Foundation director, called this team the "best that had yet appeared in the college arena."

Adolph Rupp eventually became the "winningest" college coach with an 874–190 won-loss record. A protégé of Phog Allen at Kansas University, Rupp coached basketball at Marshalltown (Iowa) and Freeport (Illinois) high schools, before going on to the college ranks at Kentucky. The Wildcat coach for forty-two years, Rupp won eighteen SEC and four national championships.

Kenny Rollins played two years at Kentucky and three years of service ball. He then returned to Kentucky to become a member of the Fabulous Five. He was All-Conference twice.

Groza and Beard were All-Americans for the second time. 1946 North Carolina All-American Jim Jordan again played on the Wildcats' team.

St. Louis University (24-3) lost the Missouri Valley Conference because of two narrow defeats by Oklahoma State (they also lost to De Paul in a divided series), but the Billikens breezed through their games against Bowling Green, Western Kentucky, and NYU to win the National Invitation Tourney. Weyand says, "the team was hailed as one of the most talented ever seen in Madison Square Garden." All-American Ed Macauley scored 24 of St. Louis' points in their 65-52 title game victory over NYU before 18,491. He was chosen the MVP of the tourney. Captain Dan Miller, ball-handling expert D. C. Wilcutt, and rebounder Joe Ossola also starred for St. Louis. First-year coach of the Billikens in 1947–48 was Edgar "Eddie" Hickey. "Easy Ed" Macauley (six feet eight inches, 175 pounds) was a hometown star for the Billikens.

Rich Koster, in an article entitled "A Team to Remember," states:

In 25 years St. Louis U. basketball has climbed some peaks. And since the Cardinals first pennant

The University of Kentucky's 1948 basketball squad—
NCAA champions. Front row: Coach Adolph Rupp,
Johnny Stough, Ralph Beard, Captain Ken Rollins,
Cliff Barker, Dale Barnstable, Assistant Coach Harry
Lancaster. Back row: Manager Humzey Yessin, Gar-
land Townes, Jim Jordan, Joe Holland, Alex Groza,
Wallace Jones, Jim Line, Roger Day, Trainer Wil-
bert "Bud" Berger. (Courtesy University of Kentucky.)

"Easy Ed" Macauley lets fly in an NBA contest be-
tween the St. Louis Bombers and the Quad-City
Blackhawks in the 1949–50 season. Blackhawk players
are Dike Eddleman (11), Marko Todorovich (21),
Dick Schultz (3), and Warren Perkins (7). (Courtesy
Murray Wier.)

in the 1920s, St. Louis has known and loved some great sports champions.

But the 1947–48 Billikens were unique. They have never been matched, and they never will be.

He notes that except for a reserve player, all of the Billikens were from the St. Louis area. Nearly half were World War II veterans. Danny Miller flew thirty missions over Germany as a B-17 gunner. D. C. Wilcutt participated in the invasion of the Phillipines.

Koster relates that the Reverend Paul C. Reinert (now president of St. Louis University) in 1948 was a young Jesuit who often traveled with the team. Reinert remembers the players in these terms:

> They were as fine a group of young men as I've ever met. . . . They weren't concerned with who got the credit or the publicity. They were a team in the best sense of the word.
>
> And I remember how the people in New York loved them.

John Flanagan, who coached all of these boys to a conference title in 1947 before giving up the reins to Hickey, notes that "they were young and wonderful, all local boys." He states they had played against each other in high school and enjoyed liking "each other after having been opponents." The players came to school and went home after practice on buses, and few had been sought by college coaches when they were high-school athletes. "That bunch of skinny, swift, and short-haired kids" were close on and off the court, and most have maintained their friendships with each other since the championship year.

The NYU team, second-place finishers in the NIT, were sparked by captain Ray Lumpp, their season's scoring record holder. Lumpp played on the 1948 Olympic gold-medalist team at London and then with the pros for five years.

The Violets (22-4) also featured a rangy forward named Dolph Schayes, an all-around performer with a deadly two-hand set shot from the corners. Schayes went on to stardom with Syracuse in professional ranks.

Baylor won the Southwest Conference as well as finishing second in the NCAA. They defeated Arizona, Border Conference champion, in an NCAA regional playoff, and then won over Washington and Kansas State in the national tournament. Robert "Jack" Robinson and Don Heathington were the Bears' leaders. Robinson, who was voted Texas' all-time best high-school basketball player, was a three-time All-League choice and was All-American in 1948. Known for his ball handling and defense, Robinson made the 1948 Olympic team.

Holy Cross was third in the NCAA. They won twenty straight before their tournament loss to Kentucky. All-American George Kaftan and Bob Cousy were on that Holy Cross team.

Another NCAA contender was Michigan, coached by Osborne "Ozzie" Cowles, former Dartmouth coach. He guided Michigan to its first undisputed Big Ten title since 1927.

A third-place finish in the NIT and the Southern Conference title went to North Carolina State. Dick Dickey, whom Young often read about in *Sport*, played four years for North Carolina State, and the team was league champ each year. Dickey was All-Conference and All-American three times.

A sharpshooting redhead from Iowa named Murray Wier broke the Big Ten scoring record with 272 points in twelve games. He had a 21.0 average for the whole season, scoring 399 in nineteen games. Wier, who had played with the Wilkinson brothers and Dick Ives in previous years, was picked on the first All-American Team by the Associated Press, Helms Foundation, *Sports Week*, Curt Gowdy, and broadcasters. Murray was picked as the Most Valuable Hawkeye in 1947 and 1948, and in the latter year he won the Chicago Tribune's silver basketball, awarded to the most valuable player in the Big Ten. He was All-Big Ten in 1948 and, along with Chuck Darling of Iowa, is a member of the All-Time All-Big Ten Team. Pops Harrison's 1948 Hawkeyes finished second in the Western Conference with an 8-4 record. The team was 15-4 overall.

Wier could fire the ball from any point on the floor, and often used a hooking action while facing the basket. He had uncanny accuracy and frequently shot while off balance. Young saw him play for Iowa and then for Tri-Cities in the NBA, when he played against the Waterloo Hawks in 1949–50. The author then played against Murray Wier's East Waterloo teams while representing city rival West. Wier's 1974 team won the state championship, and he has taken East High teams to the state tourney many times.

Also in 1947–48 Arnie Ferrin of Utah made an All-American team for the third time. The 1948 Helms Athletic Foundation All-American Team was as follows:

F	Tony Lavelli	Yale
F	Murray Wier	Iowa
F	Richard Dickey	North Carolina State
F	Duane Klueh	Indiana State

C	Ed Macauley	St. Louis
C	Jack Nichols	Washington
D	Ralph Beard	Kentucky
D	Kevin O'Shea	Notre Dame
D	Arnold Ferrin	Utah
D	Andrew Wolfe	California

Tony Lavelli was an accordion player and hook-shot specialist. In 1948 he broke the Eastern League scoring record by totaling 236 points in twelve games. Jack Nichols of Washington broke the Pacific Coast Conference record by racking up 265 points in sixteen games. O'Shea was outstanding with Notre Dame for four years. Duane Klueh played three years for Indiana State, and two of those were for John Wooden, later to be the Wizard of Westwood (coach of the highly successful basketball dynasty at UCLA). Klueh was All-Tournament in the NAIB in 1948 and 1949, in addition to his All-American selection by Helms. He is a member of the All-Time NAIA All-Tournament Team and the NAIA Hall of Fame.

The Nashville Goldblumes captured the title in the Women's AAU Nationals. Louisville won the 1948 NAIB tournament, and the Phillips 66ers were first in the Men's NAAU Tournament, as well as in the Olympic Playoffs.

Omar "Bud" Browning, All-Big Six selection three times and All-American for Oklahoma in 1935, was coach of the 66ers while they won five NAAU titles from 1944–48. As coach of the Olympic Playoffs champion, he was named mentor of the 1948 Olympic basketball team.

The Olympic team included, among others, the Phillips 66 starters and the Fabulous Five from Kentucky. In a series of exhibition games, the team raised enough money to pay all of their expenses and contribute $75,000 to the Olympic Committee.

Kieran and Daley said that Bob Kurland of the 66ers, at seven feet "undoubtedly was the tallest athlete the Olympics ever have produced." The Yanks also had one of the shortest in Joe DiPietro (four feet six inches, a weightlifter). They both won gold medals. The Americans did get a scare when they had to rally to defeat Argentina, 59 to 57, in their third game of the tournament. Otherwise they had clear sailing, and they demolished France, 65 to 21, in the final game.

Gordon "Shorty" Carpenter, who played his college basketball at Arkansas, was a member of the 66ers when they won six straight NAAU championships. He was an AAU All-American five times for Phillips and once for Denver Chevrolet.

Don Barksdale, UCLA All-American in 1947, was the first black to play for the U.S. Olympic

1948 Helms All-American, Dick Dickey of North Carolina State. (Courtesy North Carolina State University.)

basketball team. He was an AAU All-American for four seasons, playing for the Oakland Bittners and Blue and Gold Atlas. When the NBA ban on blacks was removed, he played in the pros for Baltimore and Boston.

Vince Boryla of Notre Dame and Denver Universities played AAU ball for the Denver Nuggets and was a member of the 1948 Olympic team. He was picked as an All-American for Denver University in 1949 at age twenty-eight. His college career spanned a ten-year period and was interrupted by the war.

The late Lew Beck, 1947 Oregon State All-American, captained the 1948 U.S. Olympic basketball team. He was one of the five Oilers. Another

Iowa's Murray Wier goes up for a layup as an intent referee looks on. (Courtesy Murray Wier.)

Iowa's spectacular Murray Wier, 1948 Consensus All-American. Famous for his unorthodox but accurate shooting techniques, Wier broke Andy Phillip's Big Nine scoring record with 272 points in twelve games, for a 22.6 points per game average. He received the Chicago Tribune Silver Basketball Award as the conference's MVP, and was picked on the first All-Big Nine Team, as well as on nearly everyone's All American team. Wier astounded even the most seasoned observers with his incredible shooting displays. The fiery redhead played in the NBL and NBA with the Tri-Cities Blackhawks (the franchise now called the Atlanta Hawks), and then became a highly successful basketball coach at East Waterloo High School. (Courtesy Murray Wier.)

Washington's Jack Nichols, 1948 Helms All-American. Nichols scored over five thousand points for four pro clubs from 1948–58. (Courtesy University of Washington.)

Indiana State University Coach John Wooden with his 1948 NAIB runner-up Sycamores. Left to right: Don McDonald, All-American Duane Klueh, Jim Powers, Bobby Royer, Coach John Wooden, Dan Dimich, Len Rzeszewski. Wooden moved on to UCLA as coach after that season. The Sycamores were third in the 1949 NAIB tourney. They won it in 1950—without Klueh and Wooden—under Coach John Longfellow. (Courtesy Indiana State University.)

The West Team of the 1948 College All-Stars. The East defeated the West in Madison Square Garden, 58 to 47. The players are (front row, l to r): Murray Wier, Iowa; Dan Miller, St. Louis; Gene Berce, Marquette; Richard Shrider, Ohio University; and Andy Wolfe, California; (second row) A. L. Bennett, Oklahoma A.&M.; Otto Schnellbacher, Kansas; Ed Mikan, DePaul; Jack Burmaster, Illinois; Arnold Ferrin, Utah; Thornton Jenkins, Missouri; and Alex Hannum, Southern California. Wier, Bennett, Schnellbacher, Burmaster, and Hannum were starters. Wier, Wolfe, and Ferrin were Helms All-American selections, and Dan Miller played for St. Louis' NIT champions. The West coach is Ed "Moose" Krause, who became Notre Dame's athletic director. (Courtesy Murray Wier.)

The Phillips 66ers, 1947–48. The Oilers added the Olympic Playoffs crown and their sixth consecutive NAAU title to a growing list of laurels. Kurland, R. C. Pitts, and Renick were AAU All-Americans. Those three, plus Lew Beck and Gordon Carpenter, made the Olympic team, joining the "Fabulous Five" of Kentucky that Phillips had beaten in the finals of the trials. The Oilers' season record was 62-3, and they downed the Denver Nuggets in the NAAU title game. Left to right: Bob Kurland, Ed Beisser, Gerald Tucker, Cab Renick, Jack Perrault, Lew Beck, Coach Bud Browning, Gene Jones, Buddy York, Dick Reich, R. C. Pitts, Gordon Carpenter. (Courtesy Phillips Petroleum Company.)

1949 Consensus All-American, Vince Boryla of Denver. (Courtesy University of Denver.)

66er on the Olympic squad was the 1939 and 1940 Oklahoma State All-American, Jesse "Cab" Renick.

1948-49

In the final full season of the 1940s, the Anderson Packers, coached by Murray Mendenhall, won the Eastern Division and the playoffs for the 1949 NBL championship. Don Otten of Tri-Cities (Davenport, Moline, and Rock Island) was the leading scorer in the league with 872 points. Otten, Dick Mehen of the Waterloo Hawks, Al Cervi of the Syracuse Nationals, Frank "Flash" Brian of Anderson, and Gene Englund of the Oshkosh All Stars (the Western Division champion) were named to the All-League Team. Dick Mehen of the hometown pro club was Young's favorite player. Mehen was amazingly accurate with a two-hand, over-the-head jump shot.

Denver, Dayton, Hammond, and Waterloo were new members of the National League in 1948-49. Toledo and Flint had dropped out. The NBL had reorganized after Podoloff had lured away Minneapolis, Rochester, Fort Wayne, and Indianapolis.

The Minneapolis Lakers, with the great George Mikan, Jim Pollard, and Arnie Ferrin, won the championship playoffs in the BAA after finishing second in the Western Division during the regular season. Playing the last three games with a broken hand, Mikan scored 1,698 points and averaged 28.3 for the sixty-game season. Arnie Risen of the Rochester Royals led the league in field goal percentage (42.3), and Bob Feerick of the Washington Capitols, in free throw percentage (85.9). Bob Davies of the Royals had the most assists (321). Rochester had edged Minneapolis in the Western Division by one game, and Washington had won the Eastern Division by six games over the runner-up Knicks. Joe Fulks of the Warriors broke the single-game scoring record with 63 points. Mikan, Fulks, Davies, Zaslofsky of the Stags, and Pollard made the All-NBA first team. Risen, Feerick, Bones McKinney of Washington, Kenny Sailors of Providence, and John Logan of St. Louis were on the second unit.

In August of 1949, with the backbone of the NBL broken by the loss of four of its top teams to the BAA the previous year, the BAA and NBL merged into a single, seventeen-team league called the National Basketball Association (NBA), the name of the most prestigious professional basketball league today. Providence and the Indianapolis Jets went out of business. Anderson, Denver, Syracuse, Sheboygan, Tri-Cities, and Waterloo (NBL teams) were admitted into the new circuit with the remainder of the BAA clubs. And four of the Fabulous Five (Beard, Groza, Barker, and Jones), having graduated from Kentucky, came into the NBA as the Indianapolis Olympians. Three divisions were established in the new league, the Eastern consisting of most of the old BAA East (New York, Washington, Philadelphia, Baltimore, and Boston). Syracuse's record was to count in the Eastern Division standings, but its schedule was to be similar to those in the Western Division. The latter was composed of other (i.e., in addition to Syracuse) NBL teams plus the Olympians. Minneapolis, Rochester, Fort Wayne, Chicago, and St. Louis comprised the Central Division. Koppett describes the "merger" in these terms:

> In short, what the B.A.A. had done was to invite the dying remnants of the National League to join in their own financial burial. It would have been more forthright (but perhaps sticky legally, on antitrust grounds) to refuse to admit them.

Actually the attendance of teams like Waterloo in 1949-50 was to rival what some NBA teams draw today, but Waterloo, Denver, Sheboygan, and Anderson were dropped from NBA membership after that season (Tri-Cities was to lose its franchise to Milwaukee a year later), because they were too "small-time" for Irish, Podoloff, and other NBA moguls.

At any rate, it was great while it lasted for Waterloo residents like Young who were able to see the world's best basketball teams—the Minneapolis Lakers, Rochester Royals, Indianapolis Olympians, Syracuse Nationals, New York Knicks, etc.—during the winter of 1949-50. The author was privileged to watch all of the players on the All-NBA first team (Mikan, Pollard, Groza, Davies, and Zaslofsky) and second five (Brian, Fred Schaus of Fort Wayne, Dolph Schayes of Syracuse, Cervi, and Beard), among other great stars. Moreover, playing in exhibition at the Waterloo Auditorium (Hippodrome) were Abe Saperstein's famed Harlem Globetrotters with the "Clown Prince of Basketball," Reese "Goose" Tatum. In addition to that long-limbed, loose-jointed comedian, the Trotters featured Nat "Sweetwater" Clifton, the first black to play in the NBA (1951) and an amazing ball handler; and Marques Haynes, a superlative dribbler.

Young's hometown Waterloo Hawks were coached by "Whiz Kid" Jack Smiley (who also played guard). They were led by Dick Mehen (who topped the Hawks' scorers with a 14.4

average) and Harry Boykoff. The Hawks were an exciting club but had to battle to a fifth place finish (out of six teams) in the Western Division and a 19-43 record. Waterloo had close rivalries with Indianapolis and Tri-Cities (who featured Don Otten and Murray Wier among other stars).

The 1948–49 collegiate season was the last year in the amateur ranks for Beard, Groza, Barker, and Jones, and Coach Rupp's stars closed out their careers at Kentucky by successfully defending their NCAA championship. The Wildcats (32-2) were beaten by St. Louis (with All-American Ed Macauley) in the Sugar Bowl championship game and by Loyola of Chicago in the opening round of the NIT. But they defeated Villanova, Illinois, and Oklahoma A.&M. to win the NCAA tourney at the University of Washington's Edmundson Pavilion. The win in the finale over the Aggies was by a 46-36 score. Groza, who tallied 82 points in the tourney to break a record, was named MVP for the second time, and he and Beard were first-team All-American selections for the third consecutive year. Groza, who set twenty-two SEC records, was named on the All-Time NCAA Tournament Team.

Oklahoma A.&M., NCAA runnerup, was regarded as second best in the nation. Using the patented Iba style of ball control and sound defense, the Aggies were 23 and 5 for the whole year. Their captain, Bob Harris, was named a Helms All-American. He was Bob Kurland's successor at the center position in Coach Iba's lineup.

San Francisco (25-5) won the NIT after being unseeded at the beginning of the tournament. Coached by Pete Newell, the Dons notched victories over Manhattan, Utah, Bowling Green, and Loyola of Chicago, in that order, to win the coveted title at Madison Square Garden. In the last contest, Ross Guidice sank a free throw with forty seconds remaining to provide San Francisco with the margin of victory, as they edged Loyola, 48 to 47. The champions' Don Lofgran was named the MVP. John Benington, later a successful coach, was the Dons' captain.

Illinois won the Big Ten and was third in the NCAA tourney. They were paced by All-Americans Dwight "Dike" Eddleman and Bill Erickson. "Dike" Eddleman was one of the nation's greatest all-around athletes. An Olympic placer in the high jump, he was the Illinois captain and top scorer in 1948–49, and was the punter for the victorious Illini in the 1947 Rose Bowl game against UCLA. He received eleven letters, most ever won by an Illinois athlete in modern times, and the Big Ten Medal for Athletics and Scholarship.

All-American Paul Unruh of Bradley was high scorer in the NIT tourney with eighty points and figured in one of the first-round upsets of four basketball powers (Utah, with All-American Vern Gardner, was defeated by San Francisco; Kentucky, by Loyola; St. Louis, by Bowling Green; and Western Kentucky State, by Bradley). Four New York teams—Manhattan, St. John's, NYU, and CCNY—were invited to play in the NIT this time, and all tasted defeat in a preliminary round, dubbed the "Manhattan Massacre."

Accordionist and All-American Tony Lavelli broke the Eastern League record for total points in a season with 256 in twelve games, as his team, Yale, won the conference crown. Minnesota (18-3) placed their tall center (and Iowa's nemesis), Jim McIntyre, on the *Colliers* All-American team.

The Helms Athletic Foundation's 1949 All-American Team:

F	Tony Lavelli	Yale
F	Ernie Vandeweghe	Colgate
F	Vince Boryla	Denver
F	Vern Gardner	Utah
C	Alex Groza	Kentucky
C	Ed Macauley	St. Louis
D	Ralph Beard	Kentucky
D	Robert Harris	Oklahoma A.&M.
D	William Erickson	Illinois
E	Slater Martin	Texas

Hamline (28-3) won the NAIB title to become the first school to win it twice. Hal Haskins, who later played for Waterloo, paced the Pipers and later was picked on the All-Time NAIB All-Tournament Team and as a member of the NAIA Hall of Fame.

The Nashville Goldblumes continued their dominance in Women's AAU basketball by winning the national tournament. The final game was an all-Nashville affair with the Goldblumes defeating the Business College, 35 to 17. The six-year victory string by the Phillips 66ers in the NAAU Men's Tournament was broken when the Oakland Bittners downed the defending champs, 55 to 51. Don Barksdale, UCLA All-American, led the Bittners with seventeen points in the title game.

The decade of the 1940s closed just prior to the victory by unranked CCNY in the 1950 NIT and NCAA tourneys. The double championship has never been equaled, and it was achieved by a team with no great star (although Irwin Dambrot was named an All-American).

The curtain also was drawn on the decade while most people were unaware that in some games in the last few years points had been "shaved"; in other contests the whole affair was "rigged." The

Paul Unruh rises to miss a shot against Stanford during Bradley's 46-45 win in the 1947–48 season. Unruh scored 1,822 points in his four-year collegiate career, and was All-American in 1949 and Consensus All-American in 1950. (Courtesy Bradley University.)

gan to dominate the sport. The fast break or "race-horse" basketball was refined by the high-scoring Rhode Island State five and was increasingly used. The NCAA and NIT tourneys survived the strains of war and their first full decade of existence. The NAIB became a center of attraction for the smaller schools. (All three tourneys had been started in the late 1930s.)

The professional scene featured decentralization at first. The establishment of the BAA in 1946 by powerful arena owners in large Eastern cities eventually triggered the merger of the new association with the older National League and ultimately the demise of most of the latter's teams. The synthesis, called the NBA, was an infant at the close of the decade, but was to become a giant in subsequent years.

The powers of the 1940s in collegiate basketball were Oklahoma A.&M. and Kentucky, the only two teams that won two NCAA titles. St. John's won two NIT championships, and Utah won one NCAA and one NIT crown. Hamline took the honors among the small schools in the NAIB. Col-

divulgence of that scandal in 1951 rocked the sports world in a way that was comparable to the impact of the West Point cribbing exposure of the same year, and the Black Sox episode of 1919.

SUMMARY

The 1940s had seen the game of basketball develop and change in many respects. In the 1948–49 season, one player (Paul Arizin of Villanova) scored 85 points in one game, a very high score for a *team* at the beginning of the decade. The jump shot became popular, and the broader lane and prohibiting of goal tending were reactions to the widespread employment of the lanky centers or "goons" (as their opponents called them) who be-

1949 All-American guard, Slater Martin of Texas. (Courtesy University of Texas.)

The only team to win the Grand Slam of basketball— the NCAA and NIT championships—in one season, the 1949–50 CCNY Beavers. All-American Irwin Dambrot was the MVP in the national collegiate tourney, and Ed Warner took similar honors in the NIT. (Courtesy of the City College of New York.)

or was not lacking in the 1940s with championship teams being named the "Laughing Boys" (Indiana in 1940), the "Pony Express" (Kansas in 1940), the "Iron Men" (Stanford, 1942), the "Whiz Kids" (Illinois, 1942 and 1943), the "Cinderella Kids" (Utah, 1944), and the "Fabulous Five" (Kentucky, 1948 and 1949).

There were individual stars galore. George Glamack of North Carolina, George Mikan of De-Paul, and Bob Kurland of Oklahoma A.&M. were picked on the All-Time All-American College Team by the Helms Athletic Foundation. Mikan was named the Basketball Player of the Half Century by the Associated Press. Three-time All-Americans included Stan Modzelewski of Rhode Island State, Gus Broberg of Dartmouth (including 1939), Mikan, Kurland, Arnie Ferrin of Utah, Alex Groza and Ralph Beard of Kentucky, Tony Lavelli of Yale, and Dick Dickey of North Carolina State. George Glamack, John Kotz, Andy Phillip, Gerald Tucker, Otto Graham, Dale Hall, Bill Henry, Max Morris, Leo Klier, Ernie Calverley, Sid Tanenbaum, George Kaftan, Vern Gardner, Wallace Jones, and Ed Macauley, among others, were two-time All-Americans.

In the pros, George Mikan, Bob Davies, and Joe Fulks were starring for Minneapolis, Rochester,

1949–50 All-American, Paul Arizin of Villanova. Arizin scored eighty-five points in a single game as a junior, and led the nation in scoring as a senior. (Courtesy Villanova University.)

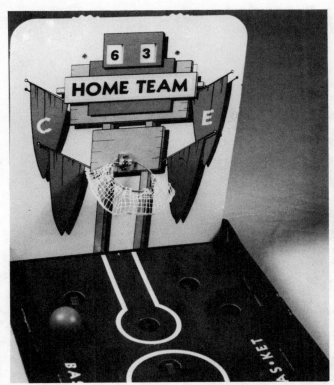

Bas-ket game. The authors played this popular Cadaco basketball game by the hours in the 1940s. (Copyright, Cadaco, Inc., Chicago, Illinois.)

and Philadelphia, respectively, and along with Dolph Schayes, who joined Syracuse in 1948–49, were ultimately to make the NBA's Silver Anniversary Team. Max Zaslofsky made the All-BAA team three times and the All-NBA Team the following year. Bob Feerick of the Capitols should not be ignored in recounting the pro stars of the decade. Al Cervi and Flash Brian from the National League and Jim Pollard who played in it for a year (along with Mikan) were great stars before and after entering the NBA.

The best professional teams were the Globetrotters; the Philadelphia Sphas in the American League; the Oshkosh All Stars, Fort Wayne Pistons, Rochester Royals, and Anderson Packers in the National League; and the Minneapolis Lakers in the NBL and BAA.

Author Young's church basketball team of 1946–47. The First Congregational Church basketball team of Waterloo, Iowa, nicknamed the "Congo Kids," won four and lost seven. Front row: Dick Walker, Jack Lane (with ball), Jerry Seaman (with ball), and Bob Young. Second row: Jim Young, Stanley Smith, Bob Keller, Coach; Bob Franklin, and "Happy" Miller. The picture was taken after a practice session in the basement gymnasium of Kingsley (elementary) School, which was across the street from the Young residence.

The United States retained its international dominance in the 1948 Olympic Games, and the Phillips 66ers claimed the lion's share of honors in the men's AAU competition.

Young and McClure had their share of heroes and heroic teams to follow, as the above narrative indicates. Iowa's Hawkeyes won the Big Ten in 1944–45 for its first undisputed title in history, and All-Americans Dick Ives and Herb Wilkinson made that Iowa team a great one. Murray Wier was everyone's All-American in 1948, when the Hawkeyes were second in the conference, and seldom has a more colorful and popular player taken the court.

Kansas tied for Big Six crowns in 1940, 1941, and 1942, and won outright championships in 1943 and 1946. The 1940 Jayhawkers were NCAA runnersup. Their leading scorer, Howard Engleman, was on the 1941 Helms All-American Team. McClure learned about most of those teams secondhand because of his youth, but he had ample opportunity to cheer for his state's stars, with two-time All-Americans Ray Evans and Charlie Black playing split (by the war) careers for the Jayhawks and starring in the late as well as early 1940s.

Young was playing church basketball for the First Congregational Church in the YMCA Junior League in Waterloo, Iowa, from the 1945–46 season through the end of the decade. After suffering through 58 to 2 and 66 to 6 losses in the first year of church league ball, the "Congo Kids," as they

1947–48 Congo Kids. The Congo Kids went through the 1946–47, 1947–48, and 1948–49 seasons with mediocre records. Shown here is the 1947–48 squad. Front row (l to r): Jim Young, Stanley Smith, Jerry Seaman, Jack Lane, and Charles "Tim" Walker. Back row: Roger Lane, Russ Oleson, Dick Walker, Bob Young, Bill Elliott, and Coach Keller.

The Congo Kids team of 1949–50, winner of the Waterloo (Iowa) YMCA Church League, Junior Division, title. The team won all ten of its league games, including some by 28-2, 31-3, 44-2, and 55-2 scores. Back row: *Jack Lane, Delbert Rossberg, *Jerry Seaman, Jim Anderson (Coach Keller between and back of Rossberg and Seaman). Front row: Clinton Dennis, *Tim Walker (captain), *Jim Young, and *Bill Elliott. (*Asterisks indicate starters.*)

came to be called, grew stronger physically and in league play each year. And their team, which began playing in late 1949, was destined to finish undefeated and win the league and playoff trophies in 1950 and 1951, along with a coveted gold basketball for each player (supplied by the parents) that Young still treasures.

In addition to the team play, there were countless hours spent shooting baskets at the Paul Barger, H. R. Gross, Dick Young, and Lew Seaman residences on their outdoor courts, and in the Young and McClure basements. At the Seaman's outdoor court, the "Tall-ies"—Bill Elliot and Jim Young—

vied with the "Not-hots"—Jack Lane and Jerry Seaman. After these games, the famished participants (four of the Congo Kids mentioned above) often feasted on Mrs. Seaman's fresh caramel rolls, or journeyed a few blocks for cokes and phosphates at Busby-Wing's drugstore. The constant pounding of the basketball on the basement floor at the Young and McClure households was accompanied by imaginary radio accounts of games starring Dick Ives, Murray Wier, Charlie Black, and Ray Evans—"broadcast" by active boys enjoying vicariously moments of athletic glory in indescribable happiness.

6

POTPOURRI

One might reasonably suppose that four sports—baseball, track and field, football, and basketball—would be more than sufficient to satiate a youngster's appetite for athletics during the spring, summer, fall, and winter. But, in truth, there were other vigorous, competitive activities bidding for his time, attention, and devotion—not all to the same degree, of course.

SWIMMING

One such activity was swimming. Despite his lack of buoyancy, Young has always loved the water. He was exposed to it before he was five-years-old when he was enrolled in the YMCA Tadpoles class. After many years of instruction at the "Y," summer camps, junior high, and high school, he developed some proficiency at it, but not to the extent that he was even thinking about competition. (Years later in his adulthood, he was still spending many a summer afternoon at the Central Missouri State outdoor pool with his family, and the McClure family usually was not too many strokes away.)

One of Young's instructors at the Waterloo "Y" was a young man named Bob Brown from the neighboring community of Cedar Falls. Brown was a competitive swimmer for the Waterloo "Y" team and later for Iowa State.

One summer day in 1948, after the London Olympiad had been held, Young was taken by his father to Brown's home in Cedar Falls at which a former Waterloo resident and his attractive wife were visiting. The former Waterloo resident was diving coach Lyle Draves, and his comely spouse was Victoria "Vicki" Manalo Draves. Mrs. Draves had just performed a phenomenal feat by winning two gold medals in the springboard and platform diving events at the Olympic Games. Her husband had been her coach as well.

Apprised in advance that Vicki would be at the Brown home, Young took along his official Olympic program and a batch of clippings, including some about the victorious woman diver. He was rewarded by Mrs. Draves' graciousness in signing his program with an appropriate message, autographing his clippings, and allowing that twelve-year-old to hold her heavy gold medals. Talk about hero worship! The double gold medalist might as well have been descending from Mount Olympus as returning from the Olympics, judging from the reaction of that awe-struck boy.

Another sports thrill stemming from the swimming and diving events at the 1948 Olympiad was the 100-meter freestyle victory achieved by Wally Ris of the United States and the University of Iowa. Ris's trick knee fortunately popped back into place during a flag ceremony before the Games. Many knowledgeable observers of the swimming scene had picked the Frenchman Alex Jany (who wore a bathing cap, of all things—this seemed unusual to a youthful American of that day) to win, but Ris was the victor in this premier swimming event. He won a second gold medal by swimming the leadoff leg in the American 800 meter freestyle relay team. The U.S. team tied a world record and defeated a stubborn Hungarian foursome.

Wally was a member of the Sigma Alpha Epsilon fraternity, to which the writer's father belonged when he attended the University of Iowa. As collegians in the 1950s, the author and his brother came to know Ris personally, as the latter was an adviser to the SAE chapter in Iowa City.

America's Vicki Draves, double gold-medalist diver in the 1948 Olympic Games. (Courtesy Vicki and Lyle Draves.)

the NAAU Indoor Meet, he anchored the winning 300 yard medley relay and 400 yard freestyle relay teams (Bill Smith also swam on those units). At the 1945 NAAU Indoor, Ris anchored the victorious relay teams in the same two events, this time competing for the Bainbridge Naval Training Center. Among other stars, Joe Verdeur (in the medley) and Adolph Kiefer (in the freestyle relay) swam with him. Wally also won the 100 yard freestyle in that 1945 national meet. He was to defend the latter crown successfully in the 1946–49 meets. In 1946 he added the NAAU Indoor 220 yard freestyle title to his laurels. His outdoor NAAU victories were in the 100 meter freestyle in 1947 and the 300 meter medley relay in 1949 (with Iowa's Duane Draves and Bowen Stassforth).

Early in the 1948 season Minnesota coach Niels Thorpe said that Ris was "the greatest free style swimmer in the world. . . ." That statement by Coach Thorpe (whose son Bill—a former teaching colleague of author Young—was a champion swim-

Ris started swimming when doctors recommended it to strengthen a knee he had injured in football. Fortunately for him, Iowa, and the United States, he took the doctor's advice. Originally Wally enrolled at the University of Illinois, but he left to enter the Navy. At the U.S. Naval Training Center at Bainbridge, Maryland, Adolph Kiefer, the backstroke star, gave him valuable instruction. After the service, Ris chose to attend Iowa because it had the only long course (fifty yards) college pool in the nation. Olympic competition is conducted over the metric equivalent of that type of course, and Wally wanted training conditions that were similar to those in London.

The tall, muscular swimmer from Chicago collected several NAAU and Big Nine titles in addition to his national collegiate championships. By 1949 Ris had won twelve NAAU titles (including five in relays and ten indoors). While swimming for Great Lakes Naval Training Center in 1944 at

Double Olympic gold medalist, Wally Ris of Iowa. (Courtesy University of Iowa Photo Service.)

mer for the Gophers during the same period) was borne out by Ris' feats later in the year. In the 1948 Big Nine meet, Ris nosed out Ohio State's ace, Bill Smith, in the 220 yard free style with a conference and national record. He also swam the 100 in :51.5, the fastest time ever recorded for the event in the long course. Moreover, in the meet finale, the 400 yard free style relay, Wally anchored Iowa's winning and record-setting team of Kenny Marsh, Duane Draves, Ervin Straub, and Ris with an amazing :50.6. At the 1948 NAAU Indoor Meet, Ris broke Johnny Weismuller's twenty-year-old record of :50.8 with a :50.5 clocking in the 100 yard freestyle event. France's Jany may have been the Olympic favorite in the 100 meters, but there were some who were not surprised when Ris defeated him!

The other 1948 Olympic champions from the United States—Bill Smith (400 meter freestyle), Jimmy McLane (1,500 meter freestyle), Allan Stack (100 meter backstroke), Joe Verdeur (200 meter breaststroke), Bruce Harlan (springboard diving), Sammy Lee (platform diving), Ann Curtis (400 meter freestyle, women), the men's 800 meter freestyle relay (Ris, McLane, Wallace Wolf, and Smith), and the women's 400 meter freestyle relay (Marie Corridon, Thelma Kalama, Brenda Helser, and Curtis) —were also heroes of the aquatic world for American youngsters of that era.

Other American medalists in the 1948 Games were:

Alan Ford	100 meter freestyle	silver
Jimmy McLane	400 meter freestyle	silver
Robert Cowell	100 meter backstroke	silver
Keith Carter	200 meter breaststroke	silver
Robert Sohl	200 meter breaststroke	bronze
Miller Anderson	springboard diving	silver
Sammy Lee	springboard diving	bronze
Bruce Harlan	platform diving	silver
Ann Curtis	100 meter freestyle	silver
Suzanne Zimmerman	100 meter backstroke	silver
Zoe Ann Olsen	springboard diving	silver
Patricia Elsener	springboard diving	bronze
Patricia Elsener	platform diving	silver

In effect, American collegiate swimmers were dominating the Olympic competition. Olympic gold medalist Bill Smith of Ohio State won seven NCAA titles in 1943 and 1947–49 in the 220 and 440 yard freestyle races. Close behind was teammate Bruce Harlan who was a six-time champion in the one-meter and three-meter diving events at the NCAA meets in 1948, 1949, and 1950. Meanwhile, Joe Verdeur of LaSalle, Olympic breaststroke champion, won his specialty (200 yards) in the 1947 and 1948 NCAA meets, and added the

Bill Smith of Ohio State, 1948 Olympic champion in the 400 meter freestyle. Smith also anchored the winning American 800 meter freestyle relay team. (Courtesy Ohio State University Photo Archives.)

Ohio State's Bruce Harlan, 1948 Olympic gold medalist in the springboard diving. (Courtesy Ohio State University Photo Archives.)

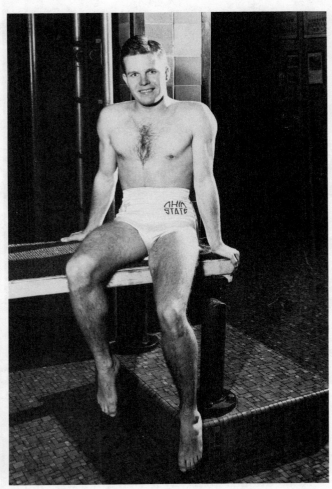

Olympic springboard-diving silver medalist, Miller Anderson of Ohio State. Anderson continued Ohio State mastery of the one-meter and three-meter diving events in the 1946 and 1947 NCAA meets by winning all four contests. Bruce Harlan took care of the 1948–50 period. (Courtesy Ohio State University Photo Archives.)

150 yard individual medley collegiate crowns in 1949 and 1950. Also Olympic gold medalists, Wally Ris of Iowa won his 100 yard freestyle event at the national collegiates in 1948 and 1949; Allan Stack of Yale won the 150 yard backstroke in 1948; and Yale's Jimmy McLane captured the 220 yard freestyle and 1,500 meter freestyle events in 1953.

Moreover, several Olympic silver medalists (in addition to Harlan and McLane who won both gold and silver medals) had also been collegiate champions: Miller Anderson of Ohio State won four NCAA golds in the two diving events at the 1946 and 1947 meets. Alan Ford of Yale won NCAA titles in 1944 in the 50 and 100 yard freestyle events, setting records that stood for many years, and he

also won the 150 yard backstroke event that year. Robert Cowell swam on Navy's winning 300 yard medley relay team at the 1944 nationals, and Robert Sohl was a member of Michigan's gold medalists in the same event at the 1947 and 1948 meets.

The NCAA team titles in the 1940s were divided among three schools. Ohio State, under Coach Mike Peppe, won five (in 1943, 1945–47, and 1949); Michigan, under Coach Matt Mann, three (1940–41 and 1948); and Yale, under Coach Bob Kiphuth, two (1942 and 1944). Matt Mann had also guided the Wolverines to team championships in 1937–39. Prior to 1937 team championships were not officially recognized by the NCAA. The authors, as youngsters in the early 1940s, knew about Matt Mann because they had read his booklet on swimming published by Wheaties, the "Breakfast of Champions" (after sending in the customary dime and two boxtops). They undoubtedly heard about the Wheaties sports library by listening on weekdays to the popular radio serial, Jack Armstrong, the All-American Boy, sponsored by General Mills.

The 1940s were a successful decade for author Young's Iowa Hawkeyes in swimming. In addition to Ris' Olympic, NAAU, and NCAA victories, the Hawkeyes' 300 yard medley relay team of Duane Draves, Bowen Stassforth (1952 Olympic silver medalist in the 200 meter breaststroke), and Ervin Straub won first place in the 1949 NCAA meet. (As mentioned, Iowa's 300 meter medley relay captured that event at the 1949 NAAU Outdoor.) Teammate Edward "Rusty" Garst was to win the NCAA 50 yard freestyle event in 1950. Coach Dave Armbruster's Iowa teams were high placers in several NCAA meets—second in 1949, fourth in 1943 and 1948, seventh in 1941, and tenth (two-way tie) in 1942.

In NAAU Indoor Meets, Wally Ris' Great Lakes Naval Training Center team won the 1944 team championship, and his 1945 Bainbridge Naval Training Center team captured the 1945 team crown. Other team victories were attained by Ohio State in 1943 and 1946–48; Yale in 1942 and the New Haven Swim Club in 1949; Michigan in 1940; and the Chicago Towers Club in 1941.

Iowa State dominated Big Eight swimming in the 1940s, winning the conference title every year the meet was held (there was no competition from 1943–46). Controlling the Big Ten were Michigan (champions in 1940–42, 1944–45, and 1948) and Ohio State (winners in 1943, 1946–47, and 1949). Yale won the Eastern Intercollegiate League in 1940–43 and 1947–49. Navy copped that conference crown in 1944 and 1946, while Army took it

1949 NCAA runner-up swimming team, the University of Iowa. Bottom row (l to r): Hutinger, Griesbach, Marsh, Stassforth, Wichman; middle row: Coach Armbruster, Korte, Maine, Ris, Draves, Straub; top row: Lehman, Wilson, Bush, Garst, Keith, Hart, Assistant Coach Counsilman. (Courtesy University of Iowa Photo Service.)

in 1945. Bob Kiphuth of Yale lost one dual meet out of sixteen in 1940, and one of nine in 1945, but his teams were otherwise undefeated in dual competition throughout the 1940s. When Coach Kiphuth retired, his dual meet record at Yale from 1918–59 was 527-12, including 182 straight victories from 1945–59. He was the 1948 men's Olympic coach and also coached the men's teams in 1932 and 1936 (he was appointed to coach the 1940 team) and the women's team in 1928.

Although his competitive days were far behind him, Johnny Weismuller, *the* Swimmer of the First Half Century, was admired greatly by Young and McClure—for his heroics and prowess demonstrated in the *Tarzan* movies as much as for previous competitive honors. For twenty years he was the most popular of all Tarzans. Weismuller starred in nineteen of the jungle pictures and never went to Africa! This, of course, did not matter to the children of the 1940s.

WRESTLING

As mentioned above, Waterloo, Iowa was, and is, a wrestling town. It has produced NCAA and NAAU champions such as Lowell Lange, Dick Hauser, Leo Thomsen, Jim Harmon, Gordon Trapp, Bill Wright, Bill Dotson, Dale Anderson, Dan Gable, and Chuck Yagla. Wrestlers from East Waterloo and West Waterloo have faced each other in the finals of the NCAA Tournament.

West High, Young's alma mater, won nineteen individual state wrestling titles in the 1940s. The twelve wrestlers who won those championships were coached by Finn Eriksen and Roy Jarrard. Eriksen guided West to its first two state team championships in 1942 and 1943 and then went into the service. With Jarrard as head coach, the "Wahawks" won their third, fourth, and fifth consecutive state team titles in 1944, 1945, and 1946. West's teams were undefeated in 1942, 1943, and 1945.

Just as Waterloo is a wrestling town, Iowa is a wrestling state. In 1947 tiny Cornell College of Mount Vernon, Iowa won both the NCAA Meet (there were no separate university and college division NCAA meets at that time) and the National AAU (NAAU) Meet. In the NCAA competition,

Cornell College wrestling team—NCAA and NAAU champions in 1947. Back row (l to r): Gordon Meredith, manager; John Gregg (121 pounds), Lowell Lange (136), Arlo Ellison (136), Leo Thomsen (128), Richard Hauser (121), Paul K. Scott, coach. Front row: Rodger Snook (145), Fred Dexter (165), Dale Thomas (175), Al Partin (Hwt.), Kent Lange (155). (Courtesy Paul Scott and Cornell College.)

Waterloo's Dick Hauser and Lowell Lange copped the titles in the 121 pound and 136 pound classes, respectively, for Cornell. Russ Bush (128 pounds), Bill Koll (145 pounds), and Bill Nelson (165 pounds) of Iowa State Teachers College (now the University of Northern Iowa—UNI) of Cedar Falls were winners, and Joe Scarpello of Iowa captured the 175 pound championship. Thus, in addition to the Cornell Rams' team title, wrestlers representing Iowa schools won six of the eight weight classes. Moreover, Hauser, Lange, Nelson, and Scarpello were all freshmen!

In the 1947 NAAU meet, Lowell Lange (135 pounds) and Dale Thomas (175 pounds) won firsts, and Dick Hauser and Rodger Snook, seconds, to give the Rams of Mount Vernon another national team championship.

In pretournament competition that season, the only blemish on the dual meet records of Cornell and Iowa State Teachers College (ISTC) was the 12-12 tie that occurred when they wrestled each other! Both schools whipped Big Six champion Iowa State. Cornell beat the Big Ten champion Illinois, 19-11, and the Eastern champion Lehigh, by 36-0.

In the 1949 NCAA meet, Oklahoma A.&M. won the team title, but Keith Young (145), Bill Nelson (155), and Bill Smith (165) of ISTC, and Lowell Lange (136) of Cornell gave Iowa schools half of the individual first places. ISTC was second in team scoring with 27 points (the Aggies had 32, with two champions).

In the 1949 NAAU Meet, however, the Panthers from ISTC won the team title with their three NCAA winners plus John Harrison (121) and Russ Bush (128) winning golds. Lange's victory at that meet gave Iowa schools six of the ten individual championships.

And Iowa collegiate dominance continued in 1950. Young, Nelson, and Smith repeated as victors in both the NCAA and NAAU, as ISTC won the first place team trophy in each of those national meets (the collegiate meet was held at Cedar Falls with co-author Young in attendance). Joe Scarpello of the University of Iowa won again at 175 in the collegiate meet, and Lange took the 136

1949 NCAA runner-up team, the University of Northern Iowa Panthers. Pictured are (front row, l to r): Bill Nelson, Coach Dave McCuskey, and Keith Young; (second row) Russ Bush, Bob Siddens, Bill Smith, Fred Stoeker, Luverne Klar, and John Harrison. (Courtesy University of Northern Iowa.)

pound division, giving Iowa schools five of the eight individual titles. John Harrison (115) and Fred Stoeker (heavyweight) of ISTC and Hauser (128) and Lange (135) of Cornell were also winners at the NAAU, so the Hawkeye state's representatives garnered seven of the ten available individual crowns! Gene Lybbert (128), Keith Young (155), and Bill Smith (165) won their weight classes to give ISTC their third straight NAAU team title in 1951.

Oklahoma A.&M. (especially), the Big Ten schools, and Michigan State (not yet a member of the latter conference), were the other major collegiate wrestling powers of the 1940s. The Aggies won six of the seven NCAA team crowns in the decade (Cornell won in 1947, and there were no meets in 1943, 1944, and 1945 because of the war).

The Oklahoma Aggies' NCAA victory in 1946 came at the expense of ISTC (25-24). The Panthers, whose lack of an entry at heavyweight may have cost them the team title, had three individual champions—Cecil Mott (121), Gerry Leeman (128), and Bill Koll (145). Leeman was voted the Outstanding Wrestler of the Meet.

Koll was a repeat victor in the 1947 and 1948 national collegiates, and he was the Outstanding Wrestler in both tourneys. In 1948 Koll (147.5) and Iowa State's Glen Brand (174) were the only NCAA champions from Iowa schools. Cornell's Lange and Hauser had suffered serious injuries in an automobile accident. Leo Thomsen, the third member of the West Waterloo-Cornell trio, upheld Cornell's colors at the 1948 NAAU Meet at Hofstra by winning the 136.5 pound class. Former Cornell wrestler, Dale Thomas (representing Marion, Iowa) captured the 175 pound division title as Navy secured the team championship.

At the 1948 Olympic trials, Bill Koll again won the Outstanding Wrestler award. At London, Bill was fifth in the lightweight class (67 kilograms o-

147.5 pounds). His teammate from ISTC, Germ Leeman, won the silver medal in the bantamweight class (57 kilos or 125.5 pounds). And Glen Brand of Iowa State College (now Iowa State University) was a gold medalist in the middleweight division (79 kilos or 174 pounds). From the Americans' standpoint, Brand shared the spotlight with a New York City patrolman, Henry Wittenberg, who was the champion in the light-heavyweight class (87 kilos or 191 pounds).

The calibre of Iowa wrestlers was also manifested by the 1940 NAAU championship at 112 pounds won by Gerald Leeman of Osage, Iowa. "Germ" was only in his junior year in high school at the time of this victory. And Waterloo's Lange and Hauser each won NAAU titles in 1946 before they graduated from West High School. Lowell Lange once worked as an ice man for Jim Young's father, and was admired as a hero by the co-author. A friendly, all-around athlete of outstanding char-

acter, Lowell was named the Most Valuable Athlete of his class, and was eventually to win three individual NCAA crowns (in 1947, 1949, and 1950 at 136 pounds) and four NAAU titles (1946, 1947, 1949, and 1950 at 135 pounds). Hauser also won an NCAA championship as a college freshman in 1947 (121 pounds) and added the 1950 and 1953 NAAU gold medals (at 128 and 125 pounds, respectively) to the one he earned in high school. Lange and Hauser probably would have won more championships had it not been for their auto accident. Lange's last two NCAA victories were won after his recovery from injuries suffered in that mishap, as were four of the Waterloo pair's NAAU wins.

In addition to Lange and Hauser, Cornell College, with fewer than a thousand students, had other wrestlers of great repute. Dale Thomas of the Rams won five NAAU freestyle wrestling, and two Greco-Roman (holds above the waist only)

1949 National AAU Meet champions, the University of Northern Iowa. Shown (l to r) are: Russ Bush, Bill Smith, John Harrison, Coach Dave McCuskey, Keith Young, and Bill Nelson. All five of these Panthers were individual champions as well! (Courtesy University of Northern Iowa.)

217

Outstanding wrestler of two NCAA meets, Bill Koll of the University of Northern Iowa. Koll won three consecutive NCAA wrestling titles in 1946, 1947, and 1948. In the latter year, he pinned all of his NCAA meet opponents to become the first wrestler to be named the national meet's Outstanding Wrestler two consecutive times. Later that year he was the Outstanding Wrestler of the Olympic Trials. (Courtesy University of Northern Iowa.)

1948 Olympic silver medalist, Gerald "Germ" Leeman of the University of Northern Iowa. At the London Games, Leeman placed second in the bantamweight class (fifty-seven kilograms or 125.5 pounds). As a junior at Osage (Iowa) High School, Germ won his first national wrestling title—an AAU championship. During World War II, Leeman starred for the Iowa Pre-Flight Seahawks in Iowa City. He won an NCAA title in 1946, and he was voted the Outstanding Wrestler of the meet. (Courtesy UNI.)

Cornell College wrestling star, Dick Hauser. As a freshman at the Mount Vernon, Iowa, college, Hauser won an NCAA championship (1947). He had won his first NAAU title the year before, as a senior at West Waterloo High School; he was to win two more NAAU crowns, in 1950 and 1953. (Courtesy Paul Scott and Cornell College.)

Lowell Lange, seven-time national champion. The West Waterloo High School state champion won his first NAAU title as a senior in high school. He went on to win three more NAAU crowns and three NCAA firsts. The Hall of Fame wrestler helped his Cornell College mates win two national team titles in 1947. (Courtesy Paul Scott and Cornell College.)

championships during his wrestling career. He was a member of two Olympic teams and placed sixth at the 1956 Olympics in Greco-Roman competition. As mentioned, Leo Thomsen of West Waterloo and Cornell won the 136.5 pound class in the 1948 NAAU meet. In 1943 Frank Preston of Coach Paul Scott's Cornell team placed first in the NAAU at 115 pounds, and teammate Walt Haloupek was second, in the 191 pound weight class, to Henry Wittenberg. With unbeaten Dale Thomas winning his division (175 pounds), the Rams were able to tie Michigan State for second place in team points. Cornell's greatest year, of course, was 1947, when Scott's forces won their two national team titles. In addition, Walt Romanowski of Cornell (130

pounds) was to be the Outstanding Wrestler in the 1951 NCAA Meet.

Meanwhile, Coach Dave McCuskey at ISTC was producing his collegiate powerhouses and training outstanding coaches of the future such as Helms Foundation Hall of Fame member, Bob Siddens. Siddens replaced Roy Jarrard at West Waterloo and turned out many more state champion teams and individuals, including national, world, and Olympic champion, Dan Gable.

McCuskey's bevy of strongmen at ISTC in the 1940s included national champions Cecil Mott, Germ Leeman, Russ Bush, Bill Koll, Bill Nelson, Bill Smith, Keith Young, John Harrison, and Fred Stoeker. Koll, Nelson, and Young won three NCAA titles each, and Bill Smith, two. Smith and Young won three NAAU crowns, and Bill Nelson and John Harrison, two. Bill Smith was to be the United States' sole Olympic wrestling champion in 1952 at Helsinki.

After twenty-one years at the Panther helm, McCuskey became head coach at the University of Iowa in 1952. He replaced Mike Howard, who had coached two-time NCAA champion Joe Scarpello, Big Ten titlist Rometo "Rummy" Macias, and Bob Geigel, among other stars. McCuskey's Hawkeye teams also included a wrestler who was to become an Olympic champion—Terry McCann. Terry won a gold medal at Rome in 1960.

The NAAU team champions in the 1940s indicate the location of some other wrestling strongholds in that decade. The winning teams were:

1940	West Side YMCA of New York*
1941	West Side YMCA of New York
1942	Crescent Club of Tulsa
1943	West Side YMCA of New York
1944	Baltimore YMCA
1945	Oklahoma City YMCA
1946	New York AC
1947	Cornell College
1948	Navy
1949–51	Iowa State Teachers College

* In 1940 Osage High School of Iowa actually had two winners and more team points than West Side "Y." But Osage's Ed Viscosil had graduated, and his affiliation was changed to "unattached," enabling West Side "Y" to win.

The victories of the West Side YMCA were in large part attributable to Henry Wittenberg, the outstanding wrestler of the decade with his 1948 Olympic title and seven NAAU championships. He was also silver medalist at 191 pounds in the 1952 Olympics. The New York policeman was voted the Outstanding U.S.A. Amateur Wrestler in

Coach Paul Scott of Cornell College and his three national champions from Waterloo, Iowa. Coach Scott (left) gives a pointer to Leo Thomsen, 1948 NAAU champion and member of the Olympic squad; seven-time national champ, Lowell Lange; and four-time national titlist, Dick Hauser. All three Ram wrestlers had won state titles for West Waterloo High School. Lange and Hauser were injured in an auto wreck, which prevented them, in 1948, from obtaining even more laurels. (Courtesy Paul Scott and Cornell College.)

NCAA wrestling champion at 175 pounds in 1947 and 1950, Iowa's Joe Scarpello. The Hawkeye grappler placed two other times in the nationals and won four Big Ten titles. (Courtesy University of Iowa.)

1941 and 1947. He had earned a bachelor's degree at CCNY in 1940 and a master's at Columbia in 1941. Wittenberg was undefeated in over 250 matches.

The two Oklahoma team championships in the NAAU competition and the six Oklahoma A.&M. NCAA first place team trophies of the 1940s give support to the assertion that Oklahoma was the wrestling capital of the United States during that decade. The East, the Big Ten schools, Michigan State, and the State of Iowa were the other major sites of wrestling power. At both the scholastic and collegiate levels, amateur wrestling was not as widespread then as it is today. But the old citadels of wrestling have ably maintained their traditions of strength, and schools like Oklahoma State (A.& M.), Oklahoma, Iowa, Iowa State, and UNI (ISTC) remain teams to be reckoned with by all challengers.

Partially because of a relative lack of television coverage, amateur wrestling in the United States, as sponsored by the schools, colleges, Wrestling Federation, and AAU is not widely understood or followed by the general public. Many immediately

Henry Wittenberg of New York, 1948 Olympic wrestling champion at 191 pounds. The light-heavyweight star won seven NAAU titles and was runnerup in his class at the 1952 Olympics. Undefeated from 1938 to 1952, he was voted the United States' Outstanding Amateur Wrestler in 1941 and 1947. (Courtesy Donald Sayenga and Amateur Athletic Union of the United States.)

Big Ten and professional wrestling star from Iowa, Bob Geigel. (Courtesy University of Iowa.)

think of the professional spectacle when the word "wrestling" is mentioned. Some do not know of the existence of amateur wrestling, or that there are sharp differences between the amateur and professional forms of the sport.

In Waterloo during the 1940s, many professional "rassling" bouts or matches were conducted at the Electric Park, a recreational complex with amusement park, ballroom, and small outdoor pugilistic arena adjacent to the Cedar River and near the giant John Deere Tractor Manufacturing Works. Many of these matches were arranged by Pinkie George, a regional promoter of some fame. World champion Lou Thesz of St. Louis, challenger Ken Fenelon of Dubuque, Strangler Lewis, the Swedish Angel, and other luminaries (including women wrestlers) were featured on Pinkie's cards. Young clipped and pasted newspaper advertisements for these evenings of entertainment into his sport scrapbook of the 1944–46 era, along with articles about the amateur wrestlers from East and West High, the Waterloo White Hawks (a Three-

I League, Class B baseball team), football teams from West and East High and Iowa University, and other foci of interest to the young Waterloo sports enthusiast.

On one occasion, Bob Young took his boys to the Electric Park to witness the "mayhem" (restrained version). They were not disappointed. But, so far as emulation and hero worship were concerned, it was the amateur wrestlers who were the most admired and respected. (To the trained eye of a wrestling fan, the amateur variety is also much more exciting than the more spectacular, but less competitive, professional version). Except for occasional unskilled, impromptu "rough-housing" at home, Bobby and Jimmy Young did not participate in this sport, but only watched and read about it.

WEIGHTLIFTING AND STRONG MEN

Growing youngsters (as well as some adults) are generally impressed with feats of strength and/or people with impressive shapes, physiques, or musculature. Those who are especially skinny or fat can easily identify with the subjects of Norman Rockwell's paintings who are trying out their new weightlifting equipment or anxiously scrutinizing the results of their new type of exercise before the bedroom mirror. Bob Hoffman, the elder statesman of weight training, has claimed that even recent American presidents and foreign potentates have been, at some time in their lives, "Bob Hoffman boys"—that is, they aspired to heights of strength and fitness and made some attempt to achieve their goals through the York Barbell program.

In the 1940s many boys shared similar aspirations. Jim Young remembers that his brother Bob sent away for information about the George Jowett strength program, and both boys pored over the advertisements and information that were sent to their home periodically after Bob's original inquiry. Jowett was one of the early strong men, and his course was in competition with those of Charles Atlas, the York Barbell Company, and others.

Readers of comic books and sports literature in those days were very familiar with the advertisements of the late Angelo Siciliano, better known as Charles Atlas. They read and reread the cartoon ad telling the well-known story of the 97 pound weakling who was humiliated in front of his girlfriend at the beach by the local bully when the latter kicked sand in his face. The reader knew, almost as a matter of conditioned response from con-

stant repetition of this theme in the ads, that the solution to the weakling's problem was for him to take the Charles Atlas course in "dynamic tension." A he-man's physique would be his, if only this course of action were followed. And the young lady's affection (if it were worth having) would soon be won again.

Most boys in the author's acquaintance assumed that the Atlas method was not effective; few actually knew anything about it. While on summer vacation in northern Minnesota one season, Young became acquainted with the employees of Gateway Hungry Jack Lodge. These cabin boys and girls (and waiters and waitresses) were students from Tilden Tech in Chicago (who often sang the praises of Mike Swistowicz, a recent Tilden graduate then headed for football stardom at Notre Dame). The author was surprised to learn that some of the young men were actually following the Atlas course. He learned from them that its essential nature was the pitting of muscle against muscle or against an immovable object, without weights and even without movement. Even armed with this knowledge, Young did not act on it, judging it as not being of much value.

But in the early 1960s, physical educators discovered that Atlas' "dynamic tension" system was indeed a very efficient and effective method of building strength, and they labeled it "isometric contraction." Even in his seventies, Atlas appeared to be a person who practiced what he preached, and his death at age eighty was mourned by many as the end of an era.

Men such as Peary Rader and Joe Weider have been leaders in the strength world for many years, but Bob Hoffman is generally recognized as having been the main promoter of American competition in the Olympic event of weightlifting. (The sport has its historical roots in ancient times.) The owner of the York Barbell Company has long sponsored the York Barbell Club in York, Pennsylvania, and top lifters from all over the nation have trained there and have been members of the organization.

The 1948 Olympic weightlifting team from the United States was no exception in this regard, and most of the team were "York men." American gold medalists in that sport at London were:

Bantamweight (123½ pounds, 56 kilograms) Joe Di Pietro
Middleweight (165¼ pounds, 75 kilograms)
Frank Spellman
Light Heavyweight (181¼ pounds, 82½ kilograms)
Stan Stanczyk
Heavyweight (unlimited) John Davis

Only in the featherweight (132¼ pounds, 60 kil-grams) and lightweight (148¼ pounds, 67½ kilograms) classes were Americans not victorious. Winners in weightlifting were then determined by the total poundages of three types of lifts—the press, snatch, and clean and jerk. In recent years the press has been eliminated.

Essentially the iron game is divided into three groups: (1) weightlifting (the recognized Olympic sport described above), (2) power lifting (competition in total poundages lifted in the bench press, squat, and dead lift), and (3) bodybuilding. The second category was not so well recognized in previous decades as it is today. Bodybuilding undoubtedly has the most devotees. An important yardstick for success in the latter area in the 1940s was the Mr. America contest. Winners of that physique competition included:

1940	John Grimek	1945	Clarence Ross
1941	John Grimek	1946	Alan Stephan
1942	Frank Leight	1947	Steve Reeves
1943	Jules Bacon	1948	George Eiferman
1944	Steve Stanko	1949	Jack Dellinger

The most famous of the Mr. Americas was Steve Reeves, who later capitalized on his title in the movie world as Hercules, among other roles.

It was not until the 1950s, however, that the author became familiar with bodybuilding. It was then that weight training came into its own as a means of improving athletic performance and fitness.

The most famous weightlifter of the 1940s was the black heavyweight John Davis, the 1948 and 1952 Olympic champion. His career spanned nineteen years—from 1938–56—and he was undefeated in fifteen of those nineteen years. Davis won six world championships (exclusive of the Olympics), his first at the age of seventeen in 1938. If his career had not been interrupted by World War II (there were no world championships in the years 1939–45), he would have won many more titles.

After a defeat at the hands of Stanley Kratkowski in the Senior National AAU Meet in 1938, John Davis did not lose for fifteen years. He won the 1939 and 1940 national titles at 181 pounds. In 1941 he went up to heavyweight and would have challenged Steve Stanko, the first lifter to total 1,000 pounds, had not Stanko contracted phlebitis that forced him to retire. Davis broke Stanko's record with 1,010 that year, and went on to hold the world record for all three individual

lifts and for the total of the three. He won the 1942 and 1943 nationals, entered the Army in late 1943, and served in the Pacific.

Davis rarely weighed over 220 pounds and employed the split style of lifting. His other important titles in the 1940s included the 1946, 1947, and 1949 world championships and the 1946, 1947, and 1948 national titles. In the next decade he added the 1950 and 1952 world titles and NAAU firsts from 1950–53.

1948 Olympic light-heavyweight champion Stanley Stanczyk ranked just behind Davis in overall honors for the 1940s. He won world titles in all the championships conducted in that decade—1946, 1947, and 1949 (like Davis, he also won in 1950 and 1952). Stanczyk also attained Senior NAAU firsts in 1947–51 and 1953.

Other outstanding American lifters of the 1940s included Joe Di Pietro, bantamweight; John Terry and Emerick Ishikawa, featherweights; 1936 Olympic champion (America's first in the sport) Anthony Terlazzo and Joseph Pitman, lightweights; Frank Spellman and John Terpak, middleweights; and Frank Kay, light heavyweight. Pete George won national titles in 1946 (lightweight) and 1949 (middleweight) and a world championship in 1947. He went on to an Olympic gold medal in 1952 and more world and national crowns.

Norbert Schemansky obtained his first major title in 1949 when he won the Senior Nationals (he won the Junior NAAU in 1946). Schemansky had placed second to Davis in the 1948 Olympics. He was to become the 1952 Olympic champion in the middle heavyweight class (198 pounds—this class was first established in 1951). He added many more gold medals in the senior nationals (eight) and world championships, and bronze Olympic medals in 1960 and 1964.

Also in the 1940s Steve Stanko and John Grimek became the only lifters to win a senior national lifting title and a Mr. America contest. John Grimek won the Senior Nationals in 1936 (and competed in the Olympics). He also secured the 1940 and 1941 Mr. America trophies. Stanko won the NAAU heavyweight championship in 1938, 1939, and 1940 and the 1944 Mr. America title. He had been forced to retire from competitive lifting (as noted above), but not from the use of weights for bodybuilding. The Mr. America contest was first held in 1938 and, like the senior nationals, has been under the auspices of the AAU,

BOXING

The great Joe Louis reigned over the heavy-weight boxers throughout the 1940s until he announced his retirement in March 1949. Boxing in the decade produced many memories, even though it apparently was, as a sport, closest to the undesirable criminal element in American society. It did, however, through amateur and professional ranks help many young men from lower social levels attain a measure of self-respect that they might not have had otherwise. The examples in the 1940s are numerous: Billy Conn, Gus Lesnevich, Tony Zale, Rocky Graziano, Jake LaMotta, Beau Jack, Ike Williams, Willie Pep, Chalky Wright, and Manuel Ortiz. All were household heroes in a sport that was painfully on the decline. It was a sport that was worldwide in its appeal and knew no boundaries of race, religion, or physical size. It asked for a measure of specialized athletic ability and a sincerity of purpose. It was a glamorous and glorious sports activity that small boys dreamed of, not because of the money or other rewards necessarily, but because of the upward mobility that was possible.

The decade's most famous example of this was "Sugar Ray" Robinson. Anyone who ever saw him in the ring, either in person or on television, could not forget the grace of his footwork or the blinding hand speed of his brilliant combinations. Unforgettable too was Robinson's slick pompadour of hair that always stood on end as soon as the fighting began. Sugar Ray beat Tommy Bell for Marty Servo's vacated welterweight championship in 1946, held it for four years, and then, to find opponents, stepped up to the middleweight class where he became champion.

To many American youngsters of all colors in the 1940s, Sugar Ray Robinson became something of a national institution. He won the national Golden Gloves featherweight title in 1939 and the lightweight title in 1940 before turning pro. In 1941 he won twenty fights and defeated Fritzie Zivic. In 1942 he won fourteen more, including one over Jake LaMotta. Although he suffered his first defeat to LaMotta in 1943, three weeks later he whipped LaMotta and then defeated the legendary Henry Armstrong. In 1944 and 1945 Robinson won thirteen fights and drew with Jose Basora. After winning the welterweight crown in his fight with Bell, Sugar Ray defeated Jimmy Doyle in his first title defense in 1947. In 1948 he defended against Bernard Docusen, and in 1949 he won twelve fights including a title bout with the colorful Kid Gavilan.

Robinson epitomized the combination of grace *and* power. Words like "beauty" and "precision" come to mind when recalling his abilities. He was a vision of gallantry in the ring and often brought to the sport of boxing values not always associated with it. He fought not only for money but for the honor and bravery in the sport. His valiance is not often witnessed in any age and was heartening to untold millions of people.

In the era of big-name boxers during the 1940s, another champion, Gus Lesnevich, reigned over the light-heavyweights alongside such champions in other weight divisions as Joe Louis, Rocky Graziano, and Sugar Ray Robinson. He broke into boxing as an amateur and became a New York Golden Gloves champion. At the age of nineteen, he turned professional, fighting as a middleweight. In his first fight, on 5 May 1934, he knocked out Justin Hoffman in the second round. He went on to win his next ten fights, four by knockouts. He followed the minor league trail of boxing the next three years, fighting in arenas in Brooklyn, Fort Lee, New Jersey; Newark, Seattle, and San Francisco. Lesnevich broke into the big time in February 1937, but he did not win as consistently as he had when he was in the minors. He defeated Tony Celli in an eight-rounder in New York, but three weeks later he was knocked out in the fifth round by Young Corbett in a feature fight in San Francisco.

After two years, he gained a reputation as a battler, and he began to gain a following and draw crowds. He was given choice fights, and finally on 17 November 1939, he gained a shot at the world's light-heavyweight title, then held by Billy Conn. Lesnevich lost the fight, a fifteen-round decision. He bounced back to defeat Dave Clark on 1 January 1940, for another chance at the title, but he lost again to Conn in a fifteen-round decision on 5 June.

Five fights and a year later, he gained the National Boxing Association's light-heavyweight title by defeating Anton Christoforidis in fifteen rounds. On 26 August 1941, he won the world's 175 pound title by defeating Tami Mauriello in fifteen rounds. He secured his title by defeating Mauriello again in fifteen rounds three months later in a return bout. But then came the war, and Lesnevich joined the Coast Guard.

He fought a few bouts while in service. When he was discharged in 1946, Lesnevich was thirty-one years old, and few boxing experts thought he could make a comeback. In his first major (non-title) fight after his discharge, Lesnevich was knocked out by Lee Oma in the sixth round. He came back, however, and knocked out Freddie Mills of London in ten rounds to retain the world's light-heavyweight crown. Shortly thereafter, he was upset by Bruce Woodcock of London, who knocked him out in the eighth round. Though the knockout was due to cuts rather than overpowering blows, sportswriters predicted that he would retire. But much to the boxing world's surprise, 1947 turned out to be Lesnevich's best year. In defense of his crown, he knocked out the highly rated Billy Fox, who had come into the fight with a record of forty-three straight victories, all by knockouts. Lesnevich then took on Melio Bettina, who was then touted as a possible rival for Joe Louis, and knocked him out in fifty-nine seconds of the first round. To make his year complete, Lesnevich twice took on his old rival, Tami Mauriello, defeating him both times, once by a knockout.

His comeback in 1947 earned him *Ring* magazine's designation as "fighter of the year." He also was awarded the Edward J. Neil Memorial Plaque that year by the Boxing Writers' Association of New York as "boxer of the year." His success continued into 1948, when he knocked out Billy Fox in the first round in defense of his title. But he lost his title to Freddie Mills in a fifteen-rounder in London that summer. He tried to regain the title the next year but lost to Joe Maxim in fifteen rounds. His last fight was as a heavyweight against Ezzard Charles for the world's title on 10 August 1949. Charles knocked him out in the seventh round. In his fifteen-year career, Lesnevich fought seventy-six fights, winning fifty-seven, twenty-one by knockouts, and losing fourteen. He fought five draws. He later was a referee in New York and New Jersey. Lesnevich died of a heart attack in February 1964, at the age of forty-nine.

Manuel Ortiz was the world bantamweight champion from 1942 until 1950 and dominated his weight division almost as completely as Joe Louis did among the heavyweights. The fierce little Mexican-American won the California amateur boxing title in 1937, captured the National Golden Gloves crown later that year, and turned pro in 1938. He fought mostly in Los Angeles throughout his career and remained active until 1955. It was in Los Angeles that Ortiz won the world bantamweight title in a twelve-round decision over Lou Salica. Through the war years and afterward, he fought numerous over-the-weight bouts, including fights with Lauro Solas, Carlos Chavez, and Willie Pep. Ortiz was a two-fisted puncher with amazing stamina. On 6 January 1947, Ortiz lost a fifteen-round decision to Harold Dade

in San Francisco for the title, but sixty-four days later, beat Dade in Los Angeles in fifteen rounds. Ortiz then held the title until Vic Toweel beat him in fifteen rounds in Johannesburg, South Africa, on 31 May 1950.

The Rocky Graziano-Tony Zale middleweight title fights and the Willie Pep-Sandy Saddler featherweight title meetings are rated among the classic battles of ring history. In 1946 Zale retained his title by knocking out Graziano in the sixth round, but Graziano won the title in 1947 by knocking out Zale in the sixth. On 10 June 1948, at Newark Zale won on a third-round knockout. These were three of the bloodiest, most ferocious battles in ring history. Graziano was Young's favorite fighter.

Zale was awarded *The Ring* magazine's Fighter of the Year medal in 1946 and was selected to its Hall of Fame in Madison Square Garden. The Edward J. Neil Trophy also went to Zale in 1946.

Sandy Saddler won three of his four encounters with Willie Pep on knockouts in the fourth, eighth, and ninth rounds. Pep took the title in their second meeting, 11 February 1949, on a fifteen-round decision.

Probably the most famous bouts of the decade were the two Billy Conn-Joe Louis fights. On 18 June 1941, at the Polo Grounds in New York, more than sixty thousand fans watched Conn box Louis to a standstill for twelve rounds, and then in the thirteenth, Conn carelessly decided to slug it out with Louis and was knocked out. After both served in the Army during World War II, they fought again on 19 June 1946 at Yankee Stadium. Louis was again victorious with a knockout in the eighth round.

The 1941 Edward J. Neil Trophy went to Joe Louis. In 1939 it had gone to Billy Conn, then light-heavyweight champion of the world. *The Ring* Magazine Merit Award went to Conn in 1940 and to Louis in 1941 (the latter had won it in 1936, 1938, and 1939 as well).

TENNIS

As was the case with wrestling, boxing, and golf, tennis was a sport that was enjoyed by the authors only in a vicarious sense. Tennis stars Don Budge, Bobby Riggs, Jack Kramer, Frank Parker, Ted Schroeder, and Pancho Gonzales dominated the men's scene; and Sarah Palfrey Cooke, Pauline Betz, Louise Brough, and Margaret Osborne duPont, the women's. Young's cheering and jeering were limited to his reactions to articles on the sport pages of the newspaper. Budge and Kramer were definitely his favorites, and the supremely confident Bobby Riggs most assuredly was not.

The Davis Cup was not contested from 1940–45 because of the war, but after the resumption of that tennis classic, the United States dominated it to the end of the decade. Runner-up Australia (in the 1946–49 period) was to turn the tables on the United States in the following decade. From 1946–49 the American victories over the Aussies in Davis Cup play were by the scores of 5-0, 4-1, 5-0, 4-1, respectively. The tennis-playing nations have competed for the Davis Cup since 1900. The winner defends the cup the following year after various elimination rounds determine the challenger to the defending champion. The challenge round consists of four singles matches and one doubles match.

American national champions among amateurs were determined by the tournament at Forest Hills, New York. In the 1940s the outdoor men's singles winners were:

Date	Winner	Runner-up
1940	Don McNeill	Bobby Riggs
1941	Bobby Riggs	Frank Kovacs
1942	Ted Schroeder	Frank Parker
1943	Joe Hunt	Jack Kramer
1944	Frank Parker	Billy Talbert
1945	Frank Parker	Billy Talbert
1946	Jack Kramer	Tom Brown, Jr.
1947	Jack Kramer	Frank Parker
1948	Pancho Gonzales	Eric Sturgess
1949	Pancho Gonzales	Ted Schroeder

The national outdoor men's doubles winners were:

1940	Jack Kramer and Ted Schroeder
1941	Jack Kramer and Ted Schroeder
1942	Gardnar Mulloy and Billy Talbert
1943	Jack Kramer and Frank Parker
1944	Don McNeill and Bob Falkenburg
1945	Gardnar Mulloy and Billy Talbert
1946	Gardnar Mulloy and Billy Talbert
1947	Jack Kramer and Ted Schroeder
1948	Gardnar Mulloy and Billy Talbert
1949	John Bromwich and Billy Sidwell (Australia)

The British champions are determined at Wimbledon. Victory at both Forest Hills and Wimbledon is considered a notable accomplishment. The Wimbledon tourney also was not held during the 1940–45 period. Subsequent men's singles winners in the 1940s were:

Date	Winner	Runner-up
1946	Yvon Petra	Geoff Brown
1947	Jack Kramer	Tom Brown, Jr.
1948	Bob Falkenburg	John Bromwich
1949	Ted Schroeder	Jaroslav Drobny

The 1946–49 Wimbledon men's doubles winners were:

1946	Jack Kramer and Tom Brown, Jr.
1947	Jack Kramer and Bob Falkenburg
1948	John Bromwich and Frank Sedgman (Australia)
1949	Pancho Gonzales and Frank Parker

Among the ranks of women tennis players, Sarah Palfrey Cooke, Pauline Betz, Margaret Osborne, and Louise Brough were dominant, as is indicated by the American and English champions of the period.

U.S. National Women's Singles Champions and Runners-up

National amateur and collegiate tennis champion, Joe Hunt of Navy. Hunt was the NCAA singles champion in 1941. Two years later, he won the U.S. Amateur singles title at Forest Hills. Like All-American Nile Kinnick and NCAA champion shot-putter and pro football star, Al Blozis, Hunt was killed in World War II. (Courtesy of the Naval Academy Athletic Association.)

Date	Winner	Runner-up
1940	Alice Marble	Helen Jacobs
1941	Sarah Palfrey Cooke	Pauline Betz
1942	Pauline Betz	Louise Brough
1943	Pauline Betz	Louise Brough
1944	Pauline Betz	Margaret Osborne
1945	Sarah Palfrey Cooke	Pauline Betz
1946	Pauline Betz	Doris Hart
1947	Louise Brough	Margaret Osborne
1948	Margaret Osborne duPont	Louise Brough
1949	Margaret Osborne duPont	Doris Hart

The U.S. national women's doubles champions are easier to report. Sarah Palfrey (later, Cooke) teamed with Alice Marble to win in 1940, and Cooke, paired with Margaret Osborne, captured the 1941 title. From 1942 through 1950 the winners were Louise Brough and Margaret Osborne with the only variety in the record book being provided by the fact that Margaret Osborne added her married name of duPont in the 1948–50 period.

The women singles winners and runners-up at Wimbledon were:

Date	Winner	Runner-up
1946	Pauline Betz	Louise Brough
1947	Margaret Osborne	Doris Hart
1948	Louise Brough	Doris Hart
1949	Louise Brough	Margaret Osborne duPont

And the women's doubles winners there were:

1946	Louise Brough and Margaret Osborne
1947	Doris Hart and Patricia Canning Todd
1948	Louise Brough and Margaret Osborne duPont
1948	Louise Brough and Margaret Osborne duPont

American women continued their dominance of the Wightman Cup matches played annually (but not from 1940–45 because of the war) between top women players in the United States and the United Kingdom. Five singles and two doubles matches are played each year, and the American women lost only one of the twenty-eight matches played in the 1946–49 period.

Professional and amateur tennis were separate before 1968. In the 1940s, one of the prominent stars in the ranks of pro tennis was Don Budge. The redhead with the powerful service won the professional singles championship in 1940 and 1942, and was second to Bobby Riggs in 1946, 1947, and 1949. In doubles he teamed with three different partners (Fred Perry in 1940 and 1941, Bobby Riggs in 1942 and 1947, and Frank Kovacs in 1949) to win the pro crown five times between 1940 and 1949. He was also second once.

A contrast in physical stature to Budge was Bobby Riggs who was often a head shorter than his opponent, but made up for it with desire. In addition to his three pro singles titles mentioned above, Riggs finished second to Budge in 1942 and second to Jack Kramer in 1948. In addition to the two pro doubles crowns won by Budge and Riggs, they were second in 1948. Riggs, with another partner, was also second in 1946.

Young's all-time favorite tennis player, Jack Kramer, won a tennis grand slam in singles and doubles at Forest Hills and Wimbledon in 1947, and then turned pro. He swept the singles and doubles (with Pancho Segura) crowns in the pro circuit in 1948.

In collegiate tennis, team champions were not recognized by the NCAA until 1946, and Southern California and William and Mary were one-two in the latter year. William and Mary proceeded to capture the team crowns in 1947 and 1948 (with Rice and San Francisco the respective runners-up), and San Francisco moved into the number one position in 1949 with three schools tied for second. Individual NCAA titlists in the 1940s included players who also made names for themselves at Forest Hills and Wimbledon—Don McNeill, Joe Hunt (who was killed in the war), Ted Schroeder, Francisco "Pancho" Segura, and Bob Falkenburg. The NCAA single champions were:

1940	Don McNeill	Kenyon
1941	Joe Hunt	Navy
1942	Ted Schroeder	Stanford
1943	Pancho Segura	Miami
1944	Pancho Segura	Miami
1945	Pancho Segura	Miami
1946	Bob Falkenburg	USC
1947	Gardner Larned	William and Mary
1948	Harry Likas	San Francisco
1949	Jack Tuero	Tulane

And the NCAA doubles champions were:

1940	Lawrence Dee and James Wade.	Stanford
1941	Charles Olewin and Charles Mattman	USC
1942	Ted Schroeder and Lawrence Dee	Stanford
1943	John Hickman and Walter Driver	Texas
1944	John Hickman and Felix Kelley	Texas
1945	Pancho Segura and Thomas Burke	Miami
1946	Bob and Tom Falkenburg	USC
1947	Sam Match and Bob Curtis	Rice
1948	Fred Kovaleski and Bernard Bartzen	William and Mary
1949	James Brink and Fred Fisher	Washington

In sum, it can be said that the 1940s were an exceptional decade in the world of men's tennis. A recent survey picked the top five tennis players of all time. The men chosen were: Bill Tilden, Don

Budge, Jack Kramer, Pancho Gonzales, and Rod Laver. Three of those five—Budge, Kramer, and Gonzales were in their prime in the 1940s. Big Bill Tilden teamed with Vincent Richards to win the men's pro doubles in 1945. As for the women, the choices were Helen Wills, Suzanne Lenglen, Alice Marble, Maureen Connolly, and Billie Jean King.

GOLF

The big names in golf in the 1940s included Byron Nelson, Ben Hogan, Sam Snead, and Jimmy Demaret in the men's professional ranks; Frank Stranahan and Willie Turnesa in the men's amateur; and Babe Didrickson Zaharias and Louise Suggs among the women. The authors became aware of the sport at the time "Lord" Byron Nelson was dueling in the sun with a golfer named Jug McSpaden. A list of the winners in the major tournaments of the time provides a good indication of the dominant players:

Anne Baxter, Dennis O'Keefe, Cary Middlecoff, Jimmy Demaret, June Havoc, and Glenn Ford in *Follow the Sun*, a screen biography of Ben Hogan.

United States Open

Year	Winner	Year	Winner
1940	Lawson Little	1947	Lew Worsham
1941	Craig Wood	1948	Ben Hogan
1942-45	Not played	1949	Cary Middlecoff
1946	Lloyd Mangrum		

The absence of Sam Snead in the above list is notable, as it has been since 1949, for Snead's Open "jinx" was as applicable in that decade as it has been in more recent years. He came very close to winning in 1947, but a relative unknown, Lew Worsham, defeated him by one stroke on the last green of their eighteen-hole playoff for the title.

Masters Tournament

Year	Winner	Year	Winner
1940	Jimmy Demaret	1946	Herman Keiser
1941	Craig Wood	1947	Jimmy Demaret
1942	Byron Nelson	1948	Claude Harmon
1943-45	Not played	1949	Sam Snead

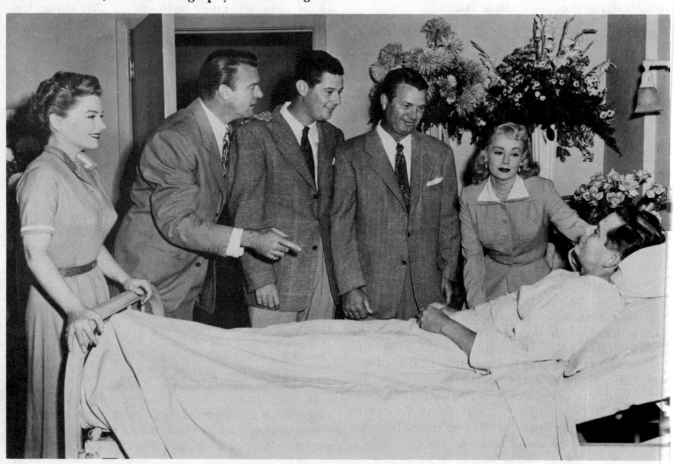

Sam Snead and Glenn Ford in *Follow the Sun.*

By way of contrast, in 1972 Jack Nicklaus won $320,542 on the pro circuit. It was not because of the latter's greater relative dominance of the game, because Nelson's $63,335 represented a record of winning eleven of nineteen tournaments in a single year—nine of them consecutively. He won fifty major tournaments in fifteen years. In one tournament, Nicklaus could win nearly the equivalent of Nelson's total earnings during the latter's best season.

Nelson retired from tournament competition at age thirty-four in 1946 after achieving most of his personal goals. He had won the U.S. Open, the PGA, and the Masters, and he held records for the most tournaments won in a year; the most consecutive tournament titles; and the most money in a season. Moreover, he had twice been named Athlete of the Year.

Ben Hogan eventually became Young's favorite golfer, especially after his remarkable comeback from near-fatal injuries in an auto accident, but the latter victories occurred in the early 1950s.

In the men's nonprofessional ranks, the U.S. Amateur and British Amateur were regarded as the prime tests of golfing success. The winners of the former tourney were:

Professional Golfers Association (PGA) Championships

1940	Byron Nelson	1945	Byron Nelson
1941	Vic Ghezzi	1946	Ben Hogan
1942	Sam Snead	1947	Jim Ferrier
1943	Not played	1948	Ben Hogan
1944	Bob Hamilton	1949	Sam Snead

British Open

1940–45	Not played	1948	Henry Cotton
1946	Sam Snead	1949	Bobby Locke
1947	Fred Daly		

1940	Dick Chapman	1947	Skee Riegel
1941	Bud Ward	1948	Willie Turnesa
1942–45	*Not played*	1949	Charles Coe
1946	Ted Bishop		

And the British Amateur champions were:

1940–45	*Not played*	1948	Frank Stranahan
1946	James Bruen	1949	S. Max McCready
1947	Willie Turnesa		

PGA Leading Money Winners					
Date	Golfer	Dollars	Date	Golfer	Dollars
1941	Ben Hogan	18,358	1946	Ben Hogan	42,556
1942	Ben Hogan	13,143	1947	Jimmy Demaret	27,936
1943	No records kept		1948	Ben Hogan	36,812
1944	Byron Nelson	37,967	1949	Sam Snead	31,593
1945	Byron Nelson	63,335			

Stranahan was well publicized as an heir to a spark-plug manufacturer's fortune and as a golfer who trained with weights. Willie Turnesa was one of several brothers who made names as golfers.

NCAA champions in the 1940s were as follows:

Date	Individual Champion		Team Champion
1940	F. Dixon Brooke	Virginina	Princeton, LSU
1941	Earl Stewart	LSU	Stanford
1942	Frank Tatum, Jr.	Stanford	Stanford, LSU
1943	Wallace Ulrich	Carleton	Yale
1944	Louis Lick	Minnesota	Notre Dame
1945	John Lorms	Ohio State	Ohio State
1946	George Hamer	Georgia	Stanford
1947	Dave Barclay	Michigan	LSU
1948	Bob Harris	San Jose	San Jose
1949	Harvie Ward	North Carolina	North Texas State

Babe Didrickson Zaharias was by far the best-known woman golfer. The Babe had been famous for her 1932 Olympic track victories, but she was an extremely versatile athlete (she was married to a professional wrestler). She won the U.S. Women's Amateur in 1946, and won the U.S. Women's Open in 1948, 1950, and 1954. Louise Suggs was the champion of the Women's Amateur in 1947, and of the U.S. Women's Open in 1949 and 1952. Other winners in the U.S. Women's Amateur (it was not held from 1942–45) were Betty Jameson in 1940 (she successfully defended her 1939 title), Mrs. Betty Hicks Newell in 1941, Grace Lenczyk in 1948, and Dorothy Porter in 1949. Patty Berg won the Women's Open in its first year (1946), and Betty Jameson captured that title in 1947.

In comparing golfers of today with those in his own era, Byron Nelson asserts that changes in the basic golf swing have been dictated by changes in equipment. He feels that power hitters of today could not use the old hickory-shafted golf clubs because of the punishment they would endure. Pros of his day "didn't hit the ball as hard and needed to use more finesse on many shots." There was no pitching wedge or sand wedge, for example, and thus golfers had to open the face of the niblick— the equivalent of today's nine iron—to obtain loft and get the ball to stop on the green.

Moreover, Nelson has observed, courses are longer and greens are larger and softer today. This increase in size is attributable to the fact that more people are playing golf. The heavier traffic would have killed the smaller greens of the past.

Golf began to flourish as people came to be more affluent and have more leisure time. The large purses and national television have given the sport more glamour, excitement, and attractiveness.

Commercial endorsements were not as large in Nelson's day, as "golf just wasn't that big then, and the game couldn't command the big purses and endorsement money it can today." In general, Byron Nelson is reluctant to compare specific golfers of the two eras because he feels that the oldsters were "playing a different game in those days."

Nelson still plays golf. Many pros believe that few men know and can demonstrate the techniques of a sound golf swing as well as he.

In September of 1974, Byron Nelson was inducted into the World Golf Hall of Fame as a charter member along with other stars of the links: Patty Berg, Walter Hagen, Ben Hogan, Bobby Jones, Francis Ouimet, Jack Nicklaus, Arnold Palmer, Gary Player, Gene Sarazen, Sam Snead, and Babe Didrickson Zaharias. The enshrinement took place in a new 2.5 million dollar building in the North Carolina sandhill country at Pinehurst.

Roberto de Vicenzo, the "globe-girdling gaucho" and winner of more tournaments than any other player in golfing history (189 as of July 1974), calls Sam Snead the best player who ever lived. De Vicenzo, who began his pro career in 1948 and won the British Open at age forty-four in 1967, claims that no one can compare with Snead. De Vicenzo cites the fact that Snead began winning tournaments in 1938, is still winning them now, and "still holds his own with the best of the kids." Roberto concludes: "Ben Hogan was a great golfer, but he stopped too soon. I rate Snead the best because of his many victories over so long a span. Golf may never see anyone like him."

HORSE RACING

The decade of the 1940s was an unusual one in the Sport of Kings, because there were four Triple Crown winners (horses victorious at the Kentucky Derby, Preakness, and Belmont Stakes—the classic races of three-year-olds). There had only been four such champions prior to 1941—Sir Barton in 1919, Gallant Fox in 1930, Omaha in 1935, and War Admiral in 1937. And since the 1940s there has been only one—Secretariat in 1973, twenty-five years after Citation accomplished the feat. The other Triple Crown winners were Whirlaway in 1941, Count Fleet in 1943, and Assault in 1946. Warren Wright was the owner of Whirlaway and Citation; Mrs. John Hertz, of Count Fleet; and Robert J. Kleberg, of Assault.

Jockey Eddie Arcaro rode Whirlaway to his three victories in 1941, and he repeated this feat with Citation in 1948. These accomplishments alone make him deserving of the honor of Jockey of the Decade, but he also rode a third Kentucky Derby winner and two other winners at the Belmont Stakes. Another famous jockey, Johnny Longden, was up on Count Fleet in 1943.

Winners of the Kentucky Derby (a mile and a quarter course at Churchill Downs in Louisville) were:

Year	Winner	Jockey	Second
1940	Gallahadion	C. Bierman	Bimelech
1941	Whirlaway	E. Arcaro	Staretor
1942	Shut Out	W. D. Wright	Alsab
1943	Count Fleet	J. Longden	Blue Swords
1944	Pensive	C. McCreary	Broadcloth
1945	Hoop Jr.	E. Arcaro	Pot o'Luck
1946	Assault	W. Mehrtens	Spy Song
1947	Jet Pilot	E. Guerin	Phalanx
1948	Citation	E. Arcaro	Coaltown
1949	Ponder	S. Brooks	Capot

The 1944 Kentucky Derby was the first one of which McClure and Young were aware at the time it was held. A picture of the 1945 winner, Hoop Jr., was mounted by Young in his first sports scrapbook. The latter also read *Sport* magazine's feature stories about Arcaro and other jockeys from time to time. The names of some of the great horses of the past such as Man O'War, Seabiscuit, Gallant Fox, and Whirlaway became known to the Young boys because of yet another popular Cadaco-Ellis parlor game ("American Derby") that they played during the period. In that game the players moved their pieces (representing great steeds of the past) around the playing board (track) a number of spaces (lengths) corresponding to the results of their throws of the dice.

The winners of the Preakness Stakes (a mile and three-sixteenths course at Pimlico in Baltimore):

Year	Winner	Jockey	Second
1940	Bimelech	F. A. Smith	Mioland
1941	Whirlaway	E. Arcaro	King Cole
1942	Alsab	B. James	Tie, Requested and Sun Again
1943	Count Fleet	J. Longden	Blue Swords
1944	Pensive	C. McCreary	Platter
1945	Polynesian	W. D. Wright	Hoop Jr.
1946	Assault	W. Mehrtens	Lord Boswell
1947	Faultless	D. Dodson	On Trust
1948	Citation	E. Arcaro	Vulcan's Forge
1949	Capot	T. Atkinson	Palestinian

And the winners of the Belmont Stakes (a mile and a half course at Belmont Park in Elmont, New York) were:

Year	Winner	Jockey	Second
1940	Bimelech	F. A. Smith	Your Chance
1941	Whirlaway	E. Arcaro	Robert Morris
1942	Shut Out	E. Arcaro	Alsab
1943	Count Fleet	J. Longden	Fairy Manhurst
1944	Bounding Home	G. L. Smith	Pensive
1945	Pavot	E. Arcaro	Wildlife
1946	Assault	W. Mehrtens	Natchez
1947	Phalanx	R. Donoso	Tide Rips
1948	Citation	E. Arcaro	Better Self
1949	Capot	T. Atkinson	Ponder

Noteworthy is the fact that four horses—Bimelech (1940), Shut Out (1942), Pensive (1944), and Capot (1949) won two of the three great races. Bimelech and Shut Out were the leading money winners among thoroughbred horses in 1940 and 1942, respectively. It should also be noted that three of the above four horses were second in the only race of the three that they did not win. Pensive was the only one of the four that lost on the last leg of the Triple Crown—the Belmont Stakes.

Arcaro was the leading money winner among jockeys in 1940, 1942, and 1948. Longden led in 1943 and 1945; Ted Atkinson, in 1944 and 1946; and the trio of Donald Meade, Doug Dodson, and Steve Brooks won the honors in 1941, 1947, and 1949, respectively.

Willie Shoemaker, picked by *Sport* as the Top Performer of the 1946–71 period (first twenty-five years of the magazine's existence), was only an apprentice jockey in 1949, but won 219 races and was the leading money winner among jockeys in 1951.

The 1940s was a good decade for Churchill Downs and the Kentucky Derby, which has been run every year since 1875. This was in spite of gasoline rationing that forced spectators to ride streetcars in 1944 (to the "Trolley Car Derby," as it was dubbed) and wartime regulations that nearly forced cancellation of the race in 1945 (it did result in a postponement of it to 17 June). The decade was dominated by the horses of Kentucky's own Calumet Farms—Whirlaway, Pensive, Citation, and Ponder. Also it was an end of an era when Colonel Matt Winn died. Colonel Winn had been the president of the Derby since 1902 and had seen his first "Running for the Roses" in 1875 from the grocery wagon of his father. He was to see seventy-five such races in his lifetime. Winn has been credited with making the Derby successful. Sports commentator and columnist Bill Corum succeeded him as president.

The authors' interest in the sport did not extend much beyond the three races described above and occasional notice of the leading jockeys in the newspapers and sports magazines.

HOCKEY

Hockey will have to be passed over with a few paragraphs, for the authors did not follow the sport with much degree of regularity or intensity during the 1940s. Despite this, as was the case with respect to other sports, Young had a favorite team and player in hockey—the Montreal Canadiens and Maurice "the Rocket" Richard. But his interest was such that he was not even aware until a later decade that he was not pronouncing "Canadiens" and "Richard" correctly. (The same was true of McClure.) Familiarity with the names of the teams and a few players like Richard of the Canadiens, Turk Broda of the Toronto Maple Leafs, and Max Bentley of the Chicago Black Hawks was nearly the extent of the authors' knowledge about the sport.

Stanley Cup winners of the 1940s indicate the dominance by Toronto of National Hockey League play during the decade:

1940	New York Rangers	1945	Toronto Maple Leafs
1941	Boston Bruins	1946	Montreal Canadiens
1942	Toronto Maple Leafs	1947	Toronto Maple Leafs
1943	Detroit Red Wings	1948	Toronto Maple Leafs
1944	Montreal Canadiens	1949	Toronto Maple Leafs

In a *Sport* article entitled "Hockey Was a Better Game in My Day," the incomparable Maurice Richard compares today's hockey with that of an earlier era. Richard claimed that in his day "shooting was more accurate. . . . Passing was cleverer. Stick handling was an art practiced not just by a few but by many. And most important, there was much more individuality . . ."

He blames expansion (of the number of NHL clubs) for what he sees as a decline in the game. The "Rocket" stated that scoring values have been downgraded by expansion and also that the game "isn't as tough as it used to be." He feels hockey is "sloppier" today and that the great forward lines of the past have disappeared. In this connection he cites those that were especially famous in 1948: the "Punch Line" of the Canadiens (Richard, Elmer Lach, and Toe Blake), the "Production Line" of the Red Wings (Gordie Howe, Ted Lind-

say, and Sid Abel), the "Kid Line" of the Maple Leafs (Howie Meeker, Vic Lynn, and Ted Kennedy), and the "Atomic Line" of the Rangers (Cal Gardner, Church Russell, and Rene Trudell).

Richard did say that the modern player was more independent and conscious of his own value than he ever was, but he thought that today's player had been spoiled by his new riches.

> Some expansion players, for example, realize that the reserves behind them aren't very talented, so they are not apt to work as hard as we used to; we knew that if we didn't produce there was plenty of good material in the minors.

He also stated that fraternizing between opposing players, such as those from different teams running a business jointly, "takes something off the competitive edge." ". . . When I played, fraternizing with the enemy was out."

SPORTS AND THE MEDIA

In this potpourri, some mention should be made of the sportswriters, sportscasters, and sports literature of the 1940s, because they contributed so much to the style and tenor of the times, hero worship, and the general perception that youngsters possessed toward the sporting life and the world around them. First and foremost among sportswriters was the venerable Grantland Rice who was as gifted with his Kiplingesque verse as he was in his colorful accounts of sporting events. Arthur Daley, John Kieran, Shirley Povich, Frank Graham, Frederick Lieb, Harold Kaese, J. G. Taylor Spink, Frank Menke, Tim Cohane, J. Roy Stockton, Tom Meany, Paul Gallico, George Trevor, and Stanley Frank were some of the other outstanding sportswriters with whom the authors were familiar by their reading of *The Sporting News, Sport,* syndicated columns on the newspaper sports pages, and books. The authors had each developed a small sports library by the end of the 1940s, when they were only thirteen.

In addition, fictional writers enriched Young and McClure's reading experiences at school. Young was especially interested in the books of the late John R. Tunis. One of the heroes in Tunis' books, which included *The Iron Duke* and *The Duke Decides,* was from Young's hometown—Waterloo, Iowa. Another favorite was Olympic gold medalist (1920 and 1924) Jackson Scholz and his fictional work on track, *Split Seconds.*

In sportscasting, mention has already been made

James Stewart, Cliff Clark, and Frank Morgan in *The Stratton Story*.

of Bill Stern, Gene Elston, and Bob Elson. Other favorites were Mel Allen of the Yankees, Red Barber of the Dodgers, Ted Husing, and boxing announcers Don Dunphy and Bill Corum (who also reported racing events on radio and in the press). Theirs was the school that has been disparagingly referred to as the "Hero Sandwich" and the "Gee-whiz" (in contrast with today's "So-what") style of journalism. It was unabashedly adulatory. It was a style that was intended to protect the athletes (and thus the tender psyches of young readers). It sacrificed realism to heroism.

Illustrative of the general thrust of this style is Grantland Rice's famous account of the Notre Dame-Army game of 1924, which one critic calls "the most influential sports story ever written."

> Outlined against a blue-grey October sky, the Four Horsemen rode again. In dramatic lore they are known as Famine, Pestilence, Destruction, and Death. These are only aliases. Their real names are Stuhldreher, Miller, Crowley, and Layden. They formed the crest of the South Bend cyclone before which another fighting Army football team was swept over the precipice of the Polo Grounds yesterday afternoon as 55,000 spectators peered down on the bewildering panorama spread on the green plain below. . . .

Randall Poe decries Rice's tendency to "hide the score" and explain "nothing about the real players on the field." Despite this writer's disagreement with most of Poe's thesis, some of the latter's description is noteworthy:

> But Rice released the sportswriter's imagination. He convinced generations of sportswriters to give up their dull habits of accuracy and let fly. He legitimatized the use of those colorful code words—*smash* for hit, *turf* for field, *ripped* for ran—which endure to this day. Rice's influence was the result not only of his technicolor style but of his sunshine philosophy. "In a two-nothing game," he said, "I tend to give the pitcher credit for pitching a good game—instead of belaboring the other team for poor hitting. You might say I go along year to year with this same philosophy."

Sportswriters like Rice were enthusiastic and not cynical. They fit the temper of the times, and they were, and still are, applauded by the authors for their efforts.

A number of feature-length motion pictures have been made about sports that have left a lasting impression on the American public. Some were frankly emotional in their appeal, while others were quite serious in their presentation of human needs and values. There have been a number of good films about baseball not the least of which was *Pride of the Yankees,* the unforgettable story of Lou Gehrig, starring Gary Cooper. It remains a film classic for movie goers. Others included *The Babe Ruth Story* with William Bendix and *The Pride of St. Louis* about Dizzy Dean's fabled career.

The Stratton Story is a film that presents Monty Stratton's fight to overcome the loss of a leg from a hunting accident at the peak of his career with the Chicago White Sox. The film was made in 1949 and took a year to produce. Stratton himself served as a technical adviser on the film to help lend accuracy to the account. Stratton had two straight 15-5 seasons in 1937 and 1938 before the accident. Films such as this one were an important part of many youngsters' lives, including Young and McClure's, in the late 1940s.

Other excellent sports movies have concerned boxing: *The Harder They Fall* with Humphrey Bogart; *Champion* with Kirk Douglas; *The Joe Louis Story; Gentleman Jim* with Errol Flynn; *Right Cross;* and probably the best ever, *Body and Soul,* with the late John Garfield.

Exciting football pictures included *Knute Rockne, Navy Blue and Gold, The Spirit of West Point* (with Glenn Davis and Doc Blanchard), and *All-American. Follow the Sun* traced the career of golfer Ben Hogan and starred Glenn Ford.

7

EPILOGUE

CONCERN FOR HEROES IN SPORTS LITERATURE

Since the authors began this study of sports heroes, many articles have been written which have underscored the importance and timeliness of the central concern of this volume. The editors of *Rotarian* magazine devoted a substantial portion of that journal's August 1974, issue to a symposium on the topic alternately titled "Where Have All the Heroes Gone?" and "Do We Need Heroes?" The articles included in the symposium were: "We Must Have Heroes" by S.L.A. Marshall, "Heroes Are Dangerous Men" by Ron Dorfman, "Heroism and Fortitude" by Josef Pieper, "The Hero and Democracy" by Sidney Hook, "The Hero As a Mirror" by Marya Mannes, and "The Decline of Greatness" by Arthur M. Schlesinger, Jr. Of the six writers, only Dorfman was negative to the idea of heroes, although Hook is favorable only if the concept is broadly defined to encompass the notion "every man a hero."

Moreover, Keith Berwick, a former UCLA history professor, has written an article for the Los Angeles Times News Service entitled "America's Plaintive Question: Where Have Heroes Gone?" He remarked that he had been part of a team of scholars touring small towns in the Western states in behalf of the National Endowment for the Humanities "to recreate the American Revolutionary experience and, if possible, to establish its relevance to present dilemmas." Berwick noted that audiences repeatedly asked the scholars the question used in the title of his article.

In the October 1974, issue of *Esquire* (devoted entirely to sports), Roger Kahn wrote an article labeled with the similar refrain: "Where Have All Our Heroes Gone?" Art Spander, in his 12 October 1974, article for *The Sporting News,* wrote on the subject: "Heroes Gone, Only Human Athletes Remain." In a 12 January 1975, article for the *Kansas City Star,* Henry C. Haskell writes under the heading "How Can We Find Great Leaders If We 'Debunk' Them?" And the writers have already referred to the article by Edward Hoagland in *The New York Times Magazine* (10 March 1974) entitled "Where Have All the Heroes Gone?"

In addition to these articles whose labels indicate the concern of their writers for the status of heroism, Young and McClure have read many articles in which the authors lamented a relative absence of the traditional hero from contemporary life. For example, Joe Robbie, owner of the Miami Dolphins, is quoted in an article entitled "Pro Football Disenchanting" as saying: "Fans regard football players as heroes. When they see their heroes involved in strikes and jumps to rival leagues they get fed up." Rich Koster, who, along with Robert Burnes of the *St. Louis Globe-Democrat,* returns again and again to this theme, writes in a column "Pro Sports: The Great Tax Write-Off": "The Wonderful World [of sport] is no longer wonderful. Its image is tarnished; it's in desperate need of heroes to replace the army of men carrying briefcases."

In another column (1 November 1974), Koster reviews articles by George Sheehan and says: "Where have all the heroes gone? Sheehan knows." Koster continues by citing Sheehan's ideas on heroes.

Koster's compatriot Bob Burnes' concern is exemplified by his article of 3 August 1974, called "The Day for the Heroes," in which he writes about the newest inductees to the Baseball Hall of Fame:

It will be a glory day for a lot of people, friends and relatives of all of the deceased honorees, the living ones themselves and for all who revere the heroes of the game. . . .

When Ford and Mantle retired, the last of the great Yankees were gone. The team today still wears the safe pin-striped uniform but it is the only connection. All the heroes are gone. . . .

You wish it could be possible to send a caravan around the baseball world with Papa [Cool Papa Bell] and Jocko [Conlan] and Mick and Whitey. Put some of their mementoes in the camper for young and old baseball fans around the country to see.

To prove perhaps that there still are some heroes left.

Columnists Mickey Herskowitz and Steve Perkins have included more than once in their question-and-answer column ("Sports Hot Line") queries from readers about Joe DiMaggio that reflect this same theme. One fan wrote to the columnists:

I had the honor this spring of playing in a pro-am celebrity tournament with Joe DiMaggio, and I realized we don't have sports heroes like him anymore, reserved and dignified and keeping his problems to himself, which is the way I remember DiMaggio as a player. Why is it today's stars are always out front and experts on everything?

The title of a recent book by Maury Allen—*Where Have You Gone, Joe DiMaggio: The Story of America's Last Hero*—underscores that fan's realization.

AP correspondent Will Grimsley writes about former restaurateur Toots Shor's statements on this subject:

"Ruth, Jack Dempsey and Joe DiMaggio—they were real heroes," the restaurateur said. "After making them, God must have discarded the mold. The heroes today are just a bunch of ice cream eaters."

Shor said modern day stars have become victims of affluence and most of them are plastic warriors, surrounded by lawyers and agents, too busy counting money in their counting houses to relate to the public.

An article distributed by the Christian Science Monitor News Service notes that Douglas Wallop, author of *The Year the Yankees Lost the Pennant* (which was made into the famous musical *Damn Yankees*), has lost much of his interest in baseball because of "the demise of his villains and the dis-

appearance of his heroes." The article notes that "fewer fans seem to follow a team with the type of passion" that characterized Wallop's previous dedication to the sport. In addition, Gerald Eskenazi, in his "Talk of the Times" article for the *Kansas City Times*, alludes to "years of growing cynicism with their heroes."

Cincinnati Reds star Johnny Bench, in lamenting the negativism of the press toward athletes, was quoted as saying:

At a time when kids need heroes the press is tearing everything down. It started with Cosell. Now everybody's trying to make a niche the same way. . . .

This all started way before Watergate. I guess it's a built-in hazard. It seems like people like to put you up as a superman, then love to tear you down. . . .

. . . it seems like anybody that goes against tradition is Howard's man.

Recent statements about the passing of heroes can also be found in literature on other aspects of popular culture. In a 11 December 1974, review of a play entitled *When You Comin' Back, Red Ryder?*, which incidentally is anti-heroic in its message, editor Bob Goddard asks the oft-repeated question and then answers it:

Where did all those Old West heroes go? They went thataway, pardner, and we're not apt to see the likes of them ever again in this day and age. But ironic echoes of that legendary time are packed with potent effect into "When You Comin' Back, Red Ryder?," this week's offering at the American Theatre.

And Clarence Page, in commenting on the acceleration of interest in Sherlock Holmes, quotes a bookstore owner to this effect:

"We need Sherlock Holmes these days," said Stuart Brent, of Chicago's Brent Bookstore. "The late Vincent Starrett (a famed Holmes expert) used to call them the greatest fairy tales ever written for grownups. He was right! This current interest is a direct result of the general anxieties grownups experience today. We need heroes again. We love Holmes because he wins without killing. It's more sophisticated, civilized, and sensible than the Vince Lombardi philosophy that says 'Win at any cost.'"

"During the Great Depression the public went wild for a new comic book character called 'Superman,'" Brent observed. "What could be finer for a guy who can't fall for the nonsense of Superman than to fall for the good sense of Sherlock Holmes? It gives us the shot in the arm that we need right now."

In an October 1974, article surveying campus

opinion ("The Class of '78"), education writer Cathy Underhill lists items that are "in" and those that are "out" with today's college students in the St. Louis area. "1940s clothes" are listed as "in" along with fraternities, Scott Joplin, and blue jeans, among others. But "Heroes" are listed as being "out" along with President Kennedy, Andy Warhol, flower children, and school pennants. Underhill concludes that students she interviewed even shun the word "hero." "There's no heroes [sic] today, nobody for us to identify with," one freshman is quoted as saying. "There's just nobody I picture as a hero. It's more traits of a lot of people, I admire," was another comment. Also: "Students are searching for someone ideal who isn't there." And: "A hero before was a person who had no apparent flaws. Now the weaknesses of public figures are open to view."

By way of emphasizing the authors' belief that the old-fashioned form of hero worship is not absent in today's sports world (albeit de-emphasized in the media): Archie Griffin, the 1974 and 1975 Heisman Trophy winner, stated before a sophisticated audience gathered in New York for his 1974 trophy acceptance speech: "If today's young people look up to the Heisman Trophy winner like I did, I promise to do everything in my power to be the greatest example." A news account of the event stated that Griffin's voice was "choked with emotion" as the Buckeye junior exclaimed that his motto in life was "the three D's, desire, dedication and determination." Griffin added that his junior high school coach had instilled these qualities in him. And reminiscent of some of the Heisman winners he emulated, Griffin concluded: "I wish I knew a way to divide this trophy with every other member of the team."

DEFINITION OF A HERO

S.L.A. Marshall defines heroism as a "selfless act with a degree of ultimate risk." His definition, by his own statement, excludes "the athlete and the sportsman." Obviously in a book about sports heroes, Marshall's meaning is not the one ascribed to the subject at hand. Ron Dorfman seems to confine heroes to a militaristic straitjacket and thus is also not helpful in a quest for applicable precision in terms. Josef Pieper, on the other hand, comes closer to the present authors' meaning when he hypothetically alludes to heroism as "exceptional ability in any sphere—football, boxing, scientific experimentation, or landing on the moon

—or similarly, . . . exceptional success . . ." His conclusion that heroism in this sense "is not less evident in the contemporary world than it was in previous epochs" is accurate, but it must be noted that this concept excludes consideration of the qualities of character or example (values) possessed by those with the exceptional ability that he requires. As mentioned, Pieper's conceptualization quoted above is stated hypothetically for purposes of analysis. He actually settles on the virtue of fortitude or courage as the essence of heroism. He is mainly focusing on the person who

risks his life for the sake of truth and good, whether in the pointedly dramatic act of martyrdom or in lifelong devotion—in acquiescence to the absolute will of God at the cost of one's own worldly comfort.

Even though the authors' study of sports is intended to be a serious one, it must be admitted that engagement in athletics is mainly a diversion and thus takes on more of a selfish than a selfless aspect. Thus, Pieper's ultimate definition should also be regarded as inapplicable. Sidney Hook refers to heroes as "the great figures in the Pantheon of thought, the men of ideas, of social vision, of scientific achievement and artistic power . . . not the soldier or the political leader . . . but the teacher . . ." Similarly, it would be too pretentious to claim these qualities or characteristics for the athletes in this study.

However, Hook then broadens his definition by recognizing that heroes "can be made by fitting social opportunities more skillfully to specific talents." He adds that "From this point of view, a hero is any individual who does his work well and makes a unique contribution to the public good." This would seem to approach very closely the concept of sports heroes in this volume. Most of the latter perform their athletic skills exceptionally well and contribute to the public good by personifying values that have long been held to be worthy of emulation. Hook's democratic conceptualization of "every man a hero" raises the significant point that the potentiality of greatness lies within us all if the concept is defined in his broad sense. Similarly Marya Mannes refers to the "continued craving for someone—hero, savior, or simply strong and honest being—to enlarge us with trust and belief, to rally us toward a higher and better plane of living." Again, her attribution of meaning to the term "hero" could be applied to certain athletes.

In sum the authors believe that a hero is one who not only performs well but also is *a model of conduct for others and exemplifies decent behavior* ("decent" in turn is defined in the natural law sense as something that does not change through the ages).

THE NEED FOR HEROES

In America the need for heroes is as great as it ever was. These are anxious times, but so were most, if not all, previous eras in their own way. Today's anxiety stems in large part from the swift, accelerating change that has placed stress upon, eroded, and even shattered institutions that are the backbone of any society—the home, church, school, and local community, among others. Much greater mobility, changing family relationships, and a movement toward homogenization of our culture are destabilizing forces that mark these times as different from previous periods of American history and create problems of rootlessness and insecurity.

As a single but not unimportant example of these changes, the father spends relatively little time with his children and thus does not have the molding effect on the latter's character as was the case in prior generations. The father is not as able to set a good example for the child as much as was his counterpart in an agricultural society when the father and child worked at home and in the fields. Today the child is affected more by his immature peers, by the groups and institutions outside the home (which have changed dramatically), and by the electronic mass media.

Today's children (and their parents and other adults) need guidance in coping with the insecurities posed by the sometimes depersonalizing forces of change. God has been, and should be, the ultimate Guide. Even with Divine Guidance, however, it is natural for people to look also to human examples of upright conduct. The plaintive cry "Where have all the heroes gone?" is a frustrated reaction to the feeling that there is a relative absence of the type of hero found in previous decades. Constant, unrelenting exposure of *national* figures by the electronic media often reveals flawed features and feet of clay. Even in a period in which many feel moral standards are declining, *local* heroes are seemingly held to higher standards of conduct than before by a community which is all too inclined to leap on every weakness and say, "I told you so." It is said that heroes reflect the nature of society. Many feel that national figures who receive so much publicity today are neither representative nor heroic. Perhaps there are as many heroic figures as before, but we do not see them. If so, that would be a tragedy of our times.

If there are eternal principles of right and wrong (such as natural law), as the writers think that there must be, genuine heroes of our age should resemble their counterparts in previous eras as to major characteristics. Today's heroes are, or should be, representative of the decent positions on moral issues. Only if values are relative, pragmatic, changing, and not universal should the *essential* nature of heroes change with the times. The authors steadfastly reject these latter assumptions.

The editors of the *Rotarian* study quote American novelist Chaim Potok: "Heroes are the inevitable concomitant of a system of value and thought that has been embraced by an aggregate of men. An idea gone public produces heroes as dividends." The *Rotarian* editors then conclude: "If our system no longer has heroes, the implication is that our values have also been dissipated." Because of the fact that heroes reflect and personify values, the *Rotarian* editors add: ". . . who we select as our heroes tells more about ourselves than about the heroes."

The need for heroes is as omnipresent as the need for values. More examples of heroism need to be brought to the fore, and each person bears a responsibility to see that this is done.

Keeping in mind the limitation imposed by differing definitions of heroism, the sentiments of the authors are echoed by most of those cited in the *Rotarian* study: Marshall says ". . . we need heroes no less and hero images the more." Pieper asserts: ". . . 'heroism' is viable in every age, today no less than in the time of Homer or in that of the *Song of the Nibelungs*," and "I cannot see why this conception of heroism . . . should lose even an iota of viability in the present age or in the future." Hook contributes this statement: "A democracy should contrive its affairs, not to give one or a few the chance to reach heroic stature, but rather to take as a regulative ideal the slogan, 'every man a hero.'" And Mannes: "The nation without heroes is a nation without a future." Finally, Schlesinger: "If our society has lost its wish for heroes and its ability to produce them, it may well turn out to have lost everything else as well."

Obviously athletic heroes cannot be equated with political heroes (although on occasion the two may correspond), but insofar as they personify outstanding qualities, they are indeed valuable in the formation of a favorable national character that is vital to the long-range survival of a society.

REASONS FOR THE EMERGENCE
OF THE SPORTS HERO
OF THE 1940S

In an article about the great North Carolina tailback Charlie "Choo Choo" Justice, Ron Fimrite refers to the "magical old football heroes of the late forties, heroes like [Justice]." He describes Justice's aspirations toward athletic heroism in these terms:

> He had for years practiced being a hero. As a boy in Asheville he had run through a broken field of women grocery shoppers, farmers' trucks and sidewalk cracks. He announced his own imagined triumphs in the hysterical style of a radio sportscaster. He had wanted nothing more than to be an All-American halfback, a football hero. And now he was one. He was Charlie (Choo Choo) Justice, the biggest hero of them all. . . .

Fimrite refers to the "phantoms, these All-America football heroes of nearly 25 years ago," and includes Justice and his All-American backfield companions Charlie Trippi, Johnny Lujack, and Doak Walker. He thinks that there are no heroes in college football today—"only superstars." He calls that period college football's "finest hour," and the authors of this study concur. In fact, as stated above, it was a conversation about these very stars that inspired the writers to pursue this subject in the first place.

What was there about these football stars of the late 1940s that made them "heroes" rather than just "superstars"? In summary form, the reasons may be these (some of the following apply to athletes of the 1940s in other sports):

1) These men appeared on the athletic scene when a nation was weary of a depression and a war and wanted entertainment, diversion, or escape. To paraphrase Fimrite: Americans didn't want their heroes in foxholes any more; they wanted them in the backfield.

2) Many of the athletes in the postwar period had fought in the war. Many were resuming an athletic career begun before or during the war. The experience of war had matured these young men. They were older and more experienced athletes as well.

3) During the war eligibility requirements had been relaxed, and some like Barney Poole were able to participate in collegiate competition more than four years. Thus many had established their reputations in college and/or service ball. They were famous before they set foot on the college campus after the war. The drumbeat of publicity by collegiate sports information bureaus and other media agents had already begun. In a phrase, there was more time for ballyhoo.

4) The T formation had not yet become overwhelmingly dominant in football. The single-wing formation was more productive of the triple-threat back, who could run, pass, and kick (usually it was the tailback in the latter formation who possessed these skills). The T formation resulted in more functional specialization. It did not make the triple-threat back extinct, as Bobby Layne of Texas illustrates, but Layne had been a single-wing performer and was converted in his senior year to a new role as T-quarterback.

5) The two-platoon system also had not yet taken hold to the extent it has today. Most of the great players of the 1940s were stars on offense and defense. Some like Trippi and Lujack were the best tacklers on the field. The fans and reporters thus could more readily digest their sports information with the smaller number of players.

6) On the professional scene, there were fewer teams in this era prior to "expansion." And the teams that did exist had been durable and long-lived. The sixteen major league baseball teams had existed without the moving of franchises since the beginning of the century. Players like Luke Appling, Joe DiMaggio, Ted Williams, and Stan Musial were also more apt to continue with the same club throughout their careers, enabling fans of those teams to identify with their players more. From the fans' standpoint, that is the stuff out of which team loyalties are made.

7) There were fewer diversions available for the fan, young and old alike in those days. There was not so much leisure time, nor was there as much affluence, and participation sports (a healthy development) did not flourish as much as they do today. In a small community, merely the introduction of a single additional form of rival entertainment such as midget auto racing or stock car racing could cause a substantial decline in attendance at minor league baseball games.

8) Related to the latter point is that times were simpler. People were less sophisticated and cynical and were apt to be satisfied with somewhat less in the way of entertainment. Not having been bombarded with first-rate athletic (and other) performances via the television tube, they did not expect as high a standard of performance by their hometown or collegiate stars. And, with this more basic life-style, there was more genuine enthusiasm for, and identification with, teams and heroes.

9) As mentioned in the first chapter, the ability to identify with sports stars possibly could be af-

fected by the racial composition of the recent crop of pro sport heroes, although the racial factor is not applicable to the writers, as McClure's idolization of Sugar Ray Robinson and Jackie Robinson illustrates. Moreover, the fact that there are black, white, and yellow stars today would seem to make it possible for more people to identify, if the athlete's skin color be that important. Admittedly, the racial factor may be an inhibiting one for some in their ability or willingness to identify, however. Perhaps more important is the variance in lifestyles of some sports heroes—their hair, dress, and social and family life, for example. It would seem that this may be more important so far as the ability of many adults today to identify with sports stars is concerned, but not so much of an obstacle for *youth,* if the generation gap theory has any validity in this respect. And yet, young people are not a homogeneous group either. Especially the life-style of an athlete like Bill Walton may "turn off" a substantial segment of the younger populace as well as a large number of adults. There were few, if any, instances of athletes refusing to stand or doff their helmets when the National Anthem was played in the 1940s.

10) Albeit this factor is a relative one, there was not so much emphasis in the press on salaries, player unions, and strikes (there were also not so many unions or strikes in the athletic world to describe). Pension funds were not such a hot item, and fans were thus not so apt to be repelled by the emphasis on playing for money rather than for the inherent value or "fun" of the game.

11) The relative absence during the 1940s of the transforming effects of the mass media (by overexposure and a more critical outlook toward athletes and their lives) has already been examined in some detail.

12) Often these stars of the 1940s *in fact* typified the values long upheld as worthy by parents for their children. Fimrite quotes a friend of Charlie Justice who said that Charlie was:

> . . . every mother's dream—clean-cut, modest, generous, didn't drink or smoke, small, boyish. . . . Charlie was a rare one. He always gave generously of his time and he was always appreciative of what athletics had done for him. He's one of the few who gave as much as he got.

And *Sport* magazine described Doak Walker in these terms:

> In his college days at Southern Methodist University, Walker neither smoked, nor drank, nor uttered anything stronger than an occasional gosh

darn. He would go to the schools in his old Dallas neighborhood and tell the kids that they should eat green vegetables, drink milk and get at least eight hours of sleep a night if they wanted to grow up to be athletes. The thing is, Doak Walker believed what he was selling. The former managing editor of this magazine, a sophisticated chap named Jack Newcombe, went to visit Doak early in Walker's marvelous pro career with the Detroit Lions. And Newcombe came back a convert to the old verities. "Doak," Newcombe wrote, "emerges as one of those rare persons who stand up in every way as a gentleman and a celebrity. Sportswriters spend their time creating heroes for their readers; rarely, if ever, do they completely believe in them. But Doak Walker has made a believer of many. I'm one of them." And Bill Rives, a former Dallas sportswriter, laid it on even thicker: "The nation fell in love with this boy," Rives wrote, "as it learned bit by bit of his strong character, his good sportsmanship, his wholesome life."

LIMITATIONS OF THIS COMPARISON

There are limitations to this attempt at comparison of eras that must be kept in mind. The fact that the writers were youngsters in the earlier period being compared is a basic one. The writers certainly admit they are not immune from the common tendency to look back on the past with rose-colored glasses, even though as social scientists they are obligated to maintain a scholar's analytical perspective.

Webster's definition of nostalgia is a "wistful or excessively sentimental, sometimes abnormal yearning for a return to . . . some past period or irrecoverable condition." Alvin Toffler, author of the bestseller, *Future Shock,* believes that the thirst for nostalgia among Americans mirrors a psychological lust for a simpler, less turbulent past. Perhaps it is a reaction to what he calls our creation of an environment so filled with accelerating change as to test the limits of human adaptive capacity.

Since World War II, and particularly in the past ten to twelve years, people have tried desperately to find something pleasant in life. It is seldom recognized, but television's Late Movies act as a sort of running commercial for the 1920s, 1930s, and 1940s especially. It has been stated that history is composed of things we would like to forget, while nostalgia is composed of things we prefer to remember. A search for our popular culture and its significance is intimately related, in the best sense, with nostalgia. It is a sort of craving for the innocence of childhood. And it takes no philosopher to know that the things of childhood should reflect our ideals—as individuals and as a society. The child's search for the heroic gesture in the 1940s is still valid in today's world.

But the fact that the authors were thirteen-years-old at the end of the 1940s does not give them the disinterested perspective of the observer who has seen the 1940s as well as the 1970s from the standpoint of adulthood. The innocence of youth undoubtedly affected the outlook of the writers in the first period being compared. Indeed there were revelations in the early 1950s that were extremely disillusioning to these maturing young men—the basketball betting scandals (involving some of Young's favorite players) and the cribbing scandal at the U.S. Military Academy are cases in point. Some of the great athletes of the 1940s have been far from heroic in their post-collegiate careers.

The introduction of television into the homes of most Americans in the 1950s brought about changes in attitudes of Americans toward sports stars, as has already been detailed in chapter 1. Other activities began taking precedence in the lives of boys who were growing into men. Participation in sports in itself diminished the time they could devote to following sports stars on local, regional, and national planes. The press of preparation for a profession or occupation reduced the time available for the type of intensive study of other athletes' activities that had contributed to the hero worship of youth.

And yet, despite this personal involvement in the decades being described, the authors think that the differences they have noted in the degree of hero worship observable in the 1940s and 1970s can be confirmed. Perhaps this is best left to those among the readers whose perspectives on these matters are more detached.

THE "TRADITIONAL" AND "MODERN" THEORIES OF SPORTS REPORTING

It is notable that the general assumptions underlying this volume are currently being subjected to a frontal assault by a school of writers that is becoming increasingly influential. The authors have already alluded to the conflict between the traditional reportorial school (disparagingly referred to as the "Hero Sandwich" and the "Gee Whiz" school of journalism—see chapters 1 and 6) and the more "modern" style of writing about sports. A recent article, syndicated by the Los An-geles Times News Service and entitled "Sportswriters Change to Trend of the '70s," describes in detail the differences in the two writing forms.

The writer of the latter article provides the traditional school with another label—"Meat and Potatoes sportswriting." It is said to consist mainly of scores and statistics such as earned-run averages, shooting percentages, and running yardage with perhaps a "few cliches" and maybe a "flowery adjective or two thrown in." The modern view, exemplified by *Sports Illustrated* articles in the eyes of that writer, is for the "more sophisticated and literate reader of today's sports page." It is said that this hypothetical modern reader wants to know more than just what happened on the field. He also wants to know what went on before or after the sporting event in the locker room, courtroom, boardroom, and bedroom.

> Racism, drugs, sex, religion, gambling, exploitation, psychology, cheating, feminism, dress styles, violence, antitrust legislation—all these subjects, and many more, have been explored in detail on the sports pages in recent months.

From the perspective of that *Los Angeles Times* writer, who clearly favors the "modern" style, the differences between the two schools of journalism appear to be as follows:

Traditional View (Gee-Whiz, Hero Sandwich, or Meat-and-Potatoes Journalism)

1. A story of a sports personality rarely included more than a "superficial, sophomoric account of the athlete's heroic on-the-field exploits, and perhaps a brief mention of his inevitably 'lovely wife' . . ."

2. The sports page was dominated with baseball statistics during the season and hot-stove league gossip in the off-season. [When was that? This sounds suspiciously like a comparison between the old *Sporting News* and *Sports Illustrated*.]

3. The sports pages contained "some of the worst writing in the newspaper . . ." [!]

4. Sportswriters functioned as sycophants or "housemen" who cheered the local team in print.

5. [This one must be quoted to reveal the unbridled arrogance of that writer.] "But the biggest single change in sportswriting has been the coming

of sociology to the sports page and the concomitant shift of the sports page away from its traditional image as the toy department of the daily newspaper —a sandbox peopled by the idiot children of journalism."

6. Sports prose was "consistently bland and hero-worshipful . . . pedestrian, cliche-ridden." Another observer, Theodore M. O'Leary, admits that "the new sports fiction is exaggerated and excessive in its denigrations" but claims that "it is a natural and overdue antidote to the silly idea that sports stadiums of America are akin to cathedrals and that competitive sports build character and are a healthy influence on contemporary life." Still a third writer called traditional sports prose a mixture of "jock worship, press-agentry and awe."

7. Grantland Rice, John Kieran, Arthur Daley, Damon Runyon, Paul Gallico, Bill Corum, Westbrook Pegler, Ring Lardner, Fred Russell, Heywood Broun, and Dick Young are typical of the writers in the traditional school.

Modern View (So-What School of Journalism)

1. A story of a sports personality probes his development as an individual, his relations with people on and off the playing field, and his attitudes toward a wide range of political, social, psychological, and individual issues.

2. Football and basketball news rivals baseball information on the sports page, and tennis, golf, and hockey receive more coverage. More obscure sports such as "river-rafting" and motorcycling receive more attention.

3. Sometimes the best writing in "very good newspapers" might well be found on the sports page. [This may be true, but not for the reasons that that writer may think.]

4. Writers today have achieved a "level of professional detachment [hoo-boy!] in print, at least [this qualification must be for the benefit of the government which is investigating "housemen" charges against sportscasters], and the rooter-as writer is a dwindling breed."

5. Presumably the coming of sociology changed all of that (see other column, number 5) and includes writing about drugs, sex, racism, feminism, violence, and other topics mentioned *supra*.

6. Sports prose is irreverent and skeptical, acerbic, trenchant, and iconoclastic. Theodore M. O'Leary describes new sports fiction as "scatalogical and profane to the point of coarseness. Its writers are well versed in sports techniques and playing field realities and jargon. It depicts most professional athletes as sexual libertarians and assumes an almost unrestricted use of stimulating drugs to hype up players for games. It recognizes courage but excludes gallantry on the playing field."

7. Red Smith and John Lardner were precursors of the new school. More recently *New York Post* writers Jimmy Cannon, Milton Gross, and Leonard Schecter typify the style, and Larry Merchant of the *Philadelphia Daily News* is given credit for making the style more pervasive.

Both the *Times* article and Randall Poe's essay in *Esquire* (quoted in Chapter 6) point to Dick Young as a representative today of the old school (and they both give him credit for being a capable sportswriter). The *Times* article relates a criticism of the modern school to the effect that it has gone too far. As an example it cites an interview with a Yankee pitcher after a World Series game during which the player was interrupted by a congratulatory telephone call from his wife. In response to the reporter's question as to the whereabouts of his wife, the pitcher responded: "Feeding the baby." The reporter's next question was "Breast or bottle?"

Dick Young is cited as one who is appalled with questions like this.

No intimacies—or sociology—for Young.

"I'm tired of this so-called in-depth crap where sportswriters ask a guy whether he wears jockey shorts or boxer shorts," Young snorts. "Too many of the young sportswriters forget they're reporters. They think they're university anthropologists or literary artists."

The *Times* writer interestingly assumes that Dick Young's criticism is echoed by most sportswriters. Thus the "modern" style is not the dominant one today, in his opinion. Also by way of balancing his prior statements casting aspersions on the intelligence of traditional writers and their readers, the *Times* article includes a critique of the modern school from writers who are basically not conservative but who object to the failure of the modernists to give the favorable, as well as the unfavorable, news about sports figures and events. And the newer stylists sometimes present "so many offbeat stories, sociological studies and in-depth analyses that they no longer provide a satisfactory accounting of the day's major sports events." Thus they have gone full circle from the critique by Poe of Grantland Rice's style which was said to "hide the score" among "brawling metaphors and foaming hype [hyperbole]."

The writers of this volume have obviously opted for Grantland Rice over Dan Jenkins (*Sports Illustrated* writer cited as illustrative of the modern school). The conflict between these two styles is significant, because the outlook of a generation toward its athletes—whether they are viewed as "heroes" or only "superstars"—will undoubtedly be affected by the way these men and women are depicted by sports journalists.

As for the values adopted by our athletes, Bill Glass and William M. Pinson, Jr., have written a provocative volume entitled *Don't Blame the Game: An Answer to Super Star Swingers and a Look at What's Right with Sports.* In the Foreword to the book, Roger Staubach says:

> I don't go along with many of the views of men such as Joe Namath, Dave Meggyesy, Bernie Parrish, Jim Bouton, and Marty Domres. I'm pleased Bill Glass has teamed with William M. Pinson, Jr. to counter their views. I agree with Glass and Pinson in most areas covered by this book. I am pleased to identify with them. So are many other professional athletes. We want our influence to count for good. We aren't self-righteous prudes, but we do believe in a God-centered morality.

SPORTS AS A CONCERN OF THE SOCIAL SCIENTIST

A person motivated by his love of sports to read this book may well have skipped the above discussion of some philosophical aspects of heroism, but those passages do illustrate that the thesis of this book is a legitimate concern of the serious scholar in the social sciences. *Political scientists* tend to leave no stone unturned in examining facets of society that have been touched by political forces and influence. Politics is involved in every significant function and aspect of our society. Sports are no exception. Whether one likes it or not, politics raises its head in the ranks of athletics. For example, despite the efforts of the Baron de Coubertin, the Olympic Games have been invaded by political forces, and it behooves us to understand them. In recent Games, the savage murders by the terrorists, the dispute over which countries should be allowed to participate, the distribution of political litera-

ture by an American woman discus thrower, the symbolic displays of political protest on the victory stand and the resultant reaction, the degree to which nations utilize their Olympic and other sports teams as an instrument of their foreign policy (to demonstrate the superiority of the *Volk* or the athletes in a "people's republic"), the informal keeping of team medal and point totals by the mass media, and the playing of the national anthems in the victory celebrations are illustrative of the political forces that have been brought to bear on an event that was intended to further amity among individual athletes and to stress participation rather than victory.

The existence or nonexistence of heroes in a society also has political implications, as is illustrated by the statements of the writers quoted from the *Rotarian* symposium (e.g., Marya Mannes' "The nation without heroes is a nation without a future").

Also, from the standpoint of the *historian*, sports history and sports heroes should be subjects of serious study by the academician. Until recent years, any history of American popular culture was viewed with a suspicious eye by much of the academic world. But the evaluation of such allegedly "low-brow" activities as American sports has fascinated some scholars, because they believe that an understanding of that subject is important and long overdue. Scholars who maintain that such things as movies, comics, radio, television, and sports are trash and of no importance miss the essential point that if an activity appeals to a substantial segment of society, then social scientists ought to understand that activity if they are to understand society itself. There is a need in American academic life for scholars to investigate all aspects of American culture, particularly when Americans are looking inward in these troubled days of the 1970s and seeking to discover a new spirit of self-reliance.

Some people seek escape in nostalgia (often mistaken for trivia). It is important that cultural historians look into those events of the past that gave people *pleasure and confidence* as well as those that gave them *pain*. Feelings of nostalgia are often used as emotional armor against the pressures of contemporary life. As stated above, the historian should find this a fruitful subject of study but should guard against identifying any "Golden Age" without the essential quality of perspective in his investigation.

By studying the problems that have confronted men in the past and their attempted solutions, man

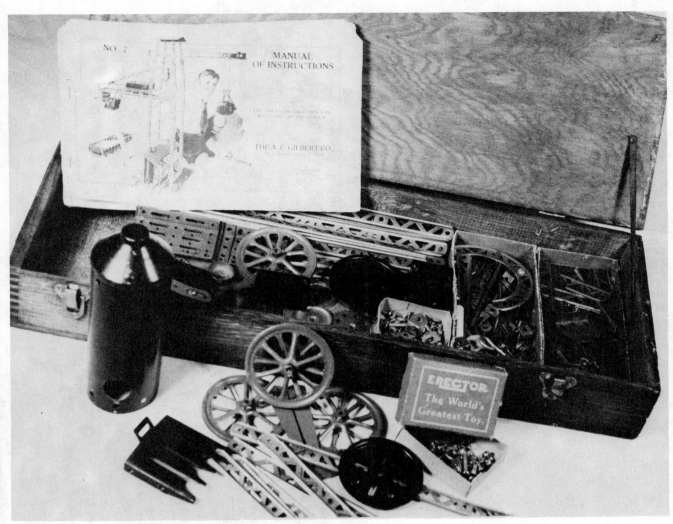

An erector set. A. C. Gilbert, the 1908 Olympic pole vault co-champion, worked his way through Yale as a magician. He invented the erector set and headed the company that made American Flyer trains. As boys, the authors derived many hours of enjoyment from A. C. Gilbert magic, chemistry, microscope, and erector sets. (From the collections of the authors.)

also gains in tolerance, appreciation, and understanding of other people's ideas and institutions. History, then, is not the mere chronicled record of the human experience. It is more than scholarly hypotheses. Hopefully, it has a sentimental side that will not only comfort people, but offer guidelines in solving the problems of the depersonalized present.

Others have stated this more cogently:

Time present and time past
Are both perhaps present in time future
And time future contained in time past.
T. S. Eliot, "Burnt Norton," *Four Quartets*

History is only a catalogue of the forgotten.
Henry Adams

Without passion there might be no errors
but without passion there would certainly
be no history.
C. V. Wedgwood

You must always know the past, for there is
no real Was, there is only Is.
William Faulkner

What is popular culture? Is it trivia? Is it an unsatisfying search for a nostalgic past that is irrecoverable? Or is it the pursuit of definitions concerning man's leisure time in a complex world that remains so confounding to the individual? Americans can send men to the moon with reasonable assurance that they will arrive and return as planned, but they are really quite ignorant about the functioning of society. Many sociologists and historians agree that one of the most important

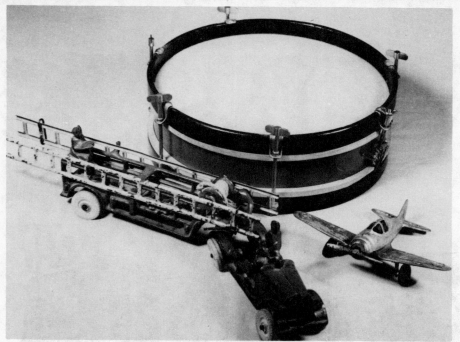

More boyhood treasures of the authors. Fire engine is
of cast iron with rubber tires.

Large-scale model Lionel train engine and bridge.
(From the collections of the authors.)

Arcade cast-iron farm implements purchased at the
Waterloo Dairy Cattle Congress in the early 1940s.
(From the collections of the authors.)

single needs in our nation is to develop a more rational process for forecasting social trends and for developing plans to deal with identified problems and needs. The study of American popular culture in our immediate past seems to be a logical step in this process of identification.

The technological age has taken a heavy toll on the individual, not only in the physical sense but also in its increase of leisure time while simultaneously dampening, in some respects, the human spirit. A search for some of the truths in American popular culture seems even more important in the 1970s when most citizens possess a fair measure of material comfort and security. What of the future? Is material comfort a sufficient reward for the human sacrifices to technological change and progress? The authors think not.

American heroes are sought as a way for the individual to achieve or maintain psychological integrity. A search for a hero, however, must never become a nonproductive fantasy or the gratification of frustrated personal desires in *imaginary* achievements. The heroics must be *genuine* in order that the individual can identify with the hero and thereby increase his feelings of self worth.

Man often feels helpless and confused in the face of great problems. His helplessness arises from the decline of an older order and its institutions of family, church, school, and community. Man seeks the familiar and takes comfort from it. Modern society has been described as a mass society in which individuals are often filled with a sense of restlessness. In seeking substitutes for the established and the traditional, for the old, warm, and intimate ways of life, they will invariably search out some form of heroic example.

BIBLIOGRAPHICAL NOTES

CHAPTER ONE

BOOK

Broeg, Bob. *Super Stars of Baseball.*

ARTICLES

Durso, Joseph. "What's Happened to Baseball?" *Saturday Review,* 14 September 1968.

Gilbert, Bil. "Confessions of a Retarded Tiger." *Sports Illustrated,* 2 June 1969.

Hemphill, Paul. "Viewpoint South." *Sport,* September 1971.

Hoagland, Edward. "Where Have All the Heroes Gone?" *The New York Times Magazine,* 10 March 1974.

Kahn, Roger. "Where Have All Our Heroes Gone?" *Esquire,* October 1974.

Kane, Martin. "An Assessment of 'Black Is Best.'" *Sports Illustrated,* 18 January 1971.

"Responsibility." *The Mentor,* 15 July 1915.

Schickel, Richard. "Growing Up in the Forties." *The New York Times Magazine,* 20 February 1972.

Silverman, Al. "1946–1971 Our 25th Anniversary." *Sport,* September 1971.

Steadman, John. "Staubach Throwback to Days of Fiction Heroes." *The Sporting News,* 29 January 1972.

"Time Out with the Editors." *Sport,* September 1971.

"Trivia." *Sports Illustrated,* 25 February 1973.

Voight, David C. "Reflections on Diamonds: American Baseball and American Culture." *Journal of Sport History,* I (Spring 1974).

RECORDS

DeWitt, Lew. *The Boy Inside of Me.*

Reid, Harold and Reid, Don. *Whatever Happened to Randolph Scott.*

Simon, Paul. *Mrs. Robinson.*

CHAPTER TWO

BOOKS

Bisher, Furman. *Strange But True Baseball Stories.*

Karst, Gene, and Jones, Martin, Jr. *Who's Who in Professional Baseball.*

Neft, David S.; Johnson, Roland T.; Cohen, Richard M.; and Deutsch, Jordan A. *The Sports Encyclopedia: Baseball.*

Paretchan, Harold R. *The World Series: The Statistical Record.*

The Sporting News (Leonard Gettleson, ed.). *Baseball's One for the Book* (published annually, now under title of *Official Baseball Record Book*).

———— (Leonard Gettleson, ed). *Official World Series Records: Complete Box Scores of All Games* (published annually).

———— (Joe Marcin, Chris Roewe, Larry Wigge, and Larry Vickrey, eds.). *Official Baseball Guide* (issued annually).

———— (Chris Roewe, Joe Marcin, and Larry Wigge, eds.). *Official Baseball Dope Book* (published annually).

Turkin, Hy, and Thompson, S. C. *The Official Encyclopedia of Baseball.*

Wallop, Douglas. *Baseball: An Informal History.*

ARTICLES

Allen, Lee. "Baseball's Greatest Achievement." *Sport,* May, 1969.

Bisher, Furman. "Love Affair with Bucs of Old." *The Sporting News,* 27 July 1974.

———. "Series Fame—and Out." *The Sporting News.* 20 October 1973.

———. "The Sportswriters' Greatest Moments of the Last 25 Years." *Sport,* December 1971.

Broeg, Bob. "Ball Park with Perfect Name." *The Sporting News,* 27 July 1974.

David, Gary F. "Record, Rewind, and Play." *All Star Baseball News,* 1 March 1974.

Falls, Joe. "Tears for Old Ball Parks." *The Sporting News,* 11 July 1970.

Graham, Frank, Jr. "When Baseball Went to War." *Sports Illustrated,* 17 April 1967.

Hemphill, Paul. "I Gotta Let the Kid Go." *Life,* 1 September 1972.

———. "Viewpoint South," *Sport,* May 1970.

Muchnick, Irvin. "How Baseball Sent Its Hop to War." *Sports Illustrated,* 24 April 1972.

Sesling, Skip. "The Cadaco Syndrome or How To Find, Buy or Cheat Your Neighbor Out of Those Discs." *All Star Baseball News,* 1 March 1974.

Spander, Art. "Fenway—A Ballpark To Savor." *The Sporting News,* 22 June 1974.

Twombly, Wells. "Those '48 Braves Were the Greatest." *The Sporting News,* 11 July 1970.

CHAPTER THREE

BOOKS

AAU. *The AAU Official Track and Field Handbook: Rules and Records.*

Grombach, John. *The 1976 Olympic Guide.*

Hanley, Reid. *Who's Who in Track and Field.*

Kieran, John, and Daley, Arthur. *The Story of the Olympic Games 776 B.C. to 1964 A.D.*

McWhirter, Norris, and McWhirter, Ross. *Guiness Book of Olympic Records.*

NCAA (Wayne Duke, ed.). *History and Records of National Collegiate Championships.*

NCAA (Don Pierce, ed.). *The Official National Collegiate Athletic Association Track and Field Guide* (published annually).

Nelson, Cordner. *Track and Field: The Great Ones.*

Schaap, Dick. *An Illustrated History of the Olympics.*

Sports Illustrated (Charles Osborne, ed.). *The Sports Illustrated Book of the Olympic Games.*

United States Olympic Committee (Asa Bushnell, ed.). *Report of the United States Olympic Committee, Games of the XIVth Olympiad.*

CHAPTER FOUR

BOOKS

Anderson, Dave. *Great Pass Receivers of the NFL.*

Broeg, Bob. *Ol' Mizzou: A Story of Missouri Football.*

Cohane, Tim. *Great College Football Coaches of the Twenties and Thirties.*

Claassen, Harold. *Football's Unforgettable Games.*

——— and Boda, Steve, Jr. *Ronald Encyclopedia of Football.*

Cummins, Tait. *Who's Who in Iowa Football.*

Danzig, Allison. *The History of American Football.*

Durant, John, and Etter, Les. *Highlights of College Football.*

Lamb, Dick, and McGrane, Bert. *75 Years with the Fighting Hawkeyes.*

McCallum, John, and Pearson, Charles H. *College Football U.S.A. 1869 . . . 1972: Official Book of the National Football Foundation.*

Mendell, Ronald L., and Phares, Timothy B. *Who's Who in Football.*

Miers, Earl Schenck. *Football.*

NCAA. *National Collegiate Sports Services College Football Modern Record Book.*

Neft, David S.; Johnson, Roland T.; Cohen, Richard M.; and Deutsch, Jordan A. *The Sports Encyclopedia: Pro Football.*

Oates, Bob, Jr., ed. *The First Fifty Years: A Celebration of the National Football League in its Fiftieth Season.*

Perry, Will. *The Wolverines: A Story of Michigan Football.*

Rice, Grantland. *The Tumult and the Shouting: My Life in Sport.*

Russell, Fred, and Leonard, George. *Big Bowl Football: The Great Postseason Classics.*

Treat, Roger. *The Official Encyclopedia of Football.*

ARTICLES

Einstein, Charles. "When Football Went to War." *Sports Illustrated,* 6 December 1971.

Jenkins, Dan. "This Year's Game of the Decade." *Sports Illustrated,* 22 November 1971.

CHAPTER FIVE

Fox, Larry. *Illustrated History of Basketball.*

Hollander, Zander. *The Modern Encyclopedia of Basketball.*

Isaacs, Neil. *All the Moves: A History of College Basketball.*

Koppett, Leonard. *Twenty Four Seconds to Shoot: An Informal History of the National Basketball Association 1945–1970.*

Liss, Howard. *The Winners: National Basketball Association Championship Playoffs.*

Mendell, Ronald L. *Who's Who in Basketball.*

Mokray, William G. *Ronald Encyclopedia of Basketball.*

The Sporting News (Nick Curran, ed.). *National Basketball Association Official Guide* (published annually).

Vecsey, George. *Harlem Globetrotters.*

Weyand, Alexander. *The Cavalcade of Basketball.*

CHAPTER SIX

Frank Menke's *The Encyclopedia of Sports,* Bob Burrill's *Who's Who in Boxing,* Nevin Gibson's *The Encyclopedia of Golf,* Harry Kariher's *Who's Who in Hockey,* and the *Official NCAA Wrestling Guide* (published annually) were helpful, as were the *United States Lawn Tennis Association Official Encyclopedia of Tennis* and Don Sayenga's 1971–72 historical series in *Amateur Wrestling News,* in which he dealt with amateur wrestling during each year of the 1940s. The authors quoted Dean Sticknoth's swimming article on "The Hawkeyes" in *The Iowa Alumni Review,* April 1948, and also "Hockey Was a Better Game in My Day," by Maurice Richard (as told to Stan Fischler) in *Sport,* November 1969.

CHAPTER SEVEN

BOOKS

Glass, Bill, and Pinson, William M., Jr. *Don't Blame the Game: An Answer to Super Star Swingers and a Look at What's Right with Sports.*

Toffler, Alvin. *Future Shock.*

ARTICLES

The August 1974 issue of *The Rotarian*—which included a symposium entitled "Do We Need Heroes?"—was of valuable assistance. The articles "We Must Have Heroes," "Heroes Are Dangerous Men," and "Heroism and Fortitude" are all from *The Great Ideas Today, 1973,* annual supplement to *The Great Books of the Western World.* "The Hero and Democracy" is from *The Hero in History;* "The Hero As Mirror" is taken from *Today's Health;* and "The Decline of Greatness" is from Arthur M. Schlesinger, Jr.'s *The Politics of Hope.*

Quoted materials were also taken from:

Fimrite, Ron. "A Long Locomotive for Choo Choo." *Sports Illustrated,* 15 October 1973.

Poe, Randall. "The Writing of Sports." *Esquire,* October 1974.

GENERAL

BOOKS

Lingeman, Richard. *Don't You Know There's a War On? The American Home Front 1941–1945.*

Time Capsule/1940: A History of the Year Condensed from the Pages of Time. Also Time Capsules for 1941, 1942, 1943, 1944, and 1945.

Wilson, Kenneth L. (Tug), and Brondfield, Jerry. *The Big Ten.*

RECORD

Greatest Moments in Sports. Produced by Bud Greenspan and James Hammerstein. Presented by Columbia Masterworks. Article by Red Smith.

NEWSPAPERS

Kansas City Star and *Times.*

New York Times.

St. Louis Globe-Democrat, especially articles by Robert L. Burnes and Rich Koster and syndicated articles in its pages by the Los Angeles Times News Service and Mickey Herskowitz and Steve Perkins.

Warrensburg (Missouri) *Daily Star-Journal.*

INDEX

Note: Page-number references to photographs are italicized.

254